WORKBOOK

Student Notes and Problems

PHYSICS 12
British Columbia

CASTLE ROCK
RESEARCH CORP

Publisher
Gautam Rao

Contributors
Lloyd Barker
David Gargus
Wayne Ladner
Blake Williams

Rao, Gautam, 1961 –

STUDENT NOTES AND PROBLEMS – Physics 12 Workbook British Columbia

1. Science – Juvenile Literature. I. Title

Published by
Castle Rock Research Corp.
2340 Manulife Place
10180 – 101 Street
Edmonton, AB T5J 3S4

1 2 3 FP 12 11 10

Dedicated to the memory of Dr. V. S. Rao

STUDENT NOTES AND PROBLEMS WORKBOOKS

Student Notes and Problems (SNAP) workbooks are a series of support resources in mathematics for students in grades 3 to 12 and in science for students in grades 9 to 12. SNAP workbooks are 100% aligned with curriculum. The resources are designed to support classroom instructions and provide students with additional examples, practice exercises, and tests. SNAP workbooks are ideal for use all year long at school and at home.

The following is a summary of the key features of all SNAP workbooks.

UNIT OPENER PAGE

- summarizes the curriculum outcomes addressed in the unit in age-appropriate language
- identifies the lessons by title
- lists the prerequisite knowledge and skills the student should know prior to beginning the unit

LESSONS

- provide essential teaching pieces and explanations of the concepts
- include example problems and questions with complete, detailed solutions that demonstrate the problem-solving process

NOTES BARS

- contain key definitions, formulas, reminders, and important steps or procedures
- provide space for students to add their own notes and helpful reminders

PRACTICE EXERCISES

- include questions that relate to each of the curriculum outcomes for the unit
- provide practice in applying the lesson concepts

REVIEW SUMMARY

- provides a succinct review of the key concepts in the unit

PRACTICE TEST

- assesses student learning of the unit concepts

ANSWERS AND SOLUTOINS

- demonstrate the step-by-step process or problem-solving method used to arrive at the correct answer

Answers and solutions for the odd-numbered questions are provided in each student workbook. A *SNAP Solutions Manual* that contains answers and complete solutions for all questions is also available.

Note to Students

Answers to problems are provided with the appropriate number of significant digits. To arrive at similar answers, follow this procedure when performing calculations:

- Use as many significant digits as possible when entering values into your calculator.
  E.g., use $9.81\ \text{m/s}^2$ versus $9.8\ \text{m/s}^2$ for the acceleration due to gravity.

- Retain all digits in your calculator for intermediate steps before reaching your final answer.

$$\text{E.g.,}\quad \vec{F} = m\vec{a}$$
$$= 10.2\ \text{kg} \times 9.81\ \text{m/s}^2$$
$$= 100.062\ \text{N}$$

- If adding or subtracting, retain the same number of decimal places as the measured number with the smallest number of decimal places.

$$\text{E.g.,}\qquad 6.48$$
$$\underline{+98.2}$$
$$104.68\ \text{m} \rightarrow 104.7\ \text{m}$$

- If multiplying or dividing, round off to the correct number of significant digits in your final answer—not in the intermediate steps.

$$\text{E.g.,}\quad W = \vec{F}d$$
$$= 100.062\ \text{N} \times 1.4\ \text{m}$$
$$= 140.0868\ \text{J}$$
$$= 1.4 \times 10^2\ \text{J}$$

Please note: Intermediate steps presented in solutions in this book do not show all of the digits that were retained in the calculator. This is done to make the solutions easier to follow when reading through them.

E.g., In the $F = ma$ example above, the answer is used to calculate the work done. Finding the force is an intermediate calculation. The solution will read as follows:

$$\vec{F} = m\vec{a} \qquad\qquad W = \vec{F}d$$
$$= 10.2\ \text{kg} \times 9.81\ \text{m/s}^2 \qquad = 100\ \text{N} \times 1.4\ \text{m}$$
$$= 100\ \text{N} \qquad\qquad = 140\ \text{J}$$
$$= 1.4 \times 10^2\ \text{J}$$

At most, in intermediate steps, one additional digit may be presented beyond what is significant. This may appear in some of the solutions shown.

In the end, no matter which approach is used to solve a problem, final answers will be different in the last digit—the digit that requires estimation and rounding. This is acceptable, since the final digit contains uncertainty.

If two answers are presented that are different in the final digit, both answers should be considered correct solutions.

CONTENTS

Vector Kinematics—Part A

Introduction to Kinematics 2
Practice Exercises 4
Uniform Motion—Graphical and Algebraic Analysis 6
Practice Exercises 10
Uniformly Accelerated Motion—Graphic Analysis 14
Practice Exercises 18
Uniformly Accelerated Motion—Algebraic Analysis 21
Practice Exercises 25
Freely Falling Objects 29
Practice Exercises 31
Motion in One Dimension—Graphical Analysis 36
Practice Exercises 37
Uniformly Accelerated Motion—Algebraic Analysis 44
Practice Exercises 46
Practice Test **52**

Vector Kinematics—Part B

Addition of Vectors on a Plane 60
Practice Exercises 63
Vector Components 65
Practice Exercises 68
Velocity Vectors and Navigation 70
Practice Exercises 72
Projectile Motion 76
Practice Exercises 78
Projectiles—Thrown at an Angle 81
Practice Exercises 82
Practice Test **87**

Dynamics

Dynamics 92
Practice Exercises 95
Newton's First Law Of Motion 96
Practice Exercises 99

Forces In Nature 101

Practice Exercises 103

Force Due To Gravity (Weight) 104

Practice Exercises 108

Applied Force or Tension 109

Practice Exercises 114

Physics Of An Inclined Plane 120

Practice Exercises 124

Newton's Third Law Of Motion 126

Practice Exercises 127

Practice Test **128**

Work, Power, and Energy

Energy 132

Practice Exercises 135

Power 139

Practice Exercises 141

Potential Energy 143

Practice Exercises 146

Kinetic Energy 148

Practice Exercises 150

Work-Energy Theorem For Net Force 151

Practice Exercises 153

Law Of Conservation Of Mechanical Energy 156

Practice Exercises 158

Law Of Conservation Of Energy 161

Practice Exercises 164

Practice Test **167**

Momentum

Momentum 172

Practice Exercises 174

Collision 178

Practice Exercises 183

Two-Dimensional Interaction 186

Practice Exercises 190

Practice Test **192**

Equilibrium

The First Condition of Equilibrium 196

Practice Exercises 200

The Second Condition of Equilibrium 204

Practice Exercises 210

Practice Test **212**

Circular Motion and Gravitation

Circular Motion 216

Practice Exercises 220

Vertical Circular Motion 223

Practice Exercises 227

Newton's Law Of Universal Gravitation 231

Practice Exercises 235

Field Explanation 238

Practice Exercises 241

Gravitational Potential Energy 243

Practice Exercises 247

Satellites: Natural And Artificial 248

Practice Exercises 249

Satellites In Orbit 250

Practice Exercises 253

Practice Test **254**

Electrostatics

Electrostatics 258

Practice Exercises 270

Field Explanation 274

Practice Exercises 279

Electric Potential Due to a Point 282

Practice Exercises 286

Electric Potential in a Uniform Electric Field 288

Practice Exercises 294

Practice Test **301**

Electric Circuits

Electric Current 306

Practice Exercises 310

Electric Circuits 314

Practice Exercises 322

Electromotive Force (EMF) 331

Practice Exercises 333

Practice Test **334**

Magnetic Forces and Fields

Magnetic Forces and Fields 338

Practice Exercises 345

Magnetic Forces on Current-Carrying Conductors 346

Practice Exercises 352

Cathode Rays 355

Practice Exercises 360

Electromagnetic Induction 364

Practice Exercises 372

Electric Generator 376

Practice Exercises 379

EMF Continued 382

Practice Exercises 385

Transformers (Induction Coil) 390

Practice Exercises 393

Power Transmission 395

Practice Test **397**

Answers and Solutions

Answers and Solutions 401

Appendix

Equations and Constants Used in this Book 469

Periodic Table of the Elements 472

Credits 473

VECTOR KINEMATICS—PART A

When you are finished this unit, you should be able to…
- Differentiate between scalar and vector quantities
- Investigate and solve problems related to uniform and uniformly accelerated motion in one dimension using both formulas and graphs

Lesson	Page	Completed on
1. Introduction to Kinematics	2	
2. Uniform Motion—Graphical and Algebraic Analysis	6	
3. Uniformly Accelerated Motion—Graphic Analysis	14	
4. Uniformly Accelerated Motion—Algebraic Analysis	21	
5. Freely Falling Objects	29	
6. Motion in One Dimension—Graphical Analysis	36	
7. Uniformly Accelerated Motion—Algebraic Analysis	46	
Practice Test	53	
Answers and Solutions	at the back of the book	

PREREQUISITE SKILLS AND KNOWLEDGE

Prior to starting this unit, you should be able to…
- Write numbers in scientific notation
- Isolate a variable and combine algebraic expressions
- Construct graphs involving relevant quantities and analyze important characteristics such as slope, intercepts, and areas under the graph.
- Perform calculations and obtain the answer to the correct number of significant figures
- Substitute the correct units for all quantities in a calculation and express the proper final unit by appropriate cancellation of units
- Determine the composition of derived units in terms of simpler units

Lesson 1 *INTRODUCTION TO KINEMATICS*

Objects are in motion everywhere. The sun moves from east to west across the sky. A plane takes off from the airport. Students walk down the hall. Rain falls from the sky. Trees sway back and forth in the wind. The hands of a clock are in uniform circular motion. Can the complex motion in these examples be described and analyzed in a meaningful way?

VECTOR QUANTITIES

Some important terms begin the study of motion.

- displacement ($\vec{d}$): the change in an object's position

- velocity ($\vec{v}$): the rate of change in an object's position

$$\vec{v} = \frac{\Delta \vec{d}}{\Delta t}$$

- acceleration ($\vec{a}$): the rate of change in an object's velocity

$$\vec{a} = \frac{\Delta \vec{v}}{\Delta t}$$

The Greek letter delta, Δ, is a symbol meaning "change in."

Rate of change involves the time of change.

A vector quantity has direction as well as magnitude.

Displacement, velocity, and acceleration are vector quantities.

Displacement, velocity, and acceleration are vector quantities. A vector quantity is a quantity that has direction as well as magnitude (size). This means that magnitude is not enough when you describe displacement, velocity, or acceleration. You must also indicate the direction of these quantities. For example, if an object is moved 20 m, you do not know its new position. However, if it is moved 20 m east, you know its new position because you know its displacement.

Because vector quantities have both magnitude and direction, both must be clearly communicated. A common convention for linear motion is to use plus or minus signs to indicate direction.

SCALAR QUANTITIES

Two additional terms are often used to describe motion:

- distance (*d*): how far an object has moved

- speed (*v*): speed can be defined in two ways:

  - the magnitude of velocity $v = \dfrac{d}{t}$

  - the distance moved divided by the time of motion (this will give average speed)

    $$\text{average speed} = \frac{\text{distance}}{\text{time}}$$

    or

    $$v_{ave} = \frac{d}{t}$$

Distance and speed are scalar quantities. A scalar quantity is a quantity that has magnitude (size) only. For example, if an object is moved 20 m, the distance moved is known, but the displacement is unknown.

Example

A person walks 20 m east, then 30 m west. What is the distance travelled by the man? What is his displacement?

Solution

The total distance travelled by the man is simply the sum of the individual distances.

$d = 20 \text{ m} + 30 \text{ m} = 50 \text{ m}$

The displacement of the man is given by the net change in his position. Consider east as the positive direction.

$\bar{d} = 20 \text{ m} + (-30 \text{ m})$
$\quad = -10 \text{ m}$
$\quad = 10 \text{ m west}$

Example

A car drives 10 km north in 20 minutes. What is the speed of the car? What is the velocity of the car?

Solution

The speed and velocity of the car have the same magnitude.

$$v = \left(\frac{10 \text{ km}}{20 \text{ min}} \right) \left(\frac{60 \text{ min}}{1.0 \text{ h}} \right) = 30 \text{ km / h}$$

The car travels north, so its velocity is simply the speed of the car combined with its direction of motion: $\bar{v} = 30 \text{ km/h north}$.

$$\text{average speed} = \frac{\text{distance}}{\text{time}}$$

average velocity

$$= \frac{\text{displacement}}{\text{time}}$$

A scalar quantity has only magnitude.

Distance and speed are scalar quantities.

PRACTICE EXERCISES

Formula: $\vec{v} = \dfrac{\vec{d}}{t}$ $\vec{a} = \dfrac{\vec{v}}{t}$ $v = \dfrac{d}{t}$ $a = \dfrac{v}{t}$

1. A man walks 275 m east, then turns around and walks 425 m west. What distance does the man travel?

2. A man walks 275 m east, then turns around and walks 425 m west. What distance does the man travel? What is the man's displacement?

3. A little girl takes her dog for a walk around a city block as described below. What is the distance travelled by the girl and dog during the walk?

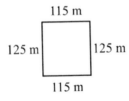

4. A little girl takes her dog for a walk around a city block as described below. What is the displacement of the girl and dog after the walk?

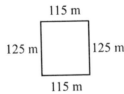

5. A student walks 11 m north and then turns around and travels 25 m south.
    The total time of travel is 52 s. What is the average speed of the student?

6. A student walks 11 m north and then turns around and travels 25 m south.
    The total time of travel is 52 s. What is the average velocity of the student?

Lesson 2   UNIFORM MOTION—GRAPHICAL AND ALGEBRAIC ANALYSIS

INSTANTANEOUS VELOCITY AND SPEED

The average velocity and average speed do not give any information about how fast an object is moving at a particular instant in time. Instead, they give an indication of how fast an object is moving, on average, over a longer duration of time.

Instantaneous speed is the speed at a precise moment in time; **instantaneous velocity** is the instantaneous speed and direction at some instant.

In this unit, motion will be described under two headings:
- motion in one dimension
- motion in two dimensions

One-dimensional motion is motion along a straight line, and **two-dimensional motion** is motion on a surface or a plane.

MOTION IN ONE DIMENSION

The following types of motion will be described:
- uniform motion
- uniformly accelerated motion

Uniform motion is motion in which the velocity (or speed) remains constant (uniform). **Uniformly accelerated motion** is motion in which the velocity (or speed) changes at the same rate. That is, the acceleration remains constant (uniform).

These two types of motion will be described graphically and algebraically.

The terms velocity and speed will be used to mean instantaneous velocity and instantaneous speed.

Uniform motion is motion in which the velocity remains constant.

Uniformly accelerated motion is motion in which the acceleration remains constant.

UNIFORM MOTION

The position-time graph for uniform motion will always be a straight line (for a given interval of time). The slope of this line represents the velocity of the object in motion.

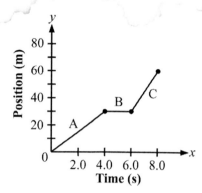

Section A of the graph describes an object moving with a constant velocity in the positive direction. This velocity in the time interval $t = 0$ to $t = 4.0$ s can be determined by calculating the slope of the graph.

$$\text{slope} = \frac{\text{rise}}{\text{run}}$$
$$= \frac{\vec{d}_2 - \vec{d}_1}{t_2 - t_1}$$
$$= \frac{30\ \text{m} - 0\ \text{m}}{4.0\ \text{s} - 0\ \text{m}}$$
$$= +7.5\ \text{m/s}$$

Because the velocity is uniform or constant, you can calculate it algebraically.

$$\vec{v} = \frac{\vec{d}}{t}$$
$$= \frac{30\ \text{m}}{4.0\ \text{s}}$$
$$= +7.5\ \text{m/s}$$

Section B shows the object moving at a constant velocity that is zero because the slope of this section is zero.

Can you tell how the object's velocity in section C compares with its velocity in section A?

Clearly, the slope is steeper, so it can be inferred that the velocity is greater. Calculate the slope of section C to confirm this inference.

$$\text{slope} = \frac{\text{rise}}{\text{run}}$$

$$= \frac{\bar{d}_2 - \bar{d}_1}{t_2 - t_1}$$

$$= \frac{60 \text{ m} - 30 \text{ m}}{8.0 \text{ s} - 6.0 \text{ m}}$$

$$= +15 \text{ m/s}$$

These calculations can be used to draw the corresponding velocity-time graph.

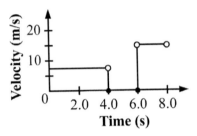

The instantaneous accelerations at $t = 4.0$ s and $t = 6.0$ s are not realistic, but they are consistent with the sharp changes in slope that occur at these same times on the position-time graph. If the accelerations at these two times are ignored, the corresponding acceleration-time graph for this motion can be drawn. Since there is no region where the velocity of the object changing, the acceleration-time graph is expected to consist of only a horizontal line located where $a = 0$ m/s^2.

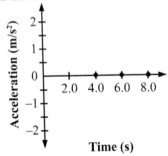

Example

An object travels at a uniform velocity of 25.0 m/s west. What is the displacement of the object after 10.0 min?

Solution

Consider west as the positive direction.

$$\bar{v} = \frac{\bar{d}}{t}$$

$$\bar{d} = \bar{v}t$$

$$= (25.0 \text{ m/s})(10.0 \text{ min})(60.0 \text{ s/min})$$

$$= (25.0 \text{ m/s})(6.00 \times 10^2 \text{ s})$$

$$= 1.50 \times 10^4 \text{ m west}$$

8

Example

After 3.0 h, an object's displacement is 3.60×10^2 km north. What is the average velocity of the object?

Solution

Consider north as the positive direction.

$$\bar{v} = \frac{\bar{d}}{t}$$
$$= \frac{3.60 \times 10^2 \text{ km}}{3.0 \text{ h}}$$
$$= 1.2 \times 10^2 \text{ km/h north}$$

Example

An object travels a distance of 5.0 m in 2.7 s. What is the average speed of the object?

Solution

$$v = \frac{d}{t}$$
$$= \frac{5.0 \text{ m}}{2.7 \text{ s}}$$
$$= 1.9 \text{ m/s}$$

PRACTICE EXERCISES

Formula: $\vec{v} = \dfrac{\vec{d}}{t}$ $\vec{d} = \vec{v}t$ $t = \dfrac{\vec{d}}{\vec{v}}$

1. An object is displaced 1.00×10^2 m west in a time of 11.2 s. What is the velocity of the object?

2. A car is travelling at a constant velocity of 10.0 m/s west. What distance will the car travel in 4.5 s?

3. A car is travelling at a constant velocity of 10.0 m/s west. What is the displacement of the car after 4.5 s have elapsed?

4. A man runs at an average velocity of 1.30 m/s south for 98.0 s and then walks at an average velocity of 0.450 m/s in the same direction for 90.0 s. What is the average velocity of the man during his total time of travel?

5. A position-time graph of an object moving east is shown. Find the velocity of the object at 8.0 s.

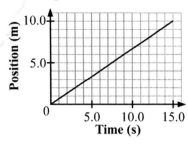

6. A position-time graph of an object moving east is shown. Find the velocity of the object at 12.0 s.

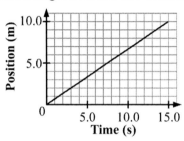

7. A position-time graph of an object moving east is shown. Find the velocity of the object at 1.0 s.

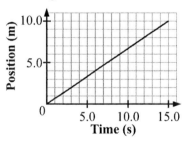

8. A velocity-time graph of an object moving south is shown. What is the displacement in 10 s?

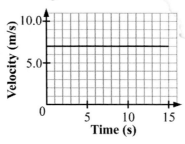

9. A velocity-time graph of an object moving south is shown. What is the distance travelled in 10 s?

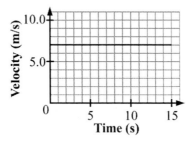

10. An object travels at a constant velocity of 8.0 m/s north for 25 minutes and then 5.0 m/s in the opposite direction for 15 minutes. What is the average velocity?

11. An object travels at a constant velocity of 8.0 m/s north for 25 minutes and then 5.0 m/s in the opposite direction for 15 minutes. What is the average speed?

12. Object A travels at a constant velocity of 2.0 m/s east, and object B travels in the same direction at a constant velocity of 3.0 m/s east. Both object A and B are initially at rest. If object B starts 1.0 min after object A, how long does it take for object B to catch object A?

Lesson 3—UNIFORMLY ACCELERATED MOTION—GRAPHICAL ANALYSIS

NOTES

When the velocity of an object changes with time, it is said to be accelerating. The object is said to accelerate whether it is speeding up or slowing down.

Both velocity and acceleration are vector quantities. If the direction of the acceleration vector is the same as the direction of the velocity vector, the object will be speeding up. If the directions are opposite, the object will be slowing down.

In uniformly accelerated motion, the acceleration of the object remains constant.

The acceleration in uniformly accelerated motion is constant.

Acceleration is defined as the rate of change in the velocity.

Acceleration is the rate of change in the velocity.

The initial and final velocities may also be denoted by $\bar{v}_0$ and $\bar{v}$ respectively.

$$\bar{a} = \frac{\Delta \bar{v}}{\Delta t}$$

or

$$\bar{a} = \frac{\bar{v}_f - \bar{v}_i}{t}$$

where

$\Delta \bar{v} = \bar{v}_f - \bar{v}_i$
$\bar{v}_f = $ final velocity
$\bar{v}_i = $ initial velocity
$\Delta t = t_f - t_i = $ time interval

The acceleration defined above is an average acceleration over the entire time interval. The defining formula emphasizes that it is an average:

$$\bar{a}_{ave} = \frac{\bar{v}_f - \bar{v}_i}{t}$$

When the motion of an object is uniformly accelerated motion, the average acceleration over the entire time interval is identical to the acceleration at any given instant of time. Instantaneous acceleration, like instantaneous velocity, is the acceleration at some precise moment in time.

For example, when a car accelerates from a stop light to the speed limit, or when a car decelerates from the speed limit to a stop, the acceleration is approximately constant or uniform, and in situations like this, the instantaneous acceleration at a particular time can be inferred by calculating the average acceleration over a larger, more conveniently measured time interval.

Example

The velocity-time graph shown represents the motion of an object that accelerates uniformly to the right.

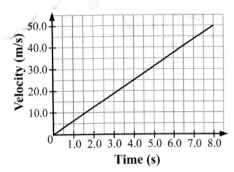

If the acceleration is constant over a given time period then the average velocity can be calculated in terms of the initial and final velocities using the formula $\vec{v}_{ave} = \dfrac{\vec{v}_f + \vec{v}_i}{2}$.

a) What is the average velocity during the 8.0 s of travel?

Solution

Consider right as the positive direction. Because the acceleration is uniform, the average velocity during the entire interval can be found from the initial and final velocity.

$$\vec{v}_{ave} = \frac{\vec{v}_f + \vec{v}_i}{2}$$
$$= \frac{50.0 \text{ m/s} + 0 \text{ m/s}}{2}$$
$$= 25.0 \text{ m/s right}$$

b) At what time does the object have an instantaneous velocity equal to the average velocity?

Solution

From the graph, the time corresponding to a velocity of 25.0 m/s can be read as 4.0 s. This is just halfway in the time interval. This useful observation can be generalized as follows.

If an object accelerates uniformly over an interval of time, the average velocity in this time interval is the same as the instantaneous velocity midway in the time interval.

c) Using the graph, determine the average acceleration over the interval $t = 0$ s to $t = 8.0$ s.

Solution

$$\vec{a} = \frac{\vec{v}_f - \vec{v}_i}{t}$$
$$= \frac{50.0 \text{ m/s} - 0 \text{ m/s}}{8.0 \text{ s}}$$
$$= 6.3 \text{ m/s}^2 \text{ right}$$

d) Calculate the average acceleration over the interval $t = 4.0$ s to $t = 8.0$ s.

Solution

$$\vec{a}_{ave} = \frac{\vec{v}_f - \vec{v}_i}{t}$$
$$= \frac{50.0 \text{ m/s} - 25.0 \text{ m/s}}{8.0 \text{ s} - 4.0 \text{ s}}$$
$$= 6.3 \text{ m/s}^2 \text{ right}$$

e) Determine the slope of this graph.

Solution

$$\text{slope} = \frac{\text{rise}}{\text{run}}$$
$$= \frac{y_2 - y_1}{x_2 - x_1}$$
$$= \frac{50.0 \text{ m/s} - 25.0 \text{ m/s}}{8.0 \text{ s} - 4.0 \text{ s}}$$
$$= 6.3 \text{ m/s}^2$$

Recall that the slope of a position-time graph represents velocity. The slope of a velocity-time graph represents acceleration.

INSTANTANEOUS VELOCITY (OR SPEED)

The slope of a position-time graph represents the velocity of the object. For the position-time graph drawn below, the line is curved because the slope (velocity) is constantly changing. The velocity can be found at any instant by drawing a tangent line to the curve at the point corresponding to the particular instant. Then, the slope of the line can be found.

Example

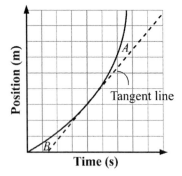

Angles *A* and *B* should be equal—this requires a good estimate.

SUMMARY: GRAPHICAL ANALYSIS

- The slope of the position-time graph is the velocity.
- The slope of the velocity-time graph is the acceleration.
- The area under a velocity-time graph is the displacement.
- Graphical representation of uniform or constant velocity:

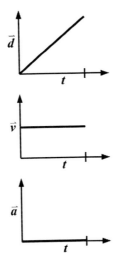

- Graphical representation of uniform or constant acceleration:

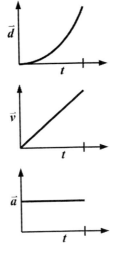

PRACTICE EXERCISES

Formula: $\bar{v} = \dfrac{\vec{d}}{t}$ $\qquad$ slope $= \dfrac{\text{rise}}{\text{run}} = \dfrac{y_2 - y_1}{x_2 - x_1}$

1. A position-time graph of an object moving east is shown.

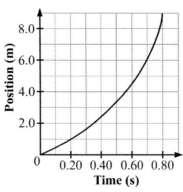

   Find the velocity of the object at 0.40 s.

2. A position-time graph of an object moving east is shown.

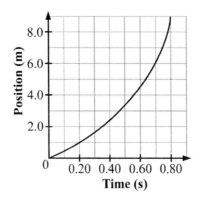

   Find the velocity of the object at 0.60 s

3. A velocity-time graph for an object that is moving north is shown.

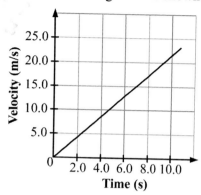

What is the acceleration of the object?

4. A velocity-time graph for an object that is moving north is shown.

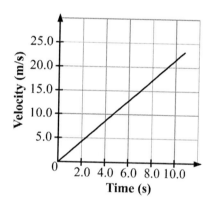

What is the object's displacement after 7.0 s?

5. A velocity-time graph for an object that is moving west is shown.

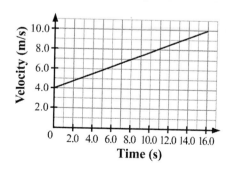

What is the acceleration of the object?

6. What is the object's displacement in 16.0 s?

7. The data below shows the velocity of an object moving north at one-second intervals.

Time (s)	Velocity (m/s)
0	12.0
1.0	15.3
2.0	18.6
3.0	21.9
4.0	25.2
5.0	28.5
6.0	31.8

Draw a velocity-time graph for the data.

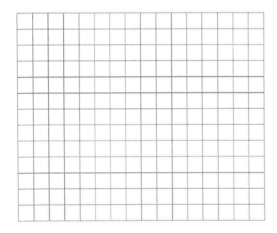

8. Using the information from question 7, what is the acceleration of the object?

9. Using the information from question 7, what is the displacement of the object during the 6.0 s described in the data table?

Lesson 4 UNIFORMLY ACCELERATED MOTION—ALGEBRAIC ANALYSIS

Acceleration is the rate of change in an object's velocity.

$$\vec{a} = \frac{\vec{v}_f - \vec{v}_i}{t}$$

where
$\vec{v}_f$ = final velocity
$\vec{v}_i$ = initial velocity

There are three additional equations that are used to describe uniformly accelerated motion:

$$\vec{d} = \left(\frac{\vec{v}_f + \vec{v}_i}{2}\right)t$$

$$\vec{d} = \vec{v}_i t + \frac{1}{2}\vec{a}t^2$$

$$\vec{v}_f^{\,2} = \vec{v}_i^{\,2} + 2\vec{a}\vec{d}$$

These equations can be derived from the graphical analysis of motion.

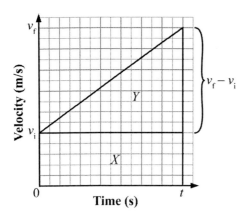

Displacement is the area under the velocity-time graph. Therefore, the displacement is the area of the rectangle X plus the area of the triangle Y.

Area of rectangle $X = \vec{v}_i t$

Area of triangle $Y = \frac{1}{2}t\left(\vec{v}_f - \vec{v}_i\right)$

$$= \frac{\vec{v}_f t}{2} - \frac{\vec{v}_i t}{2}$$

Total area of X and $Y = \vec{v}_i t + \left(\frac{\vec{v}_f t}{2} - \frac{\vec{v}_i t}{2}\right)$

Thus, $\vec{d} = \left(\frac{\vec{v}_f + \vec{v}_i}{2}\right)t$.

NOTES

$$\vec{a} = \frac{\vec{v}_f - \vec{v}_i}{t}$$

$$\vec{v}_f - \vec{v}_i = \vec{a}t$$

$$\vec{d} = \vec{v}_i t + \frac{1}{2}\vec{a}t^2$$

NOTES

Uniform acceleration implies that the velocity is changing at a constant rate. This means that a graph of the velocity over time will result in a straight but sloped line. The slope represents the magnitude of the acceleration.

The second formula for displacement can be derived in much the same way.

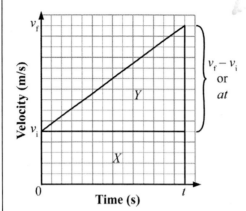

The displacement is the area under the velocity-time graph. The area is represented by a rectangle, X, and a triangle, Y.

Area of rectangle $X = \bar{v}_i t$

$$\text{Area of triangle } Y = \frac{1}{2}\bar{a}t(t)$$

$$= \frac{1}{2}\bar{a}t^2$$

$$\vec{d} = \bar{v}_i t + \frac{1}{2}\bar{a}t^2$$

The fourth equation $\vec{v}_f^2 = \vec{v}_i^2 + 2\bar{a}\vec{d}$ is derived by combining the equations $\bar{a} = \dfrac{\bar{v}_f - \bar{v}_i}{t}$ and $\vec{d} = \bar{v}_i t + \dfrac{1}{2}\bar{a}t^2$.

From equation #1,

$$\bar{a} = \frac{\bar{v}_f - \bar{v}_i}{t}$$

$$t = \frac{\bar{v}_f - \bar{v}_i}{\bar{a}}$$

Remember: average velocity can be calculated using

$$\vec{v}_{ave} = \frac{\vec{d}}{t}$$

$$= \frac{\left(\dfrac{\bar{v}_f + \bar{v}_i}{2}\right)t}{t}$$

$$= \frac{\bar{v}_f + \bar{v}_i}{2}$$

Replace t in the equation $\vec{d} = \bar{v}_i t + \dfrac{1}{2}\bar{a}t^2$ with $\dfrac{\bar{v}_f - \bar{v}_i}{\bar{a}}$:

$$\vec{d} = \bar{v}_i\left(\frac{\bar{v}_f - \bar{v}_i}{\bar{a}}\right) + \frac{1}{2}\bar{a}\left(\frac{\bar{v}_f - \bar{v}_i}{\bar{a}}\right)^2$$

$$= \left(\frac{\bar{v}_i\bar{v}_f}{\bar{a}} - \frac{\bar{v}_i^2}{\bar{a}}\right) + \left(\frac{\bar{v}_f^2}{2\bar{a}} - \frac{2\bar{v}_f\bar{v}_i}{2\bar{a}} + \frac{\bar{v}_i^2}{2\bar{a}}\right)$$

$$\vec{d} = \left(\frac{\bar{v}_f + \bar{v}_i}{2}\right)t$$

The first and fourth terms cancel; the second and fifth terms add and $-\dfrac{\bar{v}_i^2}{\bar{a}} + \dfrac{\bar{v}_i^2}{2\bar{a}}$ reduces to $-\dfrac{\bar{v}_i^2}{2\bar{a}}$.

Thus, $\quad \vec{d} = \dfrac{\vec{v}_f^{\,2}}{2\vec{a}} - \dfrac{\vec{v}_i^{\,2}}{2\vec{a}}$

$$2\vec{a}\vec{d} = \vec{v}_f^{\,2} - \vec{v}_i^{\,2}$$

$$\vec{v}_f^{\,2} = \vec{v}_i^{\,2} + 2\vec{a}\vec{d}.$$

SUMMARY—UNIFORMLY ACCELERATED MOTION

Equations	Variables				
	$\vec{v}_i$	$\vec{v}_f$	$\vec{a}$	$\vec{d}$	t
$\vec{a} = \dfrac{\vec{v}_f - \vec{v}_i}{t}$	✓	✓	✓		✓
$\vec{d} = \left(\dfrac{\vec{v}_f + \vec{v}_i}{2} \right) t$	✓	✓		✓	✓
$\vec{d} = \vec{v}_i t + \dfrac{1}{2}\vec{a}t^2$	✓		✓	✓	✓
$\vec{v}_f^{\,2} = \vec{v}_i^{\,2} + 2\vec{a}\vec{d}$	✓	✓	✓	✓	

In uniform accelerated motion, average velocity can also be calculated using $\vec{v}_{ave} = \dfrac{\vec{v}_f + \vec{v}_i}{2}$.

Each equation has four of the possible five variables that can be used to describe uniformly accelerated motion. In the mathematical analysis of uniformly accelerated motion, the equation that will be used is the first thing that must be determined. To do this, list all the given variables and the unknown variable. In this list, there must be four variables (three known and one unknown). From this list, one of the five variables from the summary will be missing. The equation to use is the equation that is also missing this variable.

Example

An object, initially travelling at a velocity of 7.0 m/s east, accelerates uniformly to a velocity of 22.0 m/s east in a time of 1.7 s. Calculate the acceleration of the object.

Solution

Consider east as the positive direction

$\vec{v}_i$	$\vec{v}_f$	$\vec{a}$	$\vec{d}$	t
7.0 m/s	22.0 m/s	?	×	1.7 s

Since $\vec{d}$ is not a concern, use the equation that does not have $\vec{d}$.

$\vec{a} = \dfrac{\vec{v}_f - \vec{v}_i}{t}$

$\quad = \dfrac{22.0 \text{ m/s} - 7.0 \text{ m/s}}{1.7 \text{ s}}$

$\quad = 8.8 \text{ m/s}^2$ or 8.8 m/s^2 east

Motion that begins from rest implies that $\vec{v}_i = 0$

Since $\vec{a}$ is not a concern, use the equation that does not have $\vec{a}$.

Example

An object accelerated north uniformly from rest in a time of 2.70 s. In this time, it travelled 20.0 m. What was the final velocity?

Solution

Consider north as the positive direction.

$\vec{v}_i$	$\vec{v}_f$	$\vec{a}$	$\vec{d}$	t
0	?	×	20.0 m	2.70 s

$$\vec{d} = \left(\frac{\vec{v}_f + \vec{v}_i}{2}\right)t \Rightarrow \vec{v}_f = \frac{2\vec{d}}{t} - \vec{v}_i$$

$$= \frac{2(20.0 \text{ m})}{2.70 \text{ s}} - 0 \text{ m/s}$$

$$= 14.8 \text{ m/s or } 14.8 \text{ m/s north}$$

Example

An object accelerates uniformly from rest at 2.00 m/s^2 west. What is the object's displacement when it reaches a velocity of 1.00×10^2 km/h ?

Solution

Consider west as the positive direction.

$$\vec{v}_f = \left(1.00 \times 10^2 \text{ km/h}\right)\left(10^3 \text{ m/km}\right)\left(\frac{1 \text{ h}}{3600 \text{ s}}\right)$$

$$= 27.8 \text{ m/s or } 27.8 \text{ m/s west}$$

Since t is not a concern, use the equation that does not have t.

$\vec{v}_i$	$\vec{v}_f$	$\vec{a}$	$\vec{d}$	t
0	27.8 m/s	2.00 m/s^2	?	×

$$\vec{v}_f^{\,2} = \vec{v}_i^{\,2} + 2\vec{a}\vec{d}$$

$$(27.8 \text{ m/s})^2 = 0 + 2(2.00 \text{ m/s}^2)(\vec{d})$$

$$\vec{d} = \frac{(27.8 \text{ m/s})^2}{2(2.00 \text{ m/s}^2)}$$

$$= 193 \text{ m or } 193 \text{ m west}$$

PRACTICE EXERCISES

Formulas: $\qquad \vec{a} = \dfrac{\vec{v}_f - \vec{v}_i}{t} \qquad \vec{d} = \left(\dfrac{\vec{v}_f + \vec{v}_i}{2}\right)t \qquad \vec{d} = \vec{v}_i t + \dfrac{1}{2}\vec{a}t^2 \qquad \vec{v}_f^{\;2} = \vec{v}_i^{\;2} + 2\vec{a}\vec{d}$

1. An object accelerates uniformly from rest to a velocity of 12.0 m/s west in 3.40 s. What is the acceleration of the object?

2. An object accelerates uniformly from rest. If the final velocity of the object after 4.7 s is 15 m/s east, what is the displacement?

3. An object initially travelling at a velocity of 2.0 m/s west accelerates uniformly at a rate of 1.3 m/s² west. During this time of acceleration, the displacement of the object is 15 m west. What is the final velocity of the object?

4. An object initially travelling at a velocity of 2.0 m/s west accelerates uniformly at a rate of 1.3 m/s² west. During this time of acceleration, the displacement of the object is 15 m west. What is the final speed of the object?

5. An object accelerates uniformly from rest for 8.10 s. If the displacement of the object in this time is 20.0 m to the right, what is the acceleration?

6. An object travels 8.0 m south in 3.2 s while uniformly accelerating at a rate of 0.71 m/s² south. What was the initial velocity of the object at the beginning of the displacement?

7. An object is displaced 25.0 m north while accelerating uniformly. If a velocity of 14.0 m/s north is reached in 1.90 s, what was the initial velocity?

8. An object accelerates uniformly from rest for 5.6 s. What is the velocity of the object in this time if the displacement is 31.0 m west?

9. An object accelerates uniformly at a rate of 0.900 m/s^2 south. This object reaches a velocity of 25.0 m/s south while its displacement is 37.0 m south. What was the initial velocity of the object?

10. A ball, starting from rest, accelerates uniformly down an incline at a rate of 1.4 m/s^2. What is the displacement of the ball in 5.0 s?

11. A ball, starting from rest, accelerates uniformly down an incline at a rate of 1.4 m/s^2. What is the velocity of the ball at 5.0 s?

12. An object was travelling at an average velocity of 9.60 m/s to the right. If the time of travel was 2.70 s, what was the displacement of the object?

13. An object was uniformly accelerated from rest at a rate of 3.10 m/s^2 south. If this object reaches a velocity of 12.4 m/s south in 4.00 s, what is the displacement of the object while accelerating?

Lesson 5   FREELY FALLING OBJECTS

A dropped pen will fall to the floor. How can this motion be described?
Does it fall to the floor with uniform motion (constant velocity), or
uniformly accelerated motion? Aristotle, the early Greek natural
philosopher, came to the conclusion that objects fall with a constant
velocity and that this velocity is proportional to the mass of the falling
object. Galileo, on the other hand, reasoned that falling objects accelerate
uniformly; that is, the rate at which they accelerate is constant.

Galileo:
Objects accelerate
uniformly at the same rate
as they fall.

Questions

1. Why did Aristotle come to the conclusion that he did?

2. How did Galileo come to his conclusion about falling objects?

The acceleration of a freely falling object is called the acceleration due to
gravity ($\vec{g}$). Near Earth's surface, this acceleration is approximately
9.81 m/s^2 . It should be noted that it varies slightly due to altitude and
latitude. However, use 9.81 m/s^2 in problem solving unless you are given
other information. The acceleration due to gravity can also be called the
gravitational field strength since $1 \text{ N/kg} = 1 \text{ m/s}^2$.

$\vec{g} = 9.81 \text{ m/s}^2$ (toward the centre of Earth)

Problems involving freely falling objects are some of the best examples
of uniformly accelerated linear motion. Therefore, the following problems
will be solved using the equations below:

$$\vec{a} = \frac{\vec{v}_\text{f} - \vec{v}_\text{i}}{t}$$

$$\vec{d} = \left(\frac{\vec{v}_\text{f} + \vec{v}_\text{i}}{2} \right) t$$

$$\vec{d} = \vec{v}_\text{i} t + \frac{1}{2} \vec{a} t^2$$

$$\vec{v}_\text{f}^{\ 2} = \vec{v}_\text{i}^{\ 2} + 2\vec{a}\vec{d}$$

Note: In these equations, $\vec{a}$ can be replaced with $\vec{g}$.

Example

A large steel ball is dropped from a height of 7.00 m above the floor.
With what velocity will the object strike the floor?

Solution
Consider down as the negative direction.

The magnitude of the
acceleration due to gravity
near Earth's surface is
approximately 9.81 m/s^2 .

Acceleration due to gravity
causes motion toward
Earth's centre and can be
considered to act in the
positive or negative
direction so long as the
convention holds
throughout the entire
problem.

$\vec{v}_i$	$\vec{v}_f$	$\vec{a}$	$\vec{d}$	t
0	?	−9.81 m/s²	−7.00 m	×

$$\vec{v}_f^{\,2} = \vec{v}_i^{\,2} + 2\vec{a}\vec{d}$$
$$= 0 + 2\left(-9.81 \text{ m/s}^2\right)\left(-7.00 \text{ m}\right)$$
$$= 137.3 \text{ m}^2/\text{s}^2$$
$$\vec{v}_f = \sqrt{137.3 \text{ m}^2/\text{s}^2}$$
$$= \pm 11.7 \text{ m/s down} \Rightarrow -11.7 \text{ m/s or } 11.7 \text{ m/s down}$$

Example

A cement block falls from the roof of a building. If the time of fall was 5.60 s, what is the height of the building?

Solution

Consider down as the negative direction.

$\vec{v}_i$	$\vec{v}_f$	$\vec{a}$	$\vec{d}$	t
0	?	−9.81 m/s²	?	5.60 s

$$\vec{d} = \vec{v}_i t + \frac{1}{2}\vec{a}t^2$$
$$= 0 + \frac{1}{2}\left(-9.81 \text{ m/s}^2\right)\left(5.60 \text{ s}\right)^2$$
$$= -154 \text{ m}$$

So the height of the building is 154 m since that is the distance that the cement block dropped.

Example

If a pen is dropped from a height of 2.50 m above the floor, how long will it take for it to strike the ground?

Solution

Consider down as the negative direction.

$\vec{v}_i$	$\vec{v}_f$	$\vec{a}$	$\vec{d}$	t
0	×	−9.81 m/s²	−2.50 m	?

$$\vec{d} = \vec{v}_i t + \frac{1}{2}\vec{a}t^2$$
$$= 0 + \frac{1}{2}\vec{a}t^2$$
$$t = \sqrt{\frac{2\vec{d}}{\vec{a}}}$$
$$= \sqrt{\frac{2\left(-2.50 \text{ m}\right)}{-9.81 \text{ m/s}^2}}$$
$$= 0.714 \text{ s}$$

PRACTICE EXERCISES

Formulas: $\vec{a} = \dfrac{\vec{v}_f - \vec{v}_i}{t}$ $\vec{d} = \left(\dfrac{\vec{v}_f + \vec{v}_i}{2}\right)t$ $\vec{d} = \vec{v}_i t + \dfrac{1}{2}\vec{a}t^2$ $\vec{v}_f^{\,2} = \vec{v}_i^{\,2} + 2\vec{a}\vec{d}$

1. A steel ball falls from a height of 15.0 m above the ground. With what velocity does it strike the ground?

2. An apple falls from a tree. If the fall took 0.50 s, from what height did the apple fall?

3. If a coin is dropped from a height of 9.50 m above the ground, what will be the velocity when it reaches the ground?

4. An object is dropped from the roof of a building. If the object takes 2.50 s to reach the ground, what is the velocity of the object when it reaches the ground?

5. An egg is thrown vertically upward from a window. If the egg is released with a velocity of 10.0 m/s and it strikes the ground at a velocity of –25.0 m/s, how long did it take the egg to reach the ground?

6. A rock was thrown vertically downward. If the rock was released with a velocity of 5.00 m/s and it hit the ground below at a velocity of 15.0 m/s, what was the rock's displacement?

7. An object is thrown vertically downward. If the object hits the ground with a velocity of 10.0 m/s and it fell for 0.880 s, with what velocity was the object released?

8. A rock is dropped from a height of 7.0 m. What is the average velocity of the rock during the fall?

9. How long does it take the rock to fall?

10. At what time is the rock actually travelling at the average velocity? (Hint: sketch a graph)

11. Hint from the previous questions that the average velocity occurs at the mid-point of the motion if the acceleration is uniform. Using this, determine how long it would take for a dropped object to hit the ground if the average velocity of the object is 12.0 m/s.

12. When an object is dropped from a height of 10.0 m above the surface of Planet X, it takes 1.20 s for the object to reach the surface. What is the acceleration of a falling object near the surface of this planet?

13. When an object is dropped from a height of 24.0 m above the surface of Planet Y, it hits the surface at a velocity of 19.6 m/s. What is the acceleration of a falling object near the surface of this planet?

14. When an object is dropped near the surface of Planet F, it reaches a velocity of 11.0 m/s in 1.50 s. What is the acceleration of a falling object near the surface of Planet F?

15. A rock, thrown vertically downward at 3.50 m/s, travels 10.0 m before hitting the ground. If it strikes the ground with a speed of 14.4 m/s, how long did it take to reach the ground?

16. A ball is thrown vertically upward off the edge of a cliff with a velocity of 10.0 m/s and strikes the ground at the base of the cliff with a velocity of –39.6 m/s. For how long is the ball in the air?

17. On Planet K, a small, dense object falls from rest, reaching a velocity of 11.0 m/s in 1.50 s. What is the acceleration due to gravity in this location?

18. A rock is thrown vertically downward, reaching a velocity of 15.0 m/s after travelling a distance of 10.0 m. What is the duration of this motion?

Lesson 6   MOTION IN ONE DIMENSION—GRAPHICAL ANALYSIS

NOTES

In this section, the motion of an object in both directions along a line is discussed.

The directions of the vector quantities have thus far always been in one direction along a line.

Consider problems in which the vector quantities are in both directions along a straight line.

Example

A ball starts up an incline with a certain velocity. The ball slows down, comes to a stop, and starts to roll back down.

In this example,
$\vec{v}_i$ is up the incline,
$\vec{a}$ is down the incline,
$\vec{v}_f$ is down the incline,
$\vec{d}$ is up the incline

Displacement becomes zero when the ball returns to its starting point and will be negative if it rolls beyond its starting point in the opposite direction.

PROBLEM SOLVING

In solving problems involving vectors in both directions along a straight line, continue to use the following equations:

$$\vec{a} = \frac{\vec{v}_f - \vec{v}_i}{t}$$

$$\vec{d} = \left(\frac{\vec{v}_f + \vec{v}_i}{2}\right)t$$

$$\vec{d} = \vec{v}_i t + \frac{1}{2}\vec{a}t^2$$

$$\vec{v}_f{}^2 = \vec{v}_i{}^2 + 2\vec{a}\vec{d}$$

Direction along a line is indicated using a positive (+) or negative (−) sign.

Indicate the direction by using positive (+) and negative (−) signs. Generally, the convention is to identify a direction to the right or up as positive (+) and a direction to the left or down as negative (−).

SUMMARY: GRAPHICAL ANALYSIS

• The slope of a position-time graph is the velocity.

• The slope of a velocity-time graph is the acceleration.

• The area under a velocity-time graph is the displacement.

Slopes may be positive (rising to the right) or negative (falling to the right). Area may be positive (above the time axis) or negative (below the time axis).

This is because displacement, velocity, and acceleration can be in either direction along any given single dimension.

PRACTICE EXERCISES

1. The position-time graph at right represents the motion of a steel ball rolling up an incline, coming to a stop, and returning back to its original position.

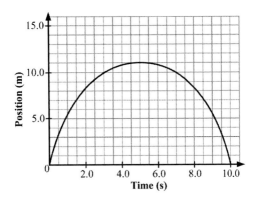

What is the velocity at 3.0 s?

2. The position-time graph at right represents the motion of a steel ball rolling up an incline, coming to a stop, and returning back to its original position.

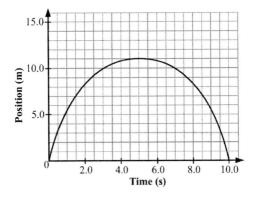

What is the velocity at 7.0 s?

3. A velocity-time graph for an object moving along a line is shown in the given graph.

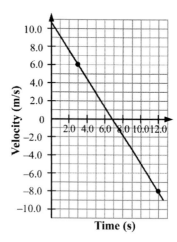

What is the acceleration at 4.0 s?

4. Using the information from question 3, what is the acceleration at 10.0 s?

5. A position-time graph for an object moving north along a line is shown.

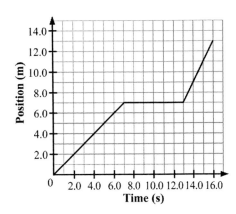

What is the displacement of the object at 16.0 s?

6. Using the information from question 5, what is the velocity at 5.0 s?

7. Using the information from question 5, what is the velocity at 9.0 s?

8. Using the information from question 5, what is the velocity at 15.0 s?

9. Using the information from question 5, what is the average velocity of the motion described?

10. Using the information from question 5, what is the acceleration at between 2.0 s and 6.0 s?

11. A velocity-time graph for an object moving along a line is shown. The object is travelling north.

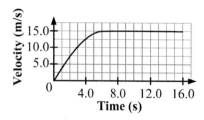

What is the velocity of the object at 7.0 s?

12. A velocity-time graph for an object moving along a line is shown. The object is travelling north.

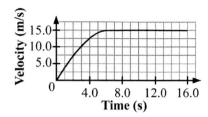

What is the acceleration of the object at 9.0 s?

13. A velocity-time graph for an object moving along a line is shown. The object is travelling north.

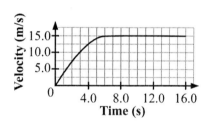

What is the displacement of the object between 8.0 s and 16.0 s?

14. A velocity-time graph for an object moving along a line is shown.

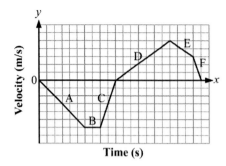

In which section is the displacement greatest?

15. A velocity-time graph for an object moving along a line is shown.

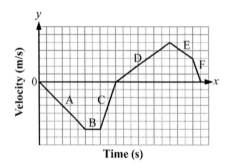

In which section is the speed of the object greatest?

16. A velocity-time graph for an object moving north along a line is shown

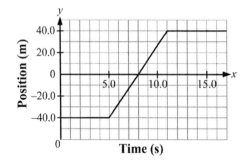

What is the velocity at 8.0 s?

17. A velocity-time graph for an object moving north along a line is shown

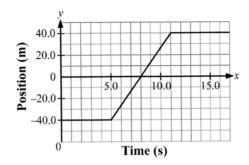

What is the velocity at 15.0 s?

18. A velocity-time graph for an object moving north along a line is shown

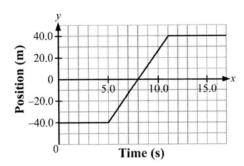

What is the displacement between 4.0 s and 15.0 s?

19. A velocity-time graph for an object moving along a line is shown.

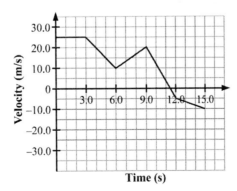

During which time interval is the object's velocity the greatest?

20. Using the information from question 19, during which time interval is the acceleration of the object zero?

21. Using the information from question 19, during which time interval is the acceleration of the object the greatest?

22. Consider the following position-time graphs.

A.
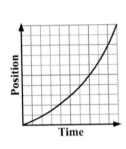

B.
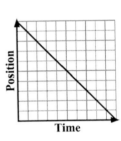

C.
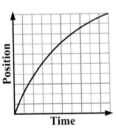

D.
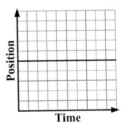

Which of these graphs represents zero velocity?

23. Using the information from question 22, which of these graphs represents motion in which the velocity is increasing?

44

24. Using the information from question 22, which of these graphs represents motion in which the velocity is decreasing?

25. Using the information from question 22, which of these graphs represents motion in which the velocity is constant?

Lesson 7 UNIFORMLY ACCELERATED MOTION—ALGEBRAIC ANALYSIS

NOTES

It is important to keep track of the direction of all vector quantities during a mathematical analysis of uniformly accelerated motion. This is particularly true when both directions along a line are involved.

The direction to the right or up is positive (+).
The direction to the left or down is negative (−).

For the cardinal points of a compass, north and east are generally positive; south and west are generally negative. This is only a convention and the sign given to direction is chosen for simplicity.

Example

A stone is thrown vertically upward with an initial velocity of 25.2 m/s. Calculate the maximum displacement (height) of this stone.

Solution

The stone will reach its maximum height at the point where its vertical velocity reaches 0 and the stone begins to fall back towards the ground. Therefore, the final velocity in this case will be 0 m/s

Although the velocity at which the stone returned is not given, when an object is thrown vertically upward, it will return with the same speed, but opposite direction.

$\bar{v}_i$	$\bar{v}_f$	$\bar{a}$	$\bar{d}$	t
25.2 m/s	0	−9.81 m/s^2	?	×

$$\bar{v}_f^{\,2} = \bar{v}_i^{\,2} + 2\bar{a}\bar{d}$$
$$0 = (25.2 \text{ m/s})^2 + 2(-9.81 \text{ m/s}^2)(\bar{d})$$
$$\bar{d} = \frac{-(25.2 \text{ m/s})^2}{2(-9.81 \text{ m/s}^2)}$$
$$= 32.4 \text{ m or } 32.4 \text{ m up}$$

Example

A stone is dropped from a height of 32.4 m above the ground. Calculate the velocity of this object when it reaches the ground.

Solution

The initial velocity in the first example and the final velocity in the second example are equal in magnitude. This will always be true when the same displacements up and down are involved.

$\bar{v}_i$	$\bar{v}_f$	$\bar{a}$	$\bar{d}$	t
0	?	−9.81 m/s^2	−32.4 m	×

$$\bar{v}_f^{\,2} = \bar{v}_i^{\,2} + 2\bar{a}\bar{d}$$
$$\bar{v}_f^{\,2} = 0 + 2(-9.81 \text{ m/s}^2)(-32.4 \text{ m})$$
$$\bar{v}_f = \sqrt{2(-9.81 \text{ m/s}^2)(-32.4 \text{ m})}$$
$$= \pm 25.2 \text{ m/s} \Rightarrow -25.2 \text{ m/s or } 25.2 \text{ m/s down}$$

Example

A stone is thrown vertically upward with an initial velocity of 11 m/s. If the stone returns to its initial position, calculate the time the stone is in the air.

Solution

$\vec{v}_i$	$\vec{v}_f$	$\vec{a}$	$\vec{d}$	t
11 m/s	−11 m/s	−9.81 m/s²	×	?

$$\vec{a} = \frac{\vec{v}_f - \vec{v}_i}{t}$$

$$t = \frac{\vec{v}_f - \vec{v}_i}{\vec{a}}$$

$$= \frac{(-11 \text{ m/s}) - 11 \text{ m/s}}{-9.81 \text{ m/s}^2}$$

$$= 2.2 \text{ s}$$

Example

A ball is rolled up a constant slope with an initial velocity of 12.0 m/s. If the ball's displacement is 0.500 m up the slope after 3.60 s, what is the velocity of the ball at this time?

Solution

Consider up the slope to be the positive direction in this case.

$\vec{v}_i$	$\vec{v}_f$	$\vec{a}$	$\vec{d}$	t
12.0 m/s	?	×	0.500 m	3.60 s

$$\vec{d} = \left(\frac{\vec{v}_f + \vec{v}_i}{2} \right) t$$

$$0.500 \text{ m} = \left(\frac{\vec{v}_f + 12.0 \text{ m/s}}{2} \right)(3.60 \text{ s})$$

$$\vec{v}_f = \frac{2(0.500 \text{ m})}{3.60 \text{ s}} - 12.0 \text{ m/s}$$

$$= -11.7 \text{ m/s or } 11.7 \text{ m/s down}$$

PRACTICE EXERCISES

Formulas: $\quad \vec{a} = \dfrac{\vec{v}_f - \vec{v}_i}{t} \qquad \vec{d} = \left(\dfrac{\vec{v}_f + \vec{v}_i}{2} \right) t \quad \vec{d} = \vec{v}_i t + \dfrac{1}{2} \vec{a} t^2 \quad \vec{v}_f^{\,2} = \vec{v}_i^{\,2} + 2 \vec{a} \vec{d}$

1. An object is thrown vertically upward with an initial velocity of 14.0 m/s. What is the displacement after 1.80 s?

2. A ball is rolled up a constant slope with an initial velocity of 9.3 m/s. What is the acceleration of the ball if its displacement is 1.9 m up the slope after 2.7 s?

3. A ball is rolled up a constant slope with an initial velocity of 9.4 m/s.
    After 3.0 s, the ball rolls down the slope with a velocity of 7.4 m/s. How far up the slope is the ball at this time?

4. An object is thrown vertically downward toward the ground with an initial velocity of 5.0 m/s. This object hits the ground with a velocity of 12.0 m/s. How long did the object take to reach the ground?

5. A ball is rolled up a constant slope. After 3.6 s, it reaches its maximum displacement of 2.6 m and then begins to roll back down. What was the initial velocity of the ball when it started up the slope?

6. An object is thrown vertically upward with an initial velocity of 10.0 m/s. What is the velocity of the object when it is on its way back down and is 5.0 m above the point of release?

7. A ball is rolled up a constant slope with an initial velocity of 2.0 m/s. After 1.5 s, the ball is 2.8 m up the incline from the point of release. What is the velocity of the ball at this time?

8. An object is thrown vertically upward. If the object has a vertical displacement up of 5.00 m after 3.00 s, what was the initial velocity?

9. A ball is rolled up a constant slope with an initial velocity of 2.2 m/s. After 2.0 s, the ball rolls down the slope with a velocity of 1.2 m/s. What is the acceleration of the ball along the incline?

10. A ball is rolled up a constant slope with an initial velocity of 2.5 m/s. When the displacement of the ball is 1.0 m up the slope, it has a velocity of 1.6 m/s down the slope. What is the acceleration of the ball?

11. A ball rolls 2.7 m up a constant slope before it comes to a stop. It then rolls back down the slope. If the initial velocity of the ball was 2.0 m/s, how long does it take the ball to roll up and down the slope?

12. While on Planet X, an object is thrown vertically upward with an initial velocity of 5.0 m/s. If this object returns to the point of release in 3.0 s, what is the acceleration of a free falling object on this planet?

13. An object is thrown vertically upward from a 30.0 m tall building. The initial velocity of the object was 20.0 m/s up .Calculate the velocity with which the object hits the ground.

14. Calculate the time it took for the object to reach the ground.

15. While riding on a roller coaster, a girl drops an object. The roller coaster was rising vertically at a velocity of 11.0 m/s and was 5.00 m above the ground when the object was dropped. How long does it take the object to reach the ground?

16. An object is thrown vertically upward. If this object takes 5.30 s to go up and down, what height did it reach?

17. An object is dropped from a height of 25.0 m above the ground. What is the average velocity of the object as it falls to the ground?

18. A stone is thrown vertically downward from the top of a 96 m building with a velocity of -5.0 m/s. This stone is observed passing by a window that has a height of 2.0 m. Assume that the direction of the stone's motion is parallel with the height of the window. If the bottom of the window is 25 m from the ground, how long does it take for the stone to pass by the window?

19 A box is floating down a river at a constant velocity of 1.00 m/s east. A student is standing on a bridge that overlooks the river. The student releases a stone, initially at rest, when the object is 4.00 m upstream from the bridge.

If the stone hits the box, from what height above the water was the object dropped?

PRACTICE TEST

1. Which of the following graphs **best** represents a velocity-time graph for a stone that is dropped from the top of a tall building (ignoring air resistance)?

   A.

   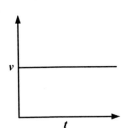

   B.

   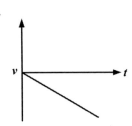

   C.

   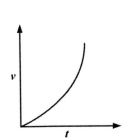

   D.

   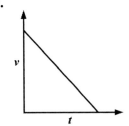

2. Which of the following graphs **best** represents a position-time graph for a stone that is dropped from the top of a tall building (ignoring air resistance)?

   A.

   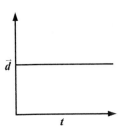

   B.

   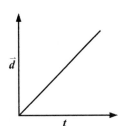

   C.

   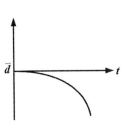

   D.

   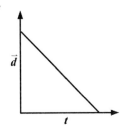

3. Which of the following graphs **best** represents an acceleration-time graph for a stone that is dropped from the top of a tall building (ignoring air resistance)?

A.
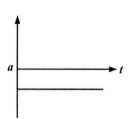

B.
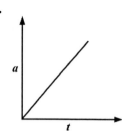

C.
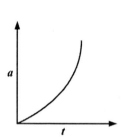

D.
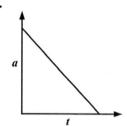

4. Which of the following graphs best represents a position-time graph for an object that is travelling along a straight horizontal line at a constant velocity of 10.0 m/s?

A.
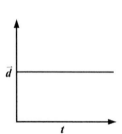

B.
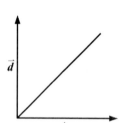

C.
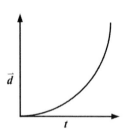

D.
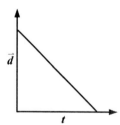

5. The position-time graph below describes an object travelling in a straight line due north.

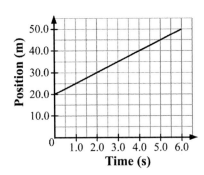

What is the velocity of the object?

A. 0.12 m/s north

B. 0.20 m/s north

C. 5.0 m/s north

D. 8.3 m/s north

6. Uniform motion is described as motion in which the

A. displacement remains constant

B. velocity remains constant

C. acceleration remains constant but not zero

D. velocity is 9.81 m/s

7. A baseball player throws a baseball straight up into the air and catches it a short time later. Which of the following velocity-time graphs best describes the motion of this ball?

A.

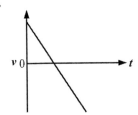

B.

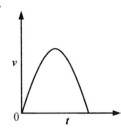

C.

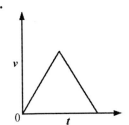

D.

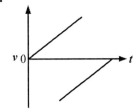

8. What is the displacement of the object during the 6.0 seconds of motion described in the graph?

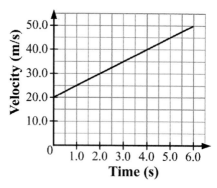

   A. +5.0 m

   B. +90 m

   C. $+1.8 \times 10^2$ m

   D. $+2.1 \times 10^2$ m

9. The motion described by the graph is **best** expressed as motion in which the

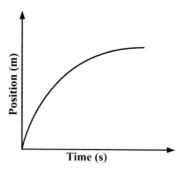

   A. object is moving at a constant velocity

   B. object is moving with increasing velocity

   C. object is moving with decreasing velocity

   D. acceleration of the object is increasing

10. If an object is thrown straight up into the air with a velocity of 8.0 m/s , what is the maximum height that it reaches?

   A. 3.3 m

   B. 6.5 m

   C. 8.5 m

   D. 9.7 m

11. A ball rolls 2.7 m up a constant slope before it stops momentarily.If the initial velocity of the ball was 2.0 m/s up the slope, what is the acceleration of the ball as it rolls up the slope?

A. -0.37 m/s^2

B. -0.74 m/s^2

C. -1.4 m/s^2

D. -9.8 m/s^2

12. A ball rolls 3.2 m up a constant slope before it stops momentarily. If the initial velocity of the ball was 2.2 m/s up the slope, how much time does it take the ball to roll up the slope?

A. 1.4 s

B. 2.9 s

C. 4.2 s

D. 6.6 s

13. An object is thrown straight up into the air from the top of a building at a velocity of 15.0 m/s, as shown in the diagram.

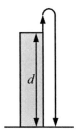

If the object hits the ground in 8.00 s, what is the height of the building?

A. 161 m

B. 194 m

C. 267 m

D. 311 m

14. An object is thrown straight up into the air from the top of a building at a velocity of 12.0 m/s, as shown in the diagram.

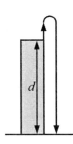

If the object hits the ground in 8.00 s, what is the speed of the object when it hits the ground?

A. 12.0 m/s

B. 66.5 m/s

C. 79.0 m/s

D. 91.5 m/s

15. A car accelerates uniformly from rest to a velocity of 105 km/h east in 9.0 s. What is the average velocity of the car during this acceleration?

A. 7.0 m/s east

B. 15 m/s east

C. 23 m/s east

D. 37 m/s east

NOTES

VECTOR KINEMATICS—PART B

When you are finished this unit, you should be able to…

• Perform vector addition and determine the resultant vector of several vectors added together

• Solve navigation problems involving the four cardinal directions

• Investigate and solve problems related to uniform and uniformly accelerated motion in one and two dimensions

Lesson	Page	Completed on
1. Addition of Vectors on a Plane	60	
2. Vector Components	65	
3. Velocity Vectors and Navigation	70	
4. Projectile Motion	76	
5. Projectiles—Thrown at an Angle	81	
Practice Test	87	
Answers and Solutions	at the back of the book	

PREREQUISITE SKILLS AND KNOWLEDGE

Prior to starting this unit, you should be able to…

• Write numbers in scientific notation

• Isolate a variable and combine algebraic expressions

• Construct graphs involving relevant quantities and analyze important characteristics such as slope, intercepts, and areas under the graph.

• Perform calculations and obtain the answer to the correct number of significant figures

• Substitute the correct units for all quantities in a calculation and express the proper final unit by appropriate cancellation of units

• Apply the ratios of sine, cosine, and tangent to right triangles

• Determine the composition of derived units in terms of simpler units

Lesson 1 ADDITION OF VECTORS ON A PLANE

Consider the following question:

A student walks 73 m north and then turns and walks 62 m east. What is the student's displacement?

Remember: Displacement is a vector quantity and is the shortest distance from the starting point to the ending point. A vector quantity has both magnitude (size) and direction.

A vector quantity is represented by a line with an arrow. The direction of the line represents the direction of the vector, and the length of the line represents the magnitude of the vector.

Direction can be expressed in a number of ways. Most commonly, angles are taken with respect to some static reference such as a horizontal or vertical line. The nature of these lines can vary immensely, from the four points of a compass, the shoreline of a river, or the horizon—the most useful choice is dependent on the particular question.

Compass direction is expressed in terms of north, east, south, and west, as shown in diagrams A and B. This is a common method that is found in most physics texts.

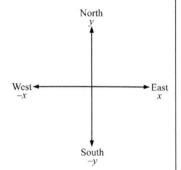

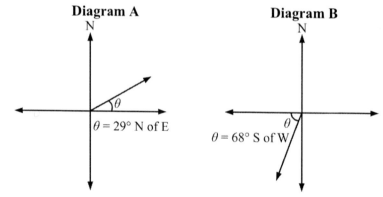

Direction may also be indicated as an angle measured counterclockwise from the positive x-axis (east), as is common in mathematics.

TAIL TO TIP VECTOR ADDITION

The two displacements (73 m north and 62 m east) can be added graphically or analytically. In both methods, a vector diagram is drawn. In the graphical method, a careful scale vector diagram is drawn. In the analytical method, a reasonable representation is drawn.

Vector diagrams require drawing the vectors tail to tip (tail to tip method). The order in which the vectors are drawn is not important.

Draw the vector $\vec{v}_1$.

Start the drawing of vector $\vec{v}_2$ at the head (tip) of this first vector, $\vec{v}_1$.

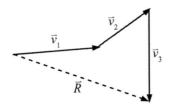

Draw the resultant vector $\vec{R}$ as shown in the diagram.

If there are more than two vectors, keep adding vectors tail to tip.

The **resultant vector** $\vec{R}$ is the arrow drawn from the tail of the first vector to the tip of the last vector and is equivalent to the sum of all of the individual vectors.

Graphical Method (ruler and protractor method)

Add the two displacements (73 m north and 62 m east) given at the beginning of this lesson.
Draw a careful scale diagram using the tail to tip method.

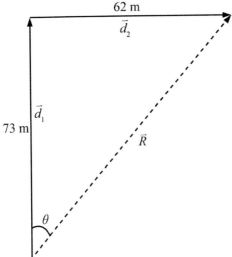

Measure the magnitude of the resultant vector (R) and the angle θ.
Scale 1.0 mm : 1.0 mm

$R = 96 \text{ mm} \Rightarrow 96 \text{ m}$
$\theta = 40.3° \approx 40°$
$\vec{R} = 96 \text{ m } 40° \text{ E of N or } 96 \text{ m } 50° \text{ N of E}$

NOTES

ANALYTICAL METHOD

Draw a vector diagram of reasonable representation using the tail to tip method.

If the vectors are perpendicular to each other, find the magnitude of the resultant vector (R) using the Pythagorean theorem.

$$c = \sqrt{a^2 + b^2}$$
$$R = \sqrt{(d_1)^2 + (d_2)^2}$$

The resultant vector is the final sum of all of the individual vectors being added.

Find the direction of the resultant vector $(\vec{R})$ using one of the trigonometric functions:

$$\sin\theta = \frac{\text{opposite}}{\text{hypotenuse}}$$
$$\cos\theta = \frac{\text{adjacent}}{\text{hypotenuse}}$$
$$\tan\theta = \frac{\text{opposite}}{\text{adjacent}}$$

Example

A student walks 73 m north and then turns and walks 62 m east. What is the student's displacement?

Solution

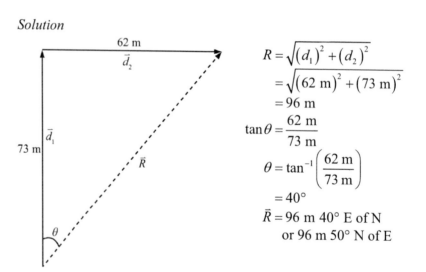

$$R = \sqrt{(d_1)^2 + (d_2)^2}$$
$$= \sqrt{(62 \text{ m})^2 + (73 \text{ m})^2}$$
$$= 96 \text{ m}$$
$$\tan\theta = \frac{62 \text{ m}}{73 \text{ m}}$$
$$\theta = \tan^{-1}\left(\frac{62 \text{ m}}{73 \text{ m}}\right)$$
$$= 40°$$
$$\vec{R} = 96 \text{ m } 40° \text{ E of N}$$
$$\text{or } 96 \text{ m } 50° \text{ N of E}$$

PRACTICE EXERCISES

Add the following displacement vectors:

1. 3.0 m south and 4.0 m south

2. 3.0 m south and 4.0 m north

3. 4.0 m east and 3.0 m south

4. 8.0 m west and 5.0 m north

5. 7.0 m east and 11.0 m north

6. 20.0 m east and 15.0 m south

7. 7.0 m south, 6.0 m east, and 8.0 m north (Hint: add collinear vectors first)

8. 15.0 m west, 12.0 m north, and 20.0 m east

Lesson 2 *VECTOR COMPONENTS*

Consider the following problem:

A student walks 75 m north and then turns and walks 62 m 32° W of N. What is the student's displacement?

The vector problems to this point have been solved using the Pythagorean theorem and basic trigonometry.

Pythagorean Theorem

$$c = \sqrt{a^2 + b^2}$$

Trigonometry Functions

$$\sin\theta = \frac{\text{opposite}}{\text{hypotenuse}} \qquad \cos\theta = \frac{\text{adjacent}}{\text{hypotenuse}} \qquad \tan\theta = \frac{\text{opposite}}{\text{adjacent}}$$

However, in this problem, the vectors are not perpendicular; therefore, they do not form a right angle. This problem may be solved using a number of methods. The component method makes use of the rectangular coordinate system. The vector is resolved into two components; one is oriented vertically and the other horizontally. The components are perpendicular to each other and can be added using the Pythagorean theorem.

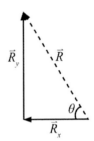

$$R = \sqrt{R_x^2 + R_y^2}$$

$$\cos\theta = \frac{R_x}{R}$$

$$\sin\theta = \frac{R_y}{R}$$

$$\tan\theta = \frac{R_y}{R_x}$$

where $\vec{R}$ = resultant vector

$\vec{R}_x$ = resultant x-component

$\vec{R}_y$ = resultant y-component

$$\cos\theta = \frac{\text{adjacent}}{\text{hypotenuse}}$$
$$= \frac{R_x}{R}$$
$$\sin\theta = \frac{\text{opposite}}{\text{hypotenuse}}$$
$$= \frac{R_y}{R}$$
$$\tan\theta = \frac{\text{opposite}}{\text{adjacent}}$$
$$= \frac{R_y}{R_x}$$
$$R = \sqrt{R_x^2 + R_y^2}$$

Recall, A student walks 75 m north and then turns and walks 62 m 32° W of N. Use the component method to find the student's displacement.

NOTES

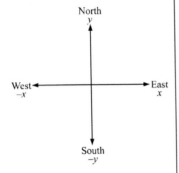

First calculate the *x*- and *y*-components of the vectors to be added together. Use the basic trigonometric relationships to find the magnitudes of these component vectors. Choose a vertical and horizontal direction to be represented by positive quantities and use these directions consistently throughout the calculation. In this case consider north and east as the positive directions.

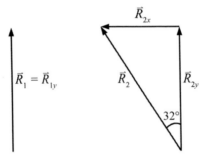

Resolve the first leg of the student's walk, 75 m north, into its *x*- and *y*-components $\left(\vec{R}_x \text{ and } \vec{R}_y \right)$. In this case there is only a vertical component associated with the displacement.

$$\vec{R}_{1y} = \vec{R}_1 = 75 \text{ m north} = 75 \text{ m}$$

Next resolve the second leg of the walk into its vertical and horizontal components, that is, break the second displacement into a component along the north-south direction and a component along the east-west direction. Use the trigonometric ratios of sine and cosine to determine the magnitude of these components.

$$\sin \theta = \frac{\text{opposite}}{\text{hypotenuse}} \qquad \cos \theta = \frac{\text{adjacent}}{\text{hypotenuse}}$$

$$\sin \theta = \frac{R_{2x}}{R_2} \qquad \cos \theta = \frac{R_{2y}}{R_2}$$

$$R_{2x} = R_2 \sin \theta \qquad R_{2y} = R_2 \cos \theta$$

$$= (62 \text{ m}) \sin 32° \qquad = (62 \text{ m}) \cos 32°$$

$$= 32.9 \text{ m} \qquad = 52.6 \text{ m}$$

Now, using north and east as the positive directions, it is possible to express the components of the displacements using only positive and negative values to denote direction.

$$\vec{R}_{1x} = 0$$
$$\vec{R}_{1y} = 75 \text{ m}$$

$$\vec{R}_{2x} = -32.9 \text{ m}$$
$$\vec{R}_{2y} = 52.6 \text{ m}$$

Add x-components to obtain $\vec{R}_x$.

$$\begin{aligned}\vec{R}_x &= \vec{R}_{1x} + \vec{R}_{2x} \\ &= 0 + \left(-32.9 \text{ m}\right) \\ &= -32.9 \text{ m or } 32.9 \text{ m west}\end{aligned}$$

Add y-components to obtain $\vec{R}_y$.

$$\begin{aligned}\vec{R}_y &= \vec{R}_{1y} + \vec{R}_{2y} \\ &= 75 \text{ m} + 52.6 \text{ m} \\ &= 127.6 \text{ m or } 127.6 \text{ m north}\end{aligned}$$

Add $\vec{R}_x$ and $\vec{R}_y$ to obtain $\vec{R}$.

$\vec{R}_y = 127.6$ m

$\vec{R}$

θ

$\vec{R}_x = -32.9$ m

$$\begin{aligned}R &= \sqrt{R_x{}^2 + R_y{}^2} \\ &= \sqrt{\left(32.9 \text{ m}\right)^2 + \left(127.6 \text{ m}\right)^2} \\ &= 1.3 \times 10^2 \text{ m}\end{aligned}$$

$$\begin{aligned}\tan\theta &= \frac{\text{opposite}}{\text{adjacent}} \\ &= \frac{R_y}{R_x} \\ &= \frac{127.6 \text{ m}}{32.9 \text{ m}} \\ \theta &= \tan^{-1}\left(\frac{127.6 \text{ m}}{32.9 \text{ m}}\right) \\ \theta &= 76° \\ \vec{R} &= 1.3 \times 10^2 \text{ m } 76° \text{ N of W}\end{aligned}$$

PRACTICE EXERCISES

Find the x- and y-components of the following displacements using the standard sign conventions.

1. 16.0 m north

2. 16.0 m 27.0° E of N

3. 20.0 m 38.0° W of N

Add the following displacement vectors.

4. 8.00 m east and 6.00 m north

5. 8.00 m east and 6.00 m 35.0° N of E

6. 12 m south and 15.0 m 55° E of N

7. 5.0 m 26° S of E and 7.0 m 58° W of N

8. 9.0 m 35° N of E and 7.0 m 25° S of E

Lesson 3 VELOCITY VECTORS AND NAVIGATION

Example

A boat travels at a velocity of 4.5 m/s north across a river. The river current is 2.0 m/s east. What is the velocity of the boat relative to the shore?

Solution

The velocity of the boat with respect to the shore is the sum of the velocity of the boat relative to water (4.5 m/s north) and the velocity of the river relative to the shore (2.0 m/s east).

These vectors are added in the same way in which displacement vectors are added. Since the velocity of the boat is measured relative to the water, and the water's velocity is measured with respect to the shore, the relative velocity of an object moving on the water with respect to the stationary shore will be the sum of the two velocities.

Draw a vector diagram.

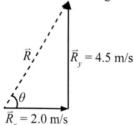

Find the magnitude of $\vec{R}$ using the Pythagorean theorem.

$$R = \sqrt{R_x^{\,2} + R_y^{\,2}}$$
$$= \sqrt{(2.0 \text{ m/s})^2 + (4.5 \text{ m/s})^2}$$
$$= 4.9 \text{ m/s}$$

Find the direction using $\tan\theta = \dfrac{\text{opposite}}{\text{adjacent}} = \dfrac{R_y}{R_x}$.

$$\tan\theta = \frac{4.5 \text{ m/s}}{2.0 \text{ m/s}}$$
$$\theta = 66°$$
$$\therefore \vec{R} = 4.9 \text{ m/s } 66° \text{ N of E}$$

Example

If a swimmer can swim with a speed of 2.5 m/s, find the angle that she must direct herself in order to cross a river directly that is flowing with a velocity of 1.5 m/s east.

Solution

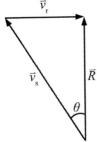

Notice that in this case, the resultant velocity will not be the hypotenuse. In this case the resultant will be the velocity vector that is directed to the north. To solve for the angle θ use the sine relation.

$$\sin \theta = \frac{\text{opposite}}{\text{hypotenuse}}$$

$$\sin \theta = \frac{v_r}{v_s}$$

$$\theta = \sin^{-1} \left(\frac{v_r}{v_s} \right)$$

$$= \sin^{-1} \left(\frac{1.5 \text{ m/s}}{2.5 \text{ m/s}} \right)$$

$$= \sin^{-1} (0.60)$$

$$= 37°$$

PRACTICE EXERCISES

1. A car is travelling in a straight line with uniform motion. The east component of this motion is 15.0 m/s, and the south component of the motion is 11.0 m/s. What is the velocity of the car?

2. A girl is moving up an escalator at a velocity of 2.00 m/s at an angle of 35.0° above the horizontal. What is the horizontal component of the girl's velocity?

3. What is the vertical component of the girl's velocity?

4. A plane flies with a velocity of 255 km/h north. If there is a strong wind of 112 km/h blowing east, what is the velocity of the plane relative to the ground?

5. A ball is thrown into the air at an angle of 40.0° above the horizontal with an initial velocity of 25.0 m/s. What is the vertical component of the initial velocity?

6. What is the horizontal component of the initial velocity?

7. A boat with a speed of 2.5 m/s is in a river with a velocity of 1.0 m/s south. What is the velocity of the boat relative to the shore when the boat is headed south?

8. What is the velocity of the boat relative to the shore when the boat is headed north?

9. What is the velocity of the boat relative to the shore when the boat is headed west?

10. An airplane is travelling east with an airspeed of 125 m/s. If a 25.0 m/s wind is blowing south, what is the velocity of the plane relative to the ground?

11. A particular boat can travel at a speed of 3.0 m/s. If the river current is 1.2 m/s east, in what direction must the boat head such that the resultant motion of the boat is north?

12. A pilot wants to fly west. If the plane has an airspeed of 95 m/s and there is a 25 m/s wind blowing north, in what direction must she steer the plane?

13. A boat is headed north in a river that flows due east at a velocity of 5.0 m/s. If the resultant velocity of this boat is 8.7 m/s 35.0° E of N, what is the speed of the boat with respect to the water?

14. A boat that can travel on still water at a speed of 5.0 m/s is headed west across a river. The river current is 2.5 m/s south. What is the velocity of the boat relative to the shore?

15. If the river is 2 395 m wide, how long does it take the boat to cross the river?

16. How far downstream is the boat when it reaches the other side of the river?

17. A boat that can travel 2.5 m/s on still water is now on a river that flows due east at a velocity of 2.0 m/s. What is the velocity of this boat with reference to a point on the shore when the boat is headed east?

18. What is the velocity of this boat with reference to a point on the shore when the boat is headed west?

19. What is the velocity of this boat with reference to a point on the shore when the boat is headed north?

20. What is the velocity of this boat with reference to a point on the shore when the boat is headed 45.0° W of N?

Lesson 4 PROJECTILE MOTION

The acceleration is g. $g = 9.81$ m/s^2

A baseball thrown by a baseball player, a football kicked by a football player, a bullet fired at a distant target, an object dropped from a plane are all examples of projectile motion.

When an object is thrown into the air, it is a projectile. You have already dealt with projectiles when they are thrown vertically upward, or when they are dropped. This section will deal with projectiles that are:

• thrown horizontally through the air

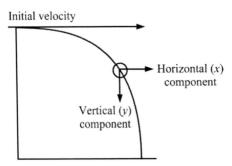

• thrown into the air at an angle

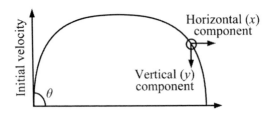

In projectile motion, the object has both a vertical and a horizontal velocity component. These two components are independent of each other except for the time of motion (i.e., the time the object travels horizontally is the same time it travels vertically). Neglect air friction,

• the horizontal motion is uniform motion, and is described by the equation

$$\bar{v} = \frac{\bar{d}}{t}$$

• the vertical motion is uniformly accelerated motion, and is described by the equations:

$$\bar{a} = \frac{\bar{v} - \bar{v}_0}{t}$$

$$\bar{d} = \left(\frac{\bar{v} + \bar{v}_0}{2} \right) t$$

$$\bar{d} = \bar{v}_0 t + \frac{1}{2} \bar{a} t^2$$

$$\bar{v}_2 = \bar{v}_{02} + 2\bar{a}\bar{d}$$

76

PROJECTILES—THROWN HORIZONTALLY

Example

An object is thrown horizontally at a velocity of 20.0 m/s from the top of a 50.0 m tall building. How far from the base of the building does the object hit the ground? (What is the range of this object?)

Solution

The question is asked to find the range of the object, which is the horizontal component of distance.

Therefore use $v = \dfrac{d}{t}$ or $d = vt$

Find t from the vertical component of distance

v_0	v	a	d	t
0	×	-9.81 m/s^2	-50.0 m	?

$$d = v_0 t + \frac{1}{2}at^2$$

$$-50.0 \text{ m} = \frac{1}{2}(-9.81 \text{ m/s}^2)(t^2)$$

$$t = \sqrt{\frac{2(50.0 \text{ m})}{9.81 \text{ m/s}^2}}$$

$$= 3.19 \text{ s}$$

Range of the object
$$d = vt$$
$$= (20.0 \text{ m/s})(3.19 \text{ s})$$
$$= 63.9 \text{ m}$$

NOTES

Range is how far the object travels horizontally.

PRACTICE EXERCISES

1. An object is thrown horizontally at a velocity of 10.0 m/s from the top of a 90.0 m building. What is the range of this object?

2. An object is thrown horizontally at a velocity of 25.0 m/s from the top of a 1.50×10^2 m building. Calculate the range of this object.

3. An object is thrown horizontally at a velocity of 18.0 m/s from the top of a cliff. If the range of this object is 100 m, how high is the cliff?

4. An object is thrown horizontally at a velocity of 20.0 m/s from the top of a cliff. If the range of this object is 48.0 m, how high is the cliff?

5. An object is thrown horizontally from the top of a building at a velocity of 15.0 m/s. If the object takes 5.50 s to reach the ground, how high is the building?

6. An object is thrown horizontally from the top of a cliff at a velocity of 20.0 m/s.

a) If the object takes 4.20 s to reach the ground, what is the range of this object?

b) What is the velocity of the object when it hits the ground? (Note: add horizontal and final vertical velocities)

7. The dots below represent the position of a projectile every 0.10 s as it is projected horizontally east along an inclined air table.

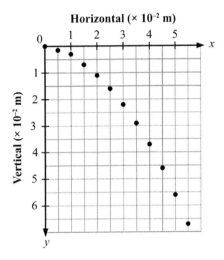

Horizontal (× 10⁻² m)

Analyze this motion by answering the following questions.

a) Complete the following table:

time (s)	displacement from t = 0 (m)		displacement during time interval (m)		average velocity during time interval (m/s)	
	horiz.	vert.	horiz.	vert.	horiz.	vert.
0						
0.10						
0.20						
0.30						
0.40						
0.50						
0.60						
0.70						
0.80						
0.90						
1.00						
1.10						

b) Using your horizontal velocity, draw a velocity-time graph on the grid below.

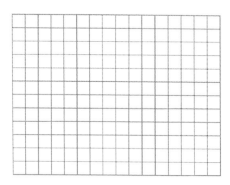

c) Using your vertical velocity, draw a velocity-time graph on the grid below.

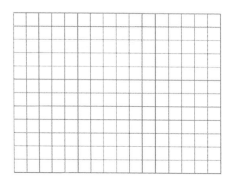

d) Using your graphs, find

    i) the horizontal acceleration

    ii) the vertical acceleration

8. An object is thrown horizontally from the top of an 85.0 m building.

    a) If the range of this object is 67.8 m, what was the horizontal velocity of the object?

    b) What is the velocity at which the object hits the ground? (Note: add the horizontal and final vertical velocities.)

Lesson 5 *PROJECTILES—THROWN AT AN ANGLE*

When both directions along a line are involved, the direction to the right or up is positive (+), and the direction to the left or down is negative (−).

NOTES

Example

An object is thrown into the air at a velocity of 20.0 m/s at an angle of 30.0° with the horizontal. What is the range of the object?

Range is how far the object travels horizontally.

Solution

The question is asked to find the range of the object, which is the horizontal component (displacement).

To do so, we first find the vertical and horizontal components of the velocity.

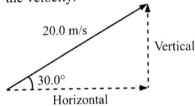

$$\sin\theta = \frac{\text{opposite}}{\text{hypotenuse}} \qquad \cos\theta = \frac{\text{adjacent}}{\text{hypotenuse}}$$

$$\sin 30.0° = \frac{\text{vertical}}{20.0 \text{ m/s}} \qquad \cos 30.0° = \frac{\text{horizontal}}{20.0 \text{ m/s}}$$

$$\text{vertical} = 10.0 \text{ m/s} \qquad \text{horizontal} = 17.3 \text{ m/s}$$

$$\bar{v}_y = (20.0 \text{ m/s})\sin 30.0° \qquad \bar{v}_x = (20.0 \text{ m/s})\cos 30.0°$$
$$= 10.0 \text{ m/s} \qquad\qquad = 17.3 \text{ m/s}$$

Find t from the vertical component.

$\bar{v}_{y(i)}$	$\bar{v}_{y(f)}$	$\bar{a}$	$\bar{d}$	t
10.0 m/s	−10.0 m/s	−9.81 m/s2	X	?

(Remember: An object will return to the ground at the same speed that it was thrown from the ground.)

$$\bar{a} = \frac{\bar{v}_{y(f)} - \bar{v}_{y(i)}}{t}$$

$$t = \frac{-10.0 \text{ m/s} - 10.0 \text{ m/s}}{-9.81 \text{ m/s}^2}$$

$$t = 2.04 \text{ s}$$

The range
$$d = v \times t$$
$$= (17.3 \text{ m/s})(2.04 \text{ s})$$
$$= 35.3 \text{ m}$$

PRACTICE EXERCISES

1. An object is thrown from the ground into the air at an angle of 40.0° from the horizontal at a velocity of 18.0 m/s. What is the range of this object?

2. An object is thrown from the ground into the air at an angle of 20.0° from the horizontal at a velocity of 15.0 m/s. What is the range of this object?

3. An object is thrown into the air with a velocity of 25.0 m/s at an angle of 32.0° to the horizontal. What is the range of this object?

4. An object is thrown from the ground into the air with a velocity of 20.0 m/s at an angle of 27.0° to the horizontal. What is the maximum height reached by this object?

5. An object is thrown from the ground into the air at an angle of 30.0° to the horizontal. If this object reaches a maximum height of 5.75 m, at what velocity was it thrown?

6. An object is projected from the ground into the air at an angle of 35.0° to the horizontal. If this object is in the air for 9.26 s, at what velocity was it thrown?

7. An object is thrown from the ground into the air at a velocity of 15.7 m/s at an unknown angle to the horizontal. If this object has a range of 25.0 m and was in the air for 2.15 s, at what angle was this object thrown?

8. An object is thrown into the air with a velocity of 30.0 m/s at an angle of 35.0° to the horizontal. What is the range of this object?

9. The dots below represent the position of a projectile every 0.10 s as it is projected at an angle up an inclined air table. Based on the motion described on the graph, complete the following data table.

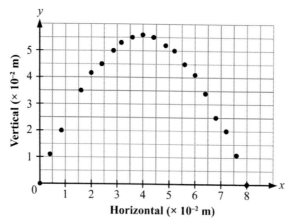

time (s)	displacement from t = 0 (m)		displacement during time interval (m)		average velocity during time interval (m/s)	
	horiz.	vert.	horiz.	vert.	horiz.	vert.
0						
0.10						
0.20						
0.30						
0.40						
0.50						
0.60						
0.70						
0.80						
0.90						
1.00						
1.10						
1.20						
1.30						
1.40						
1.50						
1.60						
1.70						
1.80						
1.90						
2.00						

b) draw a velocity-time graph using your values for horizontal velocity from the table.

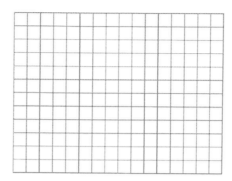

c) draw a velocity-time graph using your values for vertical velocity from the table.

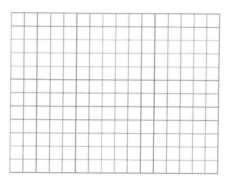

d) Using your graphs from parts b and c,

    i) find the horizontal acceleration

    ii) find the vertical acceleration

10. A ball rolls off an incline, as shown in the diagram to the right, at a velocity of 22 m/s. How far from point B will the ball hit the floor?

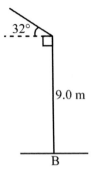

11. An object is projected from the top of a building at an angle of 28°, as shown in the diagram, at a velocity of 15 m/s. If the object hits the ground 32 m from the base of the building, how high is the building?

PRACTICE TEST

1. Linda starts walking from the corner of a vacant lot and walks 12 m 33° W of S. What is Linda's westerly displacement from the corner of the lot?

   A. +6.5 m

   C. +10 m

   B. −6.5 m

   D. −10 m

2. What is Linda's southerly displacement from the corner of the lot?

   A. +6.5 m

   C. +10 m

   B. −6.5 m

   D. −10 m

3. Marco starts walking from the corner of a vacant lot and walks 10.0 m east, stops, turns, and walks an additional 20.0 m 30.0° N of W. What is the magnitude of his resultant displacement?

   A. 12.4 m

   C. 29.1 m

   B 17.3 m

   D. 30.8 m

4. What is the direction of his displacement?

   A. 20° N of E

   C. 54° N of E

   B. 20° N of W

   D. 54° N of W

5. A pilot flies her plane with a velocity of 215 km/h east. There is a wind blowing 85 km/h south (i.e., from the north). What is the speed of the plane in reference to the ground?

   A. 130 km/h

   C. 231 km/h

   B. 197 km/h

   D. 300 km/h

6. What is the direction of her resultant displacement?

   A. 22° E of S

   C. 68° S of E

   B. 22° S of E

   D. 68° RCS

7. If we ignore air friction, when the speed of a ball is doubled, that is thrown horizontally from the roof of a building, the time that it takes to reach the ground will

   A. double

   C. remain the same

   B. half

   D. increase four times

8. If we ignore air friction, when the speed of a ball is halved, that is thrown horizontally from the roof of a building, the vertical velocity with which the ball hits the ground will

   A. half

   C. remain the same

   B. double

   D. decrease four times

9. If we ignore air friction, when we throw an object into the air at an angle above the horizontal, which of the following components remain constant?

   i) The horizontal component of the velocity
   ii) The vertical component of the velocity

   A. i only

   C. both i and ii

   B. ii only

   D. neither i nor ii

10. An object is thrown into the air at an angle of 30° above the horizontal. If we ignore air friction, what is the vertical acceleration and the vertical velocity when the object reaches its maximum displacement?

    A. $\vec{v} = 0$, $\vec{a} = 0$

    C. $\vec{v}$ = maximum, $\vec{a} = 0$

    B. $\vec{v} = 0$, $\vec{a} = -9.81$ m/s2

    D. $\vec{v}$ = maximum, $\vec{a} = -9.81$ m/s2

11. An object is thrown from ground level at a velocity of 25.0 m/s at an angle of 20.0° above the horizontal. If there is a building 25.0 m away, at what height above the ground will the object hit the building?

    A. 3.55 m

    C. 14.2 m

    B. 3.90 m

    D. 14.7 m

12. Which of the following graphs best represents the position-time graph for the vertical motion of a projectile that is thrown horizontally?

A.
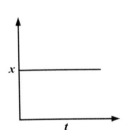

B.
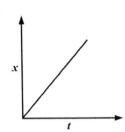

C.
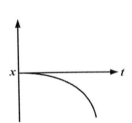

D. .
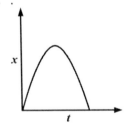

13. Which of the following graphs best represents the velocity-time graph for the horizontal motion of a projectile that is thrown into the air at an angle of 30° above the horizontal.

A.

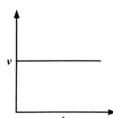

B.

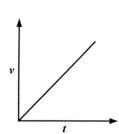

C.

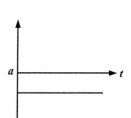

D.

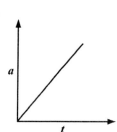

14. Which of the following graphs best represents the acceleration-time graph for the vertical motion of a projectile thrown into the air at an angle of 30° above the horizontal?

A.

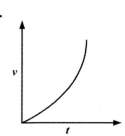

B.

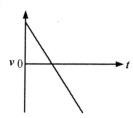

C.

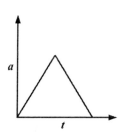

D.

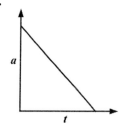

15. Meryn has a soccer ball, a baseball and a golf ball, and she is standing on a platform that is 6.0 m high. She throws the baseball horizontally and she simply drops the golf ball and the soccer ball, at the same instant in time. Which ball hits the ground first?

A. baseball

B. golf ball

C. All will reach the ground at the same time.

D. soccer ball

NOTES

DYNAMICS

When you are finished this unit, you should be able to…

- Understand Newton's three laws of motion
- Recognize the vector nature of gravitational fields and solve problems involving gravitational forces
- Analyze and solve problems that involve static and kinetic friction for objects on horizontal and inclined surfaces
- Analyze and solve problems using free-body diagrams for unbalanced forces acting on an object in various situations

Lesson	Page	Completed on
1. Dynamics	92	
2. Newton's First Law Of Motion	96	
3. Forces In Nature	101	
4. Force Due To Gravity (Weight)	104	
5. Applied Force or Tension	109	
6. Physics Of An Inclined Plane	120	
7. Newton's Third Law Of Motion	126	
Practice Test	128	
Answers and Solutions	at the back of the book	

PREREQUISITE SKILLS AND KNOWLEDGE

Prior to starting this unit, you should be able to…

- Write numbers in scientific notation
- Isolate a variable and combine algebraic expressions
- Perform calculations and obtain the answer to the correct number of significant figures
- Substitute the correct units for all quantities in a calculation and express the proper final unit by appropriate cancellation of units
- Differentiate between scalar and vector quantities
- Determine the composition of derived units in terms of simpler units

Lesson 1   DYNAMICS

NOTES

Thus far, we have been discussing kinematics—the description of how an object moves. In this section, we will discuss dynamics—*the study of forces*. Kinematics described *how* an object moves; dynamics will deal with *why* it moves.

In 1665, when Isaac Newton was 23 years old, he formulated three laws of motion. During this time, he also formulated the Law of Universal Gravitation. In this section we will discuss the Laws of Motion and, later, we will discuss the Law of Universal Gravitation. Before we start, let's look at the concept of force.

The unit of force is the Newton.

FORCE

- Symbol: $\vec{F}$
- Definition: a push or pull
- Units: Newton (N)

$\vec{F}_{net}$ **is the symbol for the net force (sum of the forces).**

Forces are vector quantities, therefore they have direction as well as magnitude.

NEWTON'S FIRST LAW OF MOTION

Newton's first law of motion states that an object continues in its state of rest or its state of velocity in a straight line unless acted on by an unbalanced force.

A Newton is equal to a $kg \cdot m/s^2$

An unbalanced force is also called the net force.

An object will remain at constant velocity unless acted on by an unbalanced force.

Example 1

A force of 7.0 N east and a force of 5.0 N south act on an object. What is the net force on the object?

Solution
- Draw a vector diagram.
- Find the magnitude of the net force (resultant vector) using the Pythagorean Theorem.
- Find the direction of the net force using one of the trigonometric functions.

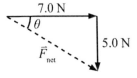

$$F_{net} = \sqrt{\left(F_1\right)^2 + \left(F_2\right)^2}$$
$$= \sqrt{\left(7.0 \text{ N}\right)^2 + \left(5.0 \text{ N}\right)^2}$$
$$\tan\theta = \frac{\text{opposite}}{\text{adjacent}}$$
$$= \frac{5.0 \text{ N}}{7.0 \text{ N}}$$
$$\theta = 36°$$
$$\vec{F}_{net} = 8.6 \text{ N } 36° \text{ S of E}$$

or

$$\vec{F}_{net} = 8.6 \text{ N } 324°$$

Example 2

A force of 3.0 N west and a force of 4.0 N 33° S of E act on an object. What is the net force on the object?

Solution

First express the directions heading counter clockwise with respect to the *x*-axis

Considering east and north direction as positive, resolve the force $F_1 = 3.0 \text{ N west}$ into *x* and *y* components.

$$\vec{F}_{1x} = F_1 \cos\theta \qquad = F_1 \sin\theta$$
$$3.0 \text{ N}\cos 180° \quad = 3.0 \text{ N}\sin 180°$$
$$= -3.0 \text{ N} \qquad = 0 \text{ N}$$

Resolve the force $\vec{F}_2 = 4.0 \text{ N } 33° \text{ S of E}$ into *x* and *y* components.

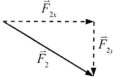

$$\overline{F}_{2x} = F_2 \cos\theta \qquad = F_2 \sin\theta$$
$$= 4.0\cos 327° \quad = 4.0\sin 327°$$
$$= 3.35 \text{ N} \qquad = -2.18 \text{ N}$$

Add *x* components.
$$\overline{F}_x = \overline{F}_{1x} + \overline{F}_{2x}$$
$$= \left(-3.0\text{N}\right) + 3.35 \text{ N}$$
$$= 0.35 \text{ N (positive indicates an east direction)}$$

Add y components.

$$\overline{F}_y = \overline{F}_{1y} + \overline{F}_{2y}$$
$$= 0 + (-2.18\ \text{N})$$
$$= -2.18\ \text{N (negative indicates a south direction)}$$

Find the magnitude of the net force (resultant vector) using the Pythagorean Theorem.

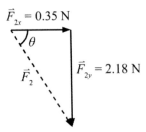

$$F_{net} = \sqrt{\left(F_x\right)^2 + \left(F_y\right)^2}$$
$$= \sqrt{\left(0.35\ \text{N}\right)^2 + \left(2.18\ \text{N}\right)^2}$$
$$= 2.2\ \text{N}$$
$$\tan\theta = \frac{F_y}{F_x}$$
$$= \frac{2.18\ \text{N}}{0.35\ \text{N}}$$
$$\theta = 81°$$
$$\overline{F}_{net} = 2.2\ \text{N } 81°\ \text{S of E}$$
$$\text{or}$$
$$= 2.2\ \text{N } 279°$$

PRACTICE EXERCISES

Note: Answers may also be expressed in angles counter clockwise with respect to the *x*-axis.

1. A force of 2.0 N east and a force of 3.0 N east act on an object. What is the net force on the object?

2. A force of 2.0 N east and a force of 3.0 N west act on an object. What is the net force on the object?

3. A force of 2.0 N east and a force of 3.0 N south act on an object. What is the net force on the object?

4. A force of 2.0 N east and a force of 3.0 N 25° N of E act on an object. What is the net force on the object?

5. Forces of 2.0 N 38° N of W and 3.0 N 61° S of W act on an object. What is the net force on the object?

6. A force of 2.0 N east, a force of 3.0 N west and a force of 4.0 N north act on an object. What is the net force on the object?

95

Lesson 2 NEWTON'S FIRST LAW OF MOTION—CONTINUED

Newton's First Law of Motion is sometimes referred to as the Law of Inertia. Inertia is the tendency for an object to remain at constant velocity. Therefore, inertia is also defined as the tendency of a body to resist a sudden change in its state of rest or its uniform motion.

Inertia is the tendency for an object to remain at a constant velocity including zero.

Let's draw on your experiences to illustrate this law. If you are in a car travelling at 50 km/h when it hits a concrete wall head on, the car will come to a sudden stop because of the extreme force acting on it. However, if you are not wearing your seat belt, you will continue at 50 km/h until forces acting on you bring you to a stop. We wear seat belts to keep us in the car—where we usually have a better chance of less severe injury.

If you are sitting at a stop light when someone runs into your car from behind at a velocity of 40 km/h, your car experiences a sudden force that causes it to increase its velocity. Your body will move too; however, your head, which is somewhat loosely attached to your body, will have a certain tendency to remain stopped (at rest). So, as your body is suddenly thrust forward, your head (remaining at rest) is caused to be snapped back—this results in whiplash injuries. Head restraints in cars are designed to help reduce these injuries.

Imagine you are standing in the aisle on a transit bus travelling at 50 km/h and the bus driver suddenly brakes hard. What will happen to you? Also, imagine you are on this same bus travelling at 30 km/h and the bus suddenly turns sharply to the right. What happens to you then?

Let's also imagine that Leo has a car that will accelerate from 0 to 100 km/h in 7.0 s. Suppose Jack goes for a ride with him, and Leo wants to show off a bit. Leo starts his car, and accelerates hard, what does Jack experience?

These are illustrations of Newton's First Law of Motion (Law of Inertia).

NEWTON'S SECOND LAW OF MOTION

The rate of change in an object's velocity is directly proportional to the net force and inversely proportional to the object's mass.

Newton's Second Law of Motion states that the rate of change in an object's acceleration is directly proportional to the net force, and inversely proportional to the object's mass.

$$a \propto F_{net}$$
$$a \propto \frac{1}{m}$$

or magnitude of acceleration $a = k \dfrac{F_{net}}{m}$

Force is the product of mass times acceleration.

k is called the proportionality constant. The above equation can be written as $a = \dfrac{F_{net}}{m}$. This is because the net force requires accelerating a 1 kg object at 1 m/s^2 is 1 N. Therefore the value of $k = 1$.

Force and acceleration are vector quantities so the above formula is usually written as: $\vec{F}_{net} = m\vec{a}$ The direction of the acceleration is in the direction of the net force acting on the object.

NOTE: Force is the product of mass times acceleration. Therefore, the unit of force (Newton) is the product of mass units (kg) and acceleration units (m/s^2).

Therefore, $1 \text{ N} = 1 \text{ kg} \cdot m/s^2$

Before we discuss this law, we need to discuss the concept of mass.

MASS

- Symbol: m
- Definition: Mass is difficult to define; it is related to the amount of matter in an object. It can be defined as the quantitative measure of an object's inertia. From your experiences, you know that the greater the mass of an object the greater its inertia. Imagine a kicking a soccer ball. It accelerates fairly easily as your foot makes contact with it.. Now, imagine kicking the soccer ball after filling it with sand. You would expect that the soccer ball would resist a change in velocity to a much greater extent than did the air filled soccer ball. So the more mass an object possesses, the more slowly it will accelerate if acted upon by some constant force.
- Units: kilogram (kg)
- Mass is a scalar quantity.

Example 1

A net force of 30 N south acts on a 10 kg object. What is the acceleration of the object?

Solution

$$\vec{F}_{net} = m\vec{a}$$

$$\vec{a} = \frac{\vec{F}_{net}}{m}$$

$$= \frac{30 \text{ N south}}{10 \text{ kg}}$$

$$= 3.0 \text{ m/s}^2 \text{ south}$$

Example 2

A 22 kg object accelerates uniformly from rest to a velocity of 2.5 m/s west in 8.7 s. What is the net force acting on the object during this acceleration?

Solution

For this problem west is considered as positive direction.

$$\bar{a} = \frac{\bar{v} - \bar{v}_0}{t}$$
$$= \frac{2.5 \text{ m/s} - 0}{8.7 \text{ s}}$$
$$= 0.29 \text{ m/s}^2 \text{ west}$$

Force acting on the object

$$\bar{F}_{net} = m\bar{a}$$
$$= (22 \text{ kg})(0.29 \text{ m/s}^2)$$
$$= 6.3 \text{ N west}$$

PRACTICE EXERCISES

Formula: $\overline{F}_{net} = m\overline{a}$

1. A net force of 9.0 N east is used to push a 20.0 kg object. What is the acceleration of the object?

2. A net force of 15.0 N north is used to pull an object. If the magnitude of acceleration of this object is 8.0 m/s^2, what is the mass of the object?

3. A 16.0 kg object is accelerated at a rate of 2.0 m/s^2 by a net force. What is the magnitude of the net force?

4. A 12.0 kg object is accelerated by a net force of 10.2 N east. What is the acceleration of the object?

5. A 5.2 kg object is accelerating at a rate of 6.0 m/s^2. What is the magnitude of the net force acting on the object?

6. If an 18 kg object has a net force of 2.0 N south acting on it, what is the acceleration of the object?

7. A 925 kg car accelerates uniformly from rest to a velocity of 25.0 m/s south in 10.0 s. What is the net force acting on the car during this acceleration?

8. A 1.08×10^3 kg car uniformly accelerates for 12.0 s from rest. During this time, the car travels 132 m north. What is the net force acting on the car during this acceleration?

9. A 1.20×10^3 kg car accelerates uniformly from 5.0 m/s east to 12 m/s east. During this acceleration, the car travels 94 m. What is the net force acting on the car during this acceleration?

10. A net force of 2.5×10^3 N north acts on an object for 5.0 s. During this time, the object accelerates from rest to a speed of 48 km/h. What is the mass of this object?

11. A net force of 6.6 N east acts on a 9.0 kg object. This object accelerates uniformly from rest to a velocity of 3.0 m/s east.

   a) How far did the object travel while accelerating?

   b) What is the time of acceleration?

Lesson 3 FORCES IN NATURE

The net force on an object is the sum of all forces acting on the object. We can identify the various forces acting on an object with descriptive terms.

- Force due to gravity (or weight) ($\overline{F}_g$)

- Normal force ($\overline{F}_N$)

- Frictional force ($\overline{F}_f$)

- Applied force or tension ($\overline{F}_T$)

FORCE DUE TO GRAVITY (WEIGHT)

- Symbol: $\overline{F}_g$

- Definition: Force due to gravity is the force, which attracts any two objects together.

- Unit: Newton (N)

Weight is a force; therefore, it is a vector quantity. In case of an object on Earth, the direction of force due to gravity (weight) is towards the center of the Earth (directed down).

If you throw an object into the air, it will return to Earth. If you drop an object from some distance from the floor, it will fall to the floor. Why is this? Earth exerts a significant pull on these objects. This pull is due to gravity. This is what we call weight. The weight of an object depends on:

1. the mass of the object.
$$m \propto F_g$$

2. the magnitude of the acceleration due to gravity (g)
$$g \propto F_g$$

Therefore, $F_g = mg$

The acceleration due to gravity near Earth's surface is taken as 9.81 m/s^2.

$\bar{g}$ can also be referred to as the gravitational field strength.

$$\vec{F}_g = m\vec{g}$$
$$\vec{g} = \frac{\vec{F}_g}{m} \text{ down}$$

Gravitational field strength is defined as the gravitational force (weight) per unit mass.

Remember, we use $\overline{F}_{net}$ to indicate for net force.

Weight is a force while mass is an intrinsic property of matter.

In order for a mass to accelerate, there must be a net force acting on it (Newton's 2nd Law of Motion). The ratio of the force per unit mass is the gravitational field strength or acceleration due to gravity.

The acceleration due to gravity or gravitational field strength near Earth's surface is 9.81 m/s^2 or 9.81 N/kg.

NOTE: m/s^2 and N/kg are equivalent units. Remember, a Newton is a kg$\cdot$m/s^2, therefore, $\dfrac{\text{N}}{\text{kg}} = \dfrac{\text{kg}\cdot\text{m/s}^2}{\text{kg}} = \text{m/s}^2$.

Example 1

What is the weight of a 12.0 kg object near Earth's surface?

Solution
The magnitude of the weight:
$$F_g = mg$$
$$= (12.0 \text{ kg})(9.81 \text{ m/s}^2)$$
$$= 118 \text{ N}$$

PRACTICE EXERCISES

Formula: $\vec{F}_g = m\vec{g}$ $F_g = mg$

1. What is the weight of a 25.0 kg object near Earth's surface?

2. What is the mass of an object if it has a weight of 80.0 N near Earth's surface?

3. What is the magnitude of the acceleration due to gravity near the surface of the Moon if an object that has a mass of 22.0 kg has a weight of 36.0 N near the Moon's surface?

4. What is the magnitude of the weight of a 72.0 kg object near Earth's surface?

5. What is the mass of an object if it has a magnitude of the weight of 127 N near Earth's surface?

Lesson 4   FORCE DUE TO GRAVITY (WEIGHT)

Although near Earth's surface we use 9.81 m/s² as the value of gravity, it is not a constant value. This value depends on the mass of Earth (or other planet). It also depends on the distance from the centre of Earth (or other planet)

$$g \propto m_1$$

$$g \propto \frac{1}{d^2}$$

Therefore, $g = \dfrac{Gm_1}{d^2}$

Earth is not a perfect sphere (ball). Earth is somewhat flatter at the poles and somewhat bulged at the equator. For this reason; the acceleration due to gravity varies with the latitude. It is less at the equator than at the poles.

Weight is often confused with mass. Weight is the force due to gravity and varies from location to location. Mass only depends on the amount of matter an object contains, and does not vary with the location.

The weight of an object varies from location to location.

The mass of an object does not depend on location.

NORMAL FORCE

The normal force is the force perpendicular to the surface of contact.

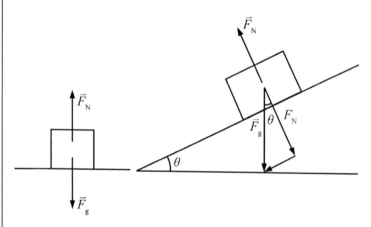

When an object is placed on a surface, the surface exerts a perpendicular force on the object. This force is the normal force..

On a horizontal surface, the magnitude of the normal force is equal to the magnitude of the weight of the object.

$$F_N = F_g = mg$$

On an incline, the magnitude of the normal force is equal to the component of the weight of the object which is perpendicular to the surface.

$$F_N = F_g \cos\theta$$
$$= mg \cos\theta$$

FRICTIONAL FORCE

Frictional forces are forces that always oppose motion. They depend on:
- the normal force
- the nature of the two surfaces

NOTE: Frictional forces do not depend on the area of contact between the two surfaces.

The nature of the surfaces is expressed as the coefficient of friction (μ).

$F_\text{f} = \mu F_\text{N}$

or $F_\text{f} = \mu mg \cos\theta$

Example 1

A 7.6 kg object is resting on a horizontal surface. What is the normal force acting on the object?

Solution

Here the normal force is upward and is equal to the magnitude of the weight.

$F_\text{N} = F_\text{g}$

$F_\text{N} = F_\text{g} = mg$

$\quad = (7.6\,\text{kg})(9.81\,\text{m/s}^2)$

$\quad = 75\,\text{N}$

Example 2

A 7.6 kg object is at rest on an inclined plane. If the inclined plane makes an angle with the horizontal of 33°, what is the magnitude of the normal force acting on the object?

Solution

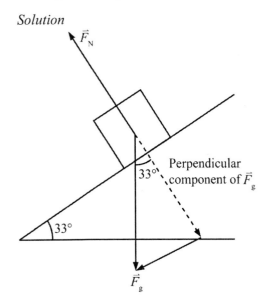

Perpendicular component of $\vec{F}_\text{g}$

The normal force is perpendicular to the surface of the inclined plane and is equal to the perpendicular component of the weight.

$$F_{g(y)} = F_g \cos \theta$$
$$F_N = F_{g(y)}$$
$$F_g = mg$$
$$= (7.6 \text{ kg})(9.81 \text{ m/s}^2)$$
$$= 75 \text{ N}$$
$$F_N = F_{g(y)}$$
$$= F_g \cos 33°$$
$$= (75 \text{ N})(0.839)$$
$$= 62 \text{ N}$$

Example 3

A 7.6 kg object is pulled along a horizontal surface. If the coefficient of friction between the surfaces is 0.20, what is the force of friction?

Solution

$$F_N = F_g$$
$$F_N = F_g = mg$$
$$= (7.6 \text{ kg})(9.81 \text{ m/s}^2)$$
$$= 75 \text{ N}$$
$$F_f = \mu F_N$$
$$= (0.20)(75 \text{ N})$$
$$= 15 \text{ N}$$

Example 4

A 7.6 kg object is pulled up an inclined plane. If the inclined plane makes an angle with the horizontal of 33°, and the coefficient of friction is 0.20, what is the magnitude of the force of friction?

Solution

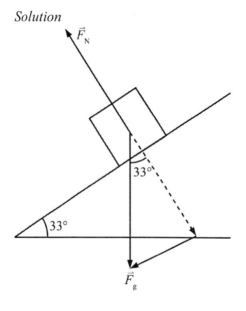

The normal force is perpendicular to the surface of the inclined plane and is equal to the perpendicular component of the weight.

$F_{g(y)} = F_g \cos\theta$

$F_g = mg$
$\quad = (7.6\,\text{kg})(9.81\,\text{m/s}^2)$
$\quad = 75\,\text{N}$

$F_N = F_{g(y)}$
$\quad = F_g \cos 33°$
$\quad = (75\,\text{N})(0.839)$
$\quad = 63\,\text{N}$

$F_{fr} = \mu F_N$
$\quad = (0.20)(63\,\text{N})$
$\quad = 13\,\text{N}$

PRACTICE EXERCISES

Formulas: $F_N = F_g = mg$ $F_{fr} = \mu F_N$ $F_{fr} = \mu mg \cos \theta$

1. A 14.0 kg object is resting on a horizontal surface. What is the magnitude of the normal force acting on the object?

2. A 9.6 kg object is pulled along a horizontal surface. If the coefficient of friction between the surfaces is 0.11, what is the force of friction?

3. A 20.0 N object is placed on a horizontal surface. A force of 3.0 N is required to keep the object moving at a constant speed. What is the coefficient of friction between the two surfaces?

4. A 16.2 kg object is at rest on an inclined plane. If the inclined plane makes an angle with the horizontal of 25.0°, what is the magnitude of the normal force acting on the object?

5. A 15.0 N object is pulled up an inclined plane. If the inclined plane makes an angle with the horizontal of 35.0°, and the coefficient of friction is 0.300, what is the magnitude of the force of friction?

Lesson 5   APPLIED FORCE OR TENSION

A force applied through a rope, for example, is referred to as a tension force (applied force). However, this force can be exerted by pushing or pulling the object directly.

The net force on an object is the sum of all forces acting on the object. To determine the net force on an object, we identify all the forces acting on the object. It can be useful to draw a free body diagram to determine the net force.

FREE BODY DIAGRAMS

Free body diagrams are diagrams that show all the forces acting on the object.

For example: An object is pulled at a constant velocity along a horizontal surface. The applied force is through a rope which makes an angle of 30.0° with the horizontal.

Free body diagram (tension on the body is F_T)

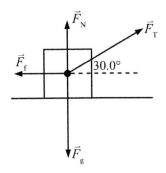

Example 1

An elevator with a mass of 9.00×10^2 kg is accelerating downward at a rate of 1.30 m/s^2. What is the tension in the cable?

Solution
Draw a free body diagram.

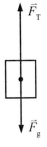

The net force on an object is the sum of all forces acting on the object.

Free body diagrams show all the forces acting on the object.

It can be useful to draw a free body diagram to determine the net force.

Find the magnitude of $\vec{F}_g$

$$F_g = mg$$
$$= (9.00 \times 10^2 \text{ kg})(9.81 \text{ m/s}^2)$$
$$= 8.83 \times 10^3 \text{ N}$$

Find the magnitude of $\vec{F}_{net}$

$$F_{net} = ma$$
$$= (9.00 \times 10^2 \text{ kg})(1.30 \text{ m/s}^2)$$
$$= 1.17 \times 10^3 \text{ N}$$

Subtract F_T from F_g because $\vec{F}_g$ and $\vec{F}_T$ are acting in opposite directions. Therefore the magnitude of the net force is

$$F_{net} = F_g - F_T$$
$$F_T = F_g - F_{net}$$
$$= (8.82 \times 10^3 \text{ N}) - (1.17 \times 10^3 \text{ N})$$
$$= 7.65 \times 10^3 \text{ N}$$

Therefore, the tension in the cable is $\vec{F}_T = 7.65 \times 10^3 \text{ N}$ upward

Example 2

An object that has a mass of 25.0 kg is pushed along a horizontal surface with a force of 95.0 N. If the force of friction is 50.0 N, what is the acceleration of the object?

Solution
Draw a free body diagram.

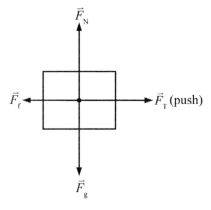

The object accelerates horizontally. Therefore, we are only concerned with the horizontal forces.

Find F_{net}

$$F_{net} = F_{app} - F_{fr}$$
$$= 95.0 \text{ N} - 50.0 \text{ N}$$
$$= 45.0 \text{ N}$$

Find magnitude of the acceleration is

$$F_{net} = ma$$
$$a = \frac{45.0 \text{ N}}{25.0 \text{ kg}}$$
$$= 1.80 \text{ m/s}^2$$

Example 3

A 3.0 kg object is thrown vertically upward with a force of 55 N. What is the acceleration of the object while the force is applied to it?

Solution

Draw a free body diagram.

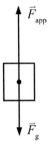

Find the magnitude of $\vec{F}_g$

$$F_g = mg$$
$$= (3.0 \text{ kg})(9.81 \text{ m/s}^2)$$
$$= 29.4 \text{ N}$$

Subtract, because $\vec{F}_g$ and $\vec{F}_{app}$ are acting in opposite directions. As the object is moving upward, find F_{net} as

$$F_{net} = F_{app} - F_g$$
$$= 55 \text{ N} - 29.4 \text{ N}$$
$$= 25.6 \text{ N}$$

Find the acceleration

$$\vec{F}_{net} = m\vec{a}$$
$$\vec{a} = \frac{25.6 \text{ N}}{3.0 \text{ kg}}$$
$$= 8.5 \text{ m/s}^2 \text{ upward}$$

Example 4

An object that has a mass of 45.0 kg is pulled along a horizontal surface by a rope that makes an angle of 32.0° with the horizontal. If the force of friction is 50.0 N and the tension in the rope is 95.0 N, what is the magnitude of acceleration of the object?

Solution

Draw a free body diagram.

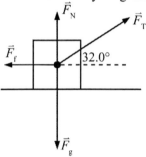

Because the object accelerates horizontally, we must find the net horizontal force. Find the horizontal component of $\vec{F}_T$.

$$\begin{aligned} F_{T(x)} &= F_T \cos \theta \\ &= (95.0 \text{ N}) \cos 32.0° \\ &= 80.6 \text{ N} \end{aligned}$$

Find the magnitude of the net horizontal force

$$\begin{aligned} F_{net} &= F_{T(x)} - F_{fr} \\ &= 80.6 \text{ N} - 50.0 \text{ N} \\ &= 30.6 \text{ N} \end{aligned}$$

Find the magnitude of acceleration

$$\begin{aligned} F_{net} &= ma \\ a &= \frac{30.6 \text{ N}}{45.0 \text{ kg}} \\ &= 0.679 \text{ m/s}^2 \end{aligned}$$

Example 5

A 75.0 kg student stands on a bathroom scale on an elevator that is accelerating upward at a rate of 1.00 m/s^2. What is the reading in Newtons (N) on the scale? (Scale reading will be the normal force $\vec{F}_N$, which is equivalent to applied tensional force $\vec{F}_T$ of the cable)

Solution

Draw a free body diagram.

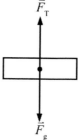

Find the magnitude of $\vec{F}_{net}$

$$F_{net} = ma$$
$$= (75.0 \text{ kg})(1.00 \text{ m/s}^2)$$
$$= 75.0 \text{ N}$$

Find magnitude of $\vec{F}_g$

$$F_g = mg$$
$$= (75.0 \text{ kg})(9.81 \text{ m/s}^2)$$
$$= 735 \text{ N}$$

Subtract, because $\vec{F}_g$ and $\vec{F}_T$ are acting in opposite directions. As the elevator is accelerating upward, find F_{net} (scale reading) as

$$F_{net} = F_T - F_g$$
$$F_T = F_{net} + F_g$$
$$= 75.0 \text{ N} - 735 \text{ N})$$
$$= 810 \text{ N}$$
$$\vec{F}_T = 810 \text{ N upward}$$

PRACTICE EXERCISES

Formulas: $\vec{F}_{net} = m\vec{a}$ $\qquad$ $F_{net} = ma$ $\qquad$ $F_{fr} = \mu F_N$ or $F_{fr} = \mu mg\cos\theta$

$F_g = mg$, $\vec{F}_g = m\vec{g}$

1. An 11.0 kg object is thrown vertically into the air with an applied force of 145 N. What is the magnitude of the initial acceleration of the object?

2. A 12.0 kg object is pushed with a horizontal force of 6.0 N east across a horizontal table. If the force of friction between the two surfaces is 2.0 N, what is the acceleration of the object?

3. A 15.0 kg object is thrown vertically into the air. If the initial acceleration of the object is 8.80 m/s^2, what is the magnitude of the applied force?

4. A 20.0 kg object is pulled horizontally along a level floor with an applied force of 27.0 N. If this object is accelerating at a rate of 0.80 m/s^2, what is the magnitude of the force of friction?

5. An object is pulled west along a horizontal frictionless surface with a steady horizontal force of 12.0 N. If the object accelerates from rest to a speed of 4.0 m/s while moving 5.0 m, what is the mass of the object?

6. A 6.3 kg object is thrown upward with an acceleration of 0.45 m/s^2. What is the magnitude of the force applied to the object?

7. What is the magnitude of tension in the cable of an 1.20×10^3 kg elevator that is

   a) accelerating downward at a rate of 1.05 m/s^2?

   b) accelerating upward at a rate of 1.05 m/s^2?

   c) moving downward at a constant velocity of 1.10 m/s^2 ?

8. An object that has a mass of 36.0 kg is pushed along a horizontal surface with a force of 85.0 N. If the magnitude of the force of friction is 72.0 N, what is the magnitude of the acceleration of the object?

9. A horizontal force of 90.0 N is required to push a 75.0 kg object along a horizontal surface at a constant speed. What is the magnitude of the force of friction?

10. A 1.0 kg object is given a push along a horizontal surface. If the velocity of the object when it is released is 0.50 m/s west, and the object slides 0.25 m before coming to a stop, what is the magnitude of the force of friction?

11. A 1.0×10^2 N box is pushed north along a horizontal surface by a 2.5×10^2 N horizontal force. If the force of friction on the box is 1.4×10^2 N, what is the acceleration of the box?

12. A 7.0 kg object rests on a horizontal frictionless surface. What is the magnitude of the horizontal force that is required to accelerate it at the rate of 2.3 m/s^2?

13. You are travelling in your car at a speed of 24.0 m/s when you slam on your brakes. The force of friction on your car tires is 1.80×10^4 N. If the mass of you and your car is 1.50×10^3 kg, how far do you skid before coming to a stop?

14. A 1.2×10^3 kg car is travelling at a velocity of 20.0 m/s east when its brakes are locked. If the force of friction is 2.5×10^4 N, what is the velocity of the car after 0.50 s?

15. A 1.0 kg box on a horizontal frictionless surface is accelerated by attaching a 1.5 kg mass as shown in the diagram. What is the magnitude of acceleration of the box? (Remember, both boxes accelerate.)

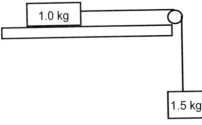

16. Two masses of 1.5 kg and 2.0 kg are hung on a frictionless pulley as shown in the diagram below.

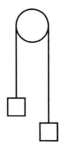

What is the acceleration of

a) the 1.5 kg mass?

b) the 2.0 kg mass?

17. A 125 N box is pulled east along a horizontal surface with a force of 60.0 N acting at an angle of 42.0° as shown in the diagram below. If the force of friction on the box is 15.0 N, what is the magnitude of acceleration?

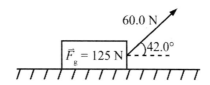

18. A 725 N student stands on a bathroom scale while riding in an elevator. The student observes that the scale reads 775 N as the elevator begins to rise. Find the acceleration of the elevator as it begins to rise. (Remember, the scale reading is the magnitude of the applied tension force, F_T.)

19. A hockey puck with a mass of 0.48 kg is shot north along the ice with an initial velocity of 3.0 m/s. After travelling 8.0 m, the puck comes to rest. What is the force of friction on the puck?

20. An 8.0 kg object is pulled vertically upward by a rope. If the tension in the rope is constant at 95 N, what is the speed of the object after 1.1 s? (Assume the object was initially at rest.)

21. Two blocks are tied together with a string as shown in the diagram below.

If a force of 20.0 N is applied to the 2.0 kg block as shown,

a) what is the magnitude of acceleration of the blocks if the surface is frictionless?

b) what is the magnitude of tension in the string joining the two blocks?

22. If the coefficient of friction between the blocks and the horizontal surface was 0.21, what would the answer to the question above be?

23. A force of 14.0 N is applied to a block as shown in the diagram below.

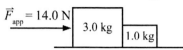

If the coefficient of friction between the blocks and the horizontal surface is 0.35,

a) what is the magnitude of acceleration of the two blocks?

b) what is the magnitude of force that the 3.0 kg block exerts on the 1.0 kg block?

24. Two students are dragging a 25.0 kg object along the hall as shown in the diagram below. If the force of friction acting on the object is 5.0 N, what is the acceleration of the object? (Be sure to include direction.)

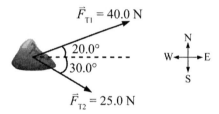

Lesson 6 *PHYSICS OF AN INCLINED PLANE*

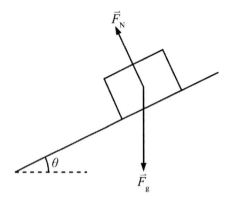

You will remember that the normal force is dependant on the weight.

$F_N = F_g \cos\theta$ or $F_N = mg\cos\theta$

If you look carefully at this equation, you will see that it is really one of the component equations:

$R_x = R\cos\theta$

$R_y = R\sin\theta$

In other words, the normal force is a component of the weight perpendicular to the surface of the plane..

When we deal with an inclined plane, it is convenient to establish the inclined plane as the *x*-axis. This means that a line drawn perpendicular (normal) to the inclined plane is the *y*-axis.

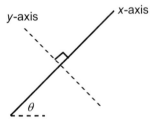

Why does an object slide down a frictionless inclined plane?

What is the force that causes an object to accelerate down a frictionless inclined plane?

Both of these situations are caused by the force due to gravity.

But, the force of gravity always acts toward the centre of Earth—straight down.

However, this force, $\vec{F}_g$, has an "*x*" component (a component that is acting along the inclined plane). It is this force that causes the object to slide down the frictionless inclined plane.

If we look at the geometry of this diagram, $\theta_2 = \theta_1$.

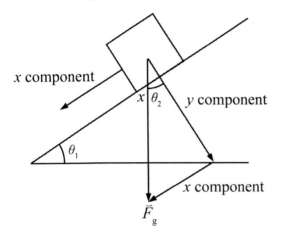

Note:
$\theta_1 + x = 90°$

But:
$\theta_2 + x = 90°$ also
$\therefore \theta_2 = \theta_1$

You will also note that θ_2 is measured from the y-axis—the perpendicular. Remember, one of the conditions of using your component equations is that the angle is to be expressed from the x-axis. If we are to express the angle in the component equations from the y-axis, the component equations switch. That is, rather than using
$R_x = R\cos\theta$
$R_y = R\sin\theta$

we use
$R_x = R\sin\theta$
$R_y = R\cos\theta$

Note that the x component of the force due to gravity in the diagram above is the opposite side of the triangle.
$$\sin\theta = \frac{\text{opposite}}{\text{hypotenuse}}$$

Therefore, opposite = (hypotenuse)($\sin\theta$)
$F_{g(x)} = F_g \sin\theta$

Going back to the equation,
$F_N = F_g \cos\theta$ or $F_N = mg\cos\theta$

F_N is equal in magnitude to the y component of the force due to gravity. And, in the diagram above, the y-component of the force due to gravity is the adjacent side of the triangle.

$$\cos \theta = \frac{\text{adjacent}}{\text{hypotenuse}}$$

Therefore, adjacent = (hypotenuse)(cosθ)
or $F_{g(y)} = F_g \cos \theta$

but $F_{g(y)}$ by definition = F_N

Therefore, $F_N = F_g \cos \theta$
or $F_N = mg \cos \theta$

Example 1

A 175 N box is sliding down a frictionless 35.0° incline as shown below. Find the parallel component of the weight that causes the box to slide. (Find $F_{g(x)}$.)

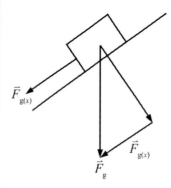

Solution

$$\begin{aligned} F_{g(x)} &= F_g \sin \theta \\ &= (175 \text{ N})(\sin 35.5°) \\ &= 1.00 \times 10^2 \text{ N} \end{aligned}$$

Example 2

A 19.2 kg box is sliding down a frictionless incline. If the incline makes an angle of 30.0° with the horizontal, what is the acceleration along the incline?

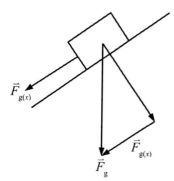

Solution

$$F_{g(x)} = F_g \sin \theta$$
$$= (19.2 \text{ kg})(9.81 \text{ m/s}^2)(\sin 30.0°)$$
$$= 94.2 \text{ N}$$

Magnitude of the net force is

$$F_{net} = F_{g(x)}$$
$$F_{net} = ma$$
$$a = \frac{F_{net}}{m}$$
$$a = \frac{94.1 \text{ N}}{19.2 \text{ kg}}$$
$$= 4.90 \text{ m/s}^2$$

The magnitude of the acceleration along the incline is 4.90 m/s²

PRACTICE EXERCISES

1. A 445 N box is sliding down a frictionless 25.0° inclined plane as shown below. Find the parallel component of the weight that causes the box to slide. (Find $F_{g(x)}$.)

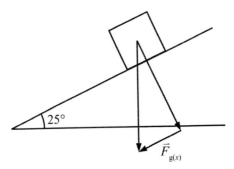

2. A 325 N box is sliding down a frictionless inclined plane. If the incline makes an angle of 30.0° with the horizontal, what is the magnitude of the acceleration along the incline?

3. A 275 N box is sliding down a 35.0° incline. If the force of friction along the incline is 96.0 N, what is the magnitude of the acceleration of the box?

4. A 435 N box is sliding down a 40.0° incline. If the acceleration of the box is 0.250 m/s^2, what is the magnitude of the force of friction on the box?

124

5. A student pulls a 125 N object up a 23.0° inclined plane as shown in the diagram below.

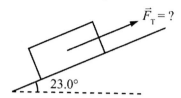

If the coefficient of friction between the object and the incline is 0.180, what amount of force must the student use to pull the object if it moves at a constant velocity? Assume that the applied force is parallel to the incline.

6. Two blocks are tied together with a string as shown in the diagram below.

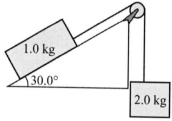

If both the pulley and the incline are frictionless,

a) what is the magnitude of the acceleration of the 1.0 kg block up the incline?

b) what is the magnitude of the tension in the string joining the two blocks?

7. If the pulley was frictionless but the coefficient of friction between the incline and the 1.0 kg block is 0.25, what would the answer to the above problem be?

Lesson 7 NEWTON'S THIRD LAW OF MOTION

Newton's Third Law of Motion states that when an object exerts a force on a second object, the second object exerts an equal and opposite force on the first.

We often see this law stated in terms of action and reaction forces.

For every action (force), there is an equal but opposite reaction (force).

For every action (force), there is an equal but opposite reaction (force).

This simply means that when you push down on your desk, your desk pushes back with an equal force. In baseball, when the bat comes in contact with the ball, the bat exerts a force on the ball; however, the ball exerts an equal force, but in the opposite direction, on the bat. You are aware of this if you have ever shot a gun. The bullet goes off in one direction, but the gun kicks back in the opposite direction.

Example 1

While standing on a horizontal frictionless surface, two students push against each other. One student has a mass of 35 kg, and the other, 45 kg. If the acceleration of the 35 kg student is 0.75 m/s^2 south, what is the acceleration of the 45 kg student?

Solution
Consider south direction as positive for this case.

$$\vec{F}_1 = -\vec{F}_2$$
$$m_1\vec{a}_1 = -m_2\vec{a}_2$$
$$(35\text{ kg})(0.75\text{ m/s}^2) = -(45\text{ kg})\vec{a}_2$$
$$\vec{a}_2 = 0.58\text{ m/s}^2 \text{ north}$$

PRACTICE EXERCISES

1. While standing on a horizontal frictionless surface, two students, Angela and Bob, push against each other. Angela has a mass of 38 kg, and, during the push, is accelerating east at a rate of 0.60 m/s^2 ^{2}. If Bob is accelerating west during the push at a rate of 0.75 m/s^2, what is his mass?

2. While standing on a horizontal frictionless surface, a 50.0 kg student pushes against a wall with an average force of 125 N east for 0.110 s. Calculate the velocity of this student at 0.110 s.

3. A 9.8×0^3 kg rocket is travelling east along a horizontal frictionless rail at a velocity of 11 m/s. The rocket then accelerates uniformly to a velocity of 22 m/s in a time of 0.75 s by the expulsion of hot gases. What is the average force at which the gases are expelled by the rocket?

4. While standing on a horizontal frictionless surface, a 45 kg student throws a 3.0 kg object to her right. During the throw, the object accelerates horizontally through a distance of 0.60 m from rest to a velocity of 9.6 m/s. Calculate the velocity of the student when the object is released.

PRACTICE TEST

1. If there is no net force acting on an moving object, it is

    i) going to be in the state of rest.
    ii) moving at constant velocity.
    iii) moving with constant acceleration.

    Which of the above conditions are correct?

    A. i only

    B. ii only

    C. i and iii only

    D. i, ii, and iii

2. In studying the relationship between the acceleration and the net force on an object, a student obtained the following graph.

    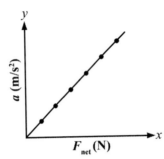

    What did the graph tell her about the relationship?

    A. $a \propto F_{net}$

    B. $a \propto \dfrac{1}{F_{net}}$

    C. $F_{net} \propto \dfrac{1}{a}$

    D. $a \propto F_{net}^{\,2}$

3. In studying the relationship between the acceleration and the mass of an object, a student obtained the following graph.

    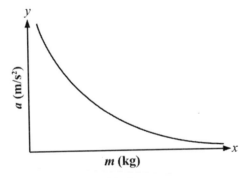

    What did this graph tell her about the relationship?

    A. $a \propto m$

    B. $a \propto m^2$

    C. $a \propto \dfrac{1}{m}$

    D. $a \propto \sqrt{m}$

4. A 75 kg student stands on a bathroom scale while riding in an elevator. What can you infer about the motion of the elevator if the scale reading is 775 N?

A. The elevator is going down at a constant velocity.

B. The elevator is going up at a constant velocity.

C. The elevator is accelerating downward.

D. The elevator is accelerating upward.

5. Which of the following statements is true about mass? (g on the moon is 1.6 m/s^2)

A. The mass of an object is 1.6 times on the moon than it is on Earth.

B. The mass of an object is less on the moon than it is on Earth.

C. The mass of an object is the same on the moon as it is on Earth.

D. The mass of the object is 6 times on the moon than it is on Earth

6. If an object has a weight of 15 N on Earth, what is the weight on planet F ($g_F = 27 \text{ m/s}^2$)?

A. 6.0 N
B. 15 N
C. 30 N
D. 41 N

7. When two objects ($m_1 = 4.5 \text{ kg}$, $m_2 = 9.0 \text{ kg}$) are dropped from the same height, which of the following statements is true about their velocities when they hit the ground? (Assume that air resistance can be ignored.)

A. m_2 has twice the velocity of m_1.

B. m_2 is travelling faster than m_1, but not twice as fast.

C. m_2 is travelling slower than m_1.

D. m_2 and m_1 are travelling at the same velocity.

8. An object that is travelling east hits a wall with a force of 12 N. What force does the wall exert on the object?

A. 12 N east
B. A force less than 12 N east
C. 12 N west
D. A force less than 12 N west

9. Mass is defined in terms of

A. inertia
B. weight
C. acceleration
D. gravity

10. If we know the net force acting on an object and the acceleration of the object, it is possible to find the

A. velocity of the object
B. force of friction on the object
C. applied force on the object
D. mass of the object

11. A student is pulling a 95.0 kg block along a horizontal surface with a force of 105 N as shown in the diagram below. If the force of friction on the block is 48.0 N, what is the magnitude of the acceleration of the block?

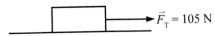

A. 0.505 m/s^2

B. 0.600 m/s^2

C. 1.11 m/s^2

D. 1.61 m/s^2

12. A 3.0 kg block is resting on a frictionless horizontal surface. If another block ($m = 7.5$ kg) is attached to the first block as shown in the diagram below, what is the magnitude of the acceleration of the 3.0 kg block?

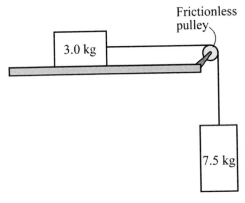

A. 2.8 m/s^2

B. 4.2 m/s^2

C. 7.0 m/s^2

D. 9.8 m/s^2

13. If the force of gravity on an object is 12.0 N, what is its mass? (Assume that the object is near Earth's surface.)

A. 0.82 N

B. 1.22 kg

C. 12.0 N

D. 118 kg

14. A 1.2×10^3 kg car is travelling at 22 m/s when its brakes are applied. If the car decelerates uniformly to rest in 9.0 s, what is the net force acting on the car?

A. −2.4 N

B. -1.7×10^2 N

C. -5.0×10^2 N

D. -2.9×10^3 N

15. A 3.0 kg object is thrown vertically upward with an applied force of 55 N. What is the acceleration of the object while the force is acting on it?

A. 8.5 m/s^2

B. 9.8 m/s^2

C. 18 m/s^2

D. 23 m/s^2

WORK, POWER, AND ENERGY

When you are finished this unit, you should be able to…

- Solve problems involving work, force, and displacement

- Perform calculations involving power and efficiency

- Define energy and differentiate between gravitational potential energy and kinetic energy

- Describe the work-energy theorem, $\left(W_{net} = \Delta E_k \right)$.

- Understand how to approach and solve problems involving the transformation of energy and the law of conservation of energy

Lesson	Page	Completed on
1. Energy	132	
2. Power	139	
3. Potential Energy	143	
4. Kinetic Energy	148	
5. Work-Energy Theorem For Net Force	151	
6. Law Of Conservation Of Mechanical Energy	156	
7. Law Of Conservation Of Energy	161	
Practice Test	167	
Answers and Solutions	at the back of the book	

PREREQUISITE SKILLS AND KNOWLEDGE

Prior to starting this unit, you should be able to…

- Write numbers in scientific notation

- Isolate a variable and combine algebraic expressions

- Perform calculations and obtain the answer to the correct number of significant figures

- Construct graphs involving relevant quantities and analyze important characteristics such as slope, intercepts, and areas under the graph.

- Substitute the correct units for all quantities in a calculation and express the proper final unit by appropriate cancellation of units

- Determine the composition of derived units in terms of simpler units

Lesson 1 ENERGY

The concept of energy was developed during the mid-1800s; however, it is a very common concept in our society today. We use the term energy when we are describing a person—we say that a person is very energetic, or that we don't have much energy today. We also talk about electricity, gasoline, wind, the sun, etc., as sources of energy. In physics, we define energy as the ability to do work.

Energy is defined as the ability to do work.

WORK

The concept of work is difficult to define; it has different meanings for different people. In physics, we will describe it as the product of force and displacement. Work is defined as the product of the component of the force parallel to the displacement multiplied by the magnitude of the displacement (i.e., distance)

Work =
Force × displacement

Work = Force × displacement

$$W = Fd$$

It is important to note the language that is used in physics to describe work. In physics, we talk about the amount of work that is done on an object. If Liam is standing holding a 30.0 kg object, he is using energy; therefore, he is doing work. However, this work is not done on the object; it is done on Liam's muscles by a force acting to contract (the length of) these muscles. In this course, we will talk of doing work on an object.
If the object does not move through some displacement, there is no work done on the object. In the same way, if there is no force acting on the object, there is no work. We do work on an object in order to overcome an opposing force (force of gravity, friction, etc.) on the object, or we do work to accelerate an object.

WORK

Symbol: W
Definition: The product of force and displacement
Formula: $W = Fd$
Units: $N \cdot m$, which is equivalent to the unit for energy called a joule (J).

SPECIAL NOTES:

• When an object is lifted at a constant velocity, work is done against gravity. The formula, $W = Fd$, can be written as:
$$W = F_g d = mgh$$

where m = mass
g = magnitude of the acceleration due to gravity
h = height (magnitude of the vertical displacement)

• In deriving this formula, $W = mgh$:
$W = F_g d$ (definition of work)

but $F_g = mg$ (force due to gravity)

- $\therefore W = mgd$
  or
  $W = mgh$
  where h = vertical displacement

- The force used in the formula $W = Fd$ is the applied force rather than the net force.

- Although work is the product of two vector quantities, it is a scalar quantity.

- When the force is not in the same direction as the displacement, we must use the component of the force that is in the direction of the displacement. (Refer to Example on page 148.)

- Work can be negative. If the force on an object is in the opposite direction to the motion, the work done on the object is negative. (Refer to Example on page 149.)

Example

A 15.0 kg object is lifted at constant velocity from the floor to height of 1.50 m. How much work is done on the object?

Solution

$$W = mgh$$
$$= (15.0\,\text{kg})(9.81\,\text{m/s}^2)(1.50\,\text{m})$$
$$= 221\,\text{J}$$

Example

A 10.0 kg object is moved horizontally 5.00 m across a level floor using a horizontal force of 3.00 N. How much work is done on the object?

Solution

$$W = Fd$$
$$= (3.00\,\text{N})(5.00\,\text{m})$$
$$= 15.0\,\text{J}$$

Example

A 3.0 kg object is held 1.2 m above the floor for 15 s. How much work is done on the object?

Solution

The is no change in gravitational potential energy since the object does not move vertically. Therefore the total work done on the object is 0.

NOTES

Example

A 50.0 kg box is pulled 11.0 m along a level surface by a rope. If the rope makes an angle with the surface of 35.0°, and the force exerted through the rope is 90.0 N, how much work is done on the box?

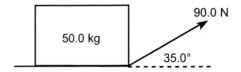

Solution

Since the object moves horizontally, we must find the horizontal component of the force.

$$\cos\theta = \frac{\text{adjacent}}{\text{hypotenuse}}$$
$$F_x = adj = (\cos\theta)(\text{hypotenuse})$$
$$= F\cos\theta$$
$$= (90.0 \text{ N})(\cos 35.0°)$$
$$= 73.7 \text{ N}$$
$$W = F_x d$$
$$= (73.7 \text{ N})(11.0 \text{ m})$$
$$= 811 \text{ J}$$

Example

A 1 385 kg car travelling at 61.0 km/h is brought to a stop after skidding 42.0 m. What is the work done on the car by the frictional forces?

Solution

Convert 61.0 km/h to m/s.

$$61.0 \text{ km/h} = \left(\frac{61.0 \text{ km}}{1.00 \text{ h}}\right)\left(\frac{1000 \text{ m}}{1.00 \text{ km}}\right)\left(\frac{1.00 \text{ h}}{3600 \text{ m}}\right)$$
$$= 16.9 \text{ m/s}$$
$$v^2 = v_0^2 + 2ad$$
$$-(16.9 \text{ m/s})^2 = (2)(a)(42.0 \text{ m})$$
$$a = -3.42 \text{ m/s}^2$$
$$F_f = F_{net} = ma$$
$$= (1385 \text{ kg})(-3.42 \text{ m/s}^2)$$
$$= -4.73 \times 10^3 \text{ N}$$
$$W = F_{fr} d$$
$$= (-4.73 \times 10^3 \text{ N})(42.0 \text{ m})$$
$$= -1.99 \times 10^3 \text{ J}$$

Note: Answer is negative because the force and the displacement are in opposite directions.

PRACTICE EXERCISES

Formulas: $W = Fd$ or $W = mgh$

1. A 20.0 N object is lifted at a constant velocity from the floor to a height of 1.50 m. How much work is done on the object?

2. A 15.0 N object is moved horizontally 3.00 m across a level floor using a horizontal force of 6.00 N. How much work is done on this object?

3. A 2.20 N object is held 2.20 m above the floor for 10.0 s. How much work is done on the object?

4. A 10.0 kg object is accelerated horizontally from rest to a speed of 11.0 m/s in 5.00 s by a horizontal force. How much work is done on this object if the object is on a frictionless surface?

5. A 90.0 N box is pulled 10.0 m along a level surface by a rope as illustrated below.

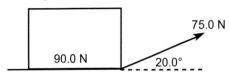

If the rope makes an angle of 20.0° with the surface, and the force exerted through the rope is 75.0 N, how much work is done on the box?

6. A 60.0 kg student runs at a constant velocity up a flight of stairs. If the vertical distance of the stairs is 3.2 m, what is the work done against gravity?

7. A 20.0 kg box is moved horizontally 9.0 m along a level frictionless surface at a constant velocity. How much work is done on the box?

8. An 80.0 kg box is pushed at a constant velocity along a frictionless incline as shown in the image below.

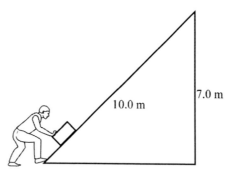

10.0 m 7.0 m

How much work is done on the box in moving it from the bottom to the top of the incline?

9. A 25.0 kg object is accelerated from rest through a distance of 6.0 m in 4.0 s across a level floor. If the force due to friction between the object and the floor is 3.8 N, what is the work done in moving the object?

10. A 1 165 kg car travelling at a speed of 55 km/h is brought to a stop while skidding 38 m. Calculate the work done on the car by the frictional force.

11. A student exerts a horizontal force of 225 N to push a heavy box along the school corridor at a constant speed of 2.00 m/s. How much work does she do in 15.0 s?

12. If a 50.0 kg box is pushed 10.0 m at a constant speed along a horizontal surface by a force of 65.0 N acting at a 30.0° angle, as shown in the image below, how much work is done on the box?

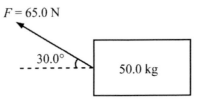

To find the work done, should you use the force of 65.0 N or should you find the horizontal component of 65.0 N? Why?

13. Given the following force-displacement graph of an object being pulled along a level surface, what is the work done in moving the object 16.0 m?

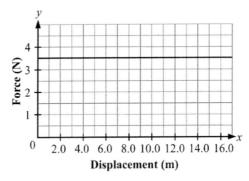

14. Given the following force-displacement graph of an object moving along a horizontal surface, what is the work done in moving the object 8.0 m?

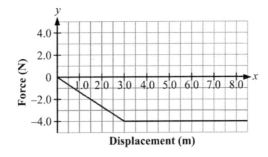

Lesson 2 POWER

Power is often confused with work. You will note that when we discussed work, we were not concerned about time. Power is concerned about time—power is the *rate* of doing work.

Symbol: P
Definition: The rate of doing work, or the rate of using energy
Formula: $P = \dfrac{W}{t}$ or $P = \dfrac{\Delta E}{t}$

Units: $\dfrac{J}{s}$, which is called a watt (W)

Note: Like work, power is a scalar quantity.

Also, a useful equation:
$P = Fv$

Derivation:
$$P = \frac{W}{t} = \frac{Fd}{t}$$

but $\dfrac{d}{t} = v$

$\therefore P = Fv$

EFFICIENCY

Efficiency is defined as

$$\text{Efficiency} = \frac{\text{work out}}{\text{work in}}$$

or

$$\text{Efficiency} = \frac{\text{power output}}{\text{power input}}$$

Efficiency is often expressed as a percentage. Therefore,

$$\% \text{ Efficiency} = \frac{\text{work out}}{\text{work in}} \times 100\%$$

or

$$\% \text{ Efficiency} = \frac{\text{power output}}{\text{power input}} \times 100\%$$

NOTES

Power is defined as the rate of doing work.

$P = \dfrac{W}{t}$ or $P = \dfrac{\Delta E}{t}$

$P = Fv$

$\% \text{ Efficiency} = \dfrac{\text{work out}}{\text{work in}} \times 100\%$

or

$\dfrac{\text{power out}}{\text{power in}} \times 100\%$

Example

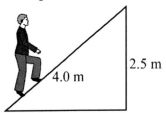

2.5 m

4.0 m

A 60.0 kg student runs at a constant velocity up the incline in 4.5 s, as illustrated in the diagram above. Calculate the power output of the student.

Solution

Find the work first. Since the work is against gravity, we use the formula

$$W = mgh$$
$$= (60.0 \text{ kg})(9.81 \text{ m/s}^2)(2.5 \text{ m})$$
$$= 1.47 \times 10^3 \text{ J}$$

$$P = \frac{W}{t}$$
$$= \frac{1.47 \times 10^3 \text{ J}}{4.5 \text{ s}}$$
$$= 3.3 \times 10^2 \text{ W}$$

Example

A 1.00×10^3 kg car accelerates from rest to a velocity of 15.0 m/s in 4.00 s. Calculate the power output of the car in this 4.00 s.

Solution

$$a = \frac{v - v_0}{t}$$
$$= \frac{15.0 \text{ m/s}}{4.00 \text{ s}}$$
$$= 3.75 \text{ m/s}^2$$

$$F_{net} = ma$$
$$= (1.00 \times 10^3 \text{ kg})(3.75 \text{ m/s}^2)$$
$$= 3.75 \times 10^3 \text{ N}$$

$$d = \left(\frac{v + v_0}{2}\right)t$$
$$= \left(\frac{15.0 \text{ m/s}}{2}\right)4.00 \text{ s}$$
$$= 30.0 \text{ m}$$

$$W = Fd$$
$$= (3.75 \times 10^3 \text{ N})(30.0 \text{ m})$$
$$= 1.13 \times 10^5 \text{ J}$$

$$P = \frac{W}{t}$$
$$= \frac{1.13 \times 10^5 \text{ J}}{4.00 \text{ s}}$$
$$= 2.81 \times 10^4 \text{ W}$$

140

PRACTICE EXERCISES

Formula: $P = \dfrac{W}{t}$

1. A 45.0 kg student runs at a constant velocity up the incline as illustrated. . If the power output of the student is 1.50×10^3 W, how long does it take the student to run the 9.0 m along the incline?

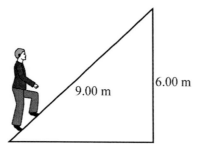

2. A 20.0 kg object is lifted vertically at a constant velocity 2.50 m in 2.00 s by a student. Calculate the power output of the student.

3. A 2.00 kg object is accelerated uniformly from rest to 3.00 m/s while moving 1.5 m across a level frictionless surface. Calculate the power output.

4. An 8.50×10^2 kg elevator (including occupants) is pulled up at a constant velocity of 1.00 m/s by a 10.0 kW electric motor. Calculate the efficiency of the electric motor.

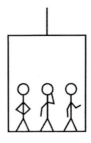

5. A 5.0 kg object is accelerated uniformly from rest to 6.0 m/s while moving 2.0 m across a level surface. If the force of friction is 4.0 N, what is the power output?

6. A 5.00×10^2 W electric motor lifts a 20.0 kg object 5.00 m in 3.50 s. What is the efficiency of the motor?

7. If a 1.00×10^2 kW electric motor has an efficiency of 82%, how long will it take to lift a 50.0 kg object to a height of 8.00 m?

Lesson 3 POTENTIAL ENERGY

There are many forms of energy: mechanical energy, thermal energy, electrical energy, nuclear energy, etc. One form of energy can be converted to other forms. For example, mechanical energy can be converted to electrical energy using an electric generator. It should be noted that when energy is changed to different forms, work is done.

In this course we will look at mechanical energy. Mechanical energy is the energy of an object as a result of its position or because of its motion. Mechanical energy has two components: potential energy and kinetic energy. Potential energy is the energy of an object that is related to its position. It is also referred to as stored energy. Kinetic energy is the energy of an object due to its motion. When one energy component is converted to another, work is done. Again, work is just the change in energy.

POTENTIAL ENERGY

This boulder has potential energy as a result of its position. It has the potential to fall to the ground and do work on the ground (i.e., by deforming the ground or changing its shape). This is gravitational potential energy or potential energy due to gravity.

When an archer pulls the string of her bow, she is doing work on the bow. If she places an arrow in this bow, the bow has the potential of doing work on the arrow. This is elastic potential energy.

When work is done against gravity, or systems like springs and bows, this work is stored in the system as potential energy.

The potential energy of an object depends on:

- the force acting on the object. If we are talking about gravitational potential energy, the potential energy depends on the gravitational force on the object.
  (Remember: $F_g = mg$)

- the displacement (change in position) of the object.
  Potential Energy = Force × displacement
  $E_p = F_g d$
  which can become
  $E_p = mgh$

NOTES

Mechanical energy:
    potential energy
       kinetic energy

Potential energy is energy due to position; in other words, potential energy is stored energy.

For gravitational potential energy:
    $E_p = mgh$

NOTES

Conservative Forces:
gravitational force
elastic force of an
ideal spring

**Friction is a
non-conservative force.**

In case of gravitational potential energy, you will note that these are the same equations that was used for work. This should be of no surprise because the potential energy of an object is changed by doing work on the object.

The force of gravity and the elastic force of an ideal spring or bow are referred to as conservative forces. When work is done moving an object against a conservative force, that work may be stored as potential energy and can be recovered. If work is done against gravity, this work is stored and can be recovered later. For example, a pile driver is lifted to a certain height—work is done against gravity on the pile driver—the pile driver now has potential energy. When the pile driver is dropped on a pile, work is done on the pile by the pile driver.

If a force is exerted on a spring to compress it, work is done against the spring. Now, this spring can be used to project an object—that is, work was done on the spring. The spring now has potential energy. When the spring is released, work is done on the object by the spring.

Friction is a non-conservative force. Work done against friction cannot be recovered. Work done against friction is converted into some other form of energy—mainly thermal energy.

Symbol: E_p

Definition: energy due to position, or stored energy

Formulas: $E_p = Fd$

or in the special (but common) case of gravitational potential energy:

$E_p = mgh$

Units: same as work, joule (J).

Example

A 15.0 kg object is lifted from the floor to a vertical height of 2.50 m. What is the potential energy (gravitational) of the object with respect to the floor?

Solution

$E_p = mgh$
$\quad = (15.0 \text{ kg})(9.81 \text{ m/s}^2)(2.50 \text{ m})$
$\quad = 368 \text{ J}$

Note: Gravitational potential energy is usually expressed in relation to some point. (Example: with respect to the floor)

144

Example

An archer pulls on the bow string with an average force of 12.0 N while drawing the arrow back a distance of 2.00×10^{-1} m. Calculate the potential energy of the bow and arrow system.

Solution

$$E_p = Fd$$
$$= (12.0 \text{ N})(2.00 \times 10^{-1} \text{ m})$$
$$= 2.40 \text{ J}$$

PRACTICE EXERCISES

Formulas: $E_p = Fd$ $E_p = F_g d$ $E_p = mgh$

1. A 25.0 N object is held 2.10 m above the ground. What is the potential energy of the object with respect to the ground?

2. An uncompressed spring is 20.0 cm in length. What is the potential energy of this spring when an average force of 65.0 N compresses it to a length of 13.5 cm?

3. A 2.75 kg box is at the top of a frictionless incline as shown in the diagram. What is the potential energy of the box with respect to the bottom of the incline?

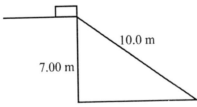

4. The bob of a pendulum has a mass of 2.0 kg. This bob is pulled sideways so that it is 0.75 m above the table top, as illustrated below.

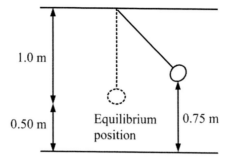

What is the potential energy of the bob with respect to the equilibrium position?

5. A 2.0×10^2 kg object is pushed to the top of an incline as illustrated. If the force applied along the incline is 6.0×10^2 N, what is the potential energy of the object when it is at the top of the incline with respect to the bottom of the incline?

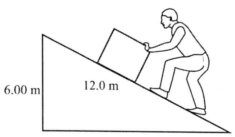

Lesson 4 KINETIC ENERGY

When an object is thrown, a force is applied and this force acts through some distance; therefore, work is done.

$$W = Fd$$

Kinetic energy is energy of motion.

However, when the object is released, it has speed; it has kinetic energy. Kinetic energy is energy of motion. The work done in accelerating this object from rest becomes kinetic energy. Kinetic energy is calculated using:

$$E_k = \frac{1}{2}mv^2$$

Derivation:

$$v^2 = v_0^2 + 2ad \qquad (v_0 = 0)$$
$$\therefore \quad v^2 = 2ad$$
$$= \frac{2Fd}{m}$$

but $\quad Fd = W = \Delta E = E_k$
when $\quad v_0 = 0$

$$\therefore \quad v^2 = \frac{2E_k}{m}$$
$$\Rightarrow E_k = \frac{1}{2}mv^2$$

The word *kinetic* comes from the Greek language for the word *motion*.

Symbol: E_k
Definition: energy of motion
Formula: $E_k = \frac{1}{2}mv^2$
Units: joule (J)

Example

A 60.0 kg student is jogging at a uniform speed of 2.70 m/s. What is the kinetic energy of the student?

Solution

$$E_k = \frac{1}{2}mv^2$$
$$= \frac{1}{2}(60.0 \text{ kg})(2.70 \text{ m/s})^2$$
$$= 219 \text{ J}$$

Example

The kinetic energy of a 2.1 kg object is 1.00×10^3 J. What is the speed of this object?

Solution

$$E_k = \frac{1}{2}mv^2$$
$$= \sqrt{\frac{2E_k}{m}}$$
$$= \sqrt{\frac{2(1.00 \times 10^3 \text{ J})}{2.10 \text{ kg}}}$$
$$= 31 \text{ m/s}$$

PRACTICE EXERCISES

Formula: $\qquad E_k = \dfrac{1}{2}mv^2$

1. A 3.0 kg object is travelling at a constant speed of 7.5 m/s. What is the kinetic energy of this object?

2. The kinetic energy of a 20.0 N object is 5.00×10^2 J. What is the speed of this object?

3. A 10.0 N object is accelerated uniformly from rest at a rate of 2.5 m/s². What is the kinetic energy of this object after it has accelerated a distance of 15.0 m?

4. An 8.0 kg object is dropped from a height of 7.0 m. What is the kinetic energy of this object as it hits the ground?

5. A 10.0 N object has kinetic energy of 3.00×10^2 J. What is the speed of the object?

6. By what factor must the kinetic energy of an object be increased to cause its speed to triple?

Lesson 5 *WORK-ENERGY THEOREM FOR NET FORCE*

The work-energy theorem for net force states that the work done by the net force on an object is equal to the change in the object's kinetic energy.

$$W = \Delta E_k$$
$$Fd = \frac{1}{2}m\left(v^2 - v_0^2\right)$$

Note that the force in this equation is the net force. We can refer to the net force as the accelerating force. When we accelerate an object, we change the kinetic energy of the object.

The work-energy theorem for net force gives us a framework to solve some motion problems.

Example

An archer exerts an average horizontal force of 55.0 N on her bow and arrow system in pulling the string back 0.350 m. If the arrow has a mass of 0.350 kg, what is the horizontal speed of the arrow as it hits the target 10.0 m away? (Note: 55.0 N is the net force on the arrow.)

Solution

$$Fd = \frac{1}{2}m\left(v^2 - v_0^2\right)$$
$$(55.0\text{N})(0.350 \text{ m}) = \frac{1}{2}(0.350 \text{ kg})\left(v^2 - 0\right)$$
$$v = \sqrt{\frac{2(55.0 \text{ N})(0.350 \text{ m})}{0.350 \text{ kg}}}$$
$$= 10.5 \text{ m/s}$$

Example

If a 985 kg car is travelling at a speed of 12.0 m/s, how much work is required to stop it?

Solution

$$W = \Delta E_k = \frac{1}{2}m\left(v^2 - v_0^2\right)$$
$$= \frac{1}{2}(985 \text{ kg})(0 - (12.0 \text{ m/s})^2)$$
$$= -7.09 \times 10^4 \text{ J}$$

NOTES

Work = Force × Displacement

$$Fd = \Delta E_k$$
(when F = net force)

or

$$Fd = \frac{1}{2}m\left(v^2 - v_0^2\right)$$

Example

A 0.85 kg puck is sliding at a speed of 5.0 m/s along a horizontal surface. The only force acting on the puck is friction. If 8.0 m farther along the surface the puck has a speed of 2.0 m/s, what is the force of friction? Note: The force of friction is the only force. Therefore, it is the net force.

Solution

$$Fd = \frac{1}{2}m\left(v^2 - v_0^2\right)$$

$$F(8.0 \text{ m}) = \frac{1}{2}(0.85 \text{ kg})\left((2.0 \text{ m/s})^2 - (5.0 \text{ m/s})^2\right)$$

$$F = -1.1 \text{ N}$$

Note: This works out to a negative force because the force of friction is in the opposite direction to the motion.

Example

A student throws a 5.0 N object vertically into the air with an average force of 9.0 N. If this force is exerted through a displacement of 0.45 m, what is the speed of the object as it leaves the student's hand?

Solution

First, find the net force by drawing a free body diagram.

$$F_{net} = F_T - F_g$$
$$= 9.0 \text{ N} - 5.0 \text{ N}$$
$$= 4.0 \text{ N}$$

$\vec{F}_T$ 9.0 N

$\vec{F}_g$ 5.0 N

We need to find the mass

$$F_g = mg$$

$$m = \frac{5.0 \text{ N}}{9.81 \text{ m/s}^2}$$
$$= 0.51 \text{ kg}$$

$$F_{net}d = \frac{1}{2}m\left(v^2 - v_0^2\right)$$

$$(4.0 \text{N})(0.45 \text{ m}) = \frac{1}{2}(0.51 \text{ kg})(v^2 - 0)$$

$$v = \sqrt{\frac{2(4.0 \text{ N})(0.45 \text{ m})}{0.51 \text{ kg}}}$$
$$= 2.7 \text{ m/s}$$

PRACTICE EXERCISES

Formulas: $\quad W = \Delta E_k \qquad W = Fd \qquad E_k = \dfrac{1}{2}mv^2 \qquad Fd = \dfrac{1}{2}m\left(v^2 - v_0^2\right)$

Note: The force in these equations is the net force. Use the work-energy theorem for net force.

1. A spring exerts an average horizontal force of 23.0 N on a 0.12 kg pebble while acting through a displacement of 5.0×10^{-2} m . What is the speed of the pebble as it leaves the spring?

2. A force of friction of 3.2 N acts on a 1.1 kg puck while it is sliding along a horizontal surface. If the initial velocity of the puck was 7.5 m/s, how far will the puck travel before coming to rest?

3. How much work is required to accelerate a 1.10×10^3 kg car from rest to 5.00 km/h along a level, frictionless surface?

4. What was the average net force exerted on a 4.5×10^{-3} kg bullet by a gun while the bullet is accelerated from rest to a speed of 1.0×10^3 m/s through a displacement of 0.70 m?

5. A student throws a 1.0 kg rock vertically into the air with an average force of 18 N. If this force was exerted through a displacement of 0.30 m, what was the speed of the rock as it left the student's hand? Is the 18 N force the applied force or the net force? (Note: Draw a free body diagram to help solve this problem.)

6. A 4.0 N box slides along a frictionless surface while travelling at a speed of 2.1 m/s. This object hits an ideal spring, as shown in the illustration, which compresses it 2.3×10^{-2} m. What is the average net force acting on the spring?

7. A 0.65 kg puck is sliding along a horizontal surface at a speed of 2.0 m/s. If the puck comes to a stop in 5.5 m, what is the force of friction acting along the surface? (Note: The force of friction is the net force on the puck.)

8. A student throws a 1.1 kg rock vertically into the air while accelerating it through a displacement of 0.36 m. If the rock leaves the student's hand at a speed of 4.2 m/s, what was the average force exerted by the student on the rock while accelerating it? (Hint: Are we asked to find the applied force or the net force? Draw a free body diagram to help solve this problem.)

9. A 15 kg box is pulled along a horizontal frictionless surface by a horizontal force of 35 N. If the box accelerates uniformly from rest, how fast is it travelling after moving 3.5 m?

10. A system containing a frictionless pulley is illustrated in the diagram. If this system is released, at what speed does the 12.0 kg object hit the floor? (Hint: Does the 12.0 kg object undergo free fall? Why or why not?)

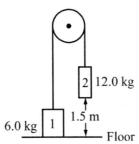

11. A 1.50×10^2 N force is pulling a 50.0 kg box along a horizontal surface. The force acts at an angle of 25.0° as shown in the diagram. If this force acts through a displacement of 12.0 m, and the coefficient of friction is 0.250, what is the speed of the box, assuming it started from rest?

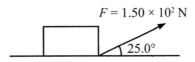

12. The battery of a calculator can provide energy at the rate of 0.0290 J/s for 275 h. If this energy could be used to accelerate a 0.145 kg baseball from rest, what speed would the ball reach?

13. A 45.0 kg box is pulled across a horizontal surface by a constant horizontal force of 192 N. If the box starts from rest, and the coefficient of friction is 0.35, what is the final speed of the box when it has travelled 8.0 m?

14. How much energy is needed to accelerate a 1.1×10^3 kg object along a horizontal frictionless surface from 15 km/h to 25 km/h in 5.0 s?

Lesson 6 LAW OF CONSERVATION OF MECHANICAL ENERGY

A force is conservative if the work done in moving an object from one point to another against the force does not depend on the path taken.

Gravitational forces are conservative.

Frictional forces are non-conservative.

The law of conservation of mechanical energy: in a frictionless system, mechanical energy is conserved.

The kinetic energy of an object, and the potential energy because of its position (gravity/spring), can be referred to as mechanical energy. If the only forces acting on an object are conservative forces, the mechanical energy of the object does not change—this is known as the law of conservation of mechanical energy.

When only conservative forces act on an object, kinetic energy is converted to potential energy or vice versa. If an object is thrown into the air, the object has kinetic energy (energy of motion) as it leaves the hand; however, eventually this object will reach its highest point where it will come to a stop. At this point, it has potential energy. The kinetic energy was changed to potential energy, and as the object returns to the hand, the potential is converted back to kinetic. However, the sum of the kinetic and potential energies is constant throughout this motion. The mechanical energy remains constant.

The law of conservation of mechanical energy states that in a frictionless system, mechanical energy is conserved.

This law can be explained in symbols as:

$$\Delta E_k + \Delta E_p = 0$$

or $\Delta E_k = -\Delta E_p$

$$\frac{1}{2}m\left(v^2 - v_0^{\,2}\right) = -mg\Delta h$$

gain in E_k = loss in E_p

$\Delta h = h_f - h_i$ Δh may be negative

If there is friction, then some mechanical energy is converted to thermal energy.

Like the work-energy theorem for net force, this law provides a framework in which to solve some motion problems.

Example

A heavy object is dropped from a vertical distance of 12.0 m above the ground. What is the speed of the object as it hits the ground?

Solution

$$\Delta E_k + \Delta E_p = 0$$

or $\Delta E_k = -\Delta E_p$

or $\dfrac{1}{2}m\left(v^2 - v_0^{\,2}\right) = -mg\Delta h$

$$\dfrac{1}{2}\left(v^2 - v_0^{\,2}\right) = -g\Delta h$$

$$\dfrac{1}{2}(v^2 - 0) = -(9.81 \text{ m}/\text{s}^2)(-12.0 \text{ m})$$

$$v = \sqrt{2(9.81 \text{ m/s}^2)(12.0 \text{ m})}$$
$$= 15.3 \text{ m/s}$$

Example

A heavy object is thrown vertically down from the top of a 1.00×10^2 m building at a velocity of 10.0 m/s. What is the speed as it reaches the ground?

Solution

$$\Delta E_k + \Delta E_p = 0$$

or $\Delta E_k = -\Delta E_p$

or $\dfrac{1}{2}m\left(v^2 - v_0^{\,2}\right) = -mg\Delta h$

$$\dfrac{1}{2}\left(v^2 - v_0^{\,2}\right) = -g\Delta h$$

$$\dfrac{1}{2}\left(v^2 - (10.0 \text{ m/s})^2\right) = -(9.81 \text{ m/s}^2)(-1.00 \times 10^2 \text{ m})$$

$$v = \sqrt{2(9.81 \text{ m/s}^2)(1.00 \times 10^2 \text{m}) + (10.0 \text{ m/s})^2}$$
$$= 45.4 \text{ m/s}$$

PRACTICE EXERCISES

Formulas: $W = Fd$ $E_p = mgh$ $E_k = \dfrac{1}{2}mv^2$ $\Delta E_k + \Delta E_p = 0$

Use the Law of Conservation of Mechanical Energy.

1. A heavy object is dropped. If this object reaches the floor at a speed of 3.2 m/s, from what height was it dropped?

2. A heavy object is dropped from a vertical height of 8.00 m above the ground. What is the speed of this object as it hits the ground?

3. A heavy object is dropped from the top of a building. If this object hits the ground with a speed of 37.0 m/s, how tall was the building?

4. A heavy object is thrown vertically down from the top of a 1.3×10^2 m building at a speed of 11.0 m/s. What is the velocity as it hits the ground?

5. A heavy box slides down a frictionless incline as shown in the diagram. If the box starts from rest at the top of the incline, what is its speed at the bottom?

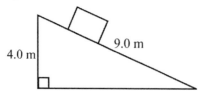

6. A pendulum is released from a position 0.25 m above the equilibrium position, as illustrated. What is the speed of the pendulum bob as it passes through the equilibrium position?

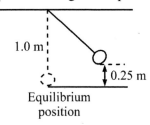

1.0 m

0.25 m

Equilibrium
position

7. A heavy box slides down a frictionless incline as shown in the diagram. If the box starts from rest at the top of the incline, what is its speed at the bottom?

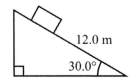

12.0 m

30.0°

8. A roller coaster car starts from rest at point A. What is the speed of this car at point C if the track is frictionless?

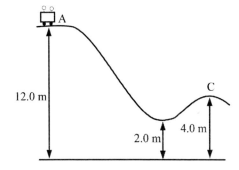

A

12.0 m

2.0 m

4.0 m

C

9. A 2.5 kg object is dropped from a height of 10.0 m above the ground. Calculate the speed of the object as it hits the ground.

10. A student running at a speed of 3.5 m/s grabs a long rope that is hanging vertically from a tree. How high can the student swing?

11. A pendulum is 1.20 m long. What is the speed of the pendulum bob when it passes through its equilibrium position if it is pulled aside until it makes a 25.0° angle to the vertical? (Hint: Is it possible to determine the vertical drop of the pendulum bob and then use the law of conservation of mechanical energy?)

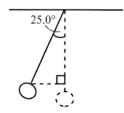

12. A 45 kg student runs with a speed of 2.0 m/s off a horizontal ledge that is 5.0 m above a swimming pool. Calculate the vertical speed of the student when she hits the water. (Hint: Can you solve this problem using your knowledge of projectile motion?)

13. A 1.0 kg box slides without friction around the loop-the-loop apparatus as shown in the diagram. If the object starts from rest at point A, and the radius of the loop is 0.75 m, what is the speed of the box at point B?

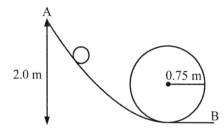

Lesson 7 LAW OF CONSERVATION OF ENERGY

There are many forms of energy: mechanical energy, thermal energy, electrical energy, etc. The Law of Conservation of Energy states that energy is neither created nor destroyed; it is converted from one form to another.

This law can be expressed in symbols as:

$\Delta E_k + \Delta E_p + \Delta TE = 0$

where TE = thermal energy.

Remember, the Law of Conservation of Mechanical Energy states that if there is no friction, mechanical energy is conserved.

$\Delta E_k + \Delta E_p = 0$

However, if there is friction, work is done against friction (to overcome it). Work done against friction = $F_f d$

Remember, F_f = force of friction

When work is done against friction, mechanical energy is changed to thermal energy (TE).

$\therefore \Delta TE = F_f d \cdot$

This means that when work is done against friction, some of the mechanical energy is changed to thermal energy.

$\Delta E_k + \Delta E_p + \Delta TE = 0$
$\therefore \Delta TE = -(\Delta E_k + \Delta E_p)$

Gain in thermal energy = Loss in mechanical energy

However, we will write this statement as

$\Delta E_k + \Delta E_p = -\Delta TE$
$\therefore \Delta E_k + \Delta E_p = -F_f d$

or $\dfrac{1}{2}m\left(v^2 - v_0^{\,2}\right) + mg\Delta h = -F_f d$

Remember, $\Delta h = h_f - h_i$ and it can be negative.

Example

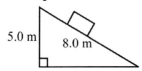

A 15.0 kg box slides down an incline as shown in the diagram. If the box starts from rest at the top of the incline and has a speed of 6.0 m/s at the bottom, what was the loss in mechanical energy (or what is the gain in thermal energy)?

Solution

$$\Delta E_k + \Delta E_p = -\Delta TE$$

$$\frac{1}{2}m\left(v^2 - v_0^{\ 2}\right) + mg\Delta h = -\Delta TE$$

$$\frac{1}{2}(15.0\text{ kg})\left[(6.0\text{ m/s})^2 - 0\right] + (15.0\text{ kg})(9.81\text{ m/s}^2)(-5.0\text{ m}) = -\Delta TE$$

$$270\text{ J} - 736\text{ J} = -\Delta TE$$

$$\Rightarrow \qquad \Delta TE = 4.7 \times 10^2 \text{ J}$$

When you apply an external force to an object within a system, you change the overall energy within that system. This change may be kinetic, potential, thermal, or any combination of these energies.

Work done by an external applied force on a system $= \Delta E_k + \Delta E_p + \Delta TE$

$$Fd = \Delta E_k + \Delta E_p + \Delta TE$$

This is an extended form of the work-energy theorem. When work is done on an object, there is a change in energy of the object. To this extent, everything that we are discussing here, including the Law of Conservation of Mechanical Energy, is a form of the work-energy theorem.

SUMMARY

- If the force in the equation $W = Fd$ is the net force,
  Work $= \Delta E_k$
  or
  $$Fd = \frac{1}{2}m\left(v^2 - v_0^{\ 2}\right)$$

- If there is no external applied force on the system, the overall energy does not change.
  $$\Delta E_k + \Delta E_p + \Delta TE = 0$$
  or
  $$\frac{1}{2}m\left(v^2 - v_0^{\ 2}\right) + mg\Delta h = -F_{fr}d$$

- If there is no friction (or friction is negligible), mechanical energy is conserved.

$$\Delta E_k + \Delta E_p = 0$$

or

$$\frac{1}{2}m\left(v^2 - v_0^{\;2}\right) = -mg\Delta h$$

- If there is an external applied force acting on the system, the overall energy changes.
Work done by an external applied force on the system =

$$\Delta E_k + \Delta E_p + \Delta TE$$

$$Fd = \frac{1}{2}m\left(v^2 - v_0^{\;2}\right) + mg\Delta h + F_f d$$

Law of Conservation of Energy:
$$\Delta E_k + \Delta E_p + \Delta TE = 0$$
or
$$\Delta E_k + \Delta E_p = -\Delta TE$$
or
$$\frac{1}{2}m\left(v^2 - v_0^{\;2}\right) + mg\Delta h = -F_{fr}d$$

Note: *TE* is the thermal energy and F_f is the force of friction.

Example

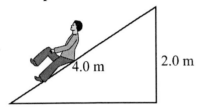

4.0 m   2.0 m

A 30.0 kg student slides down a slide as shown above. If the student's velocity at the bottom is 3.2 m/s, how much thermal energy was produced?

Solution

$$\Delta E_k + \Delta E_p + \Delta TE = 0$$

$$\frac{1}{2}m\left(v^2 - v_0^{\;2}\right) + mg\Delta h = -\Delta TE$$

$$\frac{1}{2}(30.0 \text{ kg})\left[(3.2 \text{ m/s})^2 - 0\right] + (30.0 \text{ kg})(9.81 \text{ m/s}^2)(-2.0 \text{ m}) = -\Delta TE$$

$$\Delta TE = 4.3 \times 10^2 \text{ J}$$

PRACTICE EXERCISES

Formulas: $W = Fd$ $E_p = mgh$ $E_k = \frac{1}{2}mv^2$

1. A 12 kg box initially at rest slides from the top of an incline as illustrated. If the force of friction along the incline is 5.0 N, what is the speed of the object as it reaches the bottom of the incline? (Hint: Why is the kinetic energy at the bottom not equal to the potential energy at the top?)

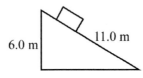

6.0 m   11.0 m

2. A 45.0 kg box initially at rest slides from the top of an incline as illustrated. If the box reaches the bottom of the incline at a speed of 5.0 m/s, what is the force of friction on the box along the incline?

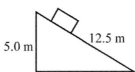

5.0 m   12.5 m

3. A constant force of 85 N accelerates a 12 kg box from a speed of 2.0 m/s to a speed of 8.0 m/s as it travels 15 m along a horizontal surface. What is the coefficient of friction between the two surfaces? Remember: $F_f = \mu F_N$. Draw a free body diagram and find the force of friction and the normal force. (Hint: There is an external applied force acting on this system.)

4. Calculate the mechanical energy converted to thermal energy when an 8.0 kg box is pushed 5.0 m along a 30.0° incline at constant velocity by an average force of 75 N parallel to the incline. How much work is done in pushing the box along the incline? What is the gravitational potential energy of the box when it is at the top of the incline? Why are these values not the same? (Hint: There is an external applied force acting on this system.)

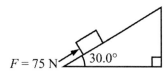

$F = 75$ N   30.0°

5. A 2.5 kg box slides from rest 0.850 m down a 30.0° incline as shown in the diagram. If the force of friction acting along the incline is 3.2 N, what is the speed of the box when it reaches the bottom of the incline?

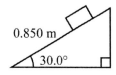

0.850 m   30.0°

6. A 18.0 N box slides from rest 0.750 m down a 30.0° incline as shown in the diagram. If the box reaches the bottom of the incline with a speed of 1.30 m/s, what was the force of friction along the incline?

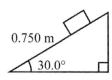

0.750 m   30.0°

7. A 115 N box slides 50.0 m along a 40.0° incline as shown in the diagram. If the force of friction along the incline is 35.0 N, what is the change in the box's gravitational potential energy?

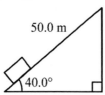

8. A 45.0 kg student starts from rest and slides 28.0 m down a water slide. What is the speed of the student at the bottom if the force of friction along the slide is 55.0 N and the vertical drop is 5.00 m?

9. A 75.0 kg box, starting from rest, slides down the incline as illustrated.

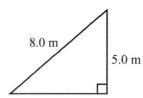

If the force due to friction along the incline is 17.9 N,

a) how much thermal energy was produced? (Hint: When work is done to overcome friction, what happens to some of the mechanical energy?)

b) what is the velocity of the box at the bottom?

PRACTICE TEST

1. When the speed of an object is doubled, its kinetic energy is

   A. quartered

   C. doubled

   B. halved

   D. quadrupled

2. Which of the following units is a unit of power?

   A. $kg \cdot m/s$

   C. $kg \cdot m^2/s^2$

   B. $kg \cdot m/s^2$

   D. $kg \cdot m^2/s^3$

3. As a heavy object falls, it

   A. gains kinetic energy and loses potential energy

   B. loses kinetic energy and gains potential energy

   C. gains both kinetic and potential energy

   D. loses both kinetic and potential energy

4. On a graph where force is plotted against displacement, the work done is indicated by the

   A. slope of the graph

   C. slope of the graph × time

   B. area under the graph

   D. area under the graph × time

5. If object A has twice the mass and half the speed of object B, then the kinetic energy of object A is

   A. one eighth that of object B

   C. one half that of object B

   B. one quarter that of object B

   D. the same as object B

6. If you are travelling along a straight level highway at 5.0 m/s and you put on your brakes and slide to a stop in distance d, how far would you slide if you have been travelling 10.0 m/s?

   A. d

   C. $2.0\,d$

   B. $\sqrt{2.0}d$

   D. $4.0\,d$

7. An object with a mass m travels a distance, d, along a horizontal surface. What is the work done by gravity on this object?

   A. mgd

   C. zero

   B. md

   D. $\dfrac{mg}{d}$

8. An object (mass = m) accelerates uniformly (acceleration = a) from rest for t seconds through a distance d. The work done on this object is

    A. mad

    C. $\dfrac{1}{2}mv^2$

    B. mgh

    D. $\dfrac{Fd}{t}$

9. When an object is travelling east at a velocity v, it has kinetic energy E. What is the kinetic energy of this object if its velocity is $3v$ east?

    A. $\sqrt{3}E$

    C. $6E$

    B. $3E$

    D. $9E$

10. Units of kinetic energy are

    A. $\mathrm{kg \cdot m/s}$

    C. $\mathrm{kg \cdot m^2/s^2}$

    B. $\mathrm{kg \cdot m/s^2}$

    D. $\mathrm{kg^2 \cdot m^2/s^2}$

11. What is the work required to accelerate an object from rest to 10.0 m/s along a frictionless surface if the mass of the object is 2.50 kg?

    A. 0 J

    C. 125 J

    B. 31.3 J

    D. 245 J

12. A projectile (mass = 10.0 g) is travelling horizontally at a velocity of 335 m/s when it hits a fixed block of wood. If the projectile penetrates the wood 3.15 cm, what is the work done on the projectile by the wood?

    A. -1.68×10^2 J

    C. 2.81×10^3 J

    B. -5.61×10^2 J

    D. 6.30×10^7 J

13. When a student runs up a flight of stairs at a velocity v, her potential energy at the top of the stairs is E_p. What is the student's potential energy at the top of the stairs if she runs up at velocity of $2v$?

    A. E_p

    C. $2E_p$

    B. $\sqrt{2}E_p$

    D. $4E_p$

14. A position-time graph for an object that is thrown vertically into the air is shown below.

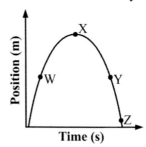

Which of the following statements is true concerning the mechanical energy of the object?

A   The mechanical energy is greatest at point X.

B   The mechanical energy is greatest at point Z.

C   The sum of the mechanical energies at points X and Z is greater than the sum of the mechanical energies at points W and Y.

D   The sum of the mechanical energies at points X and Y equal the sum of the mechanical energies at points W and Y.

15. A ball starts from rest at point A on the diagram below and rolls along the frictionless track to point B. What is the velocity of the ball at point B?

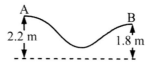

A. 2.8 m/s	**B.** 3.8 m/s
C. 5.6 m/s	**D.** 6.6 m/s

16. A student pushes against a wall with a force of 25 N for 15 s. The power output of the student is

A. 0.0 W	**B.** 1.7 W
C. 25 W	**D.** 3.8×10^{2} W

NOTES

MOMENTUM

When you are finished this unit, you should be able to…
- Define momentum and impulse
- Relate impulse to a change in velocity
- Solve problems involving momentum, mass, and velocity in one dimension
- Analyze and solve problems involving the law of conservation of momentum in one and two dimensions

Lesson	Page	Completed on
1. Momentum	172	
2. Collision	178	
3. Two-Dimensional Interaction	186	
Practice Test	192	
Answers and Solutions	at the back of the book	

PREREQUISITE SKILLS AND KNOWLEDGE

Prior to starting this unit, you should be able to…
- Write numbers in scientific notation
- Isolate a variable and combine algebraic expressions
- Perform calculations and obtain the answer to the correct number of significant figures
- Substitute the correct units for all quantities in a calculation and express the proper final unit by appropriate cancellation of units
- Differentiate between scalar and vector quantities
- Sum vector quantities to produce a resultant vector
- Determine the composition of derived units in terms of simpler units

Lesson 1 MOMENTUM

Momentum is a vector quantity.

During the 16th and 17th centuries, many scientists were convinced that there was some "quantity of motion" of objects that remained constant when they interact (collide). They discovered that this "quantity of motion" was the product of the object's mass and velocity. This quantity of motion is what we call momentum.

Symbol: $\bar{p}$

Definition: the product of the mass and the velocity of an object
$$\bar{p} = m\bar{v}$$
Units: kg m/s or $N \cdot s$

When an object accelerates, its velocity changes; therefore, its momentum changes. Change in momentum is also called *impulse*.

impulse = $\Delta\bar{p}$
or
impulse = $m\Delta\bar{v}$
Definition: the product of the net force and the time the force acts
impulse = $\bar{F}_{net}t$

When a net force acts on an object for a time period, the object accelerates —that is, its momentum changes.
$$\bar{F}_{net}t = m\Delta\bar{v}$$

Units: kg $\cdot$ m/s or N $\cdot$ s

Impulse, like momentum, is a vector quantity. The direction is the direction of the force. The equation $\bar{F}_{net}t = m\Delta\bar{v}$ shows that the longer a net force acts, the greater the change in momentum. This is why athletes are told by their coaches to follow through—keep the bat (club, etc.) in contact with the ball longer.

Newton's 2nd Law
$$\bar{F}_{net} = m\bar{a}$$
$$\bar{F}_{net} = \frac{m\Delta\bar{v}}{t}$$
$$\bar{F}_{net}t = m\Delta\bar{v}$$

Newton's First Law of Motion states that an object will remain at its state of rest or state of motion with constant velocity unless acted on by an unbalanced force. We also refer to this law as the Law of Inertia. Inertia is the tendency of an object to remain at constant velocity (including zero). Inertia depends only on the mass of the object, while momentum depends on both the mass and the velocity.

The tendency of an object to remain at a constant velocity depends on both its mass and velocity.

To help you understand this, try the following thought experiment.
- catch a tennis ball travelling at 10.0 m/s
- catch a 7.0 kg lead ball travelling at 10.0 m/s

Which one was harder to stop?

Now, try the following:
- catch a tennis ball travelling at 5.0 m/s
- catch a tennis ball travelling at 50.0 m/s

Which one was harder to stop?

Example

Calculate the momentum of a 6.2 kg object travelling at a velocity of 5.0 m/s west.

Solution

$$\bar{p} = m\bar{v}$$
$$= (6.2 \text{ kg})(5.0 \text{ m/s west})$$
$$= 31 \text{ kg} \cdot \text{m/s} \quad \text{west}$$

Example

A net force of 12.0 N north acts on an object for 2.00×10^{-3} s. Calculate the impulse.

Solution

$$\text{Impulse} = \bar{F}_{net}t$$
$$= (12.0 \text{ N north})(2.00 \times 10^{-3} \text{ s})$$
$$= 2.40 \times 10^{-2} \text{ N} \cdot \text{s} \quad \text{north}$$

Example

A net force of 14.0 N acts south on a 6.00 kg object for 1.00×10^{-1} s. What is the change in velocity of this object?

Solution

$$\bar{F}_{net}t = m\Delta\bar{v}$$
$$\Delta\bar{v} = \frac{\bar{F}_{net}t}{m}$$
$$= \frac{(14.0 \text{ N south})(1.00 \times 10^{-1} \text{ s})}{6.00 \text{ kg}}$$
$$= 0.233 \text{ m/s} \quad \text{south}$$

PRACTICE EXERCISES

Formulas: $\qquad \vec{p} = m\vec{v} \qquad\qquad \vec{F}_{net}t = \Delta\vec{p} \qquad$ **or** $\qquad \vec{F}_{net}t = m\Delta\vec{v}$

1. Calculate the momentum of a 4.0 kg object travelling at a velocity of 12.0 m/s east.

2. A 5.0 kg object has momentum of 25.0 kg·m/s west. What is its velocity?

3. An object has a velocity of 8.0 m/s south and a momentum of 36.0 kg·m/s south. What is the mass of the object?

4. An object has a velocity of 2.0 m/s east and momentum of 29 kg·m/s east. What is the magnitude of the weight of the object?

5. A 6.6 N object is travelling at a velocity of 3.0 m/s north. What is the momentum of the object? (Express answer in kg·m/s.)

6. A 7.0 kg object travels 2.6 m west in 1.1 s. If velocity is uniform, what is the momentum of the object?

7. A 5.0 kg object is dropped from a height of 2.5 m above the floor. What is the object's momentum after 0.25 s?

8. An average net force of 17.0 N acts east on an object for 2.5×10^{-2} s.. What is the impulse?

9. An average net force of 11.2 N acts west on an object producing an impulse of 7.00 N•s west. How long did the force act on the object?

10. A 26.3 kg object is travelling at 21.0 m/s north. What average net force is required to bring this object to a stop in 2.60 s?

11. An average net force of 31.6 N south is used to accelerate a 15.0 kg object uniformly from rest to 10.0 m/s. How long was the acceleration?

12. An average net force of 25.0 N acts north on an object for 7.20×10^{-1} s. What is the change in momentum of the object?

13. A 5.00 kg object accelerates uniformly from rest to a velocity of 15.0 m/s east. What is the impulse on the object?

14. An average net force caused an 11.0 kg object to accelerate uniformly from rest. If this object travels 26.3 m west in 3.20 s, what is the change in momentum of the object?

15. A 3.0 kg object is dropped from a height of 6.5 m. How far has the object fallen when its momentum is 6.0 kg·m/s down?

16. A 1.0 kg ball hits the floor with a velocity of 2.0 m/s. If this ball bounces up with a velocity of 1.6 m/s, what is the ball's change in momentum?

17. A rocket at rest with a mass of 9.5×10^3 kg. is acted on by an average net force of 1.5×10^5 N up for 15 s. What is the final velocity of the rocket?

18. Without finding the acceleration, calculate the average net force that is required to accelerate a 5.4 kg ball from rest to 3.0 m/s east in a time of 0.75 s.

19. Without finding the acceleration, calculate the time an average net force of 225 N must act on a 1.0×103 kg object to change its velocity from 2.0 m/s east to 5.0 m/s east.

20. Without finding the acceleration, calculate the change in velocity of a 15 kg object when an average net force of 95 N north acts on the object for 1.6 s.

Lesson 2 COLLISION

Elastic collisions:
Both momentum and kinetic energy are conserved.

Collisions can be classified as
- elastic
- inelastic

An elastic collision is a collision in which both kinetic energy and momentum are conserved.

An inelastic collision is a collision in which momentum is conserved, but kinetic energy is not.

Inelastic collisions: Momentum is conserved, but not kinetic energy.

Isolated System: No net external forces act on the objects.
No collision at the macroscopic level is perfectly elastic. Perfectly elastic collisions only occur at the atomic or subatomic levels. This is because collisions at the macroscopic level involve some distortion (shape change), and this creates thermal energy—i.e., some kinetic energy is converted to thermal energy. However, if the objects collide and do not stick together, there is some elastic component.

THE LAW OF CONSERVATION OF MOMENTUM

The Law of Conservation of Momentum states that in an isolated system (no net external force) the total momentum of the objects in the system after interaction (collision) is equal to the total momentum before interaction (collision).

$$\bar{P}_{sys(after)} = \bar{P}_{sys(before)}$$

The law of conservation of momentum can be derived using Newton's third law. This law states that, every action has an equal and opposite reaction.

Two objects of masses m_1 and m_2 are moving with initial velocities $\bar{v}_1$ and $\bar{v}_2$ when they collide head on (linearly). After collision their final velocities were $\bar{v}_1'$ and $\bar{v}_2'$ respectively.

According to Newton's third law,

$$\bar{F}_{reaction} = -\bar{F}_{action}$$
$$\bar{F}_{2\ on\ 1} = -\bar{F}_{1\ on\ 2}$$
$$\left(\bar{F}_{2\ on\ 1}\right)\Delta t = -\left(\bar{F}_{1\ on\ 2}\right)\Delta t \quad \text{(multiplying with } \Delta t)$$
$$\Delta \bar{p}_2 = \Delta \bar{p}_1$$
$$\Delta \bar{p}_1 + \Delta \bar{p}_2 = 0$$
$$\bar{p}_1 - \bar{p}_1' + \bar{p}_2 - \bar{p}_2' = 0$$
$$\bar{p}_1 + \bar{p}_2 = \bar{p}_1' + \bar{p}_2'$$
$$m_1\bar{v}_1 + m_2\bar{v}_2 = m_1\bar{v}_1' + m_2\bar{v}_2'$$
$$\bar{p} = \bar{p}'$$
$$\bar{P}_{sys(before)} = \bar{P}_{sys(after)} \quad \text{and vice versa}$$

In order to investigate this law, you need a system in which you can cancel out any external force.

We can use this law to do a number of mathematical calculations. In order to do these calculations, we will classify the interactions as follows:

Linear interactions
If two objects moving in a straight-line collide so that the common surface of contact is perpendicular to their velocities, the collision is said to be head-on or one-dimensional. There are two types of linear interaction:
- collisions in which the objects collide but do not stick together
- collisions in which the objects collide and stick together

Two-dimensional interactions
- collisions at 90°
- collisions at angles other than 90°

First, consider linear interactions.
In the collision problems that follow, the term *objects* is used as a general term. If these colliding objects were cars, billiard balls, curling stones, etc., the process in solving the problem would be the same.

Example: Collisions when objects do not stick together
A 0.25 kg steel ball is travelling east at a velocity of 4.5 m/s when it collides head on with a 0.30 kg steel ball travelling west at a velocity of 5.0 m/s. After collision, the 0.25 kg ball is travelling west at a velocity of 2.0 m/s. What is the velocity of the 0.30 kg ball after the collision?

Solution
Method 1

before collision

$\therefore \bar{p}_{sys(before)} = \bar{p}_1 + \bar{p}_2 = -0.375 \text{ kg} \cdot \text{m/s}$

$m_1 = 0.25$ kg	$m_2 = 0.30$ kg
$\bar{v}_1 = 4.5$ m/s	$\bar{v}_2 = -5.0$ m/s
$\bar{p}_1 = 1.13$ kg·m/s	$\bar{p}_2 = -1.5$ kg·m/s

Consider east as positive direction

after collision

$m_1 = 0.25 \text{ kg}$ $m_2 = 0.30 \text{ kg}$

$\vec{v}_1' = -2.0 \text{ m/s}$ $\vec{v}_2' = ?$

$\vec{p}_1' = -0.50 \text{ kg} \cdot \text{m/s}$ $\vec{p}_2' = ?$

$\vec{p}_{\text{sys(after)}} = \vec{p}_{\text{sys(before)}} = -0.375 \text{ kg} \cdot \text{m/s}$

$\vec{p}_{\text{sys(after)}} = \vec{p}_1' + \vec{p}_2' = -0.375 \text{ kg} \cdot \text{m/s}$

$\Rightarrow \vec{p}_2' = -0.375 \text{ kg} \cdot \text{m/s} - (-0.50 \text{ kg} \cdot \text{m/s})$

$\therefore \vec{p}_2' = 0.125 \text{ kg} \cdot \text{m/s}$

$\vec{p}_2' = m_2 \vec{v}_2'$

$\vec{v}_2' = \dfrac{\vec{p}_2'}{m_2}$

$= \dfrac{0.125 \text{ kg} \cdot \text{m/s}}{0.30 \text{ kg}}$

$= 0.42 \text{ m/s}$

The velocity of the 0.30 kg ball after the collision is 0.42 m/s east.

Steps taken to solve this problem:
• draw before and after diagrams

• write m, $\vec{v}$, $\vec{p}$ under each isolated object drawn

• using m, $\vec{v}$, $\vec{p}$ fill in as much data as possible

• calculate $\vec{p}$ where possible

• use Law of Conservation of Momentum to find $\vec{p}_{sys(after)}$

• knowing final $\vec{p}$ of object 1 and $\vec{p}_{sys(after)}$ we can calculate final $\vec{p}$ of object 2

• knowing m of object 2 and final $\vec{p}$ of object 2, use the formula $\vec{p} = mv$ to calculate final $\vec{v}$ of object 2

• Note: since objects travelled in opposite directions, one of the directions must be indicated as negative.

Method 2
Consider east direction as positive. Now, from the law of conservation of momentum

$$\bar{P}_{sys(\text{before})} = \bar{P}_{sys(\text{after})}$$
$$\bar{p}_1 + \bar{p}_2 = \bar{p}'_1 + \bar{p}'_2$$
$$m_1\bar{v}_1 + m_2\bar{v}_2 = m_1\bar{v}'_1 + m_2\bar{v}'_2$$
$$\therefore \bar{v}'_2 = \frac{m_1\bar{v}_1 + m_2\bar{v}_2 - m_1\bar{v}_1}{m_2}$$
$$= \frac{(0.25 \text{ kg})(4.5 \text{ m/s}) + (0.30 \text{ kg})(-5.0 \text{ m/s}) - (0.25)(-2.0 \text{ m/s})}{0.30 \text{ kg}}$$
$$= \frac{1.125 \text{ kg} \cdot \text{m/s} - 1.5 \text{ kg} \cdot \text{m/s} + 0.50 \cdot \text{m/s}}{0.30 \text{ kg}}$$
$$= \frac{0.125 \text{ kg} \cdot \text{m/s}}{0.30 \text{ kg}}$$
$$= 0.42 \text{ m}$$

Therefore, the velocity of the 0.30 kg ball after the collision is 0.42 m/s east.

Example: Collisions when objects stick together

A 1.1×10^3 kg car travelling east at a velocity of 25 km/h collides head on with a 1.3×10^3 kg car travelling west at a velocity of 15 km/h. During the collision, the two cars lock together. What is the velocity of the locked cars as they move together immediately after collision?

Solution

Consider east direction as positive
before collision

$$m_1 = 1.1 \times 10^3 \text{ kg}$$
$$\bar{v}_1 = 25 \text{ km/h}$$
$$\bar{p}_1 = 2.75 \times 10^4 \text{ kg} \cdot \text{km/h}$$

$$m_2 = 1.3 \times 10^3 \text{ kg}$$
$$\bar{v}_2 = -15 \text{ km/h}$$
$$\bar{p}_2 = -1.95 \times 10^4 \text{ kg} \cdot \text{km/h}$$

$$\therefore \bar{p}_{\text{before}} = \bar{p}_1 + \bar{p}_2 = 8.0 \times 10^3 \text{ kg} \cdot \text{km/h}$$

after collision

$\left(1 + 2\right)$

$m = m1 + m2 = 2.4 \times 10^3$ kg
$\vec{v}' = ?$
$\vec{p}' = 8.0 \times 10^3$ kg $\cdot$ km/h

$\therefore \vec{P}_{sys(after)} = \vec{P}_{sys(before)} = 8.0 \times 10^3$ kg $\cdot$ m/h

To find out final velocity, use momentum equation
$\vec{p}' = m\vec{v}'$

$\vec{v}' = \dfrac{\vec{p}'}{m}$

$= \dfrac{8.0 \times 10^3 \text{ kg} \cdot \text{km/h}}{2.4 \times 10^3 \text{ kg}}$

$= 3.3$ km/h east

Steps taken to solve this problem are the same as in previous example.

Note: it is not necessary to convert km/h to m/s. Because the cars stick together on collision, treat the combined cars as a single object.

Example: Explosion

A 0.050 kg bullet is fired from a 5.0 kg gun. If the velocity of the bullet is 275 m/s, what is the recoil velocity of the gun?

Before   After

$\vec{P}_{sys(before)} = \vec{P}_{sys(after)}$

$\vec{p} = \vec{p}'$

$m_g \vec{v}_g + m_b \vec{v}_b = m_g \vec{v}_g' + m_b \vec{v}_b'$

$\Rightarrow \vec{v}_g' = \dfrac{m_g \vec{v}_g + m_b \vec{v}_b - m_b \vec{v}_b'}{m_g}$

$= \dfrac{0 - \left(0.050 \text{ kg}\right)\left(275 \text{ m/s}\right)}{5.0 \text{ kg}}$ $\left(\because \vec{v}_g = 0, \vec{v}_b = 0 \text{ initially}\right)$

$= -2.75$ m/s

$= -2.8$ m/s

Note: The negative sign indicates the gun is moving in the opposite direction to the bullet.

Note: The mass before explosion is the mass of the gun and bullet.

PRACTICE EXERCISES

Formula: $\bar{p} = m\bar{v}$ $\bar{P}_{sys(after)} = \bar{P}_{sys(before)}$ $m_1\bar{v}_1 + m_2\bar{v}_2 = m_1\bar{v}_1' + m_2\bar{v}_2'$

Note: Angles (directions) are expressed first in terms of north, east, etc., and also in terms of the rectangular coordinate system.

1. A 30.0 kg object moving to the right at a velocity of 1.00 m/s collides with a 20.0 kg object moving to the left at a velocity of 5.00 m/s. If the 20.0 kg object continues to move left at a velocity of 1.25 m/s, what is the velocity of the 30.0 kg object?

2. A 4.50×10^3 kg railway car is moving east at a velocity of 5.0 m/s on a level frictionless track when it collides with a stationary 6.50×10^3 kg railway car. If the two cars lock together upon collision, how fast are they moving after collision?

3. A 925 kg car moving at a velocity of 18.0 m/s right collides with a stationary truck of unknown mass. The two vehicles lock together as a result of the collision and move off at a velocity of 6.50 m/s. What was the mass of the truck?

4. A 50.0 g bullet strikes a 7.00 kg stationary wooden block. If the bullet becomes embedded in the block, and the block with the embedded bullet moves forward at a velocity of 5.00 m/s, what was the initial velocity of the bullet?

5. A 40.0 g object moving with a velocity of 9.00 m/s to the right collides with a 55.0 g object moving with a velocity of 6.00 m/s left. If the two objects stick together upon collision, what is the velocity of the combined masses after collision?

6. A 76 kg student, standing at rest on a frictionless horizontal surface, throws a 0.20 kg object horizontally with a velocity of 22 m/s left. What was the initial velocity of the student upon release of the object?

7. A 25 kg projectile is fired horizontally from a 1.1×10^3 kg launcher. If the horizontal velocity of the projectile is 325 m/s east, what is the recoil velocity of the launcher?

8. A rail vehicle with a rocket engine is being tested on a smooth horizontal track. Starting from rest, the engine is fired for a short period of time releasing 4.5×10^2 kg of gases. It is estimated that the average velocity of the gases is 1.4×10^3 m/s right, and that the maximum velocity of the vehicle is 45 m/s left. What is the mass of this vehicle?

9. A 7.0 kg object at rest explodes into two parts. If part A has a mass of 2.0 kg and a velocity of 10.0 m/s right, what is the velocity of part B?

10. A 1.02×10^4 kg truck moving at a velocity of 15 m/s north collides head on with a 1.02×10^3 kg car moving at a velocity of 25 m/s south. If they stick together upon impact, what is the velocity of the combined masses?

11. A 225 g ball moves with a velocity of 30.0 cm/s to the right. This ball collides with a 125 g ball moving in the same direction at a velocity of 10.0 cm/s. After the collision, the velocity of the 125 g ball is 24.0 cm/s to the right.

   a) What is the velocity of the 225 g ball after the collision?

   b) Is this an elastic or inelastic collision? Provide mathematical evidence for your answer.

12. A 10.0 g object is moving with a velocity of 20.0 cm/s to the right when it collides with a stationary 30.0 g object. After collision, the 10.0 g object is moving left at a velocity of 6.00 cm/s.

   a) What is the velocity of the 30.0 g object after the collision?

   b) Is this an elastic or inelastic collision? Provide mathematical evidence for your answer.

   c) What happened to the kinetic energy that was lost?

Lesson 3 TWO-DIMENSIONAL INTERACTIONS

In the collisions that we have considered up to this point, we have assumed all motion has been along a straight line. However, most collisions are not linear. We will now consider some non-linear collisions.

Example: Collisions at 90°

A 4.0 kg object is travelling south at a velocity of 2.8 m/s when it collides with a 6.0 kg object travelling east at a velocity of 3.0 m/s. If these two objects stick together upon collision, at what velocity do the combined masses move?

Solution
before collision

$m_1 = 4.0$ kg
$\bar{v}_1 = 2.8$ m/s south
$\bar{p}_1 = 11.2$ kg·m/s south

$m_2 = 6.0$ kg
$\bar{v}_2 = 3.0$ m/s   east
$\bar{p}_2 = 18.0$ kg·m/s east

after collision

(1 + 2)

$m = m_1 + m_2 = 10.0$ kg
$\bar{v} = ?$
$\bar{p} = ?$

First find out the momentum of the system before collision ($\bar{p}_{sys(before)}$)

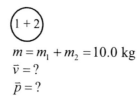

The magnitude of the resultant momentum is

$$p_R = \sqrt{p_1^2 + p_2^2}$$
$$= \sqrt{(18.0 \text{ kg} \cdot \text{m/s})^2 + (11.2 \text{ kg} \cdot \text{m/s})^2}$$
$$= 21.2 \text{ kg} \cdot \text{m/s}$$

Now, find the direction:

$$\tan\theta = \frac{p_2}{p_1}$$
$$= \frac{11.2 \text{ kg} \cdot \text{m/s}}{18.0 \text{ kg} \cdot \text{m/s}}$$
$$\theta = 31.9°$$

Therefore

$$\vec{P}_{sys(before)} = \vec{P}_R = 21.2 \text{ kg} \cdot \text{m / s } 31.9° \text{ S of E}$$

Again

$$\vec{P}_{sys(after)} = \vec{P}_{sys(before)} = \vec{P}_R$$

$$\therefore \vec{P}_{sys(after)} = \vec{p} = 21.2 \text{ kg} \cdot \text{m/s } 31.9° \text{ S of E}$$
$$= 21.2 \text{ kg} \cdot \text{m/s } 58.1 \text{ E of S}$$
$$= 21.2 \text{ kg} \cdot \text{m/s } 328°$$

Again $\vec{p} = m\vec{v}$

$$\Rightarrow \vec{v} = \frac{\vec{p}}{m}$$
$$= \frac{21.2 \text{ kg} \cdot \text{m/s } 328°}{10.0 \text{ kg}}$$
$$v = 2.1 \text{ m/s } 328°$$

Example: Collisions at Angles other than 90°

A 4.0 kg object is moving east at an unknown velocity when it collides with a 6.1 kg stationary object. After the collision, the 4.0 kg object is travelling at a velocity of 2.8 m/s 32° N of E and the 6.1 kg object is travelling at a velocity of 1.5 m/s 41° S of E. What was the velocity of the 4.0 kg object before collision?

Solution
before collision

$$m_1 = 4.0 \text{ kg} \quad m_2 = 6.1 \text{ kg}$$
$$\vec{v}_1 = ? \quad\quad \vec{v}_2 = 0$$
$$\vec{p}_1 = ? \quad\quad \vec{p}_2 = 0$$

before collision

$$m_1 = 4.0 \text{ kg}$$
$$\vec{v}_1' = 2.8 \text{ m/s } 32° \text{ N of E}$$
$$\vec{p}_1' = 11.2 \text{ kg} \cdot \text{m/s } 32° \text{ N of E}$$

$$m_2 = 6.1 \text{ kg}$$
$$\vec{v}_2' = 1.5 \text{ m/s } 41° \text{ S of E}$$
$$\vec{p}_2' = 9.15 \text{ kg} \cdot \text{m/s } 41° \text{ S of E}$$

Find east and north components of 11.2 kg·m/s 32° N of E
To solve this problem consider east and north direction as positive.

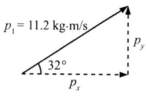

$\vec{p}'_{1x} = p'_{1x} \cos\theta$

$= (11.2 \text{ kg} \cdot \text{m/s})(\cos 32°)$

$= 9.50 \text{ kg} \cdot \text{m/s}$

$\vec{p}'_{1y} = p'_1 \sin\theta$

$= (11.2 \text{ kg} \cdot \text{m/s})(\sin 32°)$

$= 5.94 \text{ kg} \cdot \text{m/s}$

Find east and south components of 9.15 kg•m/s 41° S of E
(= 9.15 kg·m/s 319° heading counter-clockwise from x-axis)

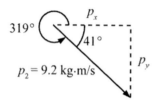

$\vec{p}'_{2x} = p'_2 \cos\theta$

$= (9.15 \text{ kg} \cdot \text{m/s})(\cos 319°)$

$= 6.91 \text{ kg} \cdot \text{m/s}$

$\vec{p}'_{2y} = p'_2 \sin\theta$

$= (9.15 \text{ kg} \cdot \text{m/s})(\sin 319°)$

$= -6.00 \text{ kg} \cdot \text{m/s}$

Do the vector addition for the components of the momentum

$\sum \vec{p}'_x = \vec{p}'_{1x} + \vec{p}'_{2x} = 9.50 \text{kg·m/s} + 6.91 \text{ kg·m/s}$

$= 16.4 \text{kg·m/s}$

$\sum \vec{p}'_y = \vec{p}'_{1y} + \vec{p}'_{2y}$

$= 5.94 \text{kg·m/s} + (-6.00 \text{ kg·m/s})$

$= -0.06 \text{ kg} \cdot \text{m/s}$

Now, find the magnitude of $\vec{p}'_R$ using Pythagoras theorem

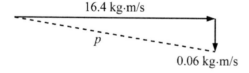

$p'_R = \sqrt{(p'_x)^2 + (p'_y)^2}$

$= \sqrt{(16.4 \text{ kg} \cdot \text{m/s})^2 + (0.06 \text{ kg} \cdot \text{m/s})^2}$

$= 16.4 \text{ kg} \cdot \text{m/s}$

Find the direction using

$\tan\theta = \dfrac{p_y}{p_x}$

$= \dfrac{0.06 \text{ kg} \cdot \text{m/s}}{16.4 \text{ kg} \cdot \text{m/s}}$

$\therefore \theta = 0.21°$

$\vec{p}_R' = 16.4 \text{ kg·m/s } 0.21° \text{ S of E}$

$\approx 16.4 \text{ kg·m/s east}$

Now form law of conservation of momentum

$\vec{p}_{\text{sys(before)}} = \vec{p}_{\text{sys(after)}} = 16.4 \text{ kg·m/s east}$

As the second object was initially stationary, the momentum of the 4.0 kg object was the momentum of the system before collision.

Therefore $\vec{p}_1 = 16.4 \text{ kg·m/s east}$

Now

$\vec{p}_1 = m_1 \vec{v}_1$

$\vec{v}_1 = \dfrac{\vec{p}_1}{m}$

$= \dfrac{16.4 \text{ kg·m/s east}}{4.0 \text{ kg}}$

$= 4.1 \text{ m/s east}$

So the velocity of the 4.0 kg object before collision was 4.1 m/s east.

PRACTICE EXERCISES

Formulas: $\bar{p} = m\bar{v}$ $\bar{P}_{sys(after)} = \bar{P}_{sys(before)}$ $m_1\bar{v}_1 + m_2\bar{v}_2 = m_1\bar{v}_1' + m_2\bar{v}_2'$ $p = \sqrt{p_1^2 + p_2^2}$

1. A 1.4×10^3 kg car is travelling westbound at a velocity of 37.0 km/h when it collides with a 2.0×10^3 kg truck travelling northbound at a velocity of 35.0 km/h. If these two vehicles lock together upon collision, what is the initial velocity of the vehicles after collision?

2. Object A has a mass of 6.2 kg and a velocity of 3.0 m/s north when it collides with object B, which has a mass of 8.0 kg and a velocity of 3.5 m/s west. If these two masses stick together upon collision, what is their velocity after collision?

3. A 4.0×10^4 kg truck moving west at a velocity of 8.0 m/s collides with a 3.0×10^4 kg truck moving south at a velocity of 5.0 m/s. If these two vehicles lock together upon collision, what is the initial velocity of the vehicles after collision?

4. A 50.0 kg object is moving east at an unknown velocity when it collides with a 60.0 kg stationary object. After the collision, the 50.0 kg object is travelling at a velocity of 6.00 m/s 50.0° N of E (or 50.0°), and the 60.0 kg object is travelling at a velocity of 6.30 m/s 38.0° S of E (or 322.0°).

    a) What was the velocity of the 50.0 kg object before collision?

    b) Is this an elastic or inelastic collision? Provide mathematical evidence for your answer.

c) What happened to the kinetic energy lost?

5. A 15.0 kg object is moving east at a velocity of 7.0 m/s when it collides with a 10.0 kg stationary object. After the collision, the 15.0 kg object is travelling at a velocity of 4.2 m/s 20.0° S of E (or 340.0°).

    a) What is the velocity of the 10.0 kg object after collision?

    b) Is this an elastic or inelastic collision? Provide mathematical evidence for your answer.

    c) What happened to the kinetic energy lost?

6. An object explodes into three equal masses. One mass moves east at a velocity of 15.0 m/s. If a second mass moves at a velocity of 10.0 m/s 45.0° S of E, what is the velocity of the third mass?

PRACTICE TEST

1. When an object is lifted vertically at a constant velocity, which of the following characteristics increases?

   i) kinetic energy
   ii) potential energy
   iii) momentum

   A. i and iii only   **B.** ii and iii only

   C. i only   **D.** ii only

2. Momentum is conserved during which of the following situations?

   i) elastic collision
   ii) inelastic collision
   iii) explosion

   A. i only   **B.** i and ii only

   C. iii only   **D.** i, ii and iii

3. When an object is at rest, which of the following characteristics may it have?

   i) kinetic energy
   ii) potential energy
   iii) momentum

   A. i and iii only   **B.** ii and iii only

   C. i only   **D.** ii only

4. Which of the following units is a unit of impulse?

   A. $kg \cdot m/s^2$ **B.** $kg \cdot m^2/s^2$

   C. N/s   **D.** $N \cdot s$

5. If an object has momentum, which of the following characteristics must it also have?

   i) kinetic energy
   ii) potential energy
   iii) mechanical energy

   A. i and iii only   **B.** ii and iii only

   C. i only   **D.** ii only

6. In an elastic collision, which of the following characteristics are conserved?

    i) kinetic energy
    ii) momentum

    A. Both i and ii

    C. Only ii

    B. Only i

    D. Neither i nor ii

7. If an object has a mass, m, and kinetic energy, E_k, its momentum is

    A. $\sqrt{\dfrac{2E_k}{m}}$

    B. $\sqrt{2E_k m}$

    C. $\dfrac{4E_k^{\,2}}{m}$

    D. $\sqrt{2E_k}$

8. When the velocity of an object is tripled, which of the following characteristics is (are) also tripled?

    i) momentum
    ii) inertia
    iii) kinetic energy
    iv) potential energy

    A. i only

    C. ii and iv only

    B. iii only

    D. i, ii, iii, and iv

9. When an object slides along a horizontal frictionless surface, which of the following characteristics remains constant?

    i) momentum
    ii) potential energy
    iii) kinetic energy

    A. i and ii only

    C. ii and iii only

    B. i and iii only

    D. i, ii, and iii

10. The impulse experienced by an object is equivalent to its change in

    A. velocity

    C. potential energy

    B. kinetic energy

    D. momentum

11. After a 1.30×10^2 kg astronaut (including equipment) connects a safety line (length = 22.0 m) to herself and to the spacecraft (mass = 2.80×10^3 kg), she pushes against the craft and moves away at a constant velocity of 9.00 m/s. How long does it take the safety line to become tight?

    A. 0.418 s

    C. 2.34 s

    B. 0.900 s

    D. 2.44 s

12. An uncharged subatomic particle that has a speed, v, and a mass, m, strikes the nucleus of a large atom. Assuming that this collision is perfectly elastic and that the particle rebounds back along the incident path, the change in momentum of the subatomic particle is closest to

A. 0

B. $\dfrac{mv}{2}$

C. mv

D. 2mv

13. A perfect elastic collision conserves

A. momentum but not kinetic energy

B. kinetic energy but not momentum

C. both momentum and kinetic energy

D. neither momentum nor kinetic energy

14. A 0.25 kg ball hits a wall at a velocity of 3.0 m/s perpendicular to the wall. If the ball rebounds at a velocity of 2.5 m/s, also perpendicular to the wall, what was the impulse on the ball during its contact with the wall?

A. 0.031 N·s

B. 0.125 N·s

C. 1.4 N·s

D. 3.8 N·s

15. A 1.1 × 103 kg car travelling east at a velocity of 25 km/h collides head on with a 2.3 × 103 kg car travelling west at a velocity of 15 km/h. During the collision, the two cars lock together. What is the velocity of the locked cars as they move off together immediately after the collision?

A. 2.1 km/h east

B. 2.1 km/h west

C. 18 km/h east

D. 18 km/h west

EQUILIBRIUM

When you are finished this unit, you should be able to…

- Recognize the difference between translational equilibrium, rotational equilibrium, and static equilibrium

- Describe torque and determine the torque on an object as a result of an applied force

- Analyze and solve problems involving objects in translational and rotational equilibrium through the application of free-body diagrams

Lesson	Page	Completed on
1. The First Condition of Equilibrium	196	
2. The Second Condition of Equilibrium	204	
Practice Test	212	
Answers and Solutions	at the back of the book	

PREREQUISITE SKILLS AND KNOWLEDGE

Prior to starting this unit, you should be able to…

- Write numbers in scientific notation

- Isolate a variable and combine algebraic expressions

- Perform calculations and obtain the answer to the correct number of significant figures

- Substitute the correct units for all quantities in a calculation and express the proper final unit by appropriate cancellation of units

- Interpret and create free-body diagrams

- Determine the composition of derived units in terms of simpler units

Lesson 1 *THE FIRST CONDITION OF EQUILIBRIUM*

Begin this lesson by considering the following examples

Example

A 20.0 kg block is suspended by a rope as shown in the diagram.

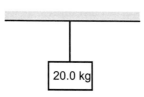

What is the net force acting on the block?

> *Solution*
>
> The net force acting on the block is zero. You will note that the block is not accelerating—it is not even moving. (Remember Newton's Second Law of Motion.)

Example

A 20.0 kg block is lifted at a constant velocity. What is the net force acting on the block?

> *Solution*
>
> The net force acting on the block is zero. You will note that the block is not accelerating. (Remember Newton's Second Law of Motion.) When the net force acting on an object is zero, we say that the object is in equilibrium. When the object is stationary, we say that it is in static equilibrium. When the object is moving at a constant velocity, we say that it is in dynamic equilibrium.
>
> In both cases, we say that the object is in translational equilibrium.

THE FIRST CONDITION OF EQUILIBRIUM

If there is no net force, there is no acceleration (no change in velocity). This is Newton's First Law of Motion.

If there is no acceleration of the object, the object is said to be in translational equilibrium.

The first condition of equilibrium is that there is no net force.

$\sum \vec{F} = 0$.

Σ is the symbol that we use for "sum of."

The first condition of equilibrium is usually expressed in terms of components.

$\sum \vec{F}_x = 0$

$\sum \vec{F}_y = 0$

If the object remains at rest, then the object is in static equilibrium. In the problems for this section, the objects will be in static equilibrium.

Translational motion is motion along a line.

The first condition of equilibrium is
$\sum \vec{F} = 0$

Note: $\sum \vec{F} = \vec{F}_{net}$

Example

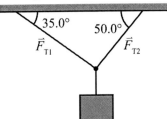

A 64.0 N object is suspended using ropes as shown in the above diagram. Calculate the magnitude of the tensions, F_{T1} and F_{T2} in the ropes.

Solution

Find the point in the system that is in static equilibrium and all the forces acting on it. In this case, it is the point where the ropes join.

Draw a free body diagram showing the forces acting on this point.

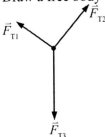

Break these forces into the *x* and *y* components.

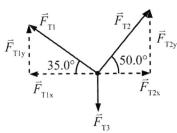

$$F_{T1(x)} = F_{T1} \cos\theta_1 \qquad\qquad F_{T2(x)} = F_{T2} \cos\theta_2$$

$$F_{T1(y)} = F_{T1} \sin\theta_1 \qquad\qquad F_{T2(y)} = F_{T2} \sin\theta_2$$

Use the first condition of equilibrium. Solve using simultaneous equations.

$$\Sigma \vec{F}_x = 0$$

$$F_{T1(x)} - F_{T21(x)} = 0$$

$$F_{T1} \cos\theta_1 - F_{T2} \cos\theta_2 = 0$$

$$F_{T1} \cos 35.0° - F_{T2} \cos 50.0° = 0$$

$$0.819(F_{T1}) - 0.643(F_{T2}) = 0$$

$$0.643(F_{T2}) = 0.819(F_{T1})$$

$$F_{T2} = \frac{0.819(F_{T1})}{0.643}$$

$$= 1.274(F_{T1})$$

$$\sum \vec{F}_y = 0$$
$$F_{T1(y)} + F_{T2(y)} - F_{T3} = 0$$
$$F_{T1} \sin \theta_1 + F_{T2} \sin \theta_2 - F_{T3} = 0$$
$$F_{T1} \sin 35.0° + F_{T2} \sin 50.0° - 64.0 \text{ N} = 0$$
$$0.574(F_{T1}) + 0.766(F_{T2}) = 64.0 \text{ N}$$
$$0.574(F_{T1}) + (0.766)(1.274 F_{T1}) = 64.0 \text{ N}$$
$$0.574(F_{T1}) + 0.976(F_{T1}) = 64 \text{ N}$$
$$1.55(F_{T1}) = 64.0 \text{ N}$$
$$(F_{T1}) = 41.3 \text{ N}$$

$$\therefore F_{T2} = (1.274)(41.3 \text{ N})$$
$$= 52.6 \text{ N}$$

Alternate Method

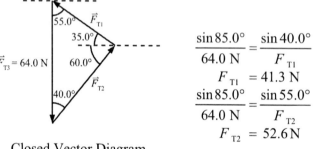

Closed Vector Diagram

$$\frac{\sin 85.0°}{64.0 \text{ N}} = \frac{\sin 40.0°}{F_{T1}}$$
$$F_{T1} = 41.3 \text{ N}$$
$$\frac{\sin 85.0°}{64.0 \text{ N}} = \frac{\sin 55.0°}{F_{T2}}$$
$$F_{T2} = 52.6 \text{ N}$$

Example

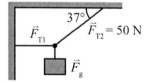

An object with a magnitude of weight F_g is suspended as shown in the diagram above. If the tension in one of the ropes is 50 N as shown, what is the value of weight of the object?

Solution

Find the point in the system that is in static equilibrium and all the forces acting on it. This is the point where the ropes join. Draw a free body diagram showing the forces acting on this point.

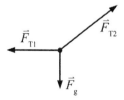

Break these forces into components if necessary.

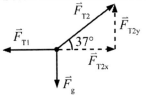

$$F_{T2(x)} = F_{T2}\cos\theta$$

$$F_{T2(y)} = F_{T2}\sin\theta$$

Use the first condition of equilibrium. Note that we do not need to use both equations.

$$\sum \vec{F}_y = 0$$
$$F_{T2(y)} - F_g = 0$$
$$F_{T2}\sin\theta = F_g$$
$$(50\ \text{N})(\sin 37°) = F_g$$
$$\therefore F_g = 30\ \text{N}$$

PRACTICE EXERCISES

Formulas: $\sum \vec{F} = 0$ $\sum \vec{F}_x = 0$ $\sum \vec{F}_y = 0$

1. $\vec{F}_{g_1}$, $\vec{F}_{g_2}$, and $\vec{F}_{g_3}$ are the weights of three objects suspended by pulleys, as illustrated. Assuming the pulleys in this system are frictionless and weightless and that magnitude of third weight is $F_{g_3} = 12$ N, what are the magnitudes of $\vec{F}_{g_1}$ and $\vec{F}_{g_2}$?

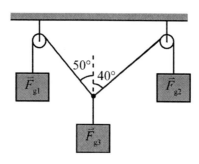

2. An object is suspended on a frictionless inclined plane by a rope parallel to the incline, as illustrated above. If the angle of the incline is 25.0° and the tension on the rope is 5 000 N, what is the weight of the object?

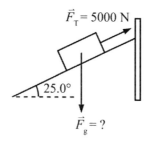

3. A 20.0 N child sitting on a playground swing is being pushed by her father. When the swing rope makes an angle of 27.0° to the vertical, what is the force exerted by her father? What is the magnitude of tension in the rope, F_T?

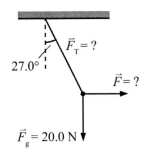

4. Two ropes are attached to a 75.0 N object as illustrated above. Find the magnitude of the tension (F_{T1} and F_{T2}) in the ropes.

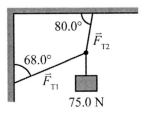

5. A 15 kg object rests on a table. A cord is attached to this object and also to a wall. Another object is hung from this cord as shown above. If the coefficient of friction between the 15 kg object and the table is 0.27, what is the maximum mass that can be hung?

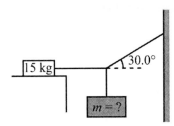

6. A 735 N mountain climber is rappelling down the face of a vertical cliff. If the rope makes an angle of 12° with the vertical face, what is the magnitude of tension in the rope?

7. In the static arrangement shown above, find F_g and F_{T2}.

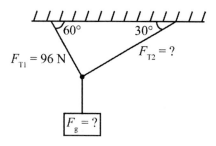

8. In the static arrangement shown above, find F_g and F_{T2}.

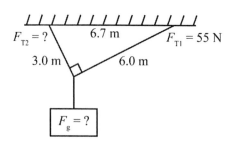

9. A 25 N block is suspended by a cord to a tree branch. In turn, a 12 N block is suspended from the first block as shown in the diagram. What are the values of F_{T1} and F_{T2}?

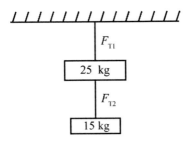

10. A 675 N object is pulled horizontally by a force of 410 N as shown in the diagram above. What is the angle θ between the rope and the vertical?

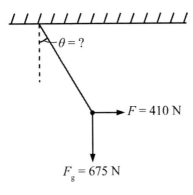

Lesson 2 THE SECOND CONDITION OF EQUILIBRIUM

NOTES

Even though an object does not change its velocity (translational equilibrium), it can still rotate. Consider a seesaw at the playground. The seesaw has no translational motion, but it can still have rotational motion. If an object is in equilibrium, it has translational and rotational equilibrium. If an object is in static equilibrium, it has no translational or rotational motion.

The first condition of equilibrium is $\sum \vec{F} = 0$.

TORQUE

The second condition of equilibrium states that in order to have no rotation, there can be no torque. For an object to have rotational equilibrium, the sum of the torques must be zero.

Think about removing a tight nut from a bolt. It will be easier to remove this nut by using a long wrench. And of course, it depends on how you apply a force to this wrench—it is best if you exert the force at right angles to the wrench.

The factors affecting the rotation of the nut are the perpendicular component of the applied force and the length of the wrench (radius of rotation). That is the distance from axis of rotation is perpendicular to the line along which the force acts.
The symbol for magnitude of torque is the Greek letter tau: τ.

Formula: $\tau = rF \sin\theta$

You will note that torque is the product of the radius of rotation, the magnitude of the force, and the direction of the force.
The unit of torque is: N·m

Torque is a vector quantity; that is, it has direction. For convenience, a torque that will cause an object to rotate counter-clockwise is considered as a positive sign, and a torque that will cause an object to rotate clockwise is considered as a negative sign.

$\tau = rF \sin\theta$

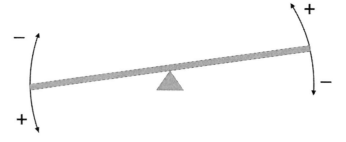

The second condition of equilibrium is expressed as

$\Sigma \tau = 0$

Before we do any problem solving, we need to look at three additional concepts:

- centre of gravity
- arbitrary position of the point of rotation
- lever arm

The second condition of equilibrium is $\Sigma \tau = 0$

CENTRE OF GRAVITY

In torque problems, we think of the weight of an object acting at one point. This one point is called the centre of gravity.
If we have a beam, the centre of gravity of the beam is the point where we could balance it.

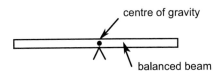

In some of the problems on torque, we will talk about a uniform beam.
For a uniform beam, the centre of gravity is at the centre of the beam.

ARBITRARY POSITION OF THE POINT OF ROTATION

In problems on torque, it is obvious that we place the point of rotation at a hinge, a fulcrum, etc. But in other problems, we must arbitrarily assign a point of rotation.

LEVER ARM

The lever arm is the perpendicular distance from the axis of rotation to the line along which the force acts.

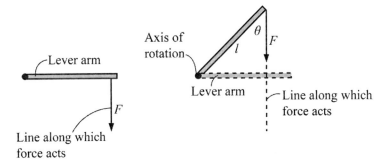

Note: In the above figure, lever arm = $r \sin\theta$
In our equation for torque, $\tau = rF \sin\theta$, $r \sin\theta =$ lever arm.

Example

A torque of 24.0 N·m is needed to tighten a nut. If a person applies a force of 100 N, what is the minimum length of wrench required?

Solution

$$\tau = rF \sin \theta$$

$$r = \frac{\tau}{F \sin \theta}$$

$$= \frac{24.0 \text{ N} \cdot \text{m}}{100 \text{ N}}$$

$$= 0.240 \text{ m or } 24.0 \text{ cm}$$

Example

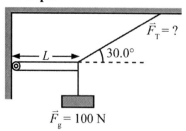

A 25.0 N uniform beam is attached to a wall by means of a hinge. Attached to the other end of this beam is a 100 N weight. A rope also helps to support the beam as shown in the diagram.

a) What is the magnitude of the tension in the rope?

Solution

This beam would rotate if the rope was not there. Therefore, we will use the second condition of equilibrium to solve the problem.

Identify the forces acting on the beam and draw a free body diagram.

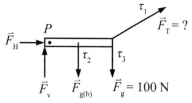

The magnitudes of the parameters are as follows,

F_T = tension in supporting rope

F_g = weight of hanging mass

$F_{g(b)}$ = weight of beam

F_H = horizontal force exerted by wall

F_V = vertical force exerted by wall

Identify the point of rotation—the hinge (point P) is the point of rotation.

Every force produces a torque except if the force acts on the point of rotation.

Identify these torques.
Use the second condition of equilibrium
$\Sigma\tau = 0$
$\tau_1 - \tau_2 - \tau_3 = 0$
$r_1F_1\sin\theta_1 - r_2F_2\sin\theta_2 - r_3F_3\sin\theta_3 = 0$

(Note: We do not know the length of the beam, so we will let L be the length of the beam.)

$L\,F_T\,\sin 30° - \frac{1}{2}L(25.0\text{ N})\sin 90° - L(100\text{ N})\sin 90° = 0$

(Note: we can divide both sides by L, and L disappears.)
$F_T\,\sin 30° - \frac{1}{2}(25.0\text{ N})\sin 90° - (100\text{ N})\sin 90° = 0$
$0.50\,F_T - 12.5\text{ N} - 100\text{ N} = 0$
$F_T = \dfrac{12.5\text{ N} + 100\text{ N}}{0.50}$
$= 225\text{ N}$

b) What are the vertical and horizontal forces that the wall exerts on the beam?

Solution
In order to solve for F_H and F_V, we will use the first condition of equilibrium. To do this, we will consider the beam to be a point.

Draw a free body diagram of the forces acting on the beam.

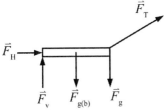

Note: we really do not know the direction of $\vec{F}_H$ and $\vec{F}_V$

Break these forces into components if required:

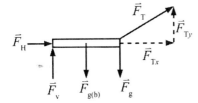

$$F_{Tx} = F_T \cos\theta$$
$$F_{Ty} = F_T \sin\theta$$

Use the first condition of equilibrium:
$$\sum \vec{F}_x = 0$$
$$F_{Tx} + F_H = 0$$
$$F_T \cos\theta = -F_H$$
$$(225 \text{ N}) \cos 30° = -F_H$$
$$(225 \text{ N})(0.866) = -F_H$$
$$\therefore F_H = -195 \text{ N}$$

$\vec{F}_H$ is toward the left

$$\sum \vec{F}_y = 0$$
$$F_{Ty} + F_V - F_{g(b)} - F_g = 0$$
$$F_T \sin\theta - F_{g(b)} - F_g + F_V = 0$$
$$(225 \text{ N}) \sin 30° - 25 \text{ N} - 100 \text{ N} + F_V = 0$$
$$112.5 \text{ N} - 25 \text{ N} - 100 \text{ N} + F_V = 0$$
$$F_V = 12.5 \text{ N}$$

$\vec{F}_V$ is upward

Example

A uniform beam 5.0 m long has a weight of 200 N on it and is suspended by three ropes, as shown below. If an 800 N object is placed as shown in the diagram, what is the magnitude of the tension in each of the ropes?

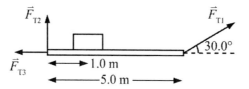

Solution
Draw a free body diagram.

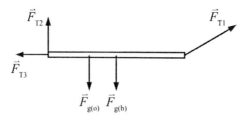

F_{T1}, F_{T2}, F_{T3} are the magnitudes of the tension in the ropes.

$F_{g(o)}$ = magnitude of weight of the object

$F_{g(b)}$ = magnitude of weight of the beam

If we are to solve this problem using the second condition of equilibrium, we must identify the torques. But, to identify the torques, we need to identify the point of rotation. In this case, there is no hinge—no obvious point of rotation. The point of rotation in this case is arbitrary—we will choose where we will place it. We will place it at the left end because there are two unknown forces at this point.

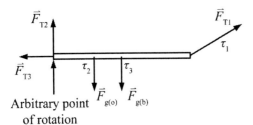

Arbitrary point
of rotation

Remember: There is no torque associated with forces acting on the point of rotation.

Use the second condition of equilibrium

$$\sum \tau = 0$$
$$\tau_1 - \tau_2 - \tau_3 = 0$$
$$r_1 F_1 \sin \theta_1 - r_2 F_2 \sin \theta_2 - r_3 F_3 \sin \theta_3 = 0$$
$$(5.0 \text{ m}) F_{T1} (\sin 30°) - (1.0 \text{ m})(800 \text{ N})$$
$$(\sin 90°) - (2.5 \text{ m})(200 \text{ N})(\sin 90°) = 0$$
$$(2.5 \text{ m}) F_{T1} - 800 \text{ N} - 500 \text{ N} \cdot \text{m} = 0$$
$$F_{T1} = \frac{800 \text{ N} \cdot \text{m} + 500 \text{ N} \cdot \text{m}}{2.5 \text{ m}} = 520 \text{ N}$$

It will be easier to find F_{T2} and F_{T3} using the first condition of equilibrium.

Draw a free body diagram.

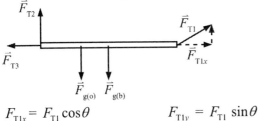

$$F_{T1x} = F_{T1} \cos \theta \qquad F_{T1y} = F_{T1} \sin \theta$$

Use the first condition of equilibrium.

$$\Sigma \vec{F}_x = 0$$
$$F_{T1x} - F_{T3} = 0$$
$$F_{T1} \cos \theta = F_{T3}$$
$$(520 \text{ N}) \cos 30° = F_{T3}$$
$$\therefore \qquad F_{T3} = 450 \text{ N}$$

$$\Sigma \vec{F}_y = 0$$
$$F_{T1y} + F_{T2} - F_{g(o)} - F_{g(b)} = 0$$
$$F_{T1} \sin \theta - F_{g(o)} + F_{g(b)} + F_{T2} = 0$$
$$(520 \text{ N}) \sin 30° - 800 \text{ N} - 200 \text{ N} + F_{T2} = 0$$
$$260 \text{ N} - 800 \text{ N} - 200 \text{ N} + F_{T2} = 0$$
$$F_{T2} = 740 \text{ N}$$

PRACTICE EXERCISES

Formulas: $\tau = rF \sin\theta$ $\qquad\qquad \Sigma\tau = 0$

1. If the torque needed to loosen a lug nut holding the wheel of a car is 45 N·m and you are using a wheel wrench that is 35 cm long, what is the magnitude of the force you exert perpendicular to the end of the wrench?

2. A beam of negligible mass is attached to a wall by means of a hinge. Attached to the centre of the beam is a 400 N weight. A rope also helps to support this beam as shown below.

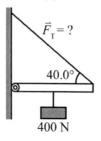

$\vec{F}_T = ?$

40.0°

400 N

   a) What is the magnitude of the tension in the rope?

   b) What are the magnitudes of the vertical and horizontal forces that the wall exerts on the beam?

3. A 650 N student stands on a 250 N uniform beam that is supported by two supports as shown below.

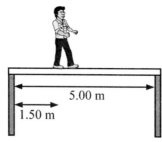

5.00 m

1.50 m

   If the supports are 5.00 m apart and the student stands 1.50 m from the left support,

   a) what is the magnitude of the force that the right support exerts on the beam?

b) what is the magnitude of the force that the left support exerts on the beam?

4. A uniform 400 N diving board is supported at two points as shown below.

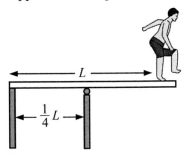

If a 75.0 kg diver stands at the end of the board, what are the forces acting on each support?

5. Find the tension in the rope supporting the 200 N hinged uniform beam shown below.

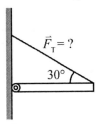

6. Find the tension in the rope supporting the 200 N hinged uniform beam shown below.

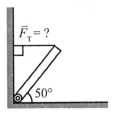

PRACTICE TEST

1. A box (mass = m) is sliding at a constant velocity down an incline as shown.

   The force of friction on this box is

   A. $F_{fr} = \mu mg \cos\theta$

   C. $F_{fr} = \mu mg$

   B. $F_{fr} = \mu mg \sin\theta$

   D. $F_{fr} = 0$

2. A uniform beam (mass = 8.0 kg, length = 5.0 m) is placed on a pivot as shown in the diagram below. If a 32 kg mass is placed 1.5 m from the pivot, where should a 42 kg mass be placed on the beam so that the beam is in static equilibrium?

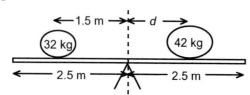

   A. 1.1 m from the pivot

   C. 2.0 m from the pivot

   B. 1.5 m from the pivot

   D. 2.5 m from the pivot

3. If a wooden beam has no rotational motion, which of the following properties are balanced?

   A. Force

   C. Acceleration

   B. Torque

   D. Radius of rotation

4. A 2.55 kg box slides down a 30.0° incline at a constant velocity. What is the force of friction between the block and the incline?

   A. 12.5 N

   C. 25.0 N

   B. 21.6 N

   D. 31.9 N

5. For an object to be in static equilibrium, which of the following conditions must be true?

   A. The velocity of the object must be zero.

   B. The acceleration of the object must be zero.

   C. The forces acting on the object must be zero.

   D. The displacement of the object must be zero

6. Two masses ($m_1 = 3.00$ kg, $m_2 = 5.00$ kg) hang from the ends of a metre stick as shown in the diagram. If the mass of the metre stick is negligible, at what distance from the left of the metre stick should a pivot be placed so that the system will be balanced?

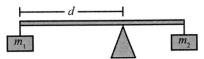

A. $d = 30.0$ cm

B. $d = 37.5$ cm

C. $d = 60.0$ cm

D. $d = 62.5$ cm

7. Given that the forces acting on a beam (length $= L$) add to zero, a student concludes the following:

i) The object must be in translational equilibrium.
ii) The object must be in rotational equilibrium.

Which of the student's conclusions is/are correct?

A. i only

B. ii only

C. both i and ii

D. neither i nor ii

8. Given that the torques acting on a beam (length $= L$) add to zero, a student concludes the following:

i) The object must be in translational equilibrium.
ii) The object must be in rotational equilibrium.

Which of the student's conclusions is/are correct?

A. i only

B. ii only

C. both i and ii

D. neither i nor ii

9. A 3.0 kg block slides down a 37° incline at a constant velocity. What is the coefficient of friction between the block and the incline?

A. 0.077

B. 0.75

C. 1.0

D. 18

10. In the static arrangement shown below, what is F_{T1} ?

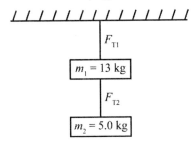

A. 49 N

B. 78 N

C. 1.3×10^2 N

D. 1.8×10^2 N

NOTES

CIRCULAR MOTION AND GRAVITATION

When you are finished this unit, you should be able to…
- Describe uniform circular motion
- Solve problems involving objects undergoing uniform circular motion
- Construct free-body diagrams for objects undergoing circular motion
- Describe Newton's law of universal gravitation
- Recognize the vector nature of gravitational fields and solve problems involving gravitational forces
- Analyze and solve problems involving gravitational potential energy relative to zero at infinity
- Solve problems involving gravitational forces and uniform circular motion

Lesson	Page	Completed on
1. Circular Motion	216	
2. Vertical Circular Motion	223	
3. Newton's Law Of Universal Gravitation	231	
4. Field Explanation	238	
5. Gravitational Potential Energy	243	
6. Satellites: Natural And Artificial	248	
7. Satellites In Orbit	250	
Practice Test	254	
Answers and Solutions	at the back of the book	

PREREQUISITE SKILLS AND KNOWLEDGE

Prior to starting this unit, you should be able to…
- Write numbers in scientific notation
- Isolate a variable and combine algebraic expressions
- Construct graphs involving relevant quantities and analyze important characteristics such as slope, intercepts, and areas under the graph.
- Perform calculations and obtain the answer to the correct number of significant figures
- Substitute the correct units for all quantities in a calculation and express the proper final unit by appropriate cancellation of units
- Interpret and create free-body diagrams
- Determine the composition of derived units in terms of simpler units

Lesson 1 CIRCULAR MOTION

UNIFORM CIRCULAR MOTION

In this unit, we will extend our study of kinematics and dynamics by studying circular motion and gravitation. We will begin by looking at uniform circular motion.

There are many examples of uniform circular motion. It can be illustrated by tying a mass to a string and whirling it in a circle on the floor at a constant speed—note that we said speed and not velocity.

We have described linear motion and how Newton's laws of motion apply to it. Now, let's describe uniform circular motion and how Newton's laws of motion are applied to it.

The speed of an object that is moving with uniform circular motion is given by

$$v = \frac{2\pi r}{T}$$

where $2\pi r$ = circumference of the circle
and T = period of motion (time of one revolution)

NOTES

The formula $v = \frac{2\pi r}{T}$ is a special case of $v = \frac{d}{t}$.

This formula is just a special case of $v = \frac{d}{t}$.

Although the speed of this mass is uniform, its velocity is not (remember velocity is a vector quantity—it has direction). For the velocity to change, the object is accelerating. This acceleration is called the centripetal acceleration $(\bar{a}_c)$, and is always directed toward the centre of the circle. The magnitude of the centripetal acceleration is found using the formula

$$a_c = \frac{v^2}{r}$$

where a_c = magnitude of centripetal acceleration
v = speed
r = radius of circle

Derivation:

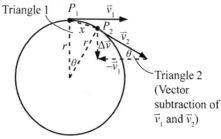

Triangle 1

Triangle 2 (Vector subtraction of $\bar{v}_1$ and $\bar{v}_2$)

p is an object that is travelling at a constant speed, v, in a circle with radius r. At $t = 0$, the object is at p_1 travelling at a velocity of v_1. At some short time later, Δt, the object is at p_2 travelling at a velocity of v_2.

The acceleration of this object is

$$a = \frac{v_2 - v_1}{\Delta t} \quad \text{or} \quad a = \frac{\Delta v}{\Delta t}$$

Triangles 1 and 2 are similar; therefore

$$\frac{\Delta v}{v_2} = \frac{x}{r} \quad \text{or} \quad \Delta v = \frac{vx}{r}$$

But,

$x = v\Delta t$ (true when Δt is small)

(this is the same as $x = vt$)

Therefore,

$$\Delta v = \frac{v(v\Delta t)}{r}$$

Now,

$$a = \frac{\Delta v}{\Delta t}$$

Therefore,

$$a_c = \frac{\frac{v^2 \Delta t}{r}}{\Delta t} \quad \text{or} \quad a_c = \frac{v^2}{r}$$

Note that the centripetal acceleration is always directed toward the centre of the circle. This is really the meaning of centripetal—centre-seeking.

Also, note that the velocity is always directed along the tangent of the circle. That is, it is perpendicular to the acceleration.

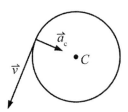

Acceleration is always directed toward the centre.

Velocity is always directed along the tangent of the circle.

If an object is accelerated toward the centre, there must be a force toward the centre (Newton's laws). This centre-seeking force is called the centripetal force. Centripetal force is a name given to any force that causes an object to move in a circle. It can be supplied through a string as in the example given. It can also be a frictional force, as when a car rounds a curve on the highway. It can be a gravitational force, as when the moon circles Earth. It can be an electrical force, as when an electron orbits a proton.

Centripetal force is a name given to any force that causes an object to move in a circle.

Circular motion is really a special case of two-dimensional motion (projectile motion). In circular motion, the force vector is always perpendicular to the velocity vector.

From Newton's Second Law of Motion, the magnitude of net force is given by

$$F_{net} = ma$$
$$F_c = ma_c$$

or

$$F_c = \frac{mv^2}{r}$$

This formula can also be expressed as

$$F_c = \frac{4\pi^2 rm}{T^2}$$

Derivation:

$$F_c = \frac{mv^2}{r}$$

But,

$$v = \frac{d}{t} \quad \text{or} \quad v = \frac{2\pi r}{T}$$

Therefore, $v^2 = \frac{4\pi^2 r^2}{T^2}$

$$F_c = \frac{m\left(\frac{4\pi^2 r^2}{T^2}\right)}{r}$$

$$F_c = \frac{4\pi^2 rm}{T^2}$$

In uniform circular motion, because the acceleration is uniform, the force that causes it must also be uniform.

Before we move on, let's discuss another force—centrifugal force. Whereas centripetal means centre-seeking, centrifugal means centre-fleeing. Centrifugal force is really an apparent force—it does not exist. It is the apparent outward force that causes a rotating object to move along a straight line. Newton's First Law of Motion tells us that you do not need a force to keep an object moving along a straight line—you only need a force to deflect the object from a straight line. Centripetal forces are very real, but centrifugal forces are only apparent (they are fictitious). What we sometimes call centrifugal force is really the object's inertia.

Centripetal means centre-seeking.
Centrifugal means centre-fleeing.

When we study motion, the motion of an object is always in reference to something else. This something else is called the frame of reference. In many cases, Earth is our frame of reference. For example, when we say that a car is travelling at a velocity of 25 m/s south, this is in reference to the fixed environment around it—the Earth. Frames of reference are classified as

- non-accelerating frames of reference (or inertial frames of reference)
- accelerating frames of reference (or non-inertial frames of reference)

Example 1

Calculate the centripetal force acting on a 1.5 kg object whirling at a speed of 2.3 m/s in a horizontal circle of radius 0.60 m.

Solution

$$F_c = \frac{mv^2}{r}$$
$$= \frac{(1.5 \text{ kg})(2.3 \text{ m/s})^2}{0.60 \text{ m}}$$
$$= 13 \text{ N}$$

Example 2

A car travelling at 14 m/s goes around an unbanked curve in the road that has a radius of 96 m. What is the centripetal acceleration?

Solution

$$a_c = \frac{v^2}{r}$$
$$= \frac{(14 \text{ m/s})^2}{96 \text{ m}}$$
$$= 2.0 \text{ m/s}^2$$

Example 3

A plane makes a complete circle with a radius of 3 622 m in 2.10 min. What is the speed of the plane?

Solution

$$v = \frac{2\pi r}{T}$$
$$= \frac{(2\pi)(3 \ 622 \text{ m})}{(2.10 \text{ min})(60 \text{ s/min})}$$
$$= 181 \text{ m/s}$$

PRACTICE EXERCISES

Formulas: $\quad v = \dfrac{2\pi r}{T} \qquad\qquad a_c = \dfrac{v^2}{r} \qquad\qquad F_c = \dfrac{mv^2}{r} \qquad F_c = \dfrac{4\pi^2 rm}{T^2}$

1. Calculate the centripetal force acting on a 925 kg car as it rounds an unbanked curve with a radius of 75 m at a speed of 22 m/s.

2. A small plane makes a complete circle with a radius of 3 282 m in 2.0 min. What is the centripetal acceleration of the plane?

3. A car with a mass of 822 kg rounds an unbanked curve in the road at a speed of 28.0 m/s. If the radius of the curve is 105 m, what is the average centripetal force exerted on the car?

4. An amusement park ride has a radius of 2.8 m. If the time of one revolution of a rider is 0.98 s, what is the speed of the rider?

5. An electron ($m = 9.11 \times 10^{-31}$ kg) moves in a circle whose radius is 2.00×10^{-2} m . If the force acting on the electron is 4.60×10^{-14} N , what is the speed of the electron?

6. A 925 kg car rounds an unbanked curve at a speed of 25 m/s. If the radius of the curve is 72 m, what is the minimum coefficient of friction between the car and the road required so that the car does not skid?

7. A 2.7×10^3 kg satellite orbits Earth at a distance of 1.8×10^7 m from Earth's centre at a speed of 4.7×10^3 m / s. What force does Earth exert on the satellite?

8. An athlete whirls a 3.7 kg shot-put in a horizontal circle with a radius of 0.90 m. If the period of rotation is 0.30 s,

   a) what is the speed of the shot-put when released?

   b) what is the magnitude of the centripetal force acting on the shot-put while it is rotated?

   c) how far would the shot-put travel horizontally if it is released 1.2 m above the ground?

9. Calculate the speed and acceleration of a point on the circumference of a $33\frac{1}{3}$ phonograph record.

    The diameter of the record is 30.0 cm. ($33\frac{1}{3}$ is the frequency that it turns—$33\frac{1}{3}$ revolutions/minute.)

10. A string requires a 135 N force in order to break it. A 2.00 kg mass is tied to this string and whirled in a horizontal circle with a radius of 1.10 m. What is the maximum speed that the mass can be whirled without breaking the string?

11. A 932 kg car is travelling around an unbanked curve that has a radius of 82 m. What is the maximum speed that this car can round this curve without skidding?

    a) if the coefficient of friction is 0.95?

    b) if the coefficient of friction is 0.40?

Lesson 2   VERTICAL CIRCULAR MOTION

Consider the motion of an object moving in a vertical circle. In such motion, the centripetal force may vary from point to point. Remember, the centripetal force is the net force acting toward the centre. To understand why the force changes from point to point, look at a mass whirled in a vertical circle at the end of a string.

NOTES

Centripetal force is the net force acting toward the centre.

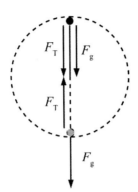

At the top position, the magnitude of the centripetal force (net force) is the sum of the tension and the weight.

$$F_c = F_T + F_g$$

At the bottom position, the magnitude of the centripetal force (net force) is the difference between the tension and the weight.

$$F_c = F_T - F_g$$

Problems involving vertical circles often involve the calculation of the minimum speed at the top of the circle so that the object does not leave the circle. In such cases, the tension (F_T) in the string is zero.

$$\therefore F_c = F_g$$

$$\frac{mv^2}{r} = mg$$

or $v = \sqrt{rg}$

Example 1

An object is swung in a vertical circle with a radius of 0.75 m. What is the minimum speed of the object at the top of the motion for the object to remain in its circular motion?

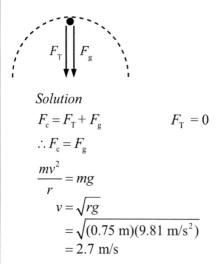

Solution

$$F_c = F_T + F_g \qquad\qquad F_T = 0$$

$$\therefore F_c = F_g$$

$$\frac{mv^2}{r} = mg$$

$$v = \sqrt{rg}$$

$$= \sqrt{(0.75\text{ m})(9.81\text{ m/s}^2)}$$

$$= 2.7\text{ m/s}$$

The speed did not depend on the mass of the object—only the radius.

Example 2

A string requires a 135 N force in order to break it. A 2.00 kg mass is tied to this string and whirled in a vertical circle with a radius of 1.10 m. What is the maximum speed that this mass can be whirled without breaking the string?

Solution

$$F_g = mg$$

$$= (2.00\text{ kg})(9.81\text{ m/s}^2)$$

$$= 19.6\text{ N}$$

$$F_c = F_T - F_g$$

$$= 135\text{ N} - 19.6\text{ N}$$

$$= 115.4\text{ N}$$

$$F_c = \frac{mv^2}{r}$$

$$= \sqrt{\frac{F_c r}{m}}$$

$$= \sqrt{\frac{(115.4\text{ N})(1.10\text{ m})}{2.00\text{ kg}}}$$

$$= 7.97\text{ m/s}$$

Example 3

A 1.7 kg object is swung from the end of a 0.60 m string in a vertical circle. If the time of one revolution is 1.1 s, what is the tension in the string?

a) when it is at the top?

Solution

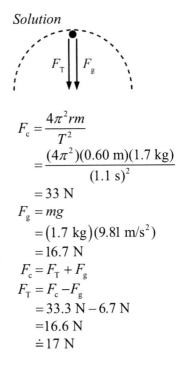

$$F_c = \frac{4\pi^2 rm}{T^2}$$
$$= \frac{(4\pi^2)(0.60 \text{ m})(1.7 \text{ kg})}{(1.1 \text{ s})^2}$$
$$= 33 \text{ N}$$
$$F_g = mg$$
$$= (1.7 \text{ kg})(9.81 \text{ m/s}^2)$$
$$= 16.7 \text{ N}$$
$$F_c = F_T + F_g$$
$$F_T = F_c - F_g$$
$$= 33.3 \text{ N} - 6.7 \text{ N}$$
$$= 16.6 \text{ N}$$
$$\doteq 17 \text{ N}$$

b) when it is at the bottom?

Solution

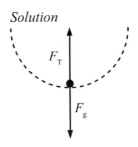

$$F_c = F_T - F_g$$
$$F_T = F_c + F_g$$
$$= 33.3 \text{ N} + 16.7 \text{ N}$$
$$= 50 \text{ N}$$

Example 4

A 826 kg car travelling at a speed of 14.0 m/s goes over a hill as shown below. If the radius of this curve is 61.0 m, what is the force exerted on the road by the car at the crest of the hill?

Solution

$$F_g = mg$$
$$= (826 \text{ kg})(9.81 \text{ m/s}^2)$$
$$= 8.10 \times 10^3 \text{ N}$$

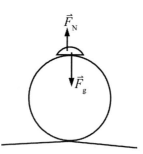

$$F_c = \frac{mv^2}{r}$$
$$= \frac{(826 \text{ kg})(14.0 \text{ m/s})^2}{61.0 \text{ m}}$$
$$= 2.65 \times 10^3 \text{ N}$$
$$F_c = F_g - F_N$$
$$F_N = F_g - F_c$$
$$= 8.10 \times 10^3 \text{ N} - 2.65 \times 10^3 \text{ N}$$
$$= 5.45 \times 10^3 \text{ N}$$

PRACTICE EXERCISES

- In solving problems with vertical circular motion, draw a free body diagram.
- In these problems, $F_c = F_{net}$
- If $F_c = F_g$, then we can use the formula $v = \sqrt{rg}$. These are problems that involve minimum speed.

---

1. You are riding your bike on a track that forms a vertical circular loop, as shown. If the diameter of the loop is 10.0 m, what is the minimum speed at the top of the loop so that you would not fall?

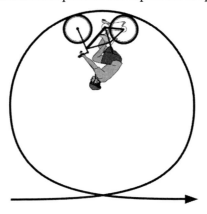

2. You are rotating a bucket of water in a vertical circle. If the radius of the rotation of the water is 0.95 m, what is the minimum velocity of the bucket at the top of its swing if the water is not to spill?

3. A student has a weight of 655 N. While riding on a roller coaster, this same student has an apparent weight of 1.96×10^3 N at the bottom of the dip that has a radius of 18.0 m. What is the speed of the roller coaster?

4. An amusement park ride spins in a vertical circle. If the diameter of this ride (circle) is 5.80 m, what minimum speed must the ride travel so that a 75.0 kg student will remain against the wall when he is in the high position?

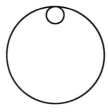

5. A string requires a 186 N force in order to break. A 1.50 kg mass is tied to this string and whirled in a vertical circle with a radius of 1.90 m. What is the maximum speed that this mass can be whirled without breaking the string?

6. A 2.2 kg object is whirled in a vertical circle whose radius is 1.0 m. If the time of one revolution is 0.97 s, what is the tension in the string (assume uniform speed)

   a) when it is at the top?

   b) when it is at the bottom?

7. A wheel-shaped space station whose radius is 48 m produces artificial gravity by rotating. Which speed must this station rotate so that the crew members have the same apparent weight in this station as they have on Earth?

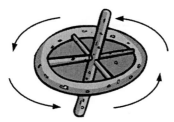

8. A 915 kg car goes over a hill, as shown. If the radius of this curve is 43 m, how fast must the car travel so that it exerts no force on the road at the crest?

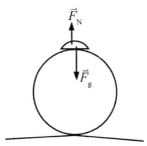

9. A 2.5 kg ball is tied to a 0.75 m string and whirled in a vertical circle (assume a constant speed of 12 m/s).

    a) Why is the tension in the string greater at its low point than at its high point?

    b) What is the tension in the string at its

        i) low point?

        ii) high point?

Lesson 3 NEWTON'S LAW OF UNIVERSAL GRAVITATION

Newton explained the dynamics of the solar system in his Law of Universal Gravitation. Newton developed this law (explanation) by bringing together his three laws of motion with Kepler's three laws of planetary motion. This was accomplished when Newton concluded that earthly objects and heavenly objects obey the same physical laws.

When an object is held above Earth's surface and dropped, it will fall to the ground. In order to explain this, Earth must be exerting an attractive force on the object. We call this force gravity.

One day when Newton was sitting under an apple tree thinking about the motion of the moon around Earth, an apple broke free from its branch and fell to the ground. Newton understood that the force that caused the apple to fall was the attractive force of the earth on the apple—gravity.
This small event started him wondering if it was also Earth's gravity that was responsible for the moon's motion around Earth. Does Earth's gravity extend that far into space? Newton hypothesized that it did, and this force was responsible for the moon's motion. By using his laws of motion and Kepler's laws, he formulated the Law of Universal Gravitation. It is this law that explains the motion of the moon around Earth, and the motion of the planets around the sun.

Consider the formulation of the Law of Universal Gravitation.

Newton's First Law of Motion explained that if a planet is moving in a circular path, it has centripetal acceleration and therefore must be a centripetal force acting on it. Newton, using Kepler's Law of Areas, showed that this force must be caused by the sun.

By considering his Second Law of Motion and Kepler's Law of Periods, Newton mathematically demonstrated that the magnitude of this force is inversely proportional to the square of the distance from the sun to the planets(R).

$$F_g \propto \frac{1}{R^2}$$

Applying Newton's Second Law in case of a planet orbiting the sun:

$$F_{net} = ma \quad \text{or} \quad F_c = \frac{m4\pi^2 R}{T^2}$$

Newton concluded that earthly objects and heavenly objects obey the same physical laws.

Newton formulated the law of universal gravitation from his laws of motion and Kepler's laws.

KEPLER'S LAW OF PERIODS

$T^2 = KR^3$

Combination: $F_c = \dfrac{m4\pi^2 R}{KR^3}$ or $F_c = \dfrac{m4\pi^2}{KR^2}$

Since: $\dfrac{m4\pi^2}{K}$ = constant for a planet

it follows: $F_g \propto \dfrac{1}{R^2}$

In case of circular motion $F_g = F_c$. Therefore, $F_g \propto \dfrac{1}{R^2}$

In general, this distance (R) is considered as r.

This is the inverse square law.

Newton demonstrated the usefulness of this law by calculating the centripetal acceleration of the moon.

Known:
- centre of Earth to the centre of the Moon $= 3.8 \times 10^8$ m
- radius of Earth $= 6.4 \times 10^6$ m
- Ratio: $= \dfrac{3.8 \times 10^8 \text{ m}}{6.4 \times 10^6 \text{ m}} = 60$

From the inverse square law, the force on an object at Earth's surface—the apple—would be $(60)^2$ times the force on an object—the apple—located where the Moon orbits. From the Second Law of Motion, the acceleration would also be $(60)^2$ times. Thus, the centripetal acceleration of the Moon should be

$(9.81 \text{ m/s}^2)\left(\dfrac{1}{(60)^2}\right) = 2.7 \times 10^{-3} \text{ m/s}^2$

If we compare this to the observed value for the centripetal acceleration of the Moon, we find it to be very close.

Newton's Third Law of Motion states that forces only exist between two objects. Newton concluded from this that the force of gravity between two objects is directly proportional to the product of their masses.
$F_g \propto m_1 m_2$

Forces only exist between two objects.
Newton's Law of Universal Gravitation:

$F_g \propto m_1 m_2$, $F_g \propto \dfrac{1}{r^2}$

By combining this with the inverse square law,

$$F_g \propto \frac{1}{r^2}$$

we get $F_g \propto \frac{m_1 m_2}{r^2}$ or $|\vec{F}_g| = \frac{Gm_1 m_2}{r^2}$

G is called Newton's gravitational constant, and has been determined to be $\left(6.67 \times 10^{-11}\right) \dfrac{\text{N} \cdot \text{m}^2}{\text{kg}^2}$. Gravitational force is always attractive.

Newton's Law of Universal Gravitation states that:
- the gravitational force between two masses is directly proportional to the product of their masses
- the gravitational force between two masses varies inversely as the square of the distance between the centres of the masses

CAVENDISH EXPERIMENT

In 1798, Cavendish measured the value G using a torsion balance.

Cavendish measured the value of G.

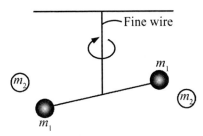

Fine wire

m_2 = large lead ball
m_1 = small lead ball

Cavendish equated the angle of rotation with force. By measuring the angle of rotation, he determined the force. Knowing the masses and the distance between them, he was able to calculate G.

Now, using Newton's Law of Universal Gravitation and the values of G, we can calculate the mass of Earth. This mass is calculated to be 5.98×10^{24} kg.

Mass of Earth is calculated to be 5.98×10^{24} kg.

Example 1

Calculate the gravitational force between two objects when they are 7.5×10^{-1} m apart. Each object has a mass of 50 kg.

Solution

$$F_g = \frac{Gm_1m_2}{r^2}$$

$$= \frac{\left(6.67 \times 10^{-11} \frac{\text{N} \cdot \text{m}^2}{\text{kg}^2}\right)(50\,\text{kg})(50\,\text{kg})}{(7.5 \times 10^{-1}\,\text{m})^2}$$

$$= 2.96 \times 10^{-7}\,\text{N}$$

$$\doteq 3.0 \times 10^{-7}\,\text{N}$$

Example 2

Calculate the gravitational force on a 6.0×10^2 kg spacecraft that is 1.6×10^4 km above Earth's surface.

Solution

$$F_g = \frac{Gm_1m_2}{r^2}$$

$$= \frac{\left(6.67 \times 10^{-11} \frac{\text{N} \cdot \text{m}^2}{\text{kg}^2}\right)(5.98 \times 10^{24}\,\text{kg})(6.00 \times 10^2\,\text{kg})}{(1.6 \times 10^7\,\text{m} + 6.37 \times 10^6\,\text{m})^2}$$

$$= 4.8 \times 10^2\,\text{N}$$

NOTE: Radius of Earth must be added to distance above Earth

PRACTICE EXERCISES

Formula: $F_g = \dfrac{Gm_1 m_2}{r^2}$

1. Two students are sitting 1.50 m apart. One student has a mass of 70.0 kg and the other has a mass of 52.0 kg. What is the gravitational force between them?

2. What gravitational force does the moon produce on Earth if the centres of Earth and the moon are 3.84×10^8 m apart and the moon has a mass of 7.35×10^{22} kg ?

3. If the gravitational force between two objects of equal mass is 2.30×10^{-8} N when the objects are 10.0 m apart, what is the mass of each object?

4. Calculate the gravitational force on a 6.50×10^2 kg spacecraft that is 4.15×10^6 m above Earth's surface.

5. The gravitational force between two objects that are 2.1×10^{-1} m apart is 3.2×10^{-6} N . If the mass of one object is 5.5×10^1 kg , what is the mass of the other object?

6. If two objects, each with a mass of 2.0×10^2 kg, produce a gravitational force between them of 3.7×10^{-6} N, what is the distance between them?

7. What is the gravitational force on a 70.0 kg object standing on Earth's surface?

8. What is the gravitational force on a 35.0 kg object standing on Earth's surface? (Use your answer from question 7 to reduce the number of calculations.)

9. What is the gravitational force on a 70.0 kg object that is 6.38×10^6 m above Earth's surface? (Use your answer from question 7 to reduce the number of calculations.)

10. What is the gravitational force on a 70.0 kg object that is 3.19×10^6 m (one-half Earth's radius) above Earth's surface? (Use your answer from question 7 to reduce the number of calculations.)

11. Three objects each with a mass of 10.0 kg are placed in a straight line 5.00×10^{-1} m apart, as shown. What is the net gravitational force on the centre object due to the other two objects?

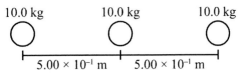

10.0 kg   10.0 kg   10.0 kg

5.00×10^{-1} m 5.00×10^{-1} m

12. Three objects A, B, and C are placed 5.00×10^{-1} m apart along a straight line, as shown. If A and B have equal masses of 10.0 kg and C has a mass of 15.0 kg, what is the net gravitational force on B due to A and C?

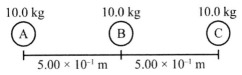

10.0 kg   10.0 kg   10.0 kg

A   B   C

5.00×10^{-1} m 5.00×10^{-1} m

13. The gravitational force between two small masses A and B when placed a short distance apart is 3.24×10^{-7} N. What is the gravitational force between these objects if the masses of both A and B are doubled and the distance between them is tripled?

Lesson 4   *FIELD EXPLANATION*

How do we explain gravitational forces—forces between two masses? How can a force exist between two objects that are not in contact? To answer these questions, scientists invented the concept of fields. A mass is surrounded by a gravitational field. The fields are invisible. Although Earth and the moon are not in physical contact, their gravitational fields do interact.

Fields are defined as spheres of influence.

Fields are defined as spheres of influence. Fields can be classified as scalar or vector. Scalar fields like scalar quantities do not have direction, but have magnitude only. Examples of scalar fields are field due to air pressure and heat fields. If you are standing near a camp fire, you are in the sphere of influence of the heat from the fire. You can measure the intensity of the heat at different points (i.e., you can measure the temperature). Temperature is a scalar quantity, and is described by the collection of these points. Therefore, the heat field is said to be a scalar field.

Vector fields, like vector quantities, have direction as well as magnitude. A gravitational field is an example of a vector field. A gravitational field is a force field, and because a force is a vector quantity, a force field is a vector field.

GRAVITATIONAL FIELDS (OR ACCELERATION DUE TO GRAVITY)

Symbol: $\vec{g}$

Gravitational fields are defined as force per unit mass.

Definition: gravitational force per unit mass: $\vec{g} = \dfrac{\vec{F}_g}{m}$

Units: $\dfrac{\text{N}}{\text{kg}}$

Other formula: $|\vec{g}| = \dfrac{GM}{r^2}$

Vector fields are represented by diagrams.

Vector fields, like vector quantities, are represented by diagrams. In field diagrams, we use arrows to represent the lines of force. The density of the arrows (lines of force) represents the magnitude of the field (the denser the lines of force, the stronger the field). The direction of the field is represented by the direction of the arrow. In case of any object on Earth this field is always directed towards the center of Earth. The diagram below represents the gravitational field around Earth.

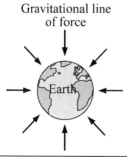

Gravitational line of force

Earth

Consider the magnitude of the gravitational field strength as shown in following two formulas:

1) $g = \dfrac{F_g}{m}$ 2) $g = \dfrac{GM}{r^2}$

The first formula is the definition of gravitational fields. The field strength (intensity) at any point around Earth can be found by using a test object (mass) and finding the weight to mass ratio of the test object at that point.

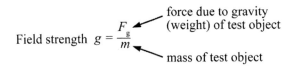

Field strength $g = \dfrac{F_g}{m}$ ← force due to gravity (weight) of test object ← mass of test object

test object: $g = \dfrac{F_g}{m}$

In the second formula, we would need to know the mass of the object producing the field and the distance from the centre of that mass.

$g = \dfrac{GM}{r^2}$ ← mass of object producing field ← distance from centre of this mass

producing object:

$g = \dfrac{GM}{r^2}$

Example 1

Calculate the magnitude of the gravitational field strength on Earth's surface.

Solution

$$g = \frac{Gm_E}{r^2}$$

$$= \frac{\left(6.67 \times 10^{-11} \dfrac{N \cdot m^2}{kg^2}\right)(5.98 \times 10^{24} \text{ kg})}{(6.38 \times 10^6 \text{ m})^2}$$

$$= 9.80 \text{ N/kg}$$

On the surface of Earth the gravitational field strength varies between 9.78 N/kg to 9.83 N/kg depending on the latitude. Therefore, the conventional standard value for g is considered as 9.81 N/kg.

NOTES

Example 2

On Earth's surface, an object has a weight (force due to gravity) of 53.7 N and a mass of 5.48 kg. Using this information, what is the magnitude of the gravitational field strength on Earth's surface?

Solution

$$g = \frac{F_g}{m}$$
$$= \frac{53.7 \text{ N}}{5.48 \text{ kg}}$$
$$= 9.80 \text{ N/kg}$$

PRACTICE EXERCISES

Formulas: $g = \dfrac{GM}{r^2}$ $F_g = mg$ $g = \dfrac{F_g}{m}$

1. Calculate the magnitude of the gravitational field strength on the surface of Mars. Mars has a radius of 3.43×10^6 m and a mass of 6.37×10^{23} kg.

2. At what distance from Earth's surface is the gravitational field strength 7.33 N/kg?

3. On the surface of Planet X, an object has a weight of 63.5 N and a mass of 22.5 kg. What is the magnitude of the gravitational field strength on the surface of Planet X?

4. On the surface of Planet Y, which has a mass of 4.83×10^{24} kg, an object has a weight of 50.0 N and a mass of 30.0 kg. What is the radius of this planet?

5. What is the magnitude of the gravitational field strength 1.276×10^7 m (twice Earth's radius) from the centre of Earth?

6. Planet B has a mass of 4.0×10^{22} kg and a radius of 6.0×10^5 m. What is the magnitude of the gravitational field strength on the surface of Planet B?

7. Two planets A and B have the same mass. However, the gravitational field strength on the surface of Planet A is 1.20 times the gravitational field strength on the surface of Planet B. How does the radius of Planet A compare with the radius of Planet B?

8. What is the magnitude of weight of a 20.0 kg object on the surface of the moon? The mass of the moon is 7.35×10^{22} kg and the radius of the moon is 1.74×10^6 m.

Lesson 5 *GRAVITATIONAL POTENTIAL ENERGY*

Previously, we discussed gravitational potential energy and introduced the equation:

$E_p = mgh$

This equation works well when we are finding the gravitational potential energy near Earth's surface. In this case, we assume that the gravitational field strength (g) has a constant value of 9.81 N/kg. However, when large distances are involved, the gravitational field (g) can no longer be assumed to remain constant.

Remember: $g = \dfrac{Gm_1}{r^2}$

m_1 = mass of object producing the field

m = mass of object that is moved

As the distance from Earth's centre (r) increases, g decreases.
The equation $E_p = mgh$ is very useful for calculating gravitational potential energy if the gravitational field strength is provided or if we are working near Earth's surface where g is known.

Recall that the E_p of a mass is just the work done on the mass in lifting it a height h. Where the gravitational force is constant, we have

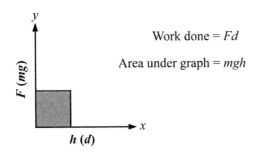

Work done = Fd

Area under graph = mgh

Work done = Fd.
Area under the curve = mgh

For those situations where g can not assumed to be 9.81 N/kg, we can reason in similar fashion. Since F_g changes with distance, the force-distance graph looks like this.

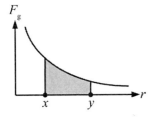

Work done is still the area under the graph, but this area is no longer easy to determine. The branch of mathematics known as calculus grew partly out of a study of problems just like this.

Using calculus, the area and hence the gravitational potential energy can be determined to be

$$E_\mathrm{p} = \frac{Gm_1m_2}{r}$$

When we discuss gravitational potential energy, we use a reference point. At this reference point, we assign the gravitational potential energy of the object as zero. When we are finding the gravitational potential energy of one object due to the gravitational force of another object, we assign the gravitational potential energy of the object due to the gravitational force of the other object as zero when the distance between them is infinite ($r = \infty$). When objects get closer together, the gravitational potential energy between them decreases. Now, the only values less than zero must be negative. That is where the negative sign in the equation $E_\mathrm{p} = -\dfrac{Gm_1m_2}{r}$ comes from.

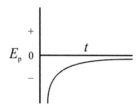

The change in the gravitational potential energy of an object of mass m_2 moving from a distance r_i to a distance r_f in a gravitational field produced by an object of mass m_1 is given by equation:

$$\Delta E_\mathrm{p} = Gm_1m_2\left(\frac{1}{r_\mathrm{i}} - \frac{1}{r_\mathrm{f}}\right)$$

This equation comes from:

$$\Delta E_\mathrm{p} = \left(E_\mathrm{p}\right)_\mathrm{f} - \left(E_\mathrm{p}\right)_\mathrm{i}$$
$$= -\frac{Gm_1m_2}{r_\mathrm{f}} - \left(-\frac{Gm_1m_2}{r_\mathrm{i}}\right)$$
$$= \frac{Gm_1m_2}{r_\mathrm{i}} - \frac{Gm_1m_2}{r_\mathrm{f}}$$
$$= \left(Gm_1m_2\right)\left(\frac{1}{r_\mathrm{i}} - \frac{1}{r_\mathrm{f}}\right)$$

Example 1

A 2.50×10^3 kg geostationary satellite (a satellite that remains in the same position above Earth's surface) is in an orbit that is 3.60×10^7 m above Earth's surface. What is the gravitational potential energy of this satellite due to the gravitational force caused by Earth? (Use gravitational potential energy = zero at $r = \infty$.)

Solution

$$E_p = -\frac{Gm_E m_s}{r}$$

$$= -\frac{\left(6.67 \times 10^{-11} \ \frac{N \cdot m^2}{kg^2}\right)(5.98 \times 10^{24} \ kg)(2.50 \times 10^3 \ kg)}{(3.60 \times 10^7 \ m + 6.38 \times 10^6 \ m)}$$

$$= -2.35 \times 10^{10} \ J$$

We could have used

$$\Delta E_p = Gm_E m_s \left(\frac{1}{r_i} - \frac{1}{r_f}\right)$$

$$\Delta E_p = \left[\left(6.67 \times 10^{-11} \frac{N \cdot m^2}{kg^2}\right)(5.98 \times 10^{24} \ kg)(2.50 \times 10^3 kg) \right.$$
$$\left. \times \left(\frac{1}{\infty} - \frac{1}{3.60 \times 10^7 m + 6.38 \times 10^6 \ m}\right)\right]$$

$$= -2.35 \times 10^{10} \ J$$

Example 2

How much work is needed to lift a 1.25×10^3 kg satellite from Earth's surface to a height of 4.00×10^6 m above Earth's surface?

Solution

$$W = \Delta E_p$$

$$\Delta E_p = Gm_E m_s \left(\frac{1}{r_i} - \frac{1}{r_f}\right)$$

$$= \left[\left(6.67 \times 10^{-11} \frac{N \cdot m^2}{kg^2}\right)(5.98 \times 10^{24} \ kg)(1.25 \times 10^3 \ kg) \right.$$
$$\left. \times \left(\frac{1}{6.38 \times 10^6 m} - \frac{1}{4.00 \times 10^6 m + 6.38 \times 10^6 \ m}\right)\right]$$

$$= -3.01 \times 10^{10} \ J$$

Example 3

A 1.10×10^3 kg object is dropped from a distance of 2.00×10^5 m onto the Moon's surface. How fast is the object travelling when it hits the Moon's surface?

Solution

$$\Delta E_k = -\Delta E_p$$

$$\Delta E_p = Gm_m m_o \left(\frac{1}{r_i} - \frac{1}{r_f} \right)$$

$$\Delta E_p = \left(6.67 \times 10^{-11} \frac{N \cdot m^2}{kg^2} \right)(7.35 \times 10^{22} \text{ kg})(1.10 \times 10^3 \text{ kg})$$

$$\times \left(\frac{1}{\left(2.00 \times 10^5 \text{m} + 1.74 \times 10^6 \text{m} \right)} - \frac{1}{1.74 \times 10^6 \text{m}} \right)$$

$$\Delta E_p = -3.20 \times 10^8 \text{ J}$$

$$\therefore \ \Delta E_k = 3.20 \times 10^8 \text{ J}$$

$$\Delta E_k = (E_k)_f - (E_k)_i$$

$$= \frac{1}{2}mv_f^2 - \frac{1}{2}mv_i^2$$

$$3.20 \times 10^8 \text{ J} = \frac{1}{2}(1.10 \times 10^3 \text{ kg})(v_f^2) - \frac{1}{2}(1.10 \times 10^3 \text{ kg})(0)$$

$$\Rightarrow v_f = 7.62 \times 10^2 \text{ m/s}$$

PRACTICE EXERCISES

Formulas: $\qquad E_p = -\dfrac{Gm_1m_2}{r} \qquad\qquad \Delta E_p = Gm_1m_2\left(\dfrac{1}{r_i} - \dfrac{1}{r_f}\right)$

1. What is the gravitational potential energy of a 5.00×10^3 kg satellite that is in an orbit that has a radius of 9.90×10^6 m around Earth? (Use gravitational potential energy = 0 at $r = \infty$.)

2. What is the work done against gravity on the satellite in problem 1 in lifting it into its orbit?

3. What is the change in the gravitational potential energy of the satellite in problem 1 as it is lifted from Earth's surface to its orbit?

4. What is the speed of a 1 750 kg meteorite when it hits the moon's surface? This meteorite had a velocity of 1.00×10^3 m/s heading directly toward the moon when it was 15 000 m above the moon's surface.

5. What is the gravitational potential energy of a 10.0 kg object when it is sitting on Earth's surface? (Use gravitational potential energy = 0 at $r =$.)

6. What is the change in the gravitational potential energy of a 2.50×10^3 kg satellite as it is lifted vertically into a circular orbit (radius $= 6.90 \times 10^6$ m) around Earth?

Lesson 6 SATELLITES: NATURAL AND ARTIFICIAL

NOTES

LAUNCHING: ESCAPE ORBITAL SPEED

In the 1600s, Newton suggested that an object could be put into an orbit around Earth if it were launched from a high hill at sufficient speed.

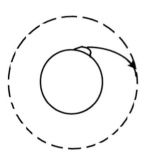

What is this speed? In our calculations, we will ignore air friction. This speed, known as *escape speed* (v_e), is found using

$$E_k = \frac{1}{2}mv^2 \quad \text{and} \quad E_p = \frac{GMm}{r}$$

m is the mass of the object that is launched and m_1 is the mass of the object from which it is launched.

To escape, the kinetic energy must equal the potential energy.

$$E_k = E_p$$

$$\frac{1}{2}mv^2 = \frac{GMm}{r}$$

$$or \quad v_e = \sqrt{\frac{2GM}{r}} = \sqrt{2gr}$$

Now find out escape speed at Earth's surface.

Method 1

$$G = 6.67 \times 10^{-11} \frac{\text{N} \cdot \text{m}^2}{\text{kg}^2}$$

$$r = 6.38 \times 10^6 \text{ m}$$

$$M = m_E = 5.98 \times 10^{24} \text{ kg}$$

$$\therefore \quad v_e = \sqrt{\frac{2Gm_E}{r}}$$

$$= \sqrt{\frac{2(6.67 \times 10^{-11} \frac{\text{N} \cdot \text{m}^2}{\text{kg}^2})(5.98 \times 10^{24} \text{kg})}{(6.38 \times 10^6 \text{ m})}}$$

$$= 1.12 \times 10^4 \text{m/s}$$

Method 2

$$v_e = \sqrt{2gr}$$

$$= \sqrt{2(9.81 \text{ m/s}^2)(6.38 \times 10^6 \text{ m})}$$

$$= 1.12 \times 10^4 \text{ m/s}$$

In the left margin:

$$E_k = \frac{1}{2}mv^2$$

and

$$E_p = \frac{Gm_1m}{r}$$

PRACTICE EXERCISES

Formulas: $v_e = \sqrt{2gr}$ $v_e = \sqrt{\dfrac{2GM}{r}}$

1. What is the escape speed at the moon's surface? ($r = 1.74 \times 10^6$ m , $M = 5.98 \times 10^{24}$ kg.)

2. What is the escape speed at Jupiter's surface? ($r = 7.18 \times 10^7$ m , mass $= 1.90 \times 10^{27}$ kg)

3. What is the mass of a planet that has an escape speed of 9.0×10^3 m/s and a radius of 7.2×10^6 m ?

4. What is the mass of a planet that has a radius of 2.57×10^6 m and an escape speed of 2.92×10^3 m/s ?

Lesson 7 SATELLITES IN ORBIT

A satellite of Earth, including the moon, is constantly falling; not *toward* Earth, but *around* Earth. Like in a falling elevator, you would appear weightless in an artificial satellite orbiting Earth.

There is a relationship between the speed of a satellite and the radius of its orbit. We can determine this relationship because we know that the gravitational force acting on the satellite is the force that keeps it moving in a circle. That is, the gravitational force is the centripetal force.

The gravitational force is the centripetal force that keeps a satellite moving in a circle.

$$F_c = F_g$$

$$F_c = F_g$$

$$\frac{m_s v^2}{r} = \frac{Gm_E m_s}{r^2}$$

$$\text{or } v = \sqrt{\frac{Gm_E}{r}}$$

where m_E = mass of Earth

m_s = mass of satellite

r = radius of satellite orbit

Note: You do not need the mass of the satellite to find its speed or radius.

PERIOD OF A SATELLITE

The time for a satellite to make one revolution is its period. It is found as in any other uniform motion.

$$v = \frac{d}{t}$$

where $d = 2\pi r$ circumference

$t = T$ period

$$\therefore v = \frac{2\pi r}{T} \qquad \begin{array}{l}\text{velocity for uniform} \\ \text{circular motion}\end{array}$$

But we have just derived

$$v = \sqrt{\frac{Gm_E}{r}}$$

$$\therefore \frac{2\pi r}{T} = \sqrt{\frac{Gm_E}{r}}$$

$$\text{or } \quad T = \frac{2\pi r^{3/2}}{\sqrt{Gm_E}}$$

Although we derived the equations using m_E, these equations work for any orbiting satellite. m_E can be the mass of the object producing the gravitational force.

Example 1

Calculate the speed of an artificial satellite in an orbit around Earth with a radius of 6.9×10^6 m.

Solution

$$v = \sqrt{\frac{Gm_E}{r}}$$

$$= \sqrt{\frac{\left(6.67 \times 10^{-11} \frac{N \cdot m^2}{kg^2}\right)(5.98 \times 10^{24} \text{ kg})}{6.9 \times 10^6 \text{ m}}}$$

$$= 7.6 \times 10^3 \text{ m/s}$$

Example 2

Geosynchronous satellites are used for communications. They are satellites that do not change position with respect to Earth. What is the height of such a satellite above Earth's surface?

Solution

The period of a geosynchronous satellite must be the same as Earth's.

$T = 1 \text{ day or } 8.64 \times 10^4$ s

$$= \frac{2\pi r^{3/2}}{\sqrt{Gm_E}}$$

$$r^{3/2} = \frac{T\sqrt{Gm_E}}{2\pi}$$

$$= \frac{\left((8.64 \times 10^4 \text{s})\sqrt{\left(6.67 \times 10^{-11} \frac{N \cdot m^2}{kg^2}\right)(5.98 \times 10^{24} \text{kg})}\right)}{2\pi}$$

$$= 2.75 \times 10^{11}$$

$$r = 4.23 \times 10^7 \text{ m}$$

$$\text{height} = r - r_E$$

$$= 4.23 \times 10^7 \text{ m} - 6.38 \times 10^6 \text{ m}$$

$$= 3.59 \times 10^7 \text{ m}$$

TOTAL ENERGY OF SATELLITES

As a rocket is launched, the combustion of fuel provides kinetic energy to the rocket, which transforms into gravitational potential energy as the rocket rises. The total mechanical energy $\left(E_p + E_k\right)$ of a satellite orbiting Earth is constant (assuming no energy is lost to friction) and can be expressed as follows:

$$E_T = \underbrace{-\frac{Gm_E m_s}{r}}_{E_p} + \underbrace{\frac{1}{2}m_s v_s^2}_{E_k}$$

where r is the distance from the satellite to the centre of Earth.

NOTES

The speed of a satellite in a stable orbit can be determined using the following formula:

$$v_s = \sqrt{\frac{Gm_E}{r}}$$

Substituting the satellite's speed into the expression for the total energy of the satellite results in this expression for the total energy:

$$E_T = -\frac{Gm_E m_s}{r} + \frac{1}{2}m_s\left(\frac{Gm_E}{r}\right)$$

$$E_T = -\frac{2Gm_E m_s}{2r} + \frac{Gm_E m_s}{2r}$$

$$E_T = -\frac{Gm_E m_s}{2r}$$

This energy is always negative. The increase in the kinetic energy a satellite falling straight to Earth from a high altitude (ignoring air resistance) can be calculated using the principles of the conservation of energy.

PRACTICE EXERCISES

Formulas: $\qquad v = \sqrt{\dfrac{Gm_E}{r}} \qquad\qquad T = \dfrac{2\pi r^{3/2}}{\sqrt{Gm_E}}$

Mass of Earth = 5.98×10^{24} kg , radius of Earth = 6.38×10^{6} m

1. Calculate the speed of the moon in its orbit around Earth. (Radius of moon's orbit $= 3.84 \times 10^{8}$ m ; moon's mass = 7.35×10^{22} kg)

2. Calculate the speed of a satellite orbiting Earth at a height of 4.40×10^{5} m above Earth's surface. (Hint: remember to add Earth's radius of 6.38×10^{6} m .)

3. Calculate the orbital speed of a satellite 5.60×10^{6} m above the surface of Jupiter. ($r_J = 7.18 \times 10^{7}$ m ; $m_J = 1.90 \times 10^{27}$ kg)

4. Calculate the speed of Earth in its orbit around the sun. (Radius of Earth's orbit $= 1.50 \times 10^{11}$ m ; mass of the sun $m_s = 1.98 \times 10^{30}$ kg)

5. Using the formula $T = \dfrac{2\pi r^{3/2}}{\sqrt{Gm}}$, calculate the time of one revolution (length of a year) on Mars. ($m_M = 6.4 \times 10^{23}$ kg ; $m_s = 1.98 \times 10^{30}$ kg ; radius of Mars' orbit $= 2.3 \times 10^{11}$ m)

PRACTICE TEST

1. When an object is travelling in a circular path, the direction of the velocity of the object at any given time is

   A. toward the centre of the circular path

   B. away from the centre of the circular path

   C. tangent to the circular path

   D. along the circular path followed by the object

2. When an object is travelling in a circular path, the direction of the acceleration of the object at any given time is

   A. toward the centre of the circular path

   B. away from the centre of the circular path

   C. tangent to the circular path

   D. along the circular path followed by the object

3. Consider the motion of a 1.0 kg mass tied to the end of a 0.70 m cord. This mass is swung clockwise in a vertical circle as illustrated. Which of the following free-body diagrams is correctly labelled to show the forces acting on the 1.0 kg mass when it is at the top of the circle (F_T = magnitude of the tension in cord)?

   A.

   B.

   C.

   D.

4. In question 3, what is the correct expression for the centripetal force acting on the 1.0 kg mass? (F_T = magnitude of the tension in cord)

   A. $F_c = F_g - F_T$ B. $F_c = F_g + F_T$

   C. $F_c = F_g$ D. $F_c = F_T$

5. If an object has a weight of 2.0 N at Earth's surface, what is the weight at a distance of one Earth radius above Earth's surface?

   A. 0.50 N   B. 1.0 N

   C. 2.0 N   D. 4.0 N

6. Which of the following graphs best represents the relationship between the gravitational field strength (g) due to Earth and the distance (r) from Earth's centre?

A.

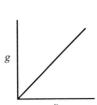

B.

C.

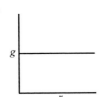

D.

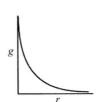

7. We cannot use the equation $E_p = mgh$ to find the gravitational potential energy of an object a large distance above Earth's surface because the

    A. mass of the object decreases as the distance above Earth's surface increases.

    B. gravitational field decreases as the distance above Earth's surface increases.

    C. both the mass and the gravitational field decrease as the distance above Earth's surface increases.

    D. gravitational potential energy is zero at an infinitely large distance from Earth's surface.

8. Which of the following graphs best represents the relationship between the tension (F_T) in the cord of an object is twirled in a horizontal circle at the end of a cord at a constant speed, and the time (t)?

A.

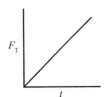

B.

C.

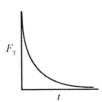

D.

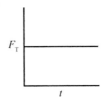

9. What is a definition of centripetal force?

    A. Applied force causing an object to travel in a circle

    B. Product of the mass and the velocity of an object travelling in a circle

    C. Net force causing an object to travel in a circle

    D. Sum of the applied force and the net force causing an object to travel in a circle

10. F_1 is the force that Earth exerts on the moon, and F_2 is the force that the moon exerts on Earth. Which of the following statements about the magnitude of these forces is true?

A. $F_1 > F_2$ **B.** $F_2 > F_1$

C. $F_1 = F_2$ **D.** $F_1 + F_2 = 0$

11. If object A has a mass of 1 100 kg and object B has a mass of 2 200 kg, which of the following statements is/are true?

   i)   On Earth, object B has twice the weight of object A.
   ii) On the Moon, object B experiences twice the gravitational force that object A experiences.
   iii) Near Earth's surface, object B experiences twice the acceleration due to gravity that object A experiences as they fall toward Earth's surface.

A. i only   **B.** i and ii only

C. ii and iii only   **D.** i, ii, and iii

12. A student predicts that the speed of a satellite in its orbit depends on the

   i)   gravitational field in the orbit
   ii) radius of the orbit
   iii) mass of the satellite

Which of the above predictions are correct?

A. i and ii only   **B.** i and iii only

C. ii and iii only   **D.** i, ii, and iii

13. A student predicts that the speed of a satellite in an orbit around Earth depends on the

   i)   mass of the satellite
   ii) mass of Earth
   iii) radius of the orbit

Which of the above predictions are correct?

A. i and ii only   **B.** i and iii only

C. ii and iii only   **D.** i, ii, and iii)

14. A car is travelling on a road that has a curve with a radius of 40.0 m. What is the maximum speed that the car can safely round the curve if the coefficient of friction between the tires and the road is 0.50?

A. 4.5 m/s   **B.** 9.0 m/s

C. 14 m/s   **D.** 20 m/s

15. What is the gravitational potential energy of a 1.25×10^3 kg satellite due to Earth's gravitational attraction when it is 4.00×10^6 m above Earth's surface? (gravitational potential energy $= 0$ at $r = \infty$)

A. -4.80×10^{10} J   **B.** 4.80×10^{10} J

C. -7.83×10^{10} J   **D.** 7.83×10^{10} J

ELECTROSTATICS

When you are finished this unit, you should be able to…
- Solve problems involving Coulomb's law
- Analyze electric fields and their effects on charged particles
- Solve problems involving electric fields and electric forces
- Define electric potential energy
- Solve problems involving electric potential energy and change in electric potential energy
- Solve problems involving electric potential difference
- Apply the law of conservation of energy to solve problems that deal with a charge in an electric field

Lesson	Page	Completed on
1. Electrostatics	258	
2. Field Explanation	274	
3. Electric Potential Due to a Point	282	
4. Electric Potential in a Uniform Electric Field	288	
Practice Test	301	
Answers and Solutions	at the back of the book	

PREREQUISITE SKILLS AND KNOWLEDGE

Prior to starting this unit, you should be able to…
- Write numbers in scientific notation
- Isolate a variable and combine algebraic expressions
- Perform calculations and obtain the answer to the correct number of significant figures
- Substitute the correct units for all quantities in a calculation and express the proper final unit by appropriate cancellation of units
- Determine the composition of derived units in terms of simpler units

Lesson 1 ELECTROSTATICS

Our study of electricity begins in 700 BC, when it was discovered that when amber (fossilized tree sap) was rubbed with fur, it would attract small pieces of leaves or straw. However, it was not until the year 1800, when Volta produced the first battery, that any practical use of electricity was developed. Today, our lives would be very different without electricity and our many electrical devices. Even more fundamental are the interatomic/intermolecular forces that hold all solids and liquids, including us, together. These interatomic/intermolecular forces are electrical in nature.

We will begin by looking at the electrical nature of matter.

Static electricity is electricity at rest.

STATIC ELECTRICITY

Amber is a form of fossilized tree sap. The early Greek civilization knew that when it was rubbed with fur, it would attract small objects—just like when you rub a plastic comb through your dry hair, the comb will attract small bits of paper (it will refer as the amber effect). Because of this, some people associated mystical properties with amber. Our word "electricity" is derived from the Greek word 'elektron' for amber.

Conductors are materials that allow electrons to flow with ease.

Insulators are materials that do not allow electrons to flow with ease.

Static electricity is electricity at rest. It is known today that other substances like glass, rubber, and plastic when rubbed with cloth will produce the same effect as amber. How can we explain this effect?

Scientists have discovered that materials can be classified as conductors and insulators. Conductors are defined as materials that allow electric charges (electrons) to flow. Insulators are defined as materials that do not allow electric charges (electrons) to flow. Metals are good examples of conductors. Amber, glass, rubber, fur, silk, and plastic are good examples of insulators. It is insulators that, when rubbed, produce the amber effect.

The amber effect is explained in terms of electron transfer.

To explain the amber effect, Benjamin Franklin, in the 18th century, suggested a model of matter in which an "electric fluid" was transferred from one object to another. When a piece of amber—or other substance such as glass, rubber, or plastic—was rubbed with cloth, electric fluid either was removed from the material, or the material gained electric fluid from the cloth used in the rubbing. Other scientists developed a two-fluid model of matter (positive and negative fluids). Although the models based on "electric fluid" could explain the amber effect, they were gradually replaced as knowledge of the structure of matter was discovered. Today, we explain the amber effect in terms of electron transfer.

We now know that matter contains both negative particles (electrons) and positive particles (protons). The protons are not free to move; therefore, they cannot be transferred by rubbing. Hence, an object can have a negative charge only if it has an excess of electrons, or a positive charge only if it has a shortage of electrons. An object is said to be neutral when it has an equal amount of positive and negative charge—an equal number of electrons and protons.

After an object has a charge placed on it, we can make it neutral by grounding it. Grounding means to provide a path for electrons to enter or leave an object. We ground the electrical panel in the basement of a home to the water main, which is buried in the earth, to maintain electrical neutrality within the home.

CHARGING BY FRICTION

When a rubber rod is rubbed with fur or wool, the rod becomes negative (i.e., the rod has gained electrons). The wool will be positive because it lost electrons.

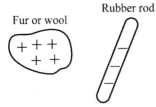

When a glass rod is rubbed with a silk cloth, the rod becomes positive because electrons are transferred from the rod to the silk, giving the silk a negative charge.

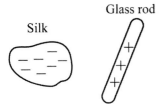

Two charged rubber rods will repel. Two charged glass rods will repel.

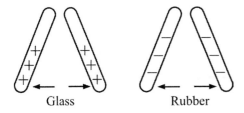

A charged rubber rod and a charged glass rod will attract.

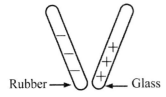

In summary, scientists have been able to identify only two types of charges (positive and negative), and they discovered that like charges repel and unlike charges attract. This is called the Law of Charges.

NOTES

A negative charge is caused by an excess of electrons.

A positive charge is caused by a shortage of electrons.

Grounding an object neutralizes its charge.

Note that we have not completely answered the question about the amber effect. Why, when an insulator is rubbed, does it attract small objects (like small bits of paper)?

To answer this question, we will introduce the topic of charging by induction.

CHARGING BY INDUCTION

If a positive charged rod is brought near but does not touch a conductor, the electrons on the neutral conductor will be attracted to its side nearest the charged rod. The neutral conductor has not gained or lost electrons, but has only rearranged the position of the electrons. This is charging by induction.

Neutral object   Positive charge rod
 (conductor)

An electroscope is an instrument used to detect the presence and nature (+ or −) of a charge.

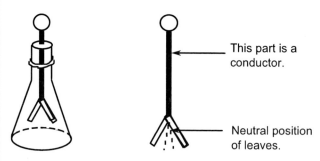

This part is a
conductor.

Neutral position
of leaves.

An electroscope may be charged by induction. When a charged rod is brought near a neutral electroscope (i.e., it has an equal number of electrons and protons), the following events will occur:

• A positively charged rod will attract electrons to the head
  of the electroscope, leaving the leaves positive.

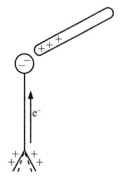

• A negatively charged rod will repel electrons from the head of the electroscope into the leaves, leaving the leaves negative.

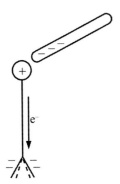

Inducing a negative charge on an electroscope

In both cases, the electroscope is neutral, but we have induced the electrons to change their relative positions without physically touching or transferring electrons to the electroscope.

Now let's look at cases where the electroscope is grounded for a brief period of time.

Case 1: a positive charged rod is brought near a neutral electroscope. While the rod is in place, the electroscope is grounded. The ground provides a path for the electrons which are attracted from the ground to the head of the electroscope. Now the electroscope has extra electrons. If the ground is removed, the extra electrons cannot escape to ground. They are trapped on the electroscope. When the rod is removed, the electroscope will have a permanent negative charge—this charge is opposite to the charge on the rod.

Inducing a positive charge on an electroscope

Case 1:

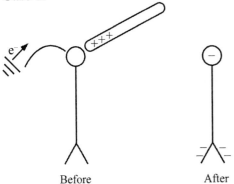

Before   After

Case 2: a positive charge is placed on the electroscope by using a negative charged rod and following the same steps. In this case, electrons are induced to leave the electroscope.

Case 2:

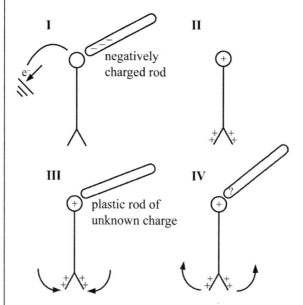

Before   After

This is called charging by induction.

How do we determine the charge on a strip of plastic if it is rubbed by a piece of cotton?

You cannot tell by looking at it, but you can use an electroscope to test for the charge. You induce a known charge on the electroscope.

For example, you rub a rubber rod with fur (you know the rod has a negative charge). You use this rod to put a positive charge on an electroscope as in case 2 above.

Diverge: move apart
Converge: come together

I

negatively charged rod

e⁻

II

III

plastic rod of unknown charge

IV

?

We now rub the plastic strip with the cotton and bring the strip near to the electroscope.

If the leaves converge (come together), the charge on the plastic is negative. If the leaves diverge (move apart), the charge on the plastic is positive.

A pith ball is a light ball with a conductive surface. A neutral pith ball is initially attracted to either a positive rod or a negative rod. This is because the pith ball is charged by induction by both a positive or negative rod.

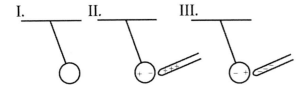

Now you know why bits of paper can be attracted to your plastic comb when you pull it through the hair on your head—your comb has an electrostatic charge (+ or –). When you bring it near a tiny piece of paper, the paper is charged by induction. This is also the secret of amber—amber does not have mystical properties, but it obtains an electrostatic charge when rubbed.

CHARGING BY CONTACT

However, if the pith ball comes in contact with the rod, the ball will instantly be repelled. Why?

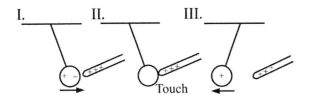

An object can obtain an electrostatic charge in three ways:

• friction

• induction

• contact

When the ball came in contact with the positive rod, the ball gave up "some electrons to the rod. The rod is still positive. However, the ball is no longer neutral; it is also positive. This is an example of charging by contact.

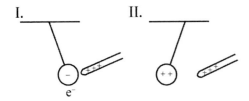

In the previous sections, we mentioned three ways an object can be charged (obtain an electrostatic charge):

NOTES

- By friction: when you rub an insulator, you are placing a charge on the rod by friction
- By induction: when you bring a charged object near a neutral conductor, the electrons are pushed or pulled to one side or the other
- By contact: A neutral object touches a charged object

Some examples of electrostatic charging are:

- When you walk across a carpeted floor, and then touch a conductor (light switch, tap, door handle), you may receive a slight shock. This is because you built up an electrostatic charge on yourself by dragging your feet on the carpet, and when you touched a conductor, this charge on your body was discharged. It is the electrons discharging (leaving) that produces the shock.

- Static cling in your clothes dryer. Here, different materials are rubbing against each other as they tumble in the dryer. In the dry atmosphere of the dryer, electrons can be transferred from one material to another by friction. They will then cling because of opposite charges.

- Thunderstorms. Clouds may become charged as a result of friction. Most lightning is the discharge between oppositely charged parts of clouds. However, a charged cloud can induce an opposite charge on the ground below, and a build-up of this induced charge may cause a sudden discharge between the cloud and the ground—this type of discharge can cause damage. Benjamin Franklin discovered that electrical charges leak off sharp points. This is the purpose of lightning rods. The rod is placed above the highest point on a building, and is grounded by a metal cable. The charge leaking from the rod helps prevent the build-up of electrical charge. If there is a build-up of charges and a sudden discharge, the discharge will strike the sharp point and follow the cable to the ground. The building will be unharmed.

- Rub a balloon on your shirt. The balloon will now stick to the wall. This is because you have charged the balloon by friction. The balloon then induces an opposite charge on the wall and the two will attract.

It should be noted that if an object is charged by friction, induction, or contact, electric charges are neither created nor destroyed—they are just moved from one place to another. This is the Law of Conservation of Charges.

You now know about forces (attractive and repulsive) between charged objects. Is there any relationship that expresses what the magnitude (size) of these forces depends on? There is a force between two negatively charged pith balls. How strong is this force? What variables does this force depend on?

Joseph Priestley suggested that the same (or a parallel) relationship exists between charges as exists between masses as expressed in Newton's Law of Universal Gravitation. Priestley came to this conclusion when he discovered that a charged pith ball placed inside a hollow charged sphere has no electrical force acting on it. He remembered that in Newton's discussion (development) of the Law of Universal Gravitation, Newton showed mathematically that if a mass is placed inside a hollow mass, there would be no gravitational force on the mass. This is because there are forces in all directions and they will cancel each other. The net force is zero.

The angle of twist is directly proportional to the force.

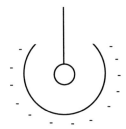

ELECTRIC FORCE LAW (COULOMB'S LAW)

Priestley suggested the Electric Force Law (Coulomb's Law) to state that:

- the electric force between two charges varies directly as the product of their charges

- the electric force between two charges varies inversely as the square of the distance between the two charges

$$F_e \, \alpha \, q_1 q_2 \qquad\qquad F_e \, \alpha \, \frac{1}{r^2}$$

F_e = electrostatic force, q_1 and q_2 = charges, r = distance

Putting these two statements together, we get:

$$F_e \, \alpha \, \frac{q_1 q_2}{r^2} \qquad \text{OR} \qquad |\vec{F}_e| = \frac{k q_1 q_2}{r^2}$$

k is Coulomb's Constant, and has been determined to be $9.00 \times 10^9 \, \dfrac{\text{N} \cdot \text{m}^2}{\text{C}^2}$

Before we can continue, we must introduce another basic unit. Up to this point, all units we have used are derived from the basic units of time (seconds), distance (metres), and mass (kilograms). Now we must introduce the unit of charge, the coulomb—its symbol is C. One coulomb is the charge on 6.25×10^{18} electrons.

Coulomb is the unit of electric charge.

If we place Coulomb's Law and Newton's Law of Universal Gravitation together, we see that they are similar.

only attractive:

$$|\vec{F}_g| = \frac{Gm_1m_2}{r^2}$$

– G has a small value

– gravitational forces are comparatively weak

either attractive or repulsive:

$$|\vec{F}_e| = \frac{kq_1q_2}{r^2}$$

– k has a large value

– electric forces are very strong

Recalling that $G = 6.67 \times 10^{-11} \dfrac{N \cdot m^2}{kg^2}$ (a very small value), one can conclude that gravity is a weak force that requires very large masses to become measurable; whereas, electrical force with a proportionality constant of $k = 9.00 \times 10^9 \dfrac{N \cdot m^2}{C^2}$ (a very large value) indicates electric forces are very large in comparison to gravitational forces, and become significant with small charges.

In 1785, a French scientist named Coulomb used a torsion balance to prove the Electric Force Law. Because of this, the Electric Force Law is today called Coulomb's Law.

The torsion balance is an instrument that has a small conducting sphere at each end of an insulating rod. Say the spheres are A and B. The rod is suspended by a thin wire. Force is required to twist this wire. The angle of twist is directly proportional to the force: $F \, \alpha \, \theta$. Therefore, by measuring the angle of twist, it was possible to determine the force producing this twist.

Coulomb used a torsion balance

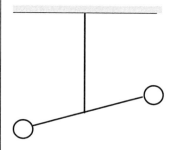

Coulomb placed a third sphere B near sphere A. By varying the distance between the two charged spheres A and B, he was able to determine that $F_e \propto \dfrac{1}{r^2}$. To double, triple, or halve the charges on the spheres A and B was more difficult.

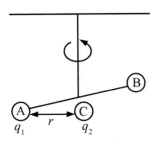

Suppose you have two identical spheres, and you put a charge of 2.0×10^{-6} C on one sphere and nothing on the other. If you allow these spheres to touch and then to separate again, what will be the charge on each sphere now?

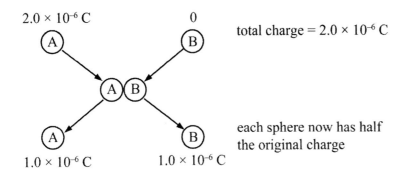

total charge $= 2.0 \times 10^{-6}$ C

each sphere now has half the original charge

Coulomb used this method to halve the charges on spheres A and B, and halve them again, etc. He was then able to demonstrate that $F_e \propto q_1 q_2$.

In solving mathematical problems involving Coulomb's Law, we always solve for the absolute value and ignore the sign on the charge. The sign on the charge is used only to determine the direction of the electric force.

Example

Calculate the electric force between charges of 1.00×10^{-6} C and 1.50×10^{-6} C when they are 5.00×10^{-1} m apart.

Solution

$$F_e = \frac{kq_1 q_2}{r^2}$$

$$= \frac{\left(9.00 \times 10^9 \, \dfrac{\text{N} \cdot \text{m}^2}{\text{C}^2}\right)(1.00 \times 10^{-6} \text{C})(1.50 \times 10^{-6} \text{C})}{(5.00 \times 10^{-1} \text{m})^2}$$

$$= 5.40 \times 10^{-2} \text{ N}$$

NOTES

Example

Two point charges of 1.8×10^{-6} C and 2.4×10^{-6} C produce a force of 2.2×10^{-3} N on each other. How far apart are these two charges?

Solution

$$Fe = \frac{kq_1kq_2}{r^2} \quad \text{or} \quad r = \sqrt{\frac{kq_1kq_2}{Fe}}$$

$$r = \sqrt{\frac{\left(9.00 \times 10^9 \, \frac{N \cdot m^2}{C^2}\right)(1.8 \times 10^{-6} \, C)(2.4 \times 10^{-6} \, C)}{2.2 \times 10^{-3}}}$$

$$= 4.2 \text{ m}$$

Example

A charge of 1.7×10^{-6} C is placed 2.0×10^{-2} m from a charge of 2.5×10^{-6} C and 3.5×10^{-2} m from a charge of -2.0×10^{-6} C as shown below.

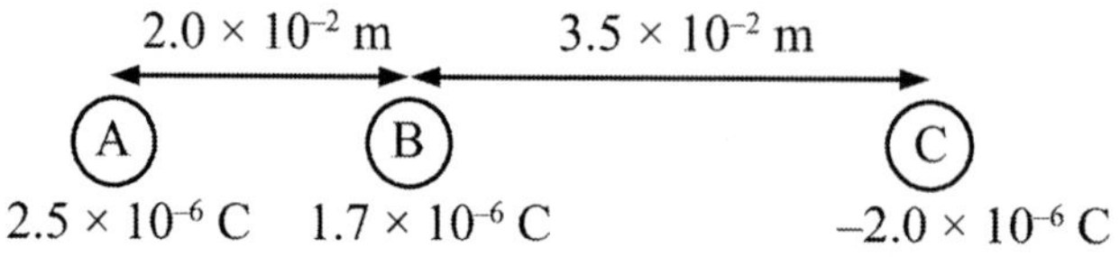

Calculate the magnitude of the net electric force on the 1.7×10^{-6} C charge.

Solution

There are two forces acting on the 1.7×10^{-6} C. We will identify the magnitude of the forces and the direction of each. Then do the vector addition to get the net force.

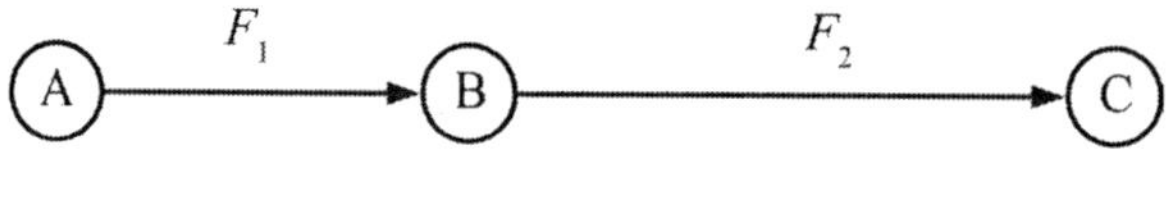

$$F_1 = \frac{kq_1q_2}{r^2}$$

$$= \frac{\left(9.00 \times 10^9 \, \frac{N \cdot m^2}{C^2}\right)(2.5 \times 10^{-6} \, C)(1.7 \times 10^{-6} \, C)}{(2.0 \times 10^{-2} \, m)^2}$$

$$= 9.6 \times 10^1 \text{ N}$$

$$F_2 = \frac{\left(9.00 \times 10^9 \, \frac{N \cdot m^2}{C^2}\right)(2.0 \times 10^{-6} \, C)(1.7 \times 10^{-6} \, C)}{(3.5 \times 10^{-2} \, m)^2}$$

$$= 2.5 \times 10^1 \text{ L}$$

Since the force $\overline{F}_1$ on B is repulsive, so it is along right direction. The force $\overline{F}_1$ on B is attractive. Therefore, this force is also along right direction. Considering right direction as positive do vector addition to get the net force

$$\overline{F}_{net} = \overline{F}_1 + \overline{F}_2$$
$$= 9.6 \times 10^1 \text{ N} + 2.5 \times 10^1 \text{ N}$$
$$= 1.21 \times 10^2 \text{ N} \quad \text{towards right}$$

Therefore, the magnitude of the net electric force on the 1.7×10^{-6} C charge is 1.21×10^{-6} N.

- We add F_1 to F_2 because the forces act in the same direction. If the forces acted in the opposite direction, we would subtract them.

- Although the third charge $\left(-2.0 \times 10^{-6} \right)$ is negative, we do not use the negative sign in the equation, but use the absolute value of the charge. Whenever we use Coulomb's law, we always use the absolute value of the charge.

- The negative sign on the charge is only used to determine whether we are dealing with a force of attraction or repulsion with respect to the other charges that may be present.

PRACTICE EXERCISES

Formula: $F_e = \dfrac{kq_1q_2}{r^2}$

Note: Problems on gravitational forces are included for comparison

1. Two students are sitting 1.50 m apart. One student has a mass of 70.0 kg and the other has a mass of 52.0 kg. What is the gravitational force between them?

2. What gravitational force does the moon exert on Earth if the centers of Earth and the Moon are 3.84×10^8 apart and the moon has a mass of 7.35×10^{22} kg?

3. Calculate the electric force between two point charges of 4.00 µC and 3.00 µC when they are 2.00 cm apart.

4. Two points of equal charge produce an electric force on each other of 3.40×10^{-2} N when placed 1.00×10^{-1} m apart. What is the charge on each point?

5. How far apart are two point charges of 2.0×10^{-6} C and 4.0×10^{-6} C if they produce an electric force on each other of 5.6×10^{-1} N?

6. Two point charged objects produce an electric force on each other of 6.20×10^{-2} N. What is the electric force if the distance between them increases to three times its original value?

7. Two point charged objects produce an electric force on each other of 4.4×10^{-3} N. What is the electric force if the charge on both objects triple and the distance between them double?

8. Three point charged objects are placed in a line as shown above. Calculate the magnitude of the net electric force on the centre charge caused by the other two charges.

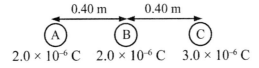

9. The electric force between two charged objects is 5.2×10^{-4} N when the objects are 3.11×10^{-1} m apart. What is the electric force between the same objects if the distance between them is changed to 4.04×10^{-1} m?

10. Three point charged objects are placed at the corner of a right-angle triangle as illustrated above. Calculate the magnitude of the net electric force on the charge marked x caused by the other two charges.

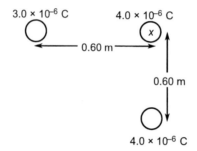

11. Two small spheres have the same mass and volume. One of the spheres has a charge of 4.00 C and the other sphere has a charge of -1.00 °C. If these two spheres are brought into brief contact with each other and then separated to a distance of 2.00×10^{-1}, what is the magnitude of the electric force between them at this distance?

12. Two small spheres, each with a mass of 2.00×10^{-5} kg, are placed 3.50×10^{-1} m apart. One sphere has a charge of -2.00 °C and is fixed in position. The other sphere has a charge of -3.00 °C but is free to move without friction. What is the magnitude of the initial acceleration caused by the electric force on the sphere that is free to move?

13. A, B, and C are three equally charged spheres.

If the distance between A and B is 1.5 cm, and the distance between B and C is 4.5 cm, how does the force that C exerts on B compare with the force that A exerts on B?

Lesson 2   FIELD EXPLANATION

Fields are defined as spheres of influence.

Scalar fields:
• heat fields
• sound fields

Vector fields:
• gravitational fields
• electric fields
• magnetic fields

Electric fields are defined as force per unit charge.

The direction of an electric field is the direction of the force on a positive test charge.

To explain the forces between objects that are not in contact, scientists invented the concept of fields. Just as a mass like Earth or the moon is surrounded by a gravitational field, an electrical charge is surrounded by an electric field. Fields are defined as spheres of influence and are classified as scalar or vector.

Heat fields are an example of scalar fields. If you are standing near a campfire, you are in the sphere of influence of the heat from the fire. You can measure the intensity of the heat at different points (i.e., you can measure the temperature). Temperature is a scalar quantity, and the field is described by the collection of these points. Therefore, the heat field is said to be a scalar field.

Vector fields, like vector quantities, have direction as well as magnitude (size). Electric fields, like gravitational fields, are vector fields.

ELECTRIC FIELDS

Symbol: $\bar{E}$

Definition: Force per unit charge $\bar{E} = \dfrac{\bar{F}_e}{q}$

Units: N/C

Other formula: $|\bar{E}| = \dfrac{kq_1}{r^2}$

Direction of electric fields: The direction of an electric field is defined as the direction that a positive test charge will move when placed in the field. A positive test charge will move away from a positive object (positive point charge) and toward a negative object (negative point charge). Therefore, the electric fields points away from positive charges and toward negative charges.

Describe the shape of electric fields in terms of lines of force.

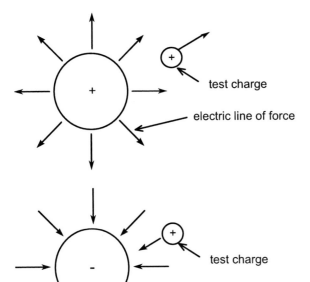

test charge

electric line of force

test charge

electric line of force

Electric fields are defined as force per unit charge.

The direction of an electric field is the direction of the force on a positive test charge.

You will remember that the strength of a vector field is represented by the density of the arrows (lines of force). The denser the lines of force, the stronger the field. Also, the direction of the field is represented by the direction of the arrows.

Let's look at the two formulas:

1. $\vec{E} = \dfrac{\vec{F}_e}{q}$

2. $|\vec{E}| = \dfrac{kq_1}{r^2}$

The first formula is the definition of an electric field. The field strength (intensity) at any point around a charged object can be found by using a test charge (positive) and finding the electric force acting on it. If we divide this electric force by the charge of the test object, we have the field strength.

$|\vec{E}| = \dfrac{\vec{F}_e}{q}$ ◀——— force on test object

◀——— charge on test object

In the second formula, we need to know the charge of the object that is producing the field and the distance from the object (charge) producing the field.

$|\vec{E}|$ = distance from object producing field

Summary:

Considering charge of the test object (test charge): $\vec{E} = \dfrac{\vec{F}_e}{q}$

Considering charge of the object producing field (point charge):

$|\vec{E}| = \dfrac{kq_1}{r^2}$

We should be aware that the form of the equations, which describe electric fields, are very similar to the form of the gravitational field equations. In solving electric field problems, we use absolute values and ignore the sign on the charge—just as we did in problems involving electric force. The sign on the charge is used to determine the direction of the field.

We describe electric fields in terms of field lines (or lines of force).

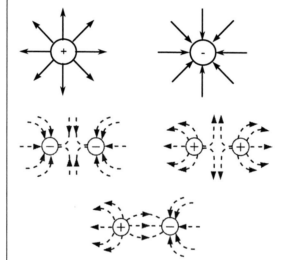

Negative charge: lines of force are drawn toward

Positive charge: lines of force are drawn away

Note that the lines of force are always drawn away from the positive charge and toward the negative charge. This is because this is the path a positive test charge would take. These lines of force also indicate like-charge repulsion, and unlike-charge attraction. Also, note the lines of force do not cross.

Example

Find the magnitude of the electric field strength 4.50×10^{-1} m from a
5.00 μC point charge.

Solution

$$|\vec{E}| = \frac{kq_1}{r^2}$$

$$= \frac{\left(9.00 \times 10^9 \, \frac{N \cdot m^2}{C^2}\right)(5.00 \times 10^{-6} \, C)}{(4.50 \times 10^{-1} \, m)^2}$$

$$= 2.22 \times 10^5 \, N/C$$

Example

What is the magnitude of the electric field strength at a point where a
2.00 μC test charge experiences an electric force of 5.30×10^{-2} N ?

$$E = |\vec{E}| \qquad = \frac{F_e}{q}$$

$$= \frac{5.30 \times 10^{-2} \, N}{2.00 \times 10^{-6} \, C}$$

$$= 2.65 \times 104 \, N/C$$

Example

What is the electric field strength midway between point charges of
-3.50 μC and 3.00 μC that are placed 4.40×10^{-1} m apart?

−3.50 μC $\qquad \vec{E}_1 \qquad\qquad \vec{E}_2 \qquad$ 3.00 μC

O ◄——————— • ◄——————— O

$\qquad\qquad\qquad 4.40 \times 10^{-1}$ m

Solution

Note: Draw a diagram and show the direction of the electric fields
using an arrow. Remember the direction of the field is the same as the
direction a positive test charge would experience an electric force at
that location.

$$\left|\vec{E}_1\right| = \frac{k_{q1}}{r^2}$$

$$= \frac{\left(9.00 \times 10^9 \, \frac{N \cdot m^2}{C^2}\right)(3.50 \times 10^{-6} \, C)}{(2.20 \times 10^{-1} m)^2}$$

$$= 6.51 \times 10^5 \, N/C$$

NOTES

$$|\bar{E}_2| = \frac{\left(9.00 \times 10^9 \, \frac{N \cdot m^2}{C^2}\right)(3.00 \times 10^{-6} \, C)}{(2.20 \times 10^{-1} \, m)^2}$$

$$= 6.51 \times 10^5 \, N/C$$

As both the lines of force are directing left, the net electrical field strength will be

$$\bar{E}_{net} = \bar{E}_1 + \bar{E}_2$$

$$= 6.51 \times 10^5 \, N/C + 5.58 \times 10^5 \, N/C$$

$$= 1.21 \times 10^6 \, N/C$$

In order to do some of the problems that follow, it is necessary to be familiar with the mass and charge of alpha particles, electrons, and protons.

	Mass	Charge
alpha particles	6.65×10^{-27} kg	3.20×10^{-19} C
electron	9.11×10^{-31} kg	-1.60×10^{-19} C
proton	1.67×10^{-27} kg	1.60×10^{-19} C

PRACTICE EXERCISES

Formulas: $|\vec{E}| = \dfrac{kq_1}{r^2}$ $\vec{E} = \dfrac{\vec{F}_e}{q}$

Note: Problems on gravitational fields are included for comparison.

1. What is the magnitude of the electric field strength 7.50×10^{-1} m from an 8.00 μC point charge?

2. Calculate the magnitude of the gravitational field strength on the surface of Mars. Mars has a radius of 3.43×10^6 and a mass of 6.37×10^{23} kg.

3. At a point, a short distance from a 4.60×10^{-6} C point charge, there is an electric field strength of 2.75×10^5 N/C. What is the distance to the point charge producing this field?

4. On the surface of Planet X an object has a weight of 63.5 N and a mass of 22.5 kg. What is the magnitude of the gravitational field strength on the surface of Planet X?

5. If an alpha particle experiences an electric force of 0.250 N at a point in space, what electric force would a proton experience at the same point?

6. What is the magnitude of the electric field strength at a point in space where a 5.20×10^{-6} C point charge experiences an electric force of 7.11×10^{-3} N?

7. What is the initial acceleration of an alpha particle when it is placed at a point in space where the magnitude of the electric field strength is 7.60×10^{4} N/C?

8. Calculate the magnitude of the electric field strength mid-way between a 4.50 μC charged object and a –4.50 μC charged object if the two charged objects are 5.00×10^{-1} m apart.

9. Calculate the magnitude of the electric field strength mid-way between a 3.0 μC point charge and a 6.0 μC point charge if the objects are 8.0×10^{-1} m apart.

10. Calculate the magnitude of the electric field strength mid-way between two 3.0 μC point charges if they are 9.0×10^{-1} m apart.

11. What is the magnitude of the electric field strength at a point in space where an electron experiences an initial acceleration of 7.50×10^{12} m/s^2 ?

12. The electric field strength at a distance of 3.00×10^{-1} m from a point charge is 3.60×10^5 N/C. . What is the electric field strength at a distance of 4.50×10^{-1} m from the same point charge?

13. At a distance of 7.50×10^{-1} m from a small charged object the electric field strength is 2.10×10^4 N/C. At what distance from this same object would the magnitude of the electric field strength be 4.20×10^4 N/C?

Lesson 3 *ELECTRIC POTENTIAL DUE TO A POINT*

If a charged object is in an electric field, it has electric potential energy ($E_{p(e)}$); in other words, work was done on the charged object to move it into its current position, and it now has the potential to move in that field .

Earlier, we discussed gravitational potential energy in a non-uniform gravitational field. The equation that described this gravitational potential energy is

$$E_{p(g)} = -\frac{Gm_1m_2}{r}$$

Recall that calculus was necessary to derive this formula.

We encounter the same problem again. In a uniform electric field (such as exists between charged parallel plates), work done in moving a charged object placed in this uniform field is equal to the electrical potential energy gained by this charged object, and this is equal to the area under the graph below (the area of a rectangle).

Work done against an electric force = $F_e d = qEd$

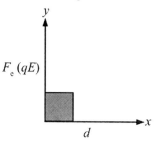

In the non-uniform electric field caused by a point charge, the electric potential energy can not be found as easily, but the reasoning is the same. Work done in moving a charged object in this non-uniform field is equal to the electrical potential energy gained and this is still the same as the area under the graph.

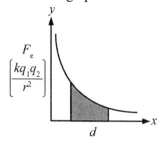

Using calculus, this area (the electrical potential energy) can be determined to be

$$E_{p(e)} = \frac{kq_1q}{r}$$

Electric potential (V) is defined as the electric potential energy per unit charge.

$$V = \frac{E_{p(e)}}{q} \qquad (q = \text{charge of test object})$$

From this definition, we can derive the equation

$$V = \frac{kq_1}{r} \qquad (q_1 = \text{charge of object producing the potential})$$

Derivation:

$$V = \frac{E_{p(e)}}{q}$$

$$V = \frac{\dfrac{kq_1 q}{r}}{q}$$

or

$$V = \frac{kq_1}{r}$$

The test charge cancels out, so we are left with the charge of the object producing the electric potential.

Note: The electric potential at a point is defined in terms of the moving of a positive charge. Therefore, V can be positive or negative.

We sometimes want to find the electric potential between two points. The electric potential between two points is the potential difference.

i.e., Given two points, A and B, the potential difference between A and B is:

$$V_{AB} \qquad = \qquad V_B \qquad - \qquad V_A$$

| Potential difference between points A and B | Electric potential at B | Electric potential at A |

When we talk of the potential at a point, we are actually talking about the potential difference between that point and infinity. The potential at infinity is assigned a value of zero.

When the electric force works on a test charge, the kinetic energy increases and the potential energy decreases. If the potential energies between two points A and B are $E_{p(eA)}$ and $E_{p(eB)}$, then the difference in potential energy denotes the negative work done.

$$V_{BA} = V_B - V_A = \frac{\left(E_{p(eB)} - E_{p(eA)} \right)}{q} = -\frac{W_{BA}}{q}$$

Example

Calculate the potential at point P given the following diagram:

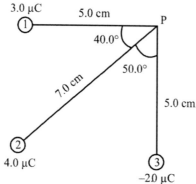

Solution

Find the potential due to each charge

$$V_1 = \frac{kq_1}{r_1}$$

$$= \frac{\left(9.00 \times 10^9 \, \frac{N \cdot m^2}{C^2} \right)(3.0 \times 10^{-6}\,C)}{5.0 \times 10^{-2}}$$

$$= 5.40 \times 10^5 \, V$$

$$V_2 = \frac{kq_2}{r_2}$$

$$= \frac{\left(9.00 \times 10^9 \, \frac{N \cdot m^2}{C^2} \right)(4.0 \times 10^{-6}\,C)}{7.0 \times 10^{-2} \, m}$$

$$= 5.14 \times 10^5 \, V$$

$$V_3 = \frac{kq_3}{r_3}$$

$$= \frac{\left(9.00 \times 10^9 \, \frac{N \cdot m^2}{C^2} \right)(-2.0 \times 10^{-6}\,C)}{5.0 \times 10^{-2} \, m}$$

$$= 3.60 \times 10^5 \, V$$

(potentials due to negative charges are negative)

Add potentials (Note: potentials are scalars)

$$V_T = V_1 + V_2 + V_3$$
$$= \left(5.40 \times 10^5 \text{ V}\right) + \left(5.14 \times 10^5 \text{ V}\right) + \left(-3.60 \times 10^5 \text{ V}\right)$$
$$= 6.9 \times 10^5 \text{ V}$$

Example 2

How much work is done against an electric field produced by a 2.5 μC charged object when an 0.025 μC charge is moved from $r = 3.0$ cm to $r = 1.0$ cm?

Solution

Find potentials at each point

$$V_1 = \frac{kq_1}{r_1}$$

$$= \frac{\left(9.00 \times 10^9 \dfrac{\text{N} \cdot \text{m}^2}{\text{C}^2}\right)(2.5 \times 10^{-6}\,\text{C})}{\left(3.0 \times 10^{-2} \text{ m}\right)}$$

$$= 7.50 \times 10^5 \text{ V}$$

$$V_1 = \frac{kq_1}{r_1}$$

$$= \frac{\left(9.00 \times 10^9 \dfrac{\text{N} \cdot \text{m}^2}{\text{C}^2}\right)(2.5 \times 10^{-6}\,\text{C})}{\left(3.0 \times 10^{-2} \text{ m}\right)}$$

$$= 7.50 \times 10^5 \text{ V}$$

$$W = q(V_2 - V_1)$$
$$= (2.5 \times 10^{-8} \text{ C})(2.25 \times 10^6 \text{ V} - 7.5 \times 10^5 \text{ V})$$
$$= 3.8 \times 10^{-2} \text{ J}$$

PRACTICE EXERCISES

Formula: $V = \dfrac{kq_1}{r}$

1. What is the potential at a distance of 6.0 cm from a 2.5 μC charge?

2. What is the potential at a distance of 25 cm from a –2.5 μC charge?

3. How much work is done against the electric field produced by a 5.0 μC charged object when a 0.030 μC charge is moved from r = 45 cm to r = 15 cm?

4. A proton is released 2.0×10^{-11} m from the centre of a 6.4×10^{-18} C fixed charged sphere. What is the speed of this proton when it is 0.50 m from this centre?

5. Three charges are located on a line as shown below:

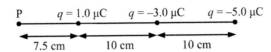

Find the potential at point P.

6. Three charges are located at the corners of a rectangle as shown below:

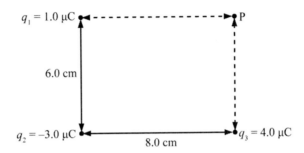

Find the potential at point P.

7. The centres of two alpha particles are held 2.5×10^{-12} m apart, then they are released. Calculate the speed of each alpha particle when they are 0.75 m apart.

8. In moving a 3.00 μC charge at a constant speed from point A to point B, 4.40×10^{-5} J of work is done. If A and B are 2.4 cm apart, what is the potential difference between A and B?

Lesson 4 ELECTRIC POTENTIAL IN A UNIFORM ELECTRIC FIELD

The electric field between parallel charged plates is uniform.

Look at the electric field between parallel charged plates:

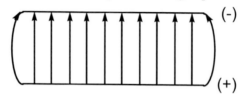

Note that the density of the lines of force is uniform; therefore, the electric field between parallel charged plates is uniform. If this field is uniform, the formula

$$|\vec{E}| = \frac{kq_1}{r^2}$$

cannot describe this field. We need a new formula to describe this uniform electric field.

However, before we describe this field, we must introduce the concept of potential difference. The concept of potential difference is developed from the concepts developed in mechanics (the study of motion and forces that change it).

An object will change its velocity when an unbalanced force acts on it— Newton's First Law of Motion. When a mass is allowed to fall in a gravitational field, the mass will accelerate from a position of high gravitational potential energy to a position of lower gravitational potential energy because of the force of gravity acting on it.

If we want to move a mass from a position of low gravitational potential energy to a position of higher gravitational potential energy, we do work on the mass against gravity. Work done against gravity can be defined in mathematical terms as:

$$W = F_g d \qquad \text{or} \qquad W = mgh$$

where   W = work

F_g = magnitude of the force due to gravity

d = magnitude of the displacement

m = mass

g = magnitude of the gravitational field strength

h = height

The change in gravitational potential energy can also be defined as:

$$E_{p(g)} = mgh$$

From this we see that the gravitational potential energy depends on:

- mass of the object ($E_{p(g)} \; \alpha \, m$)

- gravitational field strength ($E_{p(g)} \; \alpha \, g$)

- height the object is moved ($E_{p(g)} \; \alpha \, h$)

From the Law of Conservation of Energy, the loss in gravitational potential energy of an object becomes kinetic energy.

$$E_k = \frac{1}{2}mv^2$$

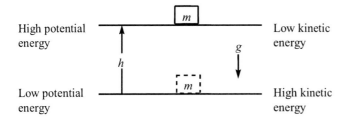

In the same way, when a charged object is allowed to move in a uniform electric field, the charge will accelerate from a position of high electrical potential energy to a position of lower electrical potential energy because of the electric force acting on it. If we want to move a charged object (e.g., a positive particle) in that field (e.g., toward a positive plate), we do work (work against an electric field) on the object. This work can be determined mathematically using the definition of work:

$$W = F_e d$$

Since $F_e = q|\vec{E}|$

it follows $W = q|\vec{E}|d$

The change in electrical potential energy can also be defined as:
$$E_{p(e)} = q|\vec{E}|d$$

From this, we see that the electrical potential energy in a uniform field depends on:

- charge of the object ($E_{p(e)} \, \alpha \, q$)

- electric field strength ($E_{p(e)} \; \alpha \, \vec{E}$)

- distance moved parallel to the force ($E_{p(e)} \; \alpha \, d$)

Again, from the Law of Conservation of Energy, the loss in electrical potential energy of a charged object becomes kinetic energy:

$$E_k = \frac{1}{2}mv^2$$

Electric potential energy depends upon:

- charge of object
- electric field
- distance

NOTES

If $V = \dfrac{\Delta E_{p(e)}}{q}$,

$\Delta E_{p(e)} = qV$,

then the Law of Conservation of Energy, as it applies electric field, becomes

$\Delta E_k = -\Delta E_{p(e)}$ or

$\dfrac{1}{2}m(v^2 - v_0^2) = -qV$

Note: A negative sign indicates that if kinetic energy is gained, electric potential energy is lost.

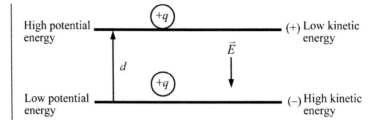

In electricity, as in mechanics, we calculate work using:

$W = Fd$

or $W = mgh$ (gravitational)

or $W = q|\vec{E}|d$ (electrical)

and we calculate kinetic energy using

$E_k = \dfrac{1}{2}mv^2$

However, in electricity we go a bit further. In electricity, we talk about the electric potential energy per unit charge. (In mechanics, we do not talk about gravitational potential energy per unit mass.)

Energy per unit charge is how we define electric potential.

ELECTRIC POTENTIAL (CONTINUED)
Symbol: V

Definition: electric potential energy per unit charge

When an electric charge is moved in an electric field, the electric potential may change. This change in the electric potential is what we call the potential difference (also called voltage).

Potential difference (also symbolized by V) is the more useful quantity when we are discussing a uniform electric field.

POTENTIAL DIFFERENCE (VOLTAGE)
Symbol: V

Definition: the change in the electric potential, or the change in the electric potential energy per unit charge.

$V = \dfrac{\Delta E_{p(e)}}{q}$

Note: Electric potential and potential difference are scalar quantities.

A battery is a source of potential difference. Just as a water pump will increase the gravitational potential energy of water, a battery will increase the electrical potential energy of a charge.

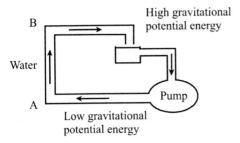

(an increase in electric potential takes place between A and B.)

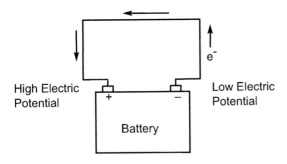

(an increase in electric potential takes place within the battery.)

The first battery was produced by Alessandro Volta in 1800. The first battery (cell) was a salt solution sandwiched between two different metals. A battery changes chemical energy into electrical energy.

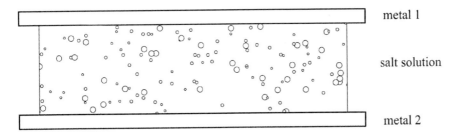

NOTES

The units for electric field can be expressed as $\dfrac{N}{C}$ or $\dfrac{V}{m}$.

Prove to yourself that they are the same.

We are now able to describe the uniform electric field between parallel plates. This field is described by the formula:

$$|\vec{E}| = \frac{V}{d}$$

where

$\vec{E}$ = electric field
V = potential difference between plates
d = distance between plates

Derivation:
In a uniform electric field,

$$\Delta E_{P(e)} = F_e d \quad (\text{remember } W = \Delta E_{p(e)})$$

$$\text{or} \quad \Delta E_{P(e)} = q|\vec{E}|d$$

$$\therefore \frac{\Delta E_{P(e)}}{q} = \vec{E}d$$

$$\text{however,} \quad V = \frac{\Delta E_{P(e)}}{q}$$

$$\therefore V = |\vec{E}|d$$

$$\text{or} \quad |\vec{E}| = \frac{V}{d}$$

Think of the parallel charged plates as extensions of the terminals of a battery. The electric field between parallel plates can be described in terms of the potential difference between the plates and the distance the plates are apart ($|\vec{E}| \; \alpha \; V$

and $|\vec{E}| \; \alpha \; \dfrac{1}{d}$).

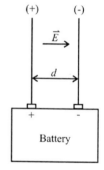

Example

Calculate the electric field strength between two parallel plates that are 6.00×10^{-2} m apart. The potential difference between the plates is 12.0 V.

Solution

$$|\vec{E}| = \frac{V}{d}$$

$$= \frac{12.0 \text{ V}}{6.00 \times 10^{-2} \text{ m}}$$

$$= 2.00 \times 10^2 \text{ V/M}$$

Example

An electron is accelerated from rest through a potential difference of 3.00×10^4 V. What is the kinetic energy gained by the electron?

Solution

$$\Delta E_k = -\Delta E_{p(e)}$$

$$V = \frac{\Delta E_{p(e)}}{q}$$

$$\Rightarrow \Delta E_{p(e)} = qV$$

$$\therefore \Delta E_k = qV$$

$$= \left(1.60 \times 10^{-19} \text{ C}\right)\left(3.00 \times 10^4 \text{ V}\right)$$

$$= 4.80 \times 10^{-15} \text{ J}$$

CATHODE-RAY TUBES

Before the widespread use of LCD and plasma screens, video was displayed using cathode-ray tubes (CRTs). In a CRT, electrons are accelerated by an electron gun toward a flat screen enclosed in a vacuum tube. The electrons are initially aimed directly at the centre of the screen, which lights up at the point it is struck with an electron. As electrons travel toward the screen, they pass between a set of two horizontal charged plates and a set of two vertical charged plates. By varying the charge in the plates, electrons can be aimed to specific points across the screen. In this way, electrons are precisely controlled to display images on televisions, computer monitors, and oscilloscopes.

PRACTICE EXERCISES

Formulas: $V = \dfrac{\Delta E_{p(e)}}{q}$ $\qquad |\vec{E}| = \dfrac{V}{d}$

1. Two parallel plates are connected to a 12.0 V battery. If the plates are 9.00×10^{-2} m apart, what is the electric field strength between them?

2. The electric field between two parallel plates is 5.0×10^3 V/m. If the potential difference between the plates is 2.0×10^2 V, how far apart are the plates?

3. Two parallel plates are 7.3 cm apart. If the electric field strength between the plates is 2.0×10^3 V/m, what is the potential difference between the plates?

4. An alpha particle gains 1.50×10^{-15} J of kinetic energy. Through what potential difference was it accelerated?

5. A proton is accelerated by a potential difference of 7.20×10^2 V. What is the change in kinetic energy of the proton?

6. What maximum speed will an alpha particle reach if it moves from rest through a potential difference of 7.50×10^3 V ?

7. A proton is placed in an electric field between two parallel plates. If the plates are 6.0 cm apart and have a potential difference between them of 7.50×10^1 V, how much work is done against the electric field when the proton is moved 3.0 cm parallel to the plates?

8. In the previous question, how much work would be done against the electric field if the proton was moved 3.0 cm perpendicular to the plates?

9. A charged particle was accelerated from rest by a potential difference of 4.20×10^2 V. If this particle increased its kinetic energy to 3.00×10^{-17} J, what potential difference would be needed to increase the kinetic energy of the same particle to 9.00×10^{-17} J?

10. An alpha particle with an initial speed of 7.15×10^4 m/s enters through a hole in the positive plate between two parallel plates that are 9.00×10^{-2} m apart, as shown above. If the electric field between the plates is 1.70×10^2 V/m, what is the speed of the alpha particle when it reaches the negative plate?

11. An electron with a speed of 5.0×10^5 m/s enters through a hole in the positive plate and collides with the negative plate at a speed of 1.0×10^5 m/s. What is the potential difference between the plates?

12. The electric field strength between two parallel plates is 9.3×10^2 V/m when the plates are 7.0 cm apart. What would the electric field strength be if the plates were 5.0 cm apart?

13. What is the electric field strength 1.00 cm from the positive charged plate if the parallel plates are 5.00 cm apart and the potential difference between the plates is 3.00×10^2 V?

14. Through what potential difference must an electron be accelerated from rest to give it a speed of 6.00×10^6 m/s?

15. If an alpha particle is accelerated from rest through a distance of 4.00 cm by a uniform electric field in 2.50×10^{-5} s, what is the electric field strength?

16. What is the potential difference between two parallel charged plates that are 7.50 cm apart if a force of 5.30×10^{-14} N is needed to move an alpha particle from the negative plate to the positive plate?

17. An electric field of 2.40×10^2 N/C is produced by two horizontal parallel plates set 4.00 cm apart. If a charged particle of 2.00 μC is moved 3.00 cm perpendicular to the electric field, what is the work done against the electric field?

18. A proton accelerates from rest from plate X to plate Y at the same time as an electron accelerates from rest from plate Y to plate X. If the potential difference between the two plates is 60.0 V,

a) what is the speed of the proton when it reaches plate Y?

b) what is the speed of the electron when it reaches plate X?

19. A charged particle was accelerated from rest by a potential difference of 2.50×10^5 V. If the particle reached a maximum speed of 2.90×10^4 m/s, what potential difference would be required to accelerate this particle from rest to a velocity of 7.25×10^4 m/s?

20. An electron is accelerated from rest through a potential difference of 5.00×10^3 V. What is the resulting speed of this electron?

21. An alpha particle is placed between two horizontal parallel charged plates that are 2.00 cm apart. The potential difference between the plates is 12.0 V.

a) What is the electric force acting on the alpha particle?

b) What is the gravitational force acting on the alpha particle?

c) If it is assumed that the electric force and the gravitational force are acting in opposite directions, what is the net force acting on the alpha particle?

d) What is the acceleration of the alpha particle?

e) What potential difference would be required between the plates so that the alpha particle becomes suspended?

22. A 0.50 kg ball is suspended in a uniform electric field ($\bar{E} = 1\,500$ N/C) as shown in the diagram below.

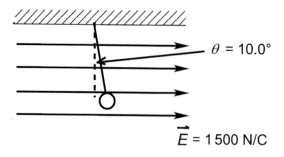

Calculate the charge on the ball.

23. An electron travelling horizontally at a speed of 8.70×10^6 m/s enters an electric field of 1.32×10^3 N/C between two horizontal parallel plates as illustrated below.

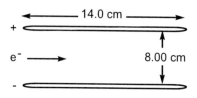

Calculate the magnitude of the vertical displacement of the electron as it travels between the plates.

PRACTICE TEST

1. A and B are identical pith balls. Ball A has a charge of –3.00 μC, and ball B has a charge of –1.00 μC.

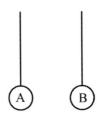

    If these two balls are brought into brief contact with each other and then separated to a distance of 2.00×10^{-2} m, what is the electric force between them?

    A. 1.35 N   **B.** 1.80 N

    C. 67.4 N   **D.** 90.0 N

2. A, B, and C represent three small charged spheres. The charges and distances are indicated in the diagram. What is the magnitude of the net electric force on sphere B that is caused by the other two charges?

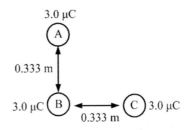

    A. 0.344 N   **B.** 0.486 N

    C. 1.03 N   **D.** 1.46 N

3. Two point charges are initially 6.0 cm apart, and are then moved so that they are 2.0 cm apart. If the initial force between these two point charges was F, what is the new force?

    A. 0.11F   **B.** 0.33F

    C. 3.0F   **D.** 9.0F

4. A and B represent small charged spheres that can move without friction. If sphere A is brought to a distance of 1.00×10^{-2} m from sphere B and released, its initial acceleration is 1.00×10^{10} m/s^2. Determine the initial acceleration of sphere A if it was brought to a distance of 3.00×10^{-2} m from sphere B.

A. 1.11×10^9 m/s^2

B. 3.33×10^9 m/s^2

C. 3.00×10^{10} m/s^2

D. 9.00×10^{10} m/s

5. A and B represent two small charged spheres that can move without friction. Their charges and masses are indicated in the diagram above. If sphere A is brought to a distance of 2.00×10^{-2} from sphere B and released, what is its initial acceleration?

$q_A = 3.00$ μC $\qquad\qquad$ $q_B = 3.00$ μC

$m_A = 5.00 \times 10^{-4}$ kg $\qquad$ $m_B = 5.00 \times 10^{-4}$ kg

A. 2.02×10^2 m/s^2

B. 8.09×10^2 m/s^2

C. 4.05×10^5 m/s^2

D. 1.35×10^{11} m/s^2

6. If a negatively charged rubber rod is used to charge an electroscope by induction, what will be the nature of the charge on the electroscope head?

A. Equal in magnitude to the charge on the rubber rod

B. Greater in magnitude than the charge on the rubber rod

C. Negative

D. Positive

7. If an alpha particle is accelerated from rest through a potential difference of 2.00×10^3 V, what is its maximum speed?

A. 3.10×10^5 m/s

B. 4.39×10^5 m/s

C. 2.65×10^7 m/s

D. 2.53×10^8 m/s

8. An electron is placed in a strong uniform electric field between two charged plates. The direction of the acceleration of the electron will be

A. in the direction of the electric field

B. in the opposite direction of the electric field

C. perpendicular to the electric field

D. unknown because the gravitational field will be in the opposite direction to the electric field

9. Which of the following phrases is a correct definition for electric potential?

    A. Electric potential energy

    B. Electric potential energy × charge

    C. Electric potential energy ÷ charge

    D. Voltage

10. When a positive point charge is moved toward another positive point charge, what happens to the potential energy of each of the point charges?

    A. both decrease   **B.** both increase

    C. both remain the same   **D.** one will increase and one will decrease

11. The direction of an electric field is defined in terms of the direction of the electric

    A. force on a positive test charge

    B. force on a negative test charge

    C. potential of a positive test charge

    D. potential of a negative test charge

12. Given two charged parallel plates as shown below, which of the following shows the correct direction of the electric field between these plates?

13. Which of the following graphs best represents the magnitude of the electric potential (V) as a function of the distance (r) from a point charge?

A.

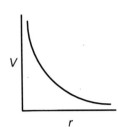

B.

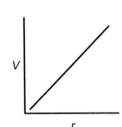

C.

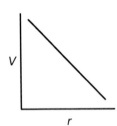

D.

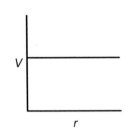

ELECTRIC CIRCUITS

When you are finished this unit, you should be able to…

- Differentiate between conventional current and electron flow
- Solve problems involving electric potential difference, current, and resistance using Ohm's law
- Construct and interpret circuit diagrams
- Use circuit diagrams to solve problems involving one source of potential difference
- Examine and solve problems related to the efficiency of electrical devices

Lesson	Page	Completed on
1. Electric Current	306	
2. Electric Circuits	314	
3. Electromotive Force (EMF)	331	
Practice Test	334	
Answers and Solutions	at the back of the book	

PREREQUISITE SKILLS AND KNOWLEGE

Prior to starting this unit, you should be able to…

- Write numbers in scientific notation
- Isolate a variable and combine algebraic expressions
- Perform calculations and obtain the answer to the correct number of significant figures
- Substitute the correct units for all quantities in a calculation and express the proper final unit by appropriate cancellation of units
- Determine the composition of derived units in terms of simpler units

Lesson 1 ELECTRIC CURRENT

ELECTRICITY

The introduction of the battery initiated new investigations in electricity: investigations that no longer involved only static charges or the discharge of these static charges. Investigations now could involve electric currents (flow of a charge through conductors).

Electric current is the rate of flow of electrical charge. In metallic conductors, it is the electrons that flow. The symbol of electric current is I.

Electric current is the rate of flow of electrical charges.

Definition: rate of flow of electrical charge $\left(I = \dfrac{q}{t} \right)$

Electric current can be described using:
conventional current
    (positive flow)
electron flow

Units: $\dfrac{C}{s}$ (which is called the ampere—A).

Charges will not move through a conductor unless there is a potential difference (voltage). In an electric circuit, there must be a voltage source and a complete pathway for the charge to flow through.

1 ampere =
$\dfrac{1 \text{ coulomb}}{s} = \dfrac{C}{s}$

Batteries in an electric circuit are voltage sources. Power companies use electric generators as voltage sources. (We will discuss generators later.) The current through a conductor depends on the potential difference and the resistance in the conductor. Current (rate of flow) will vary directly with the potential difference. It's like the current in a river. The greater the slope of the river bed, the faster the water flows. In the same way, the greater the potential difference (voltage), the greater the rate of flow (current).
$I \propto V$

Resistance in a conductor produces heat.

There is always resistance to the flow (movement) of charged particles through a conductor. This is why conductors get warm or hot when a current is flowing through them.

Current varies inversely with resistance.
$I \propto \dfrac{1}{R}$

We use R as the symbol for resistance.

The relationship $I \propto V$ and $I \propto \dfrac{1}{R}$ or $I \propto \dfrac{V}{R}$ was discovered by Ohm in 1826 and became known as Ohm's Law.

The above relationship is generally written as $I = \dfrac{V}{R}$

Ohm's Law: $V = IR$

Ohm's Law is usually written as $V = IR$.

The unit of resistance is called the ohm (symbol Ω).

ELECTRIC CURRENT

There are two ways of thinking about electric current.

- Electron flow—it is the electrons that flow through a conductor when there is an electric current. Electrons flow from the negative terminal to the positive terminal.

- Conventional current—is positive charge flow. Positive charges flow from the positive terminal to the negative terminal.

We know that it is actually the electrons that flow through a conductor; so why do we talk about conventional current? Positive charge flow has a historical basis; but also it probably goes back to our definition for the direction of an electric field and electric potential. Electric potential is defined in terms of a moving positive charge. Remember that the direction of an electric field is defined as the direction of the force on a positive test object.

Most college and university physics texts will use conventional current to describe electric current rather than electron flow. On your provincial exam, *electric current* refers to conventional current. And unless we indicate otherwise in this book, electric current will be conventional current.

Conventional current is positive charge flow.

ELECTRIC POWER

Power is the rate of doing work or using energy.

$$P = \frac{W}{t} = \frac{\Delta E}{t}$$

ΔE = energy transferred
W = work done
P = power

Power is the rate of doing work.

The unit of power is the watt (W).

From this definition of power and Ohm's Law, we can derive other relationships for power using electrical terms.

$$P = IV$$
$$P = I^2 R$$
$$P = \frac{V^2}{R}$$

Derivation:
P = power, I = current, V = potential difference, and R = resistance.

Using $P = \frac{W}{t}$ and recalling that $V = \frac{\Delta E}{q}$ or $\Delta E = Vq$, then ΔE = work or change in energy.

NOTES

Therefore, $P = \dfrac{Vq}{t}$ and $I = \dfrac{q}{t}$

Hence, $P = IV$.

Again $I = \dfrac{V}{R}$. Therefore, $P = \dfrac{V}{R}V$ or $P = \dfrac{V^2}{R}$

If $I = \dfrac{V}{R}$, then $V = IR$.

Therefore, $P = I(IR)$, or $P = I^2R$

Example

What is the electric current through a conductor if a charge of 2.0 C flows through a point in the conductor in 10 s?

Solution

$$I = \dfrac{q}{t}$$
$$= \dfrac{2.0 \text{ C}}{10 \text{ s}}$$
$$= 2.0 \times 10^{-1} \text{ A}$$

Example

Calculate the resistance in a conductor if the potential difference is 6.0 V and the current is 10 A.

Solution

$$V = IR$$
$$R = \dfrac{V}{I}$$
$$= \dfrac{6.0 \text{ V}}{10 \text{ A}}$$
$$= 6.0 \times 10^{-1} \ \Omega$$

Example

An electrical appliance uses 1.00×10^2 W when connected to a 1.20×10^2 V power line. What is the resistance in the appliance?

Solution

$$P = \dfrac{V^2}{R}$$
$$R = \dfrac{V^2}{P}$$
$$= \dfrac{(1.20 \times 10^2 \text{ V})^2}{1.00 \times 10^2 \text{ W}}$$
$$= 1.44 \times 10^2 \ \Omega$$

EFFICIENCY

Efficiency is defined as the ratio of the useful power output to the total power input. This can be expressed as follows:

$$\text{efficiency} = \frac{\text{power out}}{\text{power in}} \times 100\%$$

This can equivalently be stated as:

$$\text{efficiency} = \frac{\text{work out}}{\text{work in}} \times 100\%$$

Example

A light bulb is supplied 80.0 W of power. The bulb emits 56.0 J each second as light energy. What is the efficiency of the light bulb?

Solution

$$\text{power out} = 56.0 \text{ J/s} = 56.0 \text{ W}$$
$$\text{power in} = 80.0 \text{ W}$$
$$\text{efficiency} = \frac{\text{power out}}{\text{power in}} \times 100\%$$
$$= \frac{56.0 \text{ W}}{80.0 \text{ W}} \times 100\%$$
$$= 70.0\%$$

Consider the equation $P = IV$. This equation states that the amount of power is equal to the current (I) times the voltage (V). If the current is lowered and the voltage is increased, the same amount of power (P) can be generated.

Now, consider the equation $P = I^2 R$. This equation can be used to calculate the power loss due to resistance in the cables used to transmit power, and it implies that the power lost to heat in transmission lines can be reduced if the transmission current is decreased. Note that in the equation, current (I) is squared. If the current was reduced by a factor of 100 times, the power loss would be 100^2 or 10 000 times less. To receive the same amount of power in people's homes, the voltage must be increased to compensate for the reduction in current.

PRACTICE EXERCISES

Formulas: $I = \dfrac{q}{t}$ $\qquad$ $V = IR$ $\qquad$ $P = IV$ $\qquad$ $P = I^2R$ $\qquad$ $P = \dfrac{V^2}{R}$

1. A current of 3.60 A flows for 15.3 s through a conductor. Calculate the number of electrons that pass through a point of the conductor during this time.

2. How long would it take 2.0×10^{20} electrons to pass through a point in a conductor if the current was 10.0 A?

3. Calculate the current through a conductor if a charge of 5.60 C passes through a point in the conductor in 15.4 s.

4. What potential difference is required across a conductor to produce a current of 8.00 A if there is a resistance in the conductor of 12.0 Ω?

5. What is the heat produced in a conductor in 25.0 s if there is a current of 11.0 A and a resistance in the conductor of 7.20 Ω?

6. A particular conductor produces 1.50×10^2 J of heat in 5.50 s. If the current through the conductor is 10.0 A, what is the resistance of the conductor?

7. What is the current through a 4.00×10^2 W electric appliance when it is connected to a 1.20×10^2 V power line?

8. a) When an electric appliance is connected to a 1.20×10^2 V power line, there is a current through the appliance of 18.3 A. What is the resistance of the appliance?

   b) What is the average amount of energy given to each electron by the power line?

9. a) What potential difference is required across an electrical appliance to produce a current of 20.0 A when there is a resistance in the appliance of 6.00 Ω?

b) How many electrons pass through the electrical appliance every minute?

10. A student designed an experiment in order to measure the current through a resistor when manipulating the potential difference. The following data were recorded:

Potential difference (V)	Current (A)
3.00	0.151
6.00	0.310
9.00	0.448
12.00	0.611
15.00	0.750

a) Using the data above, draw a graph showing the relationship between the current and the potential difference.

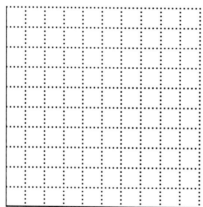

b) Using only the graph, find the resistance of the resistor.

11. If electricity cost \$0.060 per kilowatt hour, what does it cost to operate a 1.0×10^3 W appliance for 5.0 h?

12. A student forgets to turn off a 6.00×10^2 W block heater of a car when the weather turns warm. If 14 h goes by before he shuts it off, how much energy is used by the heater?

13. A 45 kg object is lifted vertically at a constant speed to a height of 9.0 m by a 7.5×10^2 W electric motor. If this motor is 25% efficient in converting electric energy to mechanical energy, how long does the motor take to lift the object?

Lesson 2   ELECTRIC CIRCUITS

An electric circuit is a pathway that allows charges to flow. In an electric circuit, there must be a voltage source—for example, a battery. The voltage source (battery) provides the electrical energy. An electric device (light bulb, toaster, radio, door bell, etc.) is placed in this circuit so that the device becomes part of the circuit. That is, the charge flows through the device, and as the charge flows, the electrical energy is converted to other forms of energy—one of these forms is heat. The reason heat is produced is that the electric device provides some resistance to the charge flow. There is usually a switch in an electric circuit. A switch is a means of breaking the pathway (circuit). If the pathway is broken, the charge cannot flow. Below is a diagram of a simple electric circuit showing the symbols for the voltage source, the electric device (resistance), and the switch.

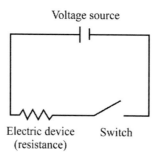

The circuits in our homes, cars, etc., have circuit breakers or fuses. These act like switches, preventing the charge from flowing through the circuit by creating a gap (break) in the pathway. Circuit breakers and fuses are heat sensitive. As the current through a conductor increases, so does the temperature of the conductor (circuit). If the current is too great, the heat produced will melt the fuse or trip the breaker.

A circuit can be described as a series or parallel circuit.

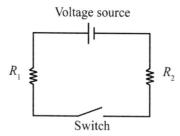

The circuit above is called a series circuit because the same amount of electrons must pass through both resistors. It is like running hurdles. You jump one hurdle, then you must jump the next. You run hurdles in series. Some Christmas lights are in series—when one light goes out, they all go out. If you look at the diagram, you can see that if one resistor burns out (like a light bulb) there is no longer a path for the electrons to flow through. Therefore, there will be no charge passing through R_2.

Parallel Circuit

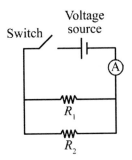

Parallel Circuit:
resistors are in parallel

The circuit above is called a parallel circuit because the charge has more than one path. The charge can travel through R_1 or R_2. If R_1 burns out, the charge can still travel through R_2. This is the type of electrical circuit in our homes.

DIRECT AND ALTERNATING CURRENT

Electric current can be direct (DC) or alternating (AC). Batteries produce direct current; that is, the conventional current always flows in the same direction through the circuit from the positive terminal to the negative terminal. Electrical generators can produce either direct current or alternating current. With alternating current, the conventional current in the circuit flows one direction and then the other—the current alternates in one direction and then the other. The circuits in our homes use alternating current. In this unit, we will study direct current (alternating current in the next unit). Many of the principles of direct current also apply to alternating current.

When drawing circuits we use the symbols:

$\vert\vert$ or $\vert\vert\vert\vert$ for direct current

Negative terminal $\longrightarrow \vert\vert \longleftarrow$ Positive terminal

$\bigotimes$ for alternating current

At this point, we will introduce Kirchhoff's current and voltage laws. The laws will apply to all DC circuits (both series and parallel).

Kirchhoff's Current and Voltage Laws apply to all DC circuits.

KIRCHHOFF'S CURRENT LAW

Series Circuit

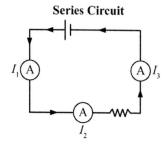

In a series circuit, because there is only one path, the current must be the same at all points.

$$I_T = I_1 = I_2 = I_3$$

Think of the charge as soldiers marching. The number of soldiers marching at any point must be the same.

Parallel Circuit

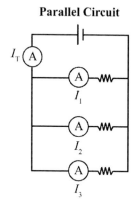

In a parallel circuit, the charge (soldiers) can take different paths. Therefore, the amount of charge (soldiers) at any point can be different.

$$I_T = I_1 + I_2 + I_3$$

Kirchhoff's Current Law is just a form of the Law of Conservation of Electric Charge.

Kirchhoff's law is stated as: The sum of the currents entering a junction equals the sum of the currents leaving the junction.

Remember, current is the movement of electrons, and if electrons move into a path, they must come out. In a way, this is just a different expression of the Law of Conservation of Electric Charge.

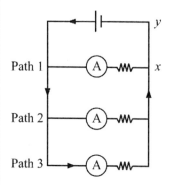

Again, if we use the soldier analogy, the soldiers that take path 1 and those that take path 2 and path 3 will come together at *x*. The soldiers marching from *x* to *y* will equal the sum of the soldiers taking path 1, path 2 and those taking path 3.

That is:
$$I_T = I_1 + I_2 + I_3 + \text{etc}$$

Kirchhoff's Voltage Law is a form of the Law of Conservation of Energy.

KIRCHHOFF'S VOLTAGE LAW

Kirchhoff's Voltage Law is stated as: The sum of the potential differences in any circuit must equal zero.

This is just a way of expressing the Law of Conservation of Energy. Remember, there is an increase in the potential across the terminals of a battery or power source. Also, remember that there is a potential loss (drop) across a resistor. Kirchhoff's Voltage Law is saying that these increases and losses must add up to zero in any circuit.

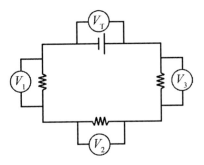

$$V_T = V_1 + V_2 + V_3$$

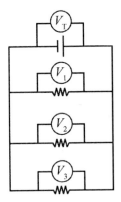

$$V_T = V_1 = V_2 = V_3$$

Note that in a parallel circuit, the potential difference is the same across all resistors in the circuit.

Kirchhoff's Laws and Ohm's Law can be used to derive equations for finding the total (equivalent) resistance in DC circuits. However, we will not derive them, but let's try to reason out these equations.

Series circuit

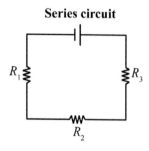

$$R_{eq} = R_1 + R_2 + R_3 \, .$$

The total resistance in a series circuit is the sum of all the resistances in the circuit. Let's again use the analogy of the marching soldiers. The charge (soldiers) must pass through all resistance. The total resistance it passes through is the sum of them all.

Parallel Circuit

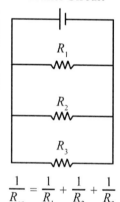

$$\frac{1}{R_{eq}} = \frac{1}{R_1} + \frac{1}{R_2} + \frac{1}{R_3}$$

Note that in a parallel circuit, the more paths there are, the less the total resistance will be. If all the charge (soldiers) has to pass through one resistor (path), a lot of friction (resistance) will be created. However, if the charge (soldiers) has a number of paths, there is more room and, therefore, less resistance.

MATHEMATICS OF CIRCUITS
Many electric circuits are a combination of series and parallel circuits or connections. Therefore we will need to be able to solve problems involving:

- Series circuits

- Parallel circuits

- Combination circuits

Example

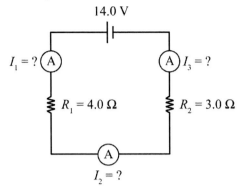

14.0 V

$I_1 = ?$

$R_1 = 4.0\ \Omega$

$I_3 = ?$

$R_2 = 3.0\ \Omega$

$I_2 = ?$

What are the values of I_1, I_2, and I_3 in this circuit?

Solution

Ohm's Law: $V_T = I_T R_T$

$R_T = R_{eq} = R_1 + R_2$
$\quad = 4.0\ \Omega + 3.0\ \Omega$
$\quad = 7.0\ \Omega$

$\therefore I_T = \dfrac{V_T}{R_T}$

$\quad = \dfrac{14.0\ \text{V}}{7.0\ \Omega}$

$\quad = 2.0\ \text{A}$

In a series circuit:

$I = I_1 = I_2 = I_3 \ldots$
$I_1 = I_2 = I_3 = 2.0\ \text{A}$

Example

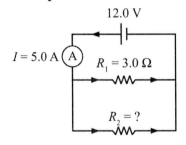

12.0 V

$I = 5.0\ \text{A}$

$R_1 = 3.0\ \Omega$

$R_2 = ?$

What is the value of R_2 in this circuit?

Solution

Ohm's Law $V = IR$

$R_{eq} = R = \dfrac{V}{I}$

$\quad = \dfrac{12.0\ \text{V}}{5.0\ \text{A}}$

$\quad = 2.4\ \Omega$

In a parallel circuit:

$$\frac{1}{R_{eq}} = \frac{1}{R_1} + \frac{1}{R_2}$$

$$\frac{1}{2.4\ \Omega} = \frac{1}{3.0\ \Omega} + \frac{1}{R_2}$$

$$\frac{1}{R_2} = \frac{1}{2.4\ \Omega} - \frac{1}{3.0\ \Omega}$$

$$= \frac{3.0 - 2.4}{7.2\ \Omega}$$

$$R_2 = 12\ \Omega$$

Example

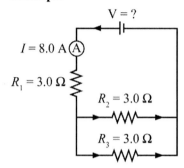

What is the potential difference supplied by the power source in this circuit?

Solution

Find equivalent resistance in the two parallel resistors first:

$$\frac{1}{R_{eq(p)}} = \frac{1}{R_2} + \frac{1}{R_3}$$

$$= \frac{1}{3.0\ \Omega} + \frac{1}{3.0\ \Omega}$$

$$= \frac{1.0 + 1.0}{3.0\ \Omega}$$

$$= 1.5\ \Omega$$

Now, add in the series resistors:

$$R_{eq(s)} = R_{eq(p)} + R_1$$

$$= 1.5\ \Omega + 3.0\ \Omega$$

$$= 4.5\ \Omega$$

Ohm's Law

$$V = IR = IR_{eq(s)}$$

$$= (8.0\ \text{A})(4.5\ \Omega)$$

$$= 36\ \text{V}$$

Example

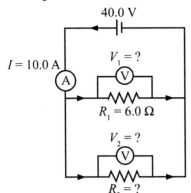

40.0 V

$I = 10.0$ A

$V_1 = ?$

$R_1 = 6.0\ \Omega$

$V_2 = ?$

$R_2 = ?$

What are the values of V_1, V_2, and R_2 in this circuit?

Solution
For a parallel circuit:
$V = V_1 = V_2 \ldots$

As $V = 40.0$ V
$V_1 = 40.0$ V
$V_2 = 40.0$ V

Ohm's Law
$V = IR$

$$R_{eq} = R = \frac{V}{I}$$
$$= \frac{40.0\ \text{V}}{10.0\ \text{A}}$$
$$= 4.0\ \Omega$$

For a parallel circuit:
$$\frac{1}{R_{eq}} = \frac{1}{R_1} + \frac{1}{R_2}$$
$$\frac{1}{4.0\ \Omega} = \frac{1}{6.0\ \Omega} + \frac{1}{R_2}$$
$$\frac{1}{R_2} = \frac{1}{4.0\ \Omega} - \frac{1}{6.0\ \Omega}$$
$$= \frac{3.0 - 2.0}{12\ \Omega}$$
$$R_2 = 12\ \Omega$$

PRACTICE EXERCISES

Formulas: For series circuits

$I_T = I_1 = I_2 = I_3 = ...$

$V = IR$ $V_T = V_1 + V_2 + V_3 + ...$

$R_{eq} = R_1 + R_2 + R_3 + ...$

For parallel circuits

$I_T = I_1 + I_2 + I_3 + ...$

$V_T = V_1 = V_2 = V_3 = ...$

$\dfrac{1}{R_{eq}} = \dfrac{1}{R_1} + \dfrac{1}{R_2} + \dfrac{1}{R_3} + ...$

1. What are the values for I_2 and I_3 in the circuit?

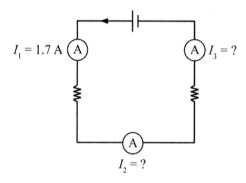

2. What is the value of I_3 in the circuit?

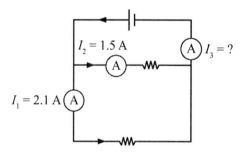

3. What is the value of V_2 in the circuit?

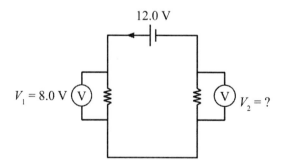

4. What is the value of V_2 in the circuit?

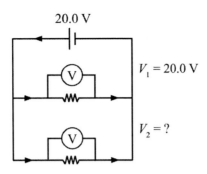

20.0 V

$V_1 = 20.0$ V

$V_2 = ?$

5. What are the values of V_2 and V_3 in the circuit?

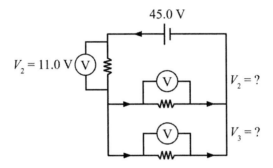

45.0 V

$V_2 = 11.0$ V

$V_2 = ?$

$V_3 = ?$

6. What is the total resistance in the circuit?

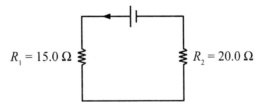

$R_1 = 15.0$ Ω

$R_2 = 20.0$ Ω

7. What is the total resistance in the circuit?

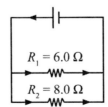

$R_1 = 6.0$ Ω

$R_2 = 8.0$ Ω

8. What is the total resistance in the circuit?

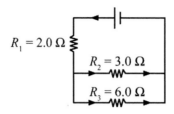

9. What is the total resistance in a circuit containing three resistors in series? The values of these resistors are 9.0 Ω, 3.0 Ω and 12.0 Ω.

10. What is the total resistance in a circuit containing three resistors in parallel? The values of these resistors are 2.0 Ω, 4.0 Ω and 8.0 Ω.

11. The total resistance in a circuit containing three resistors in parallel is 2.0 Ω. If the values of two of these resistors are 4.5 Ω and 9.0 Ω, what is the value of the third resistor?

12. The total resistance in a circuit containing three resistors in series is 12.0 Ω. If the values of two of these resistors are 6.0 Ω and 4.0 Ω, what is the value of the third resistor?

13. a) What are the values of I_1 and I_2 in the circuit?

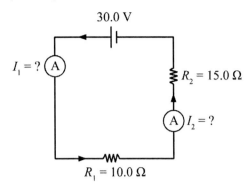

b) What is the power dissipated in R_1?

14. a) What is the value of I in the circuit?

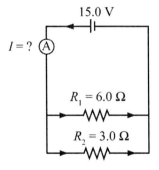

b) What is the power dissipated in R_1?

15. a) What are the values of I_1 and I_2 in the circuit?

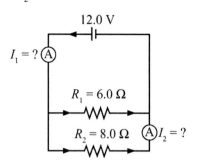

b) What is the total power dissipated in the circuit?

16. a) What are the values of I_1, I_2 and I_3 in this circuit?

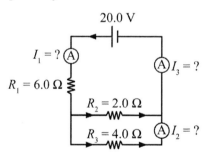

b) What is the total power dissipated in the circuit?

17. a) What is the potential difference supplied by the power source in the circuit?

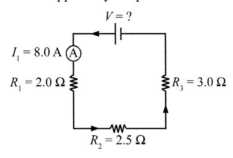

b) What is the total power dissipated by the circuit?

18. a) What is the value of I_1 in this circuit?

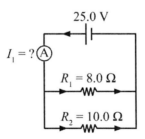

b) What is the total power dissipated in the circuit?

19. In the circuit, find R_3, I_2, I_3, and I_4.

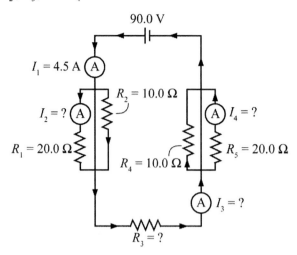

20. An electric heating coil will consume 6.0×10^2 W of power when it is connected to a 120 V outlet. A greenhouse operator has two such coils, and she wants to construct a single heater using the two coils to keep her small greenhouse at a temperature of 50.0°C during the winter months. For how many hours must this heater (two coils) operate per day if an average of 1.5×10^7 J of energy are required each winter day to maintain the desired temperature given that the coils are connected

a) in series?

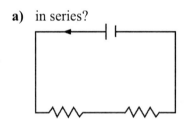

b) in parallel?

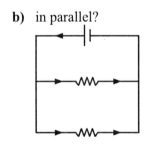

c) Which of the two arrangements is the most cost-efficient? Explain your answer.

21. A creative physics student has four 12 Ω heating coils. She constructs a water heater by placing the four coils in a circuit, as shown below.

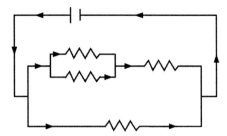

If this heater operates from a 120 V power line and is used to heat 200 kg of water (specific heat capacity = 4.18×10^3 J/kg·C) that is at an original temperature of 15° C, what will the temperature of the water be after 4.0 h? (In addition to the formulas at the back of this book, you will have to use $\Delta E = mc\Delta T$ to solve this problem. ΔE = energy used, m = mass, c = specific heat capacity, ΔT = temperature change.)

22. A physics student is testing the resistance of five equal-length conductors of 50.0 cm all made of the same material but having different cross sectional areas. She tests these conductors by constructing an electric circuit as illustrated.

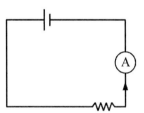

She maintains a constant voltage of 120 V across the resistors and records the current through the circuit. The following data were obtained:

A ($\times 10^{-9}$ m^2)	V (V)	I (A)	R (Ω)
2.1	120	30.0	
1.4	120	20.0	
1.1	120	15.0	
0.70	120	10.0	
0.35	120	5.0	

a) Complete the resistance column in the above table. (Show at least one calculation.)

b) Using your data from the complete table, plot a graph showing the relationship between the resistance and the cross-sectional area. (Plot resistance as a function of the cross-sectional area.)

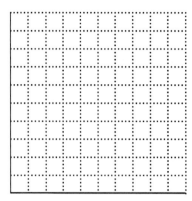

c) Plot a graph of resistance against some function of cross-sectional area that will produce a straight-line graph. Label the function of the cross-sectional area you used and show your calculated value in the above data table.

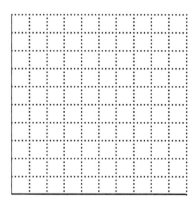

Lesson 3   ELECTROMOTIVE FORCE (EMF)

We earlier said that a battery is a source of potential difference (voltage) or electric energy. An electric generator is another source. When these devices are not connected to an external circuit, the potential difference across the terminals is called the electromotive force or emf. This name has a historical basis. At one time, it was thought that there was something that forced the current through the circuit. Electromotive force has the symbol $\mathcal{E}$. A car battery has an emf of 12 V. When a battery is part of an electric circuit, the potential difference across the terminals of the battery is less than the emf because of the internal resistance of the battery. Every battery has some internal resistance. Because of this internal resistance, the terminal voltage is always less than the emf of the battery.

$V = \mathcal{E} - Ir$

where V = terminal voltage
$\mathcal{E}$ = emf of battery
I = current through the battery
r = internal resistance

Note: Ir = drop in voltage due to internal resistance

Note: If the battery is not connected, no current flows and $V = \mathcal{E}$. This equation applies to an electric generator as well as a battery.

When there is no current flowing, the potential difference equals the emf.

When current flows from a battery (battery discharging),
$V = \mathcal{E} - Ir$

When current flows to a battery (battery charging),
$V = \mathcal{E} \pm Ir$

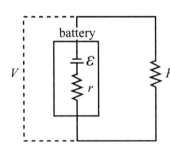

This diagram shows an external circuit with resistance R, connected to a battery. Voltage (V) across the battery terminals is given by: $V = \mathcal{E} - Ir$

When a battery goes "dead," the internal resistance becomes greater until Ir equals $\mathcal{E}$, and then the current will not flow.

When a rechargeable battery is being charged, an external voltage is applied to the battery. The voltage of this external voltage must be greater than the emf of the battery.

$V = \mathcal{E} + Ir$

V = external voltage

Example

If a 12.0 V battery has an internal resistance of 0.220 Ω, what is the terminal voltage of the battery when a current of 3.00 A flows through the battery?

Solution
$V = \mathcal{E} - Ir$
$= 12.0 \text{ V} - (3.00\text{A})(0.220 \text{ Ω})$
$= 11.3 \text{ V}$

Example

Battery

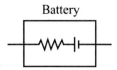

In the battery shown above, the emf is 9.0 V and when a current of 2.0 A flows through the battery, the terminal voltage is 7.0 V. What is the internal resistance of the battery?

Solution

$$V = \mathcal{E} - Ir$$
$$r = \frac{\mathcal{E} - V}{I}$$
$$= \frac{9.0 \text{ V} - 7.0 \text{ V}}{2.0 \text{ A}}$$
$$= 1.0 \ \Omega$$

Example

A 12.0 V car battery is being charged using a battery charger that is supplying 15.0 V. If the internal resistance of the battery is 1.3 Ω, what is the current through the battery?

Solution

$$V = \mathcal{E} + Ir$$
$$I = \frac{V - \mathcal{E}}{r}$$
$$= \frac{15.0 \text{ V} - 12.0 \text{ V}}{1.3 \ \Omega}$$
$$= 2.3 \text{ A}$$

PRACTICE EXERCISES

Formula: $V = \mathcal{E} \pm Ir$

1. A flashlight battery of emf 1.5 V has an internal resistance of 0.50 Ω. If there is a current of 1.0 A through the battery, what is the terminal voltage of the battery?

2. What is the emf of a battery that has a terminal voltage of 5.0 V when a current of 1.2 A flows through the battery? The battery has an internal resistance of 0.72 Ω.

3. A battery that has an emf of 24 V and an internal resistance of 0.25 Ω is being charged at a rate of 24 A. What is the voltage required to do this?

4. A battery of 12 V emf has an internal resistance of 1.0 Ω, and is connected to an external circuit that has a resistance of 4.0 Ω. What is the current through the circuit?

5. What is the internal resistance of an electric generator that has an emf of 120 V and a terminal voltage of 115 V when there is a current of 12 A through the generator?

PRACTICE TEST

1. What is the potential difference across a 5.0 Ω resistor if it carries a current of 9.0 A?

   A. 0.56 V

   C. 45 V

   B. 1.8 V

   D. 4.1×10^2 V

2. What is the total number of electrons that passes through a conductor each minute if it carries a current of 0.20 A?

   A. 0.20

   C. 1.9×10^{18}

   B. 12

   D. 7.5×10^{19}

3. If a 775 W heating coil operates for 15 minutes, how much energy does it use?

   A. 1.2 J

   C. 1.2×10^4 J

   B. 52 J

   D. 7.0×10^5 J

4. An electric circuit has three resistors as shown in the diagram below.

   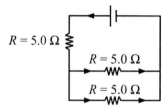

   What is their equivalent resistance?

   A. 5.0 Ω

   C. 10 Ω

   B. 7.5 Ω

   D. 15 Ω

5. Two resistors having values of 5.00 Ω and 7.50 Ω are connected in series in an electric circuit. What is their equivalent resistance?

   A. 1.50 Ω

   C. 7.50 Ω

   B. 3.00 Ω

   D. 12.5 Ω

6. If you want to determine the resistance through an electric circuit, which of the following instruments would you use?

   i)   ammeter
   ii) galvanometer
   iii) voltmeter

   A. I and II only

   C. II only

   B. I and III only

   D. III only

7. An electric circuit has three resistors, as shown in the diagram below.

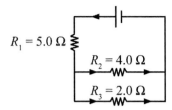

If the current through R_1 is 9.0 A, what is the current through R_2?

A. 3.0 A   **B.** 4.5 A

C. 6.0 A   **D.** 9.0 A

8. To find the resistance through a resistor in an electric circuit, an ammeter and voltmeter are used by connecting

A. both the ammeter and voltmeter into the circuit in series to the resistor

B. both the ammeter and voltmeter into the circuit in parallel to the resistor

C. the ammeter in series and the voltmeter in parallel to the resistor

D. the ammeter in parallel and the voltmeter in series to the resistor

9. When two resistors are connected in parallel in an electric circuit, both resistors will have the same

A. current flowing   **B.** power dissipated

C. resistance   **D.** voltage drop

10. If two copper conductors have the same resistance, they must also have the same

A. current flowing through them   **B.** voltage applied through them

C. length   **D.** voltage-to-current ratio

11. An electric current flows through a resistor R_1 that is in an electric circuit. If a second resistor R_2 is now placed in the circuit in series with R_1, what happens to the current through R_1?

A. The current increases if $R_1 > R_2$.   **B.** The current increases if $R_2 > R_1$.

C. The current remains the same.   **D.** The current decreases.

12. A resistor R_1, which is placed in an electric circuit, dissipates energy at a rate of P. If a second resistor R_2 is now placed in the circuit in parallel with R_1, what happens to the energy dissipated in R_1?

A. P increases if $R_1 > R_2$ **B.** P increases if $R_2 > R_1$

C. P remains the same   **D.** P decreases

13. An electric circuit has three resistors as shown in the diagram below.

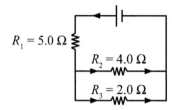

What is the total resistance of this circuit?

A. 1.0 Ω   **B.** 1.1 Ω

C. 6.3 Ω   **D.** 11 Ω

14. Using your answer to question 13, what is the terminal voltage of the battery if there is a current of 1.6 A flowing through the circuit?

A. 1.6 V   **B.** 1.8 V

C. 10 V   **D.** 18 V

MAGNETIC FORCES AND FIELDS

When you are finished this unit, you should be able to…
- Describe the magnetic fields generated by bar magnets, wires, and solenoids
- Solve problems involving the magnetic field generated by a solenoid
- Use hand rules to determine the direction of the magnetic force acting on charges and conducting wires
- Describe the motor effect and the electromagnetic principles upon which a motor operates
- Solve problems that involve charged particles and wires moving perpendicularly to magnetic fields
- Use Lenz's law to determine the direction of a current induced in a coil that is placed in a perpendicular magnetic field
- Define magnetic flux
- Apply Faraday's law to problems involving an induced emf in a coil
- Solve problems involving ideal transformers

Lesson	Page	Completed on
1. Magnetic Forces and Fields	338	
2. Magnetic Forces On Current-Carrying Conductors	346	
3. Cathode Rays	355	
4. Electromagnetic Induction	364	
5. Electric Generator	376	
6. EMF Continued	382	
7. Transformers (Induction Coil)	390	
8. Power Transmission	395	
Practice Test	397	
Answers and Solutions	at the back of the book	

PREREQUISITE SKILLS AND KNOWLEDGE

Prior to starting this unit, you should be able to…
- Write numbers in scientific notation
- Isolate a variable and combine algebraic expressions
- Perform calculations and obtain the answer to the correct number of significant figures
- Substitute the correct units for all quantities in a calculation and express the proper final unit by appropriate cancellation of units
- Determine the composition of derived units in terms of simpler units

Lesson 1 MAGNETIC FORCES AND FIELDS

Lodestone is a type of metallic rock found by the early Greeks in a place called Magnesia; hence, our modern term *magnetism*. Lodestone, in the shape of needles, was used as early as the 12th century in the navigation of ships. When a needle-like lodestone was placed on a cork floating freely in a container of water, the needle would rotate so that it was pointing north and south. These needle-like lodestones were our first compasses.

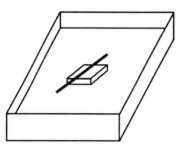

A study of magnetism was made by William Gilbert in the 1600s. Gilbert was interested in finding out why the needle-shaped lodestones always pointed north and south. He hypothesized that Earth acted like, or was, a large lodestone. He set out to test his hypothesis by constructing a model of Earth out of lodestone. He found that the needles (lodestone) would always point in the same direction. He concluded that Earth is a lodestone.

A compass needle is a small magnet. If you suspend a bar magnet by a thread, the magnet will align so that one end points north and the other end points south. This is where the terms *north pole* and *south pole* come from. Actually, the proper names are north-seeking pole and south-seeking pole. In a magnet, the north and south poles cannot be separated. If you break a magnet in two, each part will have a north pole and a south pole. Magnetic poles behave in a manner similar to electric charges, but electric charges can be isolated from each other. Magnetic poles cannot.

Magnetic poles occur in pairs.

MAGNETIC POLES
- There are two types of poles (north pole and south pole).
- Like poles repel.
- Unlike poles attract.

Why does a compass align itself north and south? Remember, Gilbert discovered that Earth acts like a lodestone (a magnet). That is, Earth has a north magnetic pole and a south magnetic pole. The north magnetic pole of Earth attracts the south pole of the magnet, and the south magnetic pole of Earth attracts the north pole of the magnet.

If the end of the magnet (compass) that points north is the north-seeking pole (N-pole), then the magnetic pole of the earth in the geographic north must be a south pole!

Magnetic fields are vector fields.

N (geographic)

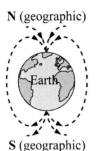

S (geographic)

Magnetic fields, like gravitational and electric fields, are vector fields. We can represent these magnetic fields with drawings:

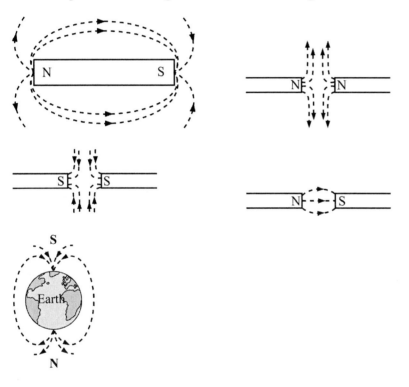

The direction of a magnetic field is defined as the direction to which the north-seeking pole of a compass needle will point.

The direction of the magnetic field is defined as the direction to which the north-seeking pole of a compass needle will point or move. A north (seeking) pole of a compass will, by definition, point to the south pole of a magnet. In all of these drawings, the field is toward the south and away from the north.

Note the similarity of the magnetic fields to electric fields.

Electric Fields Magnetic Fields

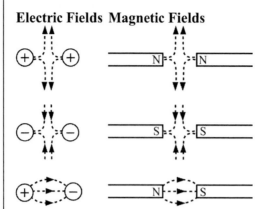

Magnetic field lines (lines of force) can be observed by placing a sheet of paper over a magnet and sprinkling iron filings on the paper. In the presence of the magnet, the iron filings become temporary magnets and will act like small compass needles. They will align themselves so that we can observe the shape of the magnetic field.

Only certain metals can become temporary magnets: cobalt, iron, and nickel. In the same way, only cobalt, iron, and nickel are attracted to magnets.

OERSTED

Hans Christian Oersted, a Danish scientist, discovered that there was a relationship between electric current and magnetism. After Alessandro Volta produced the first battery in 1800, there were many investigations and demonstrations with electric current. Oersted, while performing an electrical demonstration, accidentally discovered that an electric current will deflect a compass needle—an electric current will produce a magnetic field! (A moving charge produces a magnetic field.) The shape of the magnetic field that surrounds a current-carrying conductor can be found by putting small compass needles around the conductor. It is found that this magnetic field circles the conductor.

Oersted discovered that a current through a conductor will produce a magnetic field.

⊙ Current flowing out of page

⊗ Current flowing into page

We will use the symbol ⊙ to represent current flowing out of the page through a conductor, and the symbol ⊗ to represent current flowing into the page through a conductor.

⊙ out   ⊗ in

Magnetic fields circle a conductor.

Magnetic fields around a conductor:

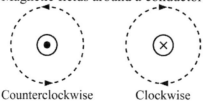

Counterclockwise   Clockwise

To obtain the direction of the magnetic field, we cannot just say that the field is directed toward the S-pole and away from the N-pole, because here, there is no S-pole or N-pole. To obtain the direction, we can remember clockwise and counterclockwise. A better method is to use the right-hand and left-hand rules. Use the right-hand rule for conventional current; use the left-hand rule for electron flow.

FIRST RIGHT-HAND RULE

Using your right hand, point your thumb in the direction of the current (positive flow); let your fingers circle the wire. The fingers will be circling the wire in the same way that the field (magnetic) circles the current-carrying conductor.

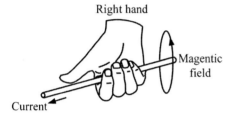

Right hand

Magentic field

Current

If a compass is placed below a current carrying conductor, which way will the needle point if the current (positive flow) is flowing into the page?

Compass points west

The compass needle will align itself as the tangent to the circular lines of force (magnetic field) and in the same direction as the magnetic field at that point.

MAGNETIC DOMAINS

Iron, cobalt, and nickel are referred to as ferromagnetic materials because they can become permanent or temporary magnets. How can we explain why ferromagnetic materials can become permanent or temporary magnets?

We have just seen that electric currents (moving charges) produce magnetic fields. We might conclude that the movement of charges within the atoms was responsible for the material's magnetic properties. If this was the case, all materials would have magnetic properties—this is true to a certain extent (other materials are called diamagnetic materials and paramagnetic materials). It is only ferromagnetic materials that can become permanent or temporary magnets. Ferromagnetic materials must have something special about the charge movement within their atoms. This special property is beyond the scope of this course, but it has to do with the spin nature of unpaired electrons in these atoms.

NOTES

Right Hand Rule: Thumb represents the direction of conventional current (positive flow), and the fingers represent the direction of the magnetic field.

Left Hand Rule: Thumb represents the direction of electron flow.

Unit of magnetic field strength is a tesla (T)

NOTES

In a ferromagnetic substance, the unpaired electrons in each atom have spins that produce a "cooperative effect" with 1015 to 1020 other atoms. This group of atoms that have cooperated is called the magnetic domain. It should be noted that although the magnetic domain contains many atoms, the dimensions of these domains are very small (about 10–6 m). This means that in a magnet there are millions of these magnetic domains. In an unmagnetized piece of material containing one of these ferromagnetic materials, the domains are randomly aligned.

In an external magnetic field, these domains will rotate so that they are in the same direction.

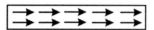

In a permanent magnet, these domains remain so that the magnetic field of each domain is in the same direction in absence of any external magnetic field.

In a temporary magnet, these domains return to a random alignment when the external magnetic field is removed.

SOLENOIDS

When a coil has many loops as compared with its length, it is called a solenoid or electromagnet. Electromagnets have many applications. They are useful because they act like permanent magnets.
The major applications of electromagnets come from the fact that they only act as magnets when an electric current is flowing through the coil. In a bar magnet, or any permanent magnet, you cannot shut them off or turn them on. With electromagnets you can.

MAGNETIC FIELD AROUND AN ELECTROMAGNET

Note that the field lines inside the magnet are straight. Inside the electromagnet, there is a uniform magnetic field. Outside the electromagnet (coil), the field is relatively weak and is the same shape as that around a bar magnet.

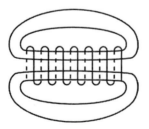

Inside an electromagnet, there is a uniform magnetic field.

SECOND RIGHT-HAND RULE

What is the direction of the magnetic field inside an electromagnet?

The second right-hand rule is used to determine the direction of the magnetic field produced inside a solenoid or electromagnet. Curl the fingers of your right hand in the direction the current (positive flow) flows in the coil. Keep your thumb straight; it will be pointing in the same direction as the north pole of a compass—in the direction of the field.

Left Hand Rule is used with electron flow.

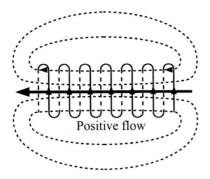

Positive flow

Magnetic field—direction your thumb points, which is the same as the direction in which the north pole of a compass points.

The direction of the magnetic field inside an electromagnet is the direction your thumb points when the fingers curl in the direction the charge is flowing.

The magnetic field produced by a solenoid or an electromagnet is very similar to magnetic fields produced by a bar magnet; therefore, the ends of the coil can be thought of as an N-pole and an S-pole.

In a solenoid, there are many loops wound tightly together. If the length of the solenoid is greater than the diameter, the magnitude of the magnetic field inside the solenoid is uniform and is found using the formula

$B = \mu_0 In$

Where n = number of loops per metre

μ_0 = permeability of free space = $4\pi \times 10^{-7} \dfrac{T \cdot m}{A}$

I = current in the solenoid

INTERACTIONS OF MAGNETIC FIELDS

We know that like poles of magnets repel and unlike poles attract.

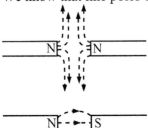

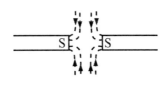

NOTES

What happens in the case of a current-carrying conductor? If two parallel current-carrying conductors are carrying current in the same direction, do the magnetic fields produced by these cause repulsion or attraction?

An ampere is defined in terms of forces between current-carrying conductors.

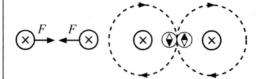

Magnetic fields between the two conductors are in opposite directions. As can be seen with the two compasses, opposite poles face one another and therefore attract one another. Depending on the current (electron flow) through the conductors, the magnetic fields will apply a force that will draw the two conductors together.

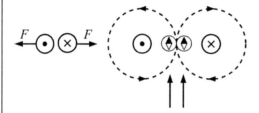

Current flowing in opposite directions through conductors will force the conductors apart. This is because the magnetic fields between the conductors are in the same direction. The magnetic lines of force will repel each other. The magnetic field forces the conductors apart (repulsion).

Because of this property (the ability of current-carrying conductors to produce magnetic forces), the unit of current, the ampere, was defined in terms of these effects. One ampere is the amount of current in each of two long, straight parallel conductors, set one metre apart, that will cause a force of 2×10^{-7} N to act on each metre of wire.

Example

An air core solenoid is 25 cm long and has 1 000 loops. If this solenoid has a diameter of 4.0 cm, and has a current of 9.0 A, what is the magnetic field in the solenoid?

Solution

$$B = \mu_0 In$$
$$= \left(4\pi \times 10^{-7} \ \frac{\text{T} \cdot \text{m}}{\text{A}} \right) (9.0 \text{A}) (4.0 \times 10^3 / \text{m})$$
$$= 4.5 \times 10^{-2} \text{ T}$$

PRACTICE EXERCISES

Formulas: $B = \mu_0 In = \mu_0 I \dfrac{N}{l}$

1. A 25.0 cm solenoid has 1 800 loops and a diameter of 3.00 cm. Calculate the magnetic field in the air core of the solenoid when a current of 1.25 A is flowing through it.

2. An air core solenoid is 25 cm long and carries a current of 0.72 A. If the magnetic field in the core is 2.1×10^{-3} T , how many turns does this solenoid have?

3. An air core solenoid is 30.0 cm long and has 775 turns. If the magnetic field in the core is 0.100 T, what is the current flowing through this solenoid?

4. What is the magnetic field near the centre of a 0.30 m long solenoid that has 800 turns of wire and carries an electric current of 2.0 A?

Lesson 2 MAGNETIC FORCES ON CURRENT-CARRYING CONDUCTORS

A current-carrying conductor will experience a force when placed in a magnetic field.

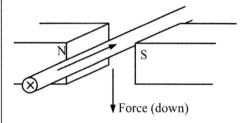

A current-carrying conductor will experience a force when placed in a magnetic field.

The magnetic field around the conductor will interact with the permanent field. In the diagram below, you will note that both the fields are in the same direction above the conductor. Therefore, the magnetic lines of force produced by the current-carrying conductor will be repelled by the magnetic lines of force produced by the permanent magnets. Below the conductor, the magnetic fields are in the opposite direction. Therefore, the magnetic lines of force between the conductor and the permanent magnet attract. Hence, the interaction of the fields above the conductor will push down, while the interaction of the field below will pull down on the conductor; therefore, the conductor will be forced down.

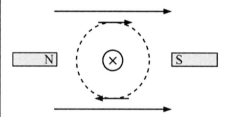

THIRD RIGHT-HAND RULE

To obtain the direction of the force on a conductor in a magnetic field, use your right hand. With this rule, keep the fingers straight and the thumb perpendicular to the fingers.

Fingers
(direction of permanent
magnetic field)

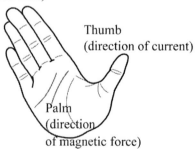

Thumb
(direction of current)

Palm
(direction
of magnetic force)

Right-hand rule for magnetic force:
fingers = magnetic field
thumb = current
palm = force

Remember that if you are considering electron flow, use the left hand rule.

Point your thumb in the direction of the current (positive flow), and your fingers in the direction of the magnetic field. The direction of your palm is the direction of the force.

MOTOR EFFECT

The right-hand rule can be used to explain the principles of the electric motor.

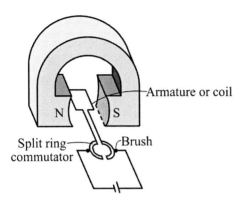

NOTES

Electric motors illustrate an application of interactions between magnetic fields.

In an actual DC motor, there are many loops of wire—these loops are called the armature.

In a simple DC motor, a loop of wire passes through a magnetic field. The ends of the loop are attached to a split ring, commutator, which turns with the loop. Fixed brushes rub on this commutator, which in turn is connected to a voltage source (battery). In the diagram below, the loop on the right side is always forced down, and in the same way, the loop on the left side is always forced up.

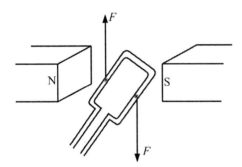

The magnitude of the magnetic force on a conductor can be calculated using:

$F_m = BIl \sin \theta$

where

B = magnitude of the magnetic field strength
I = current through the conductor
l = length of conductor
θ = the acute angle that the conductor makes with the magnetic field line.

If the conductor is perpendicular to the magnetic field, this formula can be reduced to: $F_m = B_\perp Il$ (because $\sin 90°$ is 1).

If the conductor is parallel to the magnetic field, there is no magnetic force. This is because $\sin 0°$ or $\sin 180°$ is 0.

The symbol $B_\perp$ means that the current is flowing through the conductor perpendicular to the magnetic field.

NOTES

AC motors do not require a commutator because with AC current, the current reverses itself. Most of our electric motors are AC motors because electric energy for industrial and household use is transmitted as alternating current. An example of a DC motor is the starter motor on a car.

GALVANOMETERS (ELECTRIC METERS)

Galvanometers are instruments used to detect an electric current. A galvanometer may be calibrated to measure current; in this case, it is called an ammeter. A galvanometer may also be calibrated to measure potential difference; in this case, it is called a voltmeter. These instruments also make use of the motor principle.

Galvanometers are instruments used to detect an electric current.

A current-carrying conductor in a magnetic field will experience a magnetic force. This force is directly proportional to the current flowing through the conductor. This concept is used in electric meters (galvanometers, ammeters, voltmeters) as well as other types of meters (speedometers in cars). Galvanometers form the basis of all electric meters.

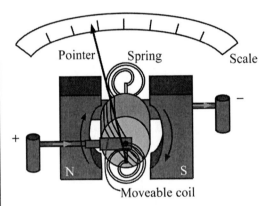

In a galvanometer, current flows through a coil, as shown above. These results in an interaction between the two magnetic fields, which causes the movable coil to rotate against a spring, resulting in a scale reading. It should be noted that a galvanometer will produce a full-scale reading with very low current through the coil.

A galvanometer is converted to an ammeter by placing a shunt (a wire) of low resistance parallel to the coil. In other words, a parallel path for the electrons is provided so that only a small fraction of the electrons flow through the movable coil.

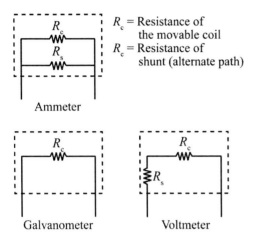

R_c = Resistance of the movable coil

R_c = Resistance of shunt (alternate path)

Ammeter

Galvanometer   Voltmeter

A galvanometer is converted to a voltmeter by placing a shunt (a wire) of high resistance in series to the coil. This reduces the current that flows through the electric meter. Remember that ammeters are placed in series in an electric circuit, while voltmeters are placed in parallel.

Right-hand rule is used for positive flow.

Left-hand rule is used for electron (negative) flow.

MOVING CHARGES IN MAGNETIC FIELDS

It is not only current-carrying conductors that are deflected by magnetic fields. Moving charges (electrons, protons, alpha particles) can also be deflected by magnetic fields. These particles are deflected in the same way as current-carrying conductors. However, to determine the direction of the deflection, you use your left hand instead of your right hand for negative particles (electrons).

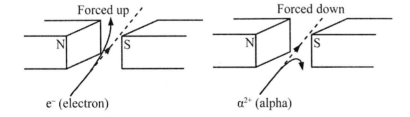

Forced up   Forced down

e^- (electron) α^{2+} (alpha)

The magnitude of the deflecting magnetic forces on moving charged particles (electrons, protons, and alpha particles) can be calculated using:
$$F_m = qvB\sin\theta$$
where
q = charge of the particle
v = speed of the particle
B = magnitude of the magnetic field strength
θ = angle at which the charge passes through the magnetic field

Like the magnetic force on conductors, this formula can be reduced to $F_m = qvB_\perp$ when the charged particles are moving perpendicular to the magnetic field. Also, like magnetic forces on conductors, the magnetic force is zero if the charged particle is moving parallel to the magnetic field.

In strong, broad magnetic fields, these charged particles can be continually deflected and end up travelling in a circle.

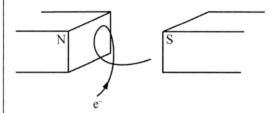

In a vacuum, charged particles can become trapped in a magnetic field. An electron moving perpendicular to the magnetic field can be forced into a circular path.

× × × × ×

× × × × ×   × indicates that
             the field is directed
× × × × ×   into the page

× × × × ×
e⁻

Example
Calculate the magnitude of the magnetic force on an electron travelling at a speed of 3.60×10^4 m/s perpendicular to a magnetic field of 4.20 T.

Solution
$$F_m = qvB_\perp$$
$$= \left(1.60 \times 10^{-19}\ \text{C}\right)\left(3.60 \times 10^4\ \text{m/s}\right)\left(4.20\ \text{T}\right)$$
$$= 2.42 \times 10^{-14}\ \text{N}$$

Example

A conductor, 3.20×10^{-1} m in length, is placed in a magnetic field of 2.10×10^{-1} T. If it is assumed that the conductor is perpendicular to the magnetic field and the magnetic force acting on the conductor is 4.00×10^{-2} N, what is the current flowing through the conductor?

Solution

$$F_m = B_\perp Il$$
$$I = \frac{F_m}{B_\perp l}$$
$$= \frac{(4.00 \times 10^{-2} \text{ N})}{(2.10 \times 10^{-1} \text{ T})(3.20 \times 10^{-1} \text{ m})}$$
$$= 5.95 \times 10^{-1} \text{ A}$$

Example

Calculate the upward acceleration of an electron that is travelling east at a speed of 8.30×10^4 m/s through a magnetic field of 3.10×10^{-1} T that is directed south.

Solution

Find the magnetic force first.

$$F_m = B_\perp Il$$
$$= \left(1.60 \times 10^{-19} \text{ C}\right)\left(8.30 \times 10^4 \text{ m/s}\right)\left(3.10 \times 10^{-1} \text{ T}\right)$$
$$= 4.12 \times 10^{-15} \text{ N}$$
$$F = ma$$
$$a = \frac{F}{m}$$
$$= \frac{4.12 \times 10^{-15} \text{ N}}{9.11 \times 10^{-31} \text{ kg}}$$
$$= 4.52 \times 10^{15} \text{ m/s}^2$$
$$\vec{a} = 4.52 \times 10^{15} \text{ m/s}^2 \text{ up}$$

PRACTICE EXERCISES

Formulas: $F_m = B_\perp Il$ $F_m = qvB_\perp$

1. A proton travelling vertically at a speed of 2.10×10^5 m/s through a horizontal magnetic field experiences a magnetic force of 9.50×10^{-14} N. What is the magnitude of the magnetic field?

2. A copper wire ($l = 0.222$ m) carries conventional current of 0.960 A north through a magnetic field ($B = 7.50 \times 10^{-4}$ T) that is directed vertically upward. What is the magnitude and direction of the magnetic force acting on the wire?

3. Calculate the magnitude and the direction of the magnetic force on an electron travelling north at a speed of 3.52×10^5 m/s through a vertically upward magnetic field of 2.80×10^{-1} T.

4. Calculate the magnitude and the direction of the magnetic force on an alpha particle travelling south at a speed of 7.40×10^4 m/s through a vertically upward magnetic field of 5.50 T.

5. Calculate the magnitude and the direction of the magnetic field that produces a magnetic force of 1.70×10^{-14} N east on a proton that is travelling 1.90×10^4 m/s north through the magnetic field.

6. An electron experiences an upward force of 7.1×10^{-14} N when it is travelling 2.7×10^5 m/s south through a magnetic field. What is the magnitude and direction of the magnetic field?

7. Calculate the magnitude and the direction of the magnetic force on an alpha particle travelling upward at a speed of 2.11×10^5 m/s through a magnetic field that is directed down.

8. A wire in the armature of an electric motor is 2.50×10^{-1} m long and is perpendicular to a magnetic field of 5.00×10^{-1} T. Calculate the magnitude of the magnetic force on the wire when it carries a current of 3.60 A.

9. An electron is accelerated from rest by a potential difference of 1.70×10^3 V, and then enters a magnetic field of 2.50×10^{-1} T, moving perpendicular to it. What is the magnitude of the magnetic force acting on the electron?

10. An electron is accelerated by a potential difference and then travels perpendicular through a magnetic field of 7.20×10^{-1} T where it experiences a magnetic force of 4.1×10^{-13} N. If it is assumed that this electron starts from rest, through what potential difference is the electron accelerated?

11. Calculate the downward acceleration of an electron that is travelling horizontally at a speed of 6.20×10^5 m/s perpendicular to a horizontal magnetic field of 2.30×10^{-1} T.

12. A solenoid lies in a horizontal plane with a current balance, WXYZ, balanced horizontally in the solenoid core at points Z and W, as shown in the diagram below.

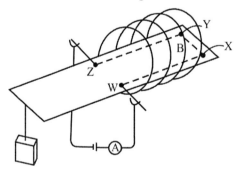

Sides WX and ZY of the current balance conductor are 7.10 cm. Side YX is 1.90 cm. A current of 6.00 A flows through the conductor on the current balance. If a mass of 1.76×10^{-2} kg is necessary to balance the current balance, what is the magnetic field strength in the solenoid?

Lesson 3   CATHODE RAYS

In the late 1800s, the electron was discovered by J.J. Thomson, who deflected fast-moving electrons by a magnetic field. This was done by investigating an electric discharge across a spark gap in a vacuum (or in gases at very low pressure).

CATHODE RAY TUBE (CRT)

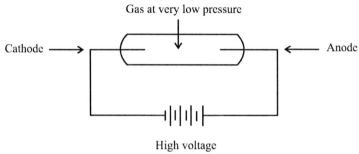

The electrodes of the CRT are connected to a source of high potential difference.

The term *cathode ray* is used because it was determined that the discharge originated at the negative electrode (cathode). This was determined because the tube glowed with greater intensity opposite the cathode as indicated in the diagram below.

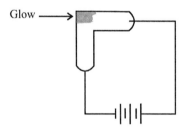

Over a few years, a number of scientists discovered different properties of the discharge that became known as the cathode ray.

J.J. Thomson determined that cathode rays were particles, and that they had a characteristic charge-to-mass (q/m) ratio. He measured this charge-to-mass ratio to be 1.76×10^{11} C/kg. This particle became known as the electron. The cathode ray was discovered to be a beam of electrons.

NOTES

J.J. Thomson determined the charge/mass ratio of the electron.

The cathode ray is a beam of electrons.

THOMSON EXPERIMENT

In Thomson's experiment, cathode rays pass through a magnetic field. The magnetic field was found to deflect the rays.

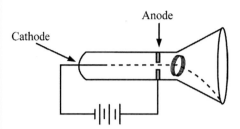

The anode is a circular disk with a hole in it. The electrons are accelerated between the cathode and the anode (this part of the tube can be called an electron gun or accelerator). Under high voltage, the electrons have high kinetic energy (high speed) when they reach the anode. A beam of electrons with high energy passes through the hole in the anode; it then passes through a magnetic field. The electrons may be deflected up or down by the magnetic field. The deflection is in an arc (part of a circle). The force that causes an object to move in a circle is called centripetal force. The formula for calculating centripetal force is:

Centripetal force is a force that causes an object to move in an arc or circle.

$$F_c = \frac{mv^2}{r}$$

m = mass
v = speed
r = radius of the circle (arc)

In this case, the force causing the electrons to deflect in an arc (circle) is the magnetic force (F_m). Therefore, $F_c = F_m$.

$$F_c = \frac{mv^2}{r} \text{ and } F_m = qvB_\perp \text{ ; but } F_c = F_m$$

Therefore, $qvB_\perp = \frac{mv^2}{r}$ or $qB_\perp = \frac{mv}{r}$

and $\frac{q}{m} = \frac{v}{B_\perp r}$

The charge-to-mass ratio that Thomson measured was q/m. The r and B in this formula can be measured, but the speed of the electron is difficult to determine. We can find the speed today by using:

$V = \frac{\Delta E}{q}$ to find the change in energy of the accelerated electron and

$E_k = \frac{1}{2}mv^2$ to find the speed

However, to use these equations, we need the mass and the charge of the electron. Thomson had neither. He found the speed by passing the electrons through both a magnetic field and an electric field.

The electric field and magnetic field were adjusted so that the magnetic and electric forces acting on the electrons were equal, but in opposite directions. In this case, the electrons travelled in a straight line (no deflection).

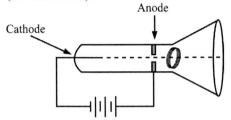

$$F_e = F_m$$
$$q|\vec{E}| = qvB_\perp$$

therefore, $v = \dfrac{|\vec{E}|}{B_\perp}$

Thomson obtained the speed of the electron as the ratio of the field strength. Now, with the speed of the electrons, he could return to:

$$F_c = F_m$$
$$qvB_\perp = \frac{mv^2}{r}$$
$$\frac{q}{m} = \frac{v}{B_\perp r}$$

and with v, B, and R, he could calculate the charge/mass ratio.

SUMMARY

Types of forces used in this section:

$\vec{F}_g$: $\quad F_g = mg$

$\vec{F}_e$: $\quad F_e = q|\vec{E}|$

$\vec{F}_m$: $\quad F_m = qvB_\perp$

$\vec{F}_c$: $\quad F_c = \dfrac{mv^2}{r}$

Thomson's method was to equate forces.

- When he used only a magnetic field, the electrons were deflected.

Deflection (magnetic field only)

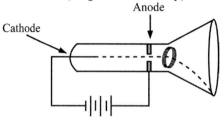

$$F_m = F_c$$
$$qvB_\perp = \frac{mv^2}{r}$$

- When he used both a magnetic field and an electric field, he balanced the forces so there was no deflection.

No deflection
(both a magnetic field and an electric field)

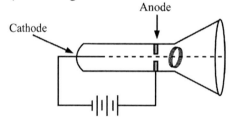

$$F_e = F_m$$
$$q \mid \bar{E} \mid = qvB_\perp$$
$$\therefore v = \frac{\mid \bar{E} \mid}{B_\perp}$$

Example

Charged particles are travelling horizontally at 3.60×10^6 m/s when they enter a vertical magnetic field of 7.10×10^{-1} T. If the radius of the arc of the deflected particles is 9.50×10^{-2} m, what is the charge-to-mass ratio of the particles?

Solution

$$F_m = F_c$$
$$qvB_\perp = \frac{mv^2}{r}$$
$$\frac{q}{m} = \frac{v}{B_\perp r}$$
$$= \frac{3.60 \times 10^6 \text{ m/s}}{(7.10 \times 10^{-1} \text{ T})(9.50 \times 10^{-2} \text{ m})}$$
$$= 5.34 \times 10^7 \text{ C/kg}$$

Example

What is the speed of an electron that passes through an electric field of 6.30×10^3 N/C and a magnetic field of 7.11×10^{-3} T undeflected? Assume the electric and magnetic fields are perpendicular to each other.

Solution

$$F_m = F_e$$
$$qvB_\perp = q\,|\bar{E}|$$
$$v = \frac{|\bar{E}|}{B_\perp}$$
$$= \frac{6.30 \times 10^3 \text{ N/C}}{7.11 \times 10^{-3} \text{ T}}$$
$$= 8.86 \times 10^5 \text{ m/s}$$

Example

An electron travelling vertically enters a horizontal magnetic field of 7.20×10^{-2} T. If the electron is deflected in an arc of radius 3.70×10^{-3} m, what is the kinetic energy of the electron?

Solution

$$F_m = F_c$$
$$qvB_\perp = \frac{mv^2}{r}$$
$$v = \frac{qB_\perp r}{m}$$
$$= \frac{(1.60 \times 10^{-19} \text{ C})(7.20 \times 10^{-2} \text{ T})(3.70 \times 10^{-3} \text{ m})}{9.11 \times 10^{-31} \text{ kg}}$$
$$= 4.68 \times 10^7 \text{ m/s}$$
$$E_k = \frac{1}{2}mv^2$$
$$= \frac{1}{2}(9.11 \times 10^{-31} \text{ kg})(4.68 \times 10^7 \text{ m/s})^2$$
$$= 9.97 \times 10^{-16} \text{ J}$$

PRACTICE EXERCISES

Formulas: You have to derive your own formulas by equating forces.

$$F_e = q\,|\bar{E}\,| \qquad\qquad F_c = \frac{mv^2}{r} \qquad\qquad F_m = qvB_\perp$$

1. An alpha particle travels through a magnetic field of 4.22×10^{-1} T perpendicular to the field. If the radius of the arc of the deflected particles is 1.50×10^{-3} m , what is the speed of the particles?

2. A proton travels through a magnetic field at a speed of 5.40×10^5 m/s perpendicular to the field. If the radius of the arc of the deflected proton is 7.20×10^{-3} m , what is the magnetic field strength?

3. Calculate the charge-to-mass ratio of a particle that is travelling 3.60×10^5 m/s and is deflected in an arc with a radius of 7.40×10^{-2} m as it travels through a perpendicular magnetic field of 6.10×10^{-1} T .

4. Alpha particles travel undeflected through magnetic and electric fields that are perpendicular to each other. The speed of the alpha particles is 7.80×10^5 m/s and the strength of the magnetic field is 2.20×10^{-1} T . If it is assumed that the alpha particles are travelling perpendicular to these fields, what is the strength of the electric field?

5. Positive charged particles travel undeflected through magnetic and electric fields that are perpendicular to each other. The magnetic field strength is 6.50×10^{-1} T and the strength of the electric field is 2.10×10^{5} N/C. If it is assumed the charged particles are travelling perpendicular to these fields, what is the speed of the charged particles?

6. Alpha particles travel through a magnetic field of 3.60×10^{-1} T and are deflected in an arc with a radius of 8.20×10^{-2} m. If it assumed that the alpha particles are travelling perpendicular to the field, what is the energy of each alpha particle?

7. In a CRT (cathode ray tube), electrons are accelerated from rest by a potential difference of 2.50×10^{3} V. What is the maximum speed of the electrons?

8. In a CRT, an electron reaches a maximum speed of 4.75×10^{7} m/s. If this electron is accelerated from rest, what is the potential difference across the tube?

9. In a CRT, electrons are accelerated from rest by a potential difference of 1.40×10^3 V. These electrons enter a magnetic field with a strength of 2.20×10^{-2} T. If it is assumed that the electrons are travelling perpendicular to the field, what is the radius of the arc of the deflected electrons?

10. Electrons are accelerated from rest in a CRT. These electrons now pass through a magnetic field of 1.40×10^{-2} T and through an electric field of 4.20×10^5 N/C. The fields are perpendicular to each other, and the electrons are not deflected. If it is assumed the electrons are travelling perpendicular to these fields, what is the potential difference across the CRT?

11. A negatively charged particle with a mass of 8.4×10^{-27} kg is travelling at a velocity of 5.6×10^5 m/s perpendicularly through a magnetic field of 2.8×10^{-1} T. If the radius of the path of the particle is 3.5 cm, how many excess electrons does this particle carry?

12. Alpha particles travel at a speed of 3.00×10^6 m/s through a magnetic field. If the magnetic field strength is 4.2×10^{-2} T, what is the radius of the path followed by the alpha particles when the magnetic field is parallel to the direction the alpha particles travel?

13. A proton moves through a 0.75 T magnetic field in a circle with a radius of 0.30 m. What is the rotational speed of this proton?

14. Electrons are accelerated from rest through a potential difference. These electrons are then deflected along an arc of radius 0.77 m when they travel through a 2.2×10^{-4} T magnetic field. What is the accelerating voltage?

15. An ion with a charge to mass ratio of 1.10×10^4 C/kg travels perpendicular to a magnetic field ($B = 9.10 \times 10^{-1}$ T) in a circular path ($r = 0.240$ m) . How long does it take the ion to complete one revolution?

Lesson 4 ELECTROMAGNETIC INDUCTION

Magnetic field out of
the plane of the page

Magnetic field into
the plane of the page

The process of producing
an induced emf in a
conductor by the use of a
magnetic field is
electromagnetic induction.

Oersted discovered that an electric current will produce a magnetic field. This led to the question, "Could a magnetic field produce an electric current?" Faraday and Henry independently discovered that a magnetic field could produce an electric current.

One way of producing an electric current through a conductor is to move a conducting rod through a magnetic field as shown in (2) below.

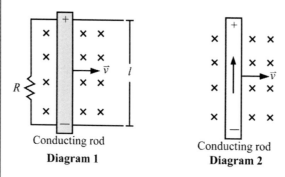

Conducting rod   Conducting rod
Diagram 1   **Diagram 2**

In this method, an emf is induced in the rod (i.e., the charges move to different ends of the rod, leaving one end positive and the other end negative). When this rod becomes part of an electric circuit as shown in (1) above, it will act like a battery (a voltage source), causing charge to move in the circuit.

The process of producing an induced emf in a conductor by use of a magnetic field is known as electromagnetic induction. When a conductor in which an emf is induced is part of a circuit, the induced emf will cause a charge to flow through the conductor. This flow of charge is called an induced current.

There are a number of ways that an electric current can be produced using a magnetic field. Faraday produced an electric current by using an induction coil as shown below.

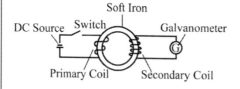

Faraday discovered that when the switch of his induction coil was being closed or was being opened, the galvanometer deflected, indicating a brief current through the secondary coil. It should be noted that when the switch remained closed or open, there was no deflection (i.e., no current was in secondary coil). It should also be noted that while the switch was being closed, the galvanometer deflected in one direction, but while the switch was being opened, the deflection was in the opposite direction.

In a similar demonstration, you can connect a galvanometer to an air core solenoid and move a magnet in and out of the solenoid.

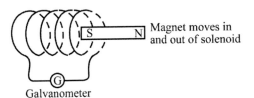

Magnet moves in and out of solenoid

Galvanometer

Again, it should be noted that an electric current is produced (induced) in the solenoid when it is moving relative to the magnetic field. When the magnet is pushed into the solenoid, the deflection is in one direction; but when the magnet is pulled out of the solenoid, the deflection is in the opposite direction. (It doesn't matter whether the magnet is moved while the solenoid is kept stationary or whether the solenoid is moved while the magnet remains stationary.)

The direction of the induced current can be found using Lenz's Law. Lenz's Law states that the induced current flows in a direction as to produce a magnetic force that opposes the direction of the applied force (motion).

Lenz's Law is really an application of the law of conservation of energy. Energy cannot be created. You cannot get electrical energy from nothing. It must come from somewhere.

Lenz's Law:
The induced current flows in a direction as to produce a magnetic force that opposes the direction of the applied force.

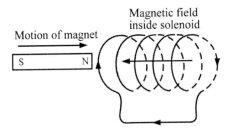

Magnetic field inside solenoid

Motion of magnet

For example, when a magnet is pushed into the coil, a current is induced in the coil. Lenz's Law tells us that the current flows in such a way that the magnetic field inside the coil opposes the magnetic field of the magnet. Therefore, the current in the coil must flow in the direction indicated in the diagram above. To see this, use your hand to indicate the direction of the magnetic field inside the coil. Your thumb points in the direction of the north-seeking pole (or pole that is equivalent to the north-seeking pole). Your fingers will point in the same direction that conventional current must flow through the windings of the coil. Note that this field opposes the magnetic field of the magnet. If this was not the case, that is, if the magnetic field in the coil did not oppose the magnetic field of the magnet, you would be getting energy from nothing.

Use the right-hand rule if you are considering positive flow (conventional current).

Use the left-hand rule if you are considering electron flow.

Remember, in this book, current is positive flow (conventional current). Therefore, use the right-hand rule.

Hand rules indicate the magnetic field inside the coil.

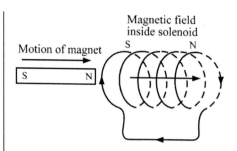

Magnetic field
inside solenoid

Motion of magnet

The above diagram must be wrong. If the current in the conductor is as indicated in the above diagram, the magnetic field would attract the magnet. That is, no work (no energy) would be required to slide the magnet into the coil, but electric energy would be produced. This is energy from nothing! Impossible!

Energy must be put into the system to get energy out.

The magnetic field produced by the induced current must oppose the magnetic field of the magnet producing the current—Lenz's Law.

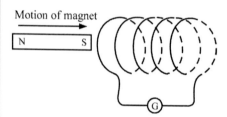

Motion of magnet

In what direction is the induced current through G in the diagram above?
Right

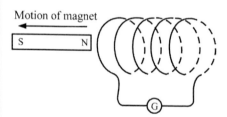

Motion of magnet

In what direction is the induced current through G in the diagram above?
Right

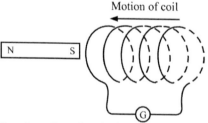

Motion of coil

In what direction is the induced current through G in the diagram above?
Right

In the same way, if a conducting rod is moved through a magnetic field, the magnetic field of an induced current opposes the magnetic field that produced the induced current (Lenz's Law).

Conducting rod

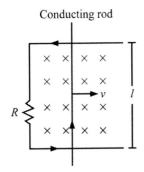

Direction of current
- palm opposite v (speed)
- fingers into page
- thumb will point up in direction of the current

Lenz's Law tells us that the magnetic force on the conducting rod must be in the opposite direction to its motion (opposite to v). If we use our right hand (opened) and point the palm opposite to v and our fingers in the direction of the magnetic field, our thumb will point in the direction of the induced current. In the diagram above, the current flows counter-clockwise through the circuit.

Conducting rod

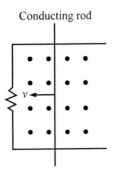

In what direction is the induced current flowing in the circuit above? Counter-clockwise.

Now let's turn our attention to the magnitude of this induced current. The magnitude of this current depends on the induced emf.

$$I = \frac{V}{R} = \frac{\mathcal{E}}{R} \text{ (Ohm's law)}$$

Before we discuss the magnitude of the induced current, we will introduce the concept of magnetic flux.

MAGNETIC FLUX

What is magnetic flux? Faraday explained magnetic flux in terms of magnetic field lines. The density of these lines represents the magnetic field strength.

The magnetic flux through a loop depends on the orientation (angle) of the loop and the magnetic field lines as well as the area of the loop.

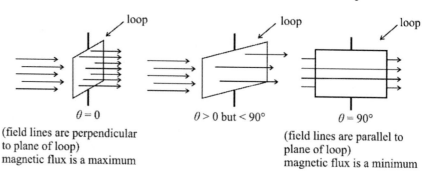

$\theta = 0$
(field lines are perpendicular to plane of loop)
magnetic flux is a maximum

$\theta > 0$ but $< 90°$

$\theta = 90°$
(field lines are parallel to plane of loop)
magnetic flux is a minimum

That is, the magnetic flux depends on the number of field lines that pass through the loop. We see that when the field lines are perpendicular to the plane of the loop, there will be more lines that pass through the loop. When the field lines are parallel to the plane of the loop, there are no lines that pass through the loop. This means that the magnetic flux depends on:

- the magnitude of the strength of the magnetic field, B (the greater the field strength, the greater the number of lines)
- the area of the loop, A (the greater the area of the loop, the greater the number of lines that pass through it)
- the orientation, θ (When the plane of the loop is perpendicular to the field, there is a maximum number of lines. When the plane of the loop is parallel to the field, there are no lines passing through the loop)

Magnetic Flux
Symbol: Φ
$\Phi = BA\cos\theta$
B = magnitude of the magnetic field strength (number of lines)
A = area of loop
θ = angle of field to a perpendicular to the plane of the loop

Units of magnetic flux are $T \cdot m^2$ or webers (Wb).

Faraday's explanation of how an induced current is produced by using a magnetic field involved a changing magnetic flux. He said that the faster the change, the greater the induced current. That is, the induced current depends on the rate of change of the magnetic flux. And, the induced current depends on the induced emf (Ohm's law).

$$\mathcal{E} = \frac{\Delta\Phi}{\Delta t}$$

On your data sheet, you will find the equation

$$\varepsilon = -N\frac{\Delta\Phi}{\Delta t}$$

The negative sign relates to Lenz's Law.

N is the number of loops in the coil (solenoid) that is moved through a magnetic field.

Note: It does not need to be a loop that moves (rotates) in the magnetic field. It can be a conductor cutting through a magnetic field as indicated earlier.

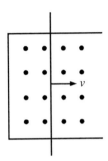

This equation, $\varepsilon = -N\frac{\Delta\Phi}{\Delta t}$ is an algebraic expression of Faraday's Law of Induction.

Faraday's Law of Induction is the basis of electric generators.

Example

A square loop of wire is perpendicular to a 1.50 T magnetic field. If each side of the wire is 2.10 cm, what is the magnetic flux through the loop?

Solution

$$\text{area} = l \times w$$
$$= \left(2.10\times10^{-2} \text{ m}\right)\left(2.10\times10^{-2} \text{ m}\right)$$
$$= 4.41\times10^{-4} \text{ m}^2$$
$$\Phi = BA\cos\theta$$
$$= \left(1.50 \text{ T}\right)\left(4.41\times10^{-4} \text{ m}^2\right)$$
$$= 6.62\times10^{-4} \text{ Wb}$$

NOTES

Example

A 1.80 cm diameter circular coil that contains 50 turns of wire is perpendicular to a 0.250 T magnetic field. If the magnetic field is reduced to zero in a time of 0.100 s, what is the average induced emf in the coil?

Solution

$$\begin{aligned}\text{area} &= \pi r^2 \\ &= \pi\left(0.900\times10^{-2}\ \text{m}\right)^2 \\ &= 2.54\times10^{-4}\ \text{m}^2\end{aligned}$$

$$\begin{aligned}\Phi &= B_{\text{f}}A\cos\theta \\ &= 0\end{aligned}$$

$$\begin{aligned}\Phi_{\text{o}} &= B_{\text{o}}A\cos\theta \\ &= (0.250\ \text{T})\left(2.54\times10^{-4}\ \text{m}^2\right) \\ &= 6.36\times10^{-5}\ \text{Wb}\end{aligned}$$

$$\begin{aligned}\Delta F &= \Phi_{\text{f}} - \Phi_{\text{o}} \\ &= 0 - 6.36\times10^{-5}\ \text{Wb} \\ &= -6.36\times10^{-5}\ \text{Wb}\end{aligned}$$

The minus sign tells us that the flux is decreasing.

$$\begin{aligned}\varepsilon &= -N\frac{\Delta\Phi}{\Delta t} \\ &= -50\left(\frac{-6.36\times10^{-5}\ \text{Wb}}{0.100\ \text{s}}\right) \\ &= 3.18\times10^{-2}\ \text{V}\end{aligned}$$

Remember, this sign relates to the direction of the current—do not worry about the signs here.

Example

A circular loop of wire (radius = 2.5 cm) is placed in a magnetic field (B = 0.02 T), as shown in the diagram below.

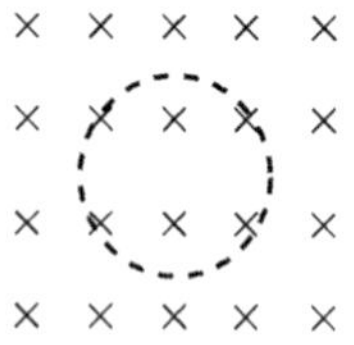

This field is then decreased to 0.010 T in 0.10 s.

a) What is the average emf induced in the loop?

Solution

$$\begin{aligned}\text{area} &= \pi r^2 \\ &= \pi\left(2.5\times10^{-2}\ \text{m}\right)^2 \\ &= 1.96\times10^{-3}\ \text{m}^2\end{aligned}$$

$$\Delta F = \Phi_f - \Phi_o$$
$$= (BA)_f - (BA)_o$$
$$= (0.010 \text{ T})(1.96 \times 10^{-3} \text{ m}^2) - (0.02 \text{ T})(1.96 \times 10^{-3} \text{ m}^2)$$
$$= -1.96 \times 10^{-5} \text{ Wb}$$

$$\mathcal{E} = -N \frac{\Delta\Phi}{\Delta t}$$
$$= -\left(\frac{-1.96 \times 10^{-5} \text{ Wb}}{0.10 \text{ s}} \right)$$
$$= 1.96 \times 10^{-4} \text{ V}$$
$$= 2.0 \times 10^{-4} \text{ V}$$

b) What is the direction of the current through the loop?

Solution
Use Lenz's Law—the induced current through the loop produces a magnetic flux through the loop to oppose the change in the magnetic flux caused by the external magnetic flux.

In this problem, we are decreasing the magnetic flux into the page. Therefore, the current in the loop will be in a direction as to produce a magnetic flux into the page.

Use the right hand rule—point thumb into the page. The direction of the induced current in the loop will be the direction that your fingers curl around your thumb.

Conventional current is clockwise.

PRACTICE EXERCISES

Formulas: $\Phi = BA\cos\theta$ $\varepsilon = -N\dfrac{\Delta\Phi}{\Delta t}$

1. A magnetic field $\left(B = 3.2\times10^{-3}\ \text{T}\right)$ passes perpendicular through a circular loop of wire $\left(\text{radius} = 5.0\ \text{cm}\right)$. What is the magnetic flux through the loop?

2. A circular coil with 200 turns and a radius of 6.0 cm is rotated in a uniform magnetic field $\left(B = 3.6\times10^{-4}\ \text{T}\right)$. At $t = 0$, the coil is perpendicular to the field, and at $t = 0.015$ s, the coil is parallel to the field. What is the average emf induced in the coil?

3. A square-shaped piece of wire with an area of $2.5\times10^{-3}\ \text{m}^2$ is perpendicular to a uniform magnetic field $\left(B = 2.2\times10^{-2}\ \text{T}\right)$ as shown in diagram (a) below.

Diagram a   Diagram b

area = 2.5 × 10⁻³ m²   collapsed (area = 0)

If the square collapses in a time of 0.100 s, as shown in diagram (b) above, what is the average induced emf as it collapses, and what is the direction of the induced current? (Remember to use conventional current.)

4. Find the average emf induced in a circular coil with 50 turns and a radius of 0.050 m if the magnetic flux through the loops is changing at a rate of 15 Wb/s?

5. A square-shaped coil with 100 turns (area of each square loop = 4.0×10^{-3} m^2) is perpendicular to a uniform magnetic field. When the coil is rotated through 90° in 0.12 s, the average induced emf is 0.92 V. What is the magnetic field strength?

6. A circular coil with 10 turns and a diameter of 25 cm is placed perpendicular to a uniform magnetic field $\left(B = 2.7 \times 10^{-3} \text{ T}\right)$. If the direction of the magnetic field is reversed in 0.30 s, what is the average emf induced in the coil?

7. A magnet is quickly removed from a circular coil (25 turns, area = 5.0×10^{-3} m^2). This changes the magnetic field within the coil at a rate of 0.40 T/s. What is the average emf induced in the coil?

8. A square-shaped piece of wire $\left(\text{area} = 7.2 = 10^3 \text{ m}^2\right)$, as shown in the diagram below, has a resistance of 12.0 Ω.

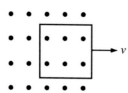

Assume that the magnetic field drops uniformly from 1.6 T to 0 T in 0.050 s as the loop is pulled from the magnetic field.

a) What is the average emf induced in the loop?

b) What is the current induced in the loop?

c) What is the direction of the electron flow in the loop?

9. A square-shaped piece of wire (4.0 cm per side), as shown in the diagram below, is placed in a magnetic field $(B = 0.20 \text{ T})$.

The magnetic field is increased to 0.50 T in 0.30 s.

a) Find the current through the loop if the resistance of the loop is 2.0 Ω.

b) Find the direction of the electron flow through the loop.

Lesson 5 ELECTRIC GENERATOR

Electric generators are an application of interactions between magnetic fields.

An electric generator is a device that converts mechanical energy into electrical energy. It makes use of the principle of electromagnetic induction. A loop of wire (actually a number of loops) is rotated through a magnetic field. This changes the magnetic flux, which induces an emf, which in turn induces a current to flow. In a sense, a generator works opposite to the electric motor. In a motor, a current-carrying conductor passes through a magnetic field. The interaction between magnetic fields causes the loop to rotate.

In a generator, again, there is a loop of wire, but now this loop is mechanically rotated in a magnetic field. This produces (induces) a current in the loop—electromagnetic induction.

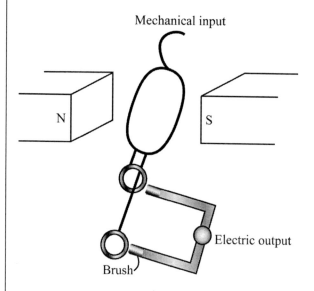

Motor: electrical energy to mechanical energy
Generator: mechanical energy to electrical energy

Energy from wind or falling water can be used to rotate the loop.

The generator described above is known as an AC generator, because the current will alternate back and forth. The alternator in a car is an example of an AC generator.

SUMMARY

- We have used Lenz's Law to determine the direction of the induced current through a conductor.
- We have used Faraday's Law of magnetic induction to determine the magnitude of the emf produced by an electric generator (and Ohm's law to determine the current).

BACK EMF

In the electric motor, there are loops of wire that are rotating in a magnetic field. These loops (armature) rotate because of the interactions of magnetic fields. But, no matter why the loops (armature) rotate, there is an emf induced in the wire loops and, therefore, an induced current.

The direction of the induced emf will oppose the voltage across the motor—this is Lenz's Law. The emf that is induced in this way is called the back emf. It is called the back emf because the induced emf is always in the opposite direction to the voltage applied across the motor.

When a motor is first turned on in your home, you might notice that the lights dim for an instant. This is because when the motor is first turned on, the loops are not rotating, and if they are not rotating, there is no induced back emf. As the motor very quickly gains speed, the induced back emf builds very quickly. This means that when the motor is first turned on, the only voltage causing the electrons to move in the loops is the voltage applied across the motor. But, as the loops start to rotate, the induced back emf opposes the voltage across the motor. This will lower the voltage in the wire loop circuit; if we apply Ohm's law, it lowers the current drawn by the motor.

By the time the motor reaches its operating speed, the current drawn by the motor has decreased. When there is a lot of current drawn by the motor, it takes away from other circuits in our homes—therefore, the lights dim initially when the motor is turned on.

Formula: $V_{back} = \varepsilon - Ir$

where V_{back} = back emf

ε = emf supplied by power source

I = current through the motor when it reaches full speed

r = resistance of motor

Example

A 120 V motor draws 10.0 A when it reaches its full operating speed. If the armature of this motor has a resistance of 5.2 Ω, what is the back emf when it reaches its full operating speed?

Solution

$$V_{back} = \varepsilon - Ir$$
$$= 120 \text{ V} - (10.0 \text{ A})(5.2 \text{ } \Omega)$$
$$= 120 \text{ V} - 52 \text{ V}$$
$$= 68 \text{ V}$$

Example

A 120 V motor draws 12.0 A when the motor is operating at full speed. If the armature of this motor has a resistance of 6.0 Ω, what is

a) the current when the motor is initially turned on (remember, no back emf)?

Solution
Initially
$$V_{back} = 0$$
$$V_{back} = \mathcal{E} - Ir$$
$$0 = 120 \text{ V} - I(6.0 \text{ Ω})$$
$$I = \frac{120 \text{ V}}{6.0 \text{ Ω}}$$
$$= 20 \text{ A}$$

b) the back emf when the armature reaches its full operating speed?

Solution
$$V_{back} = \mathcal{E} - Ir$$
$$= 120 \text{ V} - (12.0 \text{ A})(6.0 \text{ Ω})$$
$$= 120 \text{ V} - 72 \text{ V}$$
$$= 48 \text{ V}$$

Example

A 120 V motor draws 3.50 A when it reaches its full operating speed. If it draws 15.0 A when it is initially turned on, what is

a) the resistance of the armature?

Solution
$$V_{back} = \mathcal{E} - Ir$$
$$r = \frac{\mathcal{E} - V_{back}}{I}$$
$$r = \frac{120 \text{ V} - 0}{15.0 \text{ A}}$$
$$= \frac{120 \text{ V}}{15.0 \text{ A}}$$
$$= 8.00 \text{ Ω}$$

When the motor is initially turned on, the $V_{back} = 0$.

b) the back emf when it reaches its full operating speed?

Solution
$$V_{back} = \varepsilon - Ir$$
$$= 120 \text{ V} - (3.50 \text{ A})(8.00 \text{ Ω})$$
$$= 120 \text{ V} - 28 \text{ V}$$
$$= 92 \text{ V}$$

PRACTICE EXERCISES

Formula: $V_{back} = \varepsilon - Ir$

1. A 120 V DC motor draws 12.0 A when it reaches its full operating speed. If the resistance of the armature of this motor is 6.0 Ω, what is the back emf when it reaches its full operating speed?

2. A 120 V motor draws 15.0 A when it reaches its full operating speed and 40.0 A when it is initially turned on. What is the

   a) resistance of the armature?

   b) back emf when it reaches its full operating speed?

3. A 120 V motor draws 9.0 A when it reaches its full operating speed. If the resistance of the armature is 5.0 Ω, what is the

   a) back emf when the motor is operating at full speed?

   b) back emf when the motor is initially turned on?

   c) current when the motor is initially turned on?

4. The armature of a 120 V motor slows down because of an increased load (for example, an electric lawnmower enters thick, tall grass). The resistance of the armature is 6.0 Ω, and the current drawn by the motor when operating at full speed is 3.6 A. The current drawn by the motor when the increased load is applied is 8.4 A.

   a) Explain why the motor (armature) gets hotter when the increased load slows it down.

   b) Explain why the current through the armature increases when the load is increased.

   c) What is the back emf when the motor is operating at full speed?

   d) slowed down because of the increased load?

5. The back emf in a motor is 90.0V when the armature of the motor is turning at 1 000 rev/min. What is the back emf in the same motor when the motor is turning 500 rev/min?

6. The current drawn by a 120 V motor when the motor is turned on is 10.0 A and 3.0 A when it is operating at its full speed.

a) What is the resistance of the armature?

b) What is the back emf when the motor is operating at full speed?

Lesson 6   EMF CONTINUED

As we have said, it is not only a loop of wire that is rotated in a magnetic field that produces an induced emf; a straight conductor that is moved through a magnetic field will also induce an emf. When we are dealing with a straight conductor, it is more convenient to use the formula $\mathcal{E} = B_\perp lv$ to find the emf.

$\mathcal{E}$ = emf

B = magnitude of the magnetic field strength

l = length of the conductor

v = speed of the conductor

To return to problem 5 in the previous assignment, we could use $\mathcal{E} = B_\perp lv$ to see that as the speed is halved, the emf is halved.

Derivation of $\varepsilon = B_\perp lv$ (Method 1)

To derive this equation, we can use the concept of magnetic flux.

Magnetic flux

Symbol: Φ

Definition: $\Phi = B_\perp A$

where $B_\perp$ = magnetic field component perpendicular to the conductor

A = area through which the magnetic field passes

Units: $T \cdot m^2$ or   weber (Wb)

Faraday's Law of Induction: The induced emf is proportional to the rate of change in the magnetic flux.

$$\varepsilon = \frac{\Delta \Phi}{\Delta t}$$

Now let's return to our circuit:

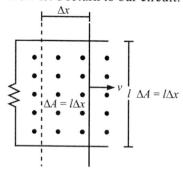

Change in magnetic flux: $\Delta F = B_\perp l \Delta x$

Rate of change in magnetic flux:

$$\frac{\Delta \Phi}{\Delta t} = \frac{B_\perp l \Delta x}{\Delta t}$$

but $v = \dfrac{\Delta x}{\Delta t}$

Remember:

$\mathcal{E} = V$

if there is no current flowing.

$$\therefore \frac{\Delta \Phi}{\Delta t} = B_\perp l v$$

or $\mathcal{E} = B_\perp l v$

Derivation of $\mathcal{E} = B_\perp l v$ (Method 2)

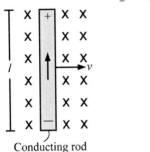

Conducting rod

Remember:
$$\mathcal{E} = V$$
if there is no current.

When a conducting rod is moved through a magnetic field, the charge in the rod experiences a magnetic force.

$$F_m = qvB_\perp$$

This charge would move to the upper end of the rod, leaving the top end positive. Because of the difference in charge between the ends of this rod, there is a potential difference (induced voltage). When the charge was forced through this rod, work was done.

$W = Fd$
or $\Delta E = Fl = F_m l$ (l = length of conductor)

But: $F_m = qvB_\perp$
and $\Delta E = qV$

$\therefore qV = qvB_\perp l$
$\quad V = B_\perp l v$
or $\mathcal{E} = B_\perp l v$

Example

A conducting rod 25.0 cm long moves perpendicular to a magnetic field ($B = 0.20$ T) at a speed of 1.0 m/s. Calculate the induced emf in the rod.

Solution
$\varepsilon = B_\perp l v$
$\quad = (0.20 \text{ T})(25.0 \times 10^{-2} \text{ m})(1.0 \text{ m/s})$
$\quad = 5.0 \times 10^{-2} \text{ V}$

Example

The conducting rod in the diagram below is 15 cm long and is moving at a speed of 2.0 m/s perpendicularly to a 0.30 T magnetic field.

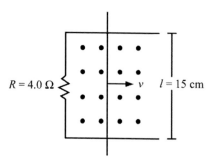

If the resistance in the circuit is 4.0 Ω, what is the magnitude and direction of the conventional current through the circuit?

Solution

$\mathcal{E} = B_\perp lv$

$\quad = (0.30 \text{ T})(15\times10^{-2} \text{ m})(2.0 \text{ m/s})$

$\quad = 9.0\times10^{-2} \text{ V}$

$I = \dfrac{\mathcal{E}}{R}$

$\quad = \dfrac{9.0\times10^{-2} \text{ V}}{4.0 \text{ } \Omega}$

$\quad = 2.3\times10^{-2} \text{ A clockwise}$

PRACTICE EXERCISES

Formula: $\mathcal{E} = B_{\perp} l v$

1. A conducting rod 0.35 m long moves perpendicular to a magnetic field $(B = 0.75 \text{ T})$ at a speed of 1.5 m/s. Calculate the induced emf in the rod.

2. A conducting rod 0.28 m long moves perpendicular to a magnetic field at a speed of 0.80 m/s. If the induced emf is 0.075 V, what is the magnitude of the magnetic field?

3. A conducting rod is 22.0 cm long. It is moving at a speed of 1.25 m/s perpendicular to a 0.150 T magnetic field.

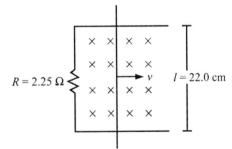

If the resistance in the circuit is 2.25 Ω, what is the magnitude and direction of the current through the circuit?

385

4. The conducting rod in the diagram below is 15 cm long and is moving at a speed of 0.95 m/s perpendicular to the magnetic field.

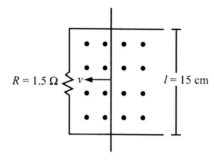

If the resistance in the circuit is 1.5 Ω and a current of 5.6×10^{-2} A is induced in the circuit,

a) what is the magnitude of the magnetic field?

b) what is the direction of the induced current?

5. The conducting rod in the diagram below is 30.0 cm long and is moved perpendicular to a 0.950 T magnetic field.

If the resistance in the circuit is 3.25 Ω, what force is required to move the rod at a constant speed of 1.50 m/s?

6. A plane with a wing span of 6.25 m is flying horizontally at a speed of 95.0 m/s. Given that the vertical component of Earth's magnetic field is 4.70×10^{-6} T, what is the induced emf between the tips of the wings?

7. The conducting rod in the diagram below is 30.0 cm long and is moving at a speed of 3.00 m/s perpendicular to a 0.600 T magnetic field.

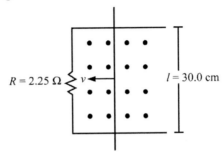

$R = 2.25\ \Omega$ v $l = 30.0$ cm

If the resistance in the circuit is 2.25 Ω, what is the electric energy dissipated in the resistor in 15.0 s?

8. The conducting rod in the diagram below is 1.2 m long and is moving at a speed of 2.5 m/s perpendicular to a 0.75 T magnetic field.

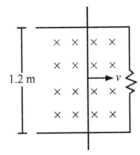

1.2 m v

If the current in the circuit is 0.45 A, what is the resistance in the circuit?

9. The conducting rod in the diagram below is 1.0 m long. It is moved at a speed of 3.0 m/s perpendicular to a 0.95 T magnetic field.

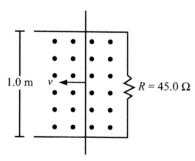

If the resistance in the circuit is 45.0 Ω, how much work is done against the magnetic field in 1.0×10^{-2} s ?

10. The conducting rod in the diagram below is 0.50 m long. It is moved at a constant speed perpendicular to a 0.65 T magnetic field.

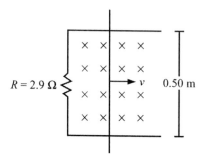

If the resistance in the circuit is 2.9 Ω and the induced current is 5.2×10^{-2} A , what is the speed of the conducting rod?

11. A rectangular piece of wire is moved at a speed of 1.80 m/s perpendicular to a 1.30 T magnetic field, as shown below.

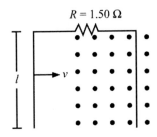

If the length of the side moving perpendicular to the field is 0.625 m and the resistance in the circuit is 1.50 Ω,

a) what is the induced current?

b) what is the direction of the current?

12. A rectangular piece of wire wound 5 times is moved at a speed of 2.7 m/s perpendicular to a 1.1 T magnetic field as shown below.

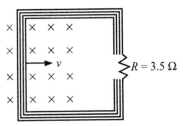

If the length of the side of the wire moving perpendicular to the field is 0.18 m and the resistance in the circuit is 3.5 Ω,

a) what is the induced current?

b) what is the direction of the current?

Lesson 7 TRANSFORMERS (INDUCTION COIL)

Another important application of electromagnetic induction is the transformer. A transformer is a device that is used to convert a potential difference to a higher or lower value.

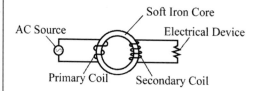

A transformer consists of a primary coil and a secondary coil. The primary coil is connected to either an AC source (as shown above) or to a DC source; however, if it is connected to a DC source, the current must fluctuate. This can be done by opening and closing a switch. Note that the transformer is similar to Faraday's apparatus.

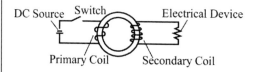

The electrical device in the diagrams above could be, for example, the picture tube of a TV, a spark plug in a car, or an electric circuit in your home.

When a transformer is used to increase the potential difference, it is called a step-up transformer. In a step-up transformer, the secondary coil has more turns than the primary coil. A step-up transformer is used to convert 120 V household voltage to 15 000 V in your TV to activate the picture tube.

When a transformer is used to decrease the potential difference, it is called a step-down transformer. In a step-down transformer, the secondary coil has fewer turns than the primary coil. A step-down transformer is used by companies that supply electric energy. High voltages are required to transport this energy; however, before it is fed into homes, it must be reduced. Step-down transformers are used to reduce the voltage before it enters homes. You might also use a step-down transformer to charge batteries.

The purpose of the alternating current or the fluctuating current is to produce a magnetic field in the soft iron. Because the current in the primary coil is changing, this magnetic field is changing. The changing magnetic field in the soft iron induces an AC current in the secondary coil.

Although a transformer will increase or decrease the voltage, energy is conserved—you cannot get something for nothing. Therefore, energy must be conserved in a transformer. To understand this, let's consider the transformer equation:

$$\frac{V_p}{V_s} = \frac{N_p}{N_s}$$

(ratio of the voltages = ratio of the number of turns)

The energy (or power) output must equal the energy (or power) input— Law of Conservation of Energy.

That is, $I_p V_p = I_s V_s$ (remember $P = IV$)

$$\frac{I_s}{I_p} = \frac{N_p}{N_s}$$

or $\dfrac{I_s}{I_p} = \dfrac{V_p}{V_s} = \dfrac{N_p}{N_s}$

From this, we see that as the number of turns increases, the voltage increases but the current decreases.

In the problems that follow, we will assume that the transformers are ideal. That is, no electrical energy is converted to other forms of energy. The efficiency of transformers is usually very high.

Example

A step-up transformer is used to convert 1.20×10^2 V to 1.50×10^4 V. If the primary coil has 24 turns, how many turns does the secondary coil have?

Solutions

$$\frac{V_p}{V_s} = \frac{N_p}{N_s}$$

$$\frac{1.20 \times 10^2 \text{ V}}{1.50 \times 10^4 \text{ V}} = \frac{24}{N_s}$$

$$N_s = 3\ 000$$

NOTES

Example

A step-up transformer has 1.00×10^3 turns on its primary coil and 1.00×10^5 turns on its secondary coil. If the transformer is connected to a 1.20×10^2 V power line, what is the step-up voltage?

Solution

$$\frac{V_p}{V_s} = \frac{N_p}{N_s}$$

$$\frac{1.20 \times 10^2 \text{ V}}{V_s} = \frac{1.00 \times 10^3}{1.00 \times 10^5}$$

$$V_s = 1.20 \times 10^4 \text{ V}$$

Example

A step-down transformer reduces the voltage from 1.20×10^2 V to 12.0 V. If the primary coil has 5.00×10^2 turns and draws 3.00×10^{-2} A,

a) what is the power delivered to the secondary coil?

Solution

$$P_p = I_p V_p$$
$$= \left(3.00 \times 10^{-2} \text{ A}\right)\left(1.20 \times 10^2 \text{ V}\right)$$
$$= 3.60 \text{ W}$$
$$P_s = P_p$$
$$= 3.60 \text{ W}$$

b) what is the current in the secondary coil?

Solution

$$\frac{I_s}{I_p} = \frac{V_p}{V_s}$$

$$\frac{I_s}{3.00 \times 10^{-2} \text{ A}} = \frac{1.20 \times 10^2 \text{ V}}{12.0 \text{ V}}$$

$$I_s = 0.300 \text{ A}$$

or

$$P_s = I_s V_s$$
$$I_s = \frac{3.60 \text{ W}}{12.0 \text{ V}}$$
$$= 0.300 \text{ A}$$

PRACTICE EXERCISES

Formula: $$\frac{I_s}{I_p} = \frac{V_p}{V_s} = \frac{N_p}{N_s}$$

1. Currents of 0.25 A and 0.95 A flow through the primary and secondary coils of a transformer, respectively. If there are 1.0×10^3 turns in the primary coil, how many turns are in the secondary coil?

2. A step-down transformer has coils of 1.20×10^3 and 1.50×10^2 turns. If the transformer is connected to a 1.20×10^2 V power line and the current in the secondary coil is 5.00 A, what is the current in the primary coil?

3. Near Franco's home, the voltage of the power line is 3.6×10^3 V. The transformer between his home and the line reduces this voltage to 1.20×10^2 V. If the transformer is to deliver 2.4×10^3 J of energy each second to Franco's home, what is the current in

   a) the primary coil?

   b) the secondary coil?

4. A step-down transformer $\left(N_p = 1.50 \times 10^2, N_s = 25\right)$ is connected to a 1.20×10^2 V primary line. If there is a 75 Ω electrical device placed in the secondary circuit, what is the current in the primary coil?

5. If the voltage and current of the primary coil is 1.20×10^2 V and 3.0 A, what is the power delivered to the secondary coil?

6. If the power delivered to the secondary coil of a step-up transformer is 50.0 W from a 1.20×10^2 V power line, what is the current in the primary coil?

7. A transformer $\left(N_p = 5.5 \times 10^2, N_s = 36\right)$ is connected to a 1.20×10^2 V power line. If the current in the primary coil is 1.0 A, what is the power in the secondary coil?

8. A 1.0×10^2 W transformer $\left(N_s = 1.5 \times 10^3\right)$ has an input voltage of 9.0 V and an output current of 0.65 A. How many turns are there in the primary coil?

Lesson 8 POWER TRANSMISSION

One major application of transformers is in the transmission of electric power. At the generator, there are step-up transformers that will increase the voltage to a very high voltage (100 000 V to 500 000 V) and at the user end, before the electric power enters our homes and other buildings, there are step-down transformers that reduce the voltage to 120 V. Why is electric power transmitted at very high voltages? There are two reasons for this. Let's review the power equations first.

$$P = IV$$
$$P = I^2R$$
$$P = \frac{V^2}{R}$$

$P = IV$ tells us that the power delivered through a line is the product of the current flowing and the voltage.

$P = I^2R$ and $P = \dfrac{V^2}{R}$ introduce the concept of resistance. If there is resistance, there is heat produced—there is electric energy and, therefore, electric power lost.

$P = I^2R$ allows us to determine this power loss. $P = \dfrac{V^2}{R}$ allows us to calculate the power that flows through the line—the power delivered.

Now, let's return to the power transmitted through the lines. In this transmission, it is important to keep the power loss to a minimum. Now remember, $P = I^2R$. There is not a lot that can be done to lower the resistance significantly; but we see from the equation that if electric power is delivered using low current, the power loss is lower than if it were delivered at a high current. For example, if the electric current were reduced by a factor of 100, the energy loss would be reduced by a factor of $(100)^2$ or 10 000 times. But in order to reduce the current, the voltage is increased by using a step-up transformer.

There is a second reason why electric power is transmitted at high voltages. Let's say that transformers were not used and electric power was transmitted at 120 V. Again, remember we cannot do a lot to change the resistance of the line. Sure we can make it bigger (greater cross-sectional area), but this makes it heavier and therefore harder to support. It also makes it more expensive (more material). There is a limit as to the amount of current that flows through a wire safely. In the wires in our homes, this limit is approximately 20 A to 25 A.

NOTES

Suppose each one of us were to use 100 W (one 100 W light bulb), the current through the transmission lines would be (assuming voltage through the lines is 120 V):

$$P = IV$$

$$I = \frac{P}{V} = \frac{100 \text{ W}}{120 \text{ V}} = 0.833 \text{ A}$$

This does not seem too bad; but, there are communities with a lot of people. Let's use a community that has 100 000 people, each using electric energy at a rate of 100 W. This community would require $0.833 \text{ A} \times 100\ 000 = 83\ 300 \text{ A}$

Now, if each line carried 25 A, this community would require

$$\frac{83\ 300 \text{ A}}{25 \text{ A}} = 3\ 332 \text{ lines}$$

This is not practical.

Therefore, power is transmitted through power lines at a very high voltage and with very low current.

PRACTICE TEST

1. An electric current is induced in a circuit containing an air core solenoid, as shown below, by suddenly pushing a magnet into the coil.

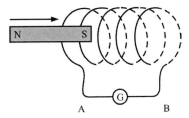

   Which of the following statements is true?

   i)   A magnetic field is induced in the solenoid to attract the magnet.
   ii) The current (conventional) will flow from A to B through G.

   A. Both i and ii are true   **B.** Neither i nor ii is true

   C. Only i is true   **D.** Only ii is true

2. Which of the following statements about magnetic fields is true?

   i)   They can be produced by moving protons.
   ii) They are vector fields.
   iii) They can be expressed in N/A·m.

   A. i and ii only   **B.** i and iii only

   C. ii and iii only   **D.** i, ii, and iii

3. A "step-up" transformer has ten turns on its secondary coil to every one turn on its primary coil. Which of the following statements is true?

   i)   The power dissipated each minute by the secondary coil is ten times that dissipated by the primary coil.
   ii) The current in the secondary coil is ten times that of the primary coil.

   A. Both i and ii are true   **B.** Neither i nor ii is true

   C. Only i is true   **D.** Only ii is true

4. A "step-up" transformer can be used to increase

   A. voltage only

   B. voltage and current

   C. voltage and the power dissipated

   D. voltage, current, and the power dissipated

5. If a transformer is to operate from a DC source rather than an AC source, what additional apparatus is required?

   A. A spark gap in the primary circuit   **B.** A spark gap in the secondary circuit

   C. A switch in the primary circuit   **D.** A switch in the secondary circuit

6. Lenz's Law is an example of conservation of

    A. electric charges   **B.** electric energy

    C. energy   **D.** forces

7. A conducting rod AB decelerates from 3.0 m/s to 1.0 m/s as it slides to the right along the conducting rails through a magnetic field as shown in the diagram. Which of the following statements is true concerning the induced current (conventional) through the described circuit?

    A. The current will increase in a clockwise direction.

    B. The current will decrease in a clockwise direction.

    C. The current will increase in a counter-clockwise direction.

    D. The current will decrease in a counter-clockwise direction.

8. If an alpha particle is travelling east through a magnetic field that is directed west, what is the direction of the magnetic force on the alpha particle?

    A. Up   **B.** Down

    C. No force   **D.** North

9. A proton is travelling east through Earth's magnetic field at the equator. What is the direction of the magnetic force on the proton?

    A. Up   **B.** Down

    C. No force   **D.** North

10. Electrons are induced to flow counter-clockwise through a conducting loop that is placed on your desk using a downward magnetic field. Which of the following statements is true concerning the magnetic field?

    i)   A constant magnetic field is directed into the loop.
    ii) An increasing magnetic field is directed into the loop.
    iii) A decreasing magnetic field is directed into the loop.

    A. I only   **B.** II only

    C. III only   **D.** None are true

11. A conductor carries electrons north. What is the direction of the magnetic field due to this conductor at a distance of 0.50 cm above this conductor?

    A. East   **B.** West

    C. Up   **D.** Down

12. Voltage is induced in the conducting loop by rotating it clockwise. If the period of rotation was cut in half, the induced voltage would

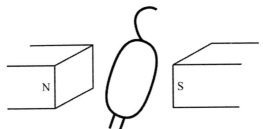

A. halve

B. remain the same

C. double

D. quadruple

13. Mechanical energy can be converted to electric energy by a
  i) generator
  ii) motor
  iii) transformer

A. i only

B. ii only

C. i and iii only

D. ii and III only

14. Electric energy can be converted to mechanical energy by a
  i) generator
  ii) motor
  iii) transformer

A. i only

B. ii only

C. i and iii only

D. ii and iii only

15. The principle of electromagnetic induction is used in the operation of a
  i) generator
  ii) motor
  iii) transformer

A. i only

B. iii only

C. i and ii only

D. i and iii only

16. The magnetic force acting on a charged particle that is travelling through a perpendicular magnetic field is F. What is the magnetic force on this particle if both its mass and velocity are halved?

A. $F/4$

B. $F/2$

C. $2F$

D. $4F$

17. In the diagram, the north pole of the magnet is quickly moved down into the conducting loop and then is quickly pulled back up out of the conducting loop. As viewed from above, the induced current in the loop is

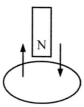

   A. always clockwise   **B.** always counter-clockwise

   C. first clockwise, then counter-clockwise   **D.** first counter-clockwise, then clockwise

18. The charge-to-mass ratio of the electron was determined partially by balancing the

   A. gravitational and electric forces

   B. gravitational and magnetic forces

   C. electric and magnetic forces

   D. gravitational, electric, and magnetic forces

19. Cathode rays are a beam of

   A. alpha particles   **B.** electrons

   C. photons   **D.** protons

20. A student makes the following statements about cathode rays.

   i) Cathode rays can be deflected by electric fields.
   ii) Cathode rays can be deflected by magnetic fields.
   iii) Cathode rays travel at a speed of 3.00×10^8 m/s through a vacuum.

   The student is correct about

   A. Statements i and ii only   **B.** Statements i, ii, and iii

   C. Statement i only   **D.** Statement ii only

21. Charged particles are deflected by a magnetic field when they travel perpendicular to the field. This deflection can be increased by

   i) decreasing the mass of the particles
   ii) increasing the charge on the particles
   iii) increasing the mass of the particles

   A. I only   **B.** II only

   C. I and II only   **D.** II and III only

22. Electrons pass without deflection through superimposed electric and magnetic fields. Knowing only the strength of each field, we could calculate the

   A. speed of electrons   **B.** charge of an electron

   C. mass of an electron   **D.** charge-to-mass ratio of an electron

Student Notes and Problems

ANSWERS AND SOLUTIONS

CASTLE ROCK

RESEARCH CORP

VECTOR KINEMATICS— PART A

Lesson 1—Introduction to Kinematics

PRACTICE EXERCISES
ANSWERS AND SOLUTIONS

---

1. Total distance $d = 275 \text{ m} + 425 \text{ m} = 700 \text{ m}$
    Direction does not matter in the case of the scalar distance.

3. Distance travelled does not involve the directions.
    $d = 115 \text{ m} + 125 \text{ m} + 115 \text{ m} + 125 \text{ m}$
    $= 480 \text{ m}$

5. Average speed is a measure of the rate that distance was covered in some period of time (t). In the case of speed and distance, direction does not apply.
    total distance $= d$
    $= 11 \text{ m} + 25 \text{ m}$
    $= 36 \text{ m}$

    average speed $= \dfrac{\text{total distance}}{\text{total time}}$
    $= \dfrac{d}{t}$
    $= \dfrac{36 \text{ m}}{52 \text{ s}}$
    $= 0.69 \text{ m/s}$

Lesson 2—Uniform Motion

PRACTICE EXERCISES
ANSWERS AND SOLUTIONS

---

1. Consider west as the positive direction.
    $\vec{v} = \dfrac{\vec{d}}{t}$
    $= \dfrac{1.00 \times 10^2 \text{ m}}{11.2 \text{ s}}$
    $= 8.93 \text{ m/s}$ or 8.93 m/s west

3. Consider west as the positive direction.
    $\vec{v} = \dfrac{\vec{d}}{t}$
    $\vec{d} = \vec{v}t$
    $= (10.0 \text{ m/s})(4.5 \text{ s})$
    $= 45 \text{ m}$ or 45 m west

5. Velocity is constant throughout this particular motion and is equal to the slope of the graph. Consider east as the positive direction.
    slope $= \dfrac{\text{rise}}{\text{run}}$
    $= \dfrac{\Delta \vec{d}}{\Delta t}$
    $= \dfrac{10.0 \text{ m} - 0 \text{ m}}{15.0 \text{ s} - 0 \text{ s}}$
    $= 0.677 \text{ m/s}$ or 0.667 m/s east

9. The distance travelled does not involve the direction. The object travelled at a constant speed of 7.0 m/s (the velocity is read from the graph and the directionality is ignored) throughout its entire motion.
    $d = vt$
    $= (7.0 \text{ m/s})(10 \text{ s})$
    $= 70 \text{ m}$

    distance $= 70 \text{ m}$

11. Speed involves the scalar distance without any direction attached.
    Total distance:
    $d = 1.2 \times 10^4 \text{ m} + 4.5 \times 10^3 \text{ m}$
    $= 1.65 \times 10^4 \text{ m}$

    Total time:
    $t = 25 \text{ min} + 15 \text{ min}$
    $= 40 \text{ min}$
    $= (40 \text{ min})(60 \text{ s/min})$
    $= 2.4 \times 10^3 \text{ min}$

    Average speed:
    $v_{\text{ave}} = \dfrac{d}{t}$
    $= \dfrac{1.65 \times 10^4 \text{ m}}{2.4 \times 10^3 \text{ s}}$
    $= 6.9 \text{ m/s}$

Lesson 3—Uniformly Accelerated Motion—Graphical Analysis

PRACTICE EXERCISES
ANSWERS AND SOLUTIONS

1. Draw a tangent line at 0.40 s.

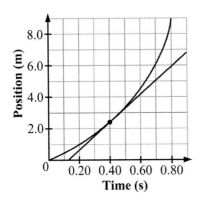

Find the slope of this tangent line. Consider east as the positive direction.

$$slope = \frac{rise}{run}$$
$$= \frac{(5.9-0)\,m}{(0.80-0.14)\,s}$$
$$= 8.9 \text{ m/s or } 8.9 \text{ m/s east}$$

3. Acceleration is the slope of the velocity-time graph. Consider north as the positive direction.

$$slope = \frac{rise}{run}$$
$$= \frac{(15.0-0)\,m/s}{(7.0-0)\,s}$$
$$= 2.1 \text{ m/s}^2 \text{ or } 2.1 \text{ m/s}^2 \text{ north}$$

5. Acceleration = slope

$$slope = \frac{rise}{run}$$
$$= \frac{(10.0-4.0)\,m/s}{(16.0-0)\,s}$$
$$= 0.38 \text{ m/s}^2 \text{ west}$$

7. Velocity-time graph

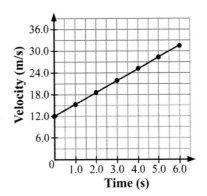

9. Consider north as the positive direction.
Displacement = area

$$A_{tot} = A_{rectangle} + A_{triangle}$$
$$= (l \times w) + \frac{1}{2}(l \times w)$$
$$= (6.0 \text{ s} \times 12.0 \text{ m/s}) + \frac{1}{2}(6.0 \text{ s} \times 19.8 \text{ m/s})$$
$$= 1.3 \times 10^2 \text{ m north}$$

Lesson 4—Uniformly Accelerated Motion—Algebraic Analysis

PRACTICE QUESTIONS
ANSWERS AND SOLUTIONS

1.

$\vec{v}_i$	$\vec{v}_f$	$\vec{a}$	$\vec{d}$	t
0	12.0 m/s	?	×	3.40 s

Consider west as the positive direction.

$$\vec{a} = \frac{\vec{v}_f - \vec{v}_i}{t}$$
$$= \frac{12.0 \text{ m/s} - 0}{3.40 \text{ s}}$$
$$= 3.53 \text{ m/s}^2 \text{ or } 3.53 \text{ m/s}^2 \text{ west}$$

3.

$\vec{v}_i$	$\vec{v}_f$	$\vec{a}$	$\vec{d}$	t
2.0 m/s	?	1.3 m/s²	15 m	×

Consider west as the positive direction.

$$\vec{v}_f^2 = \vec{v}_i^2 + 2\vec{a}\vec{d}$$
$$= (2.0 \text{ m/s})^2 + 2(1.3 \text{ m/s}^2)(15 \text{ m})$$
$$= 43.0 \text{ m}^2/\text{s}^2$$
$$\vec{v}_f = 6.6 \text{ m/s or } 6.6 \text{ m/s west}$$

5.

$\vec{v}_i$	$\vec{v}_f$	$\vec{a}$	$\vec{d}$	t
0	×	?	20.0 m	8.10 s

Consider right as the positive direction.

$$\vec{d} = \vec{v}_i t + \frac{1}{2}\vec{a}t^2$$

$$20.0\text{ m} = \frac{1}{2}(\vec{a})(8.10\text{ s})^2$$

$$\vec{a} = 0.610\text{ m/s}^2 \text{ or } 0.610\text{ m/s}^2 \text{ right}$$

7.

$\vec{v}_i$	$\vec{v}_f$	$\vec{a}$	$\vec{d}$	t
?	14.0 m/s	×	25.0 m	1.90 s

Consider north as the positive direction.

$$\vec{d} = \left(\frac{\vec{v}_f + \vec{v}_i}{2}\right)t$$

$$25.0\text{ m} = \left(\frac{14.0\text{ m/s} + \vec{v}_i}{2}\right)1.90\text{ s}$$

$$\vec{v}_i = \frac{2(25.0\text{ m})}{1.90\text{ s}} - 14.0\text{ m/s}$$

$$= 12.3\text{ m/s or } 12.3\text{ m/s north}$$

9.

$\vec{v}_i$	$\vec{v}_f$	$\vec{a}$	$\vec{d}$	t
?	25.0 m/s	0.900 m/s^2	37.0 m	×

Consider south as the positive direction.

$$\vec{v}_f^{\,2} = \vec{v}_i^{\,2} + 2\vec{a}\vec{d}$$

$$(25.0\text{ m/s})^2 = \vec{v}_i^{\,2} + 2(0.900\text{ m/s}^2)(37.0\text{ m})$$

$$\vec{v}_i^{\,2} = (25.0\text{ m/s})^2 - 2(0.900\text{ m/s}^2)(37.0\text{ m})$$

$$= 558.4\text{ m}^2/\text{s}^2$$

$$\vec{v}_i = \sqrt{558.4\text{ m}^2/\text{s}^2}$$

$$= 23.6\text{ m/s or } 23.6\text{ m/s south}$$

11. Consider the direction of the acceleration down the incline as the positive direction.

$$\vec{a} = \frac{\vec{v}_f - \vec{v}_i}{t}$$

$$1.4\text{ m/s}^2 = \frac{\vec{v}_f - 0}{5.0\text{ s}}$$

$$\vec{v}_f = (1.4\text{ m/s}^2)(5.0\text{ s})$$

$$= 7.0\text{ m/s or } 7.0\text{ m/s down the incline}$$

13.

$\vec{v}_i$	$\vec{v}_f$	$\vec{a}$	$\vec{d}$	t
0	12.4 m/s	3.10 m/s^2	?	4.00 s

Consider south as the positive direction.

Use any formula except $\vec{a} = \dfrac{\vec{v}_f - \vec{v}_i}{t}$.

$$\vec{d} = \vec{v}_i t + \frac{1}{2}\vec{a}t^2$$

$$= 0 + \frac{1}{2}(3.10\text{ m/s}^2)(4.00\text{ s})^2$$

$$= \frac{1}{2}(3.10\text{ m/s}^2)(4.00\text{ s})^2$$

$$= 24.8\text{ m or } 24.8\text{ m south}$$

Lesson 5—Freely Falling Objects

PRACTICE QUESTIONS
ANSWERS AND SOLUTIONS

NOTE: For all practice exercises in this section consider up as the positive direction and down as the negative direction.

1.

$\vec{v}_i$	$\vec{v}_f$	$\vec{a}$	$\vec{d}$	t
0	?	−9.81 m/s^2	−15.0 m	×

$$\vec{v}_f^{\,2} = \vec{v}_i^{\,2} + 2\vec{a}\vec{d}$$

$$= 0 + 2\vec{a}\vec{d}$$

$$\vec{v}_f = \sqrt{2\vec{a}\vec{d}}$$

$$= \sqrt{2(-9.81\text{ m/s}^2)(-15.0\text{ m})}$$

$$= \pm 17.2\text{ m/s} \Rightarrow -17.2\text{ m/s or } 17.2\text{ m/s down}$$

3.

$\vec{v}_i$	$\vec{v}_f$	$\vec{a}$	$\vec{d}$	t
0	?	−9.81 m/s^2	−9.50 m	×

$$\vec{v}_f^{\,2} = \vec{v}_i^{\,2} + 2\vec{a}\vec{d}$$

$$= 0 + 2\vec{a}\vec{d}$$

$$\vec{v}_f = \sqrt{2\vec{a}\vec{d}}$$

$$\sqrt{2(-9.81\text{ m/s}^2)(-9.50\text{ m})}$$

$$= \pm 13.7\text{ m/s} \Rightarrow -13.7\text{ m/s or } 13.7\text{ m/s down}$$

5.

$\vec{v}_i$	$\vec{v}_f$	$\vec{a}$	$\vec{d}$	t
10.0 m/s	−25.0 m/s	−9.81 m/s²	×	?

$$\vec{a} = \frac{\vec{v}_f - \vec{v}_i}{t}$$

$$-9.81 \text{ m/s}^2 = \frac{(-25.0 \text{ m/s}) - (+10.0 \text{ m/s})}{t}$$

$$t = \frac{(-25.0 \text{ m/s}) - 10.0 \text{ m/s}}{-9.81 \text{ m/s}^2}$$

$$= 3.57 \text{ s}$$

7.

$\vec{v}_i$	$\vec{v}_f$	$\vec{a}$	$\vec{d}$	t
?	−10.0 m/s	−9.81 m/s2	×	0.880 s

$$\vec{a} = \frac{\vec{v}_f - \vec{v}_i}{t}$$

$$-9.81 \text{ m/s}^2 = \frac{(-10.0 \text{ m/s}) - \vec{v}_i}{0.880 \text{ s}}$$

$$\vec{v}_i = (-10.0 \text{ m/s}) - (-9.81 \text{ m/s}^2)(0.880 \text{ s})$$

$$= -1.37 \text{ m/s or } 1.37 \text{ m/s down}$$

9.

$\vec{v}_i$	$\vec{v}_f$	$\vec{a}$	$\vec{d}$	t
0 m/s	?	−9.81 m/s²	−7.0 m	×

$$\vec{d} = \vec{v}_i t + \frac{1}{2}\vec{a}t^2$$

$$= 0 + \frac{1}{2}\vec{a}t^2$$

$$t = \sqrt{\frac{2\vec{d}}{\vec{a}}}$$

$$= \sqrt{\frac{2(-7.0 \text{ m})}{-9.81 \text{ m/s}^2}}$$

$$= 1.2 \text{ s}$$

11.

$\vec{v}_i$	$\vec{v}_f$	$\vec{a}$	$\vec{v}_{ave}$	t
0	?	−9.81 m/s²	−12.0 m/s	?

$$\vec{v}_{ave} = \frac{\vec{v}_f + \vec{v}_i}{2}$$

$$= \frac{\vec{v}_f + 0}{2}$$

$$\vec{v}_f = 2\vec{v}_{ave}$$

$$= 2(-12.0 \text{ m/s})$$

$$= -24.0 \text{ m/s}$$

$$\vec{a} = \frac{\vec{v}_f - \vec{v}_i}{t}$$

$$t = \frac{\vec{v}_f - \vec{v}_i}{\vec{a}}$$

$$= \frac{-24.0 \text{ m/s} - 0}{-9.81 \text{ m/s}^2}$$

$$= 2.45 \text{ s}$$

13.

$\vec{v}_i$	$\vec{v}_f$	$\vec{a}$	$\vec{d}$	t
0 m/s	−19.6 m/s	?	−24.0 m	×

$$\vec{v}_f^2 = \vec{v}_i^2 + 2\vec{a}\vec{d}$$

$$= 0 + 2\vec{a}\vec{d}$$

$$\vec{a} = \frac{\vec{v}_f^2}{2\vec{d}}$$

$$\vec{a} = \frac{(-19.6 \text{ m/s})^2}{2(-24.0 \text{ m})}$$

$$= -8.00 \text{ m/s}^2 \text{ or } 8.00 \text{ m/s}^2 \text{down}$$

15.

$\vec{v}_i$	$\vec{v}_f$	$\vec{a}$	$\vec{d}$	t
−3.50 m/s	−14.4m/s	−9.81 m/s²	−10.0 m	?

$$\vec{d} = \left(\frac{\vec{v}_f + \vec{v}_i}{2}\right)t$$

$$-10.0 \text{ m} = \left(\frac{(-14.4 \text{ m/s}) + (-3.50 \text{ m/s})}{2}\right)t$$

$$t = \frac{2(-10.0 \text{ m})}{-17.9 \text{ m/s}}$$

$$t = 1.12 \text{ s}$$

It is interesting to note that any of the kinematic formulas that involve time could have been used to generate the same result.

17.

$\vec{v}_i$	$\vec{v}_f$	$\vec{a}$	$\vec{d}$	t
0	−11.0 m/s	?	×	1.50 s

$$\vec{a} = \frac{\vec{v}_f - \vec{v}_i}{t}$$

$$= \frac{(-11.0 \text{ m/s}) - 0}{1.50 \text{ s}}$$

$$= -7.33 \text{ m/s}^2 \text{ or } 7.33 \text{ m/s}^2 \text{ down}$$

Lesson 6—Motion in One Dimension—Graphical Analysis

PRACTICE QUESTIONS
ANSWERS AND SOLUTIONS

1. Velocity = slope of position-time graph.
Draw a tangent line and find the slope.

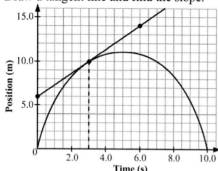

$$slope = \frac{rise}{run}$$
$$= \frac{y_2 - y_1}{x_2 - x_1}$$
$$slope = \frac{(14.0 - 5.0)\,m}{(6.0 - 0)\,s}$$
$$= 1.5\ m/s$$
$$= 1.5\ m/s\ up$$

3. Acceleration = slope of velocity-time graph
Slope is constant; therefore acceleration is uniform.

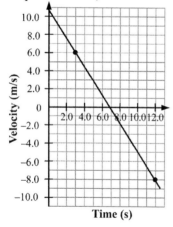

$$slope = \frac{rise}{run}$$
$$= \frac{y_2 - y_1}{x_2 - x_1}$$
$$= \frac{\big((-8.0) - 6.0\big)\ m/s}{(12.0 - 3.0)\ s}$$
$$\cong -1.6\ m/s^2$$

5. Displacement is read from the graph as
13.0 m north

7. Velocity = slope of position-time graph
Determine the slope at $t = 9.0$ s.

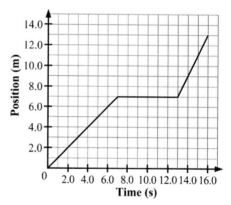

The graph is a straight horizontal line in the region
of $t = 9$ s, therefore slope = 0 m/s.

9.

$$\vec{v}_{ave} = \frac{\vec{d}}{t}$$
$$= \frac{13.0\ m\ north}{16.0\ s}$$
$$= 0.813\ m/s\ north$$

11. Read the velocity from a velocity-time graph.
$\vec{v} = 15.0$ m/s north

13. Displacement = area under velocity-time graph
area $= l \times w$
$$= (16.0\ s - 8.0\ s) \times 15.0\ m/s$$
$$= 1.20 \times 10^2\ m\ or\ 1.20 \times 10^2\ m\ north$$

15. Since speed is a scalar quantity, only the magnitude
of the velocity is important. The object has the
largest speed in region B of the graph.

---

17. Velocity = slope of position-time graph.

slope = 0 m/s

19. Read velocity from velocity-time graph.

Greatest velocity is 25.0 m/s is in the interval $t = 0$ to $t = 3.0$ s.

21. The greatest (i.e., steepest) slope is in the interval $t = 9.0$ s to $t = 12.0$ s.

23. The slope of a position-time graph gives the velocity. In order for velocity to be increasing, the slope must be increasing. This is only true in the case of graph A.

25. A constant velocity would be represented by a straight line in a position-time graph. This is true in the cases of graphs B and D.

Lesson 7—Uniform Accelerated Motion—Algebraic Analysis

PRACTICE EXERCISES
ANSWERS AND SOLUTIONS

NOTE: For all practice exercises in this lesson involving projectile motion, consider up as the positive direction and down as the negative direction.

1.

$\vec{v}_i$	$\vec{v}_f$	$\vec{a}$	$\vec{d}$	t
14.0 m/s	×	−9.81 m/s^2	?	1.80 s

$$\vec{d} = \vec{v}_i t + \frac{1}{2}\vec{a}t^2$$
$$= (14.0 \text{ m/s})(1.80 \text{ s}) + \frac{1}{2}(-9.81 \text{ m/s}^2)(1.80 \text{ s})^2$$
$$= 9.31 \text{ m or } 9.31 \text{ m up}$$

3.

$\vec{v}_i$	$\vec{v}_f$	$\vec{a}$	$\vec{d}$	t
9.4 m/s	−7.4 m/s	×	?	3.0 s

Consider up the slope as the positive direction.

$$\vec{d} = \left(\frac{\vec{v}_f + \vec{v}_i}{2}\right)t$$
$$= \left(\frac{(-7.4 \text{ m/s}) + 9.4 \text{ m/s}}{2}\right)3.0 \text{ s}$$
$$= 3.0 \text{ m or } 3.0 \text{ m up the slope}$$

5.

$\vec{v}_i$	$\vec{v}_f$	$\vec{a}$	$\vec{d}$	t
?	0	×	2.6 m	3.6 s

Consider up the slope as the positive direction.

$$\vec{d} = \left(\frac{\vec{v}_f + \vec{v}_i}{2}\right)t$$
$$2.6 \text{ m} = \left(\frac{0 + \vec{v}_i}{2}\right)3.6 \text{ s}$$
$$\vec{v}_i = \frac{2(2.6 \text{ m})}{3.6 \text{ s}}$$
$$= 1.4 \text{ m/s or } 1.4 \text{ m/s up the slope}$$

7.

$\vec{v}_i$	$\vec{v}_f$	$\vec{a}$	$\vec{d}$	t
2.0 m/s	?	×	2.8 m	1.5 s

Consider up the slope as the positive direction.

$$\vec{d} = \left(\frac{\vec{v}_f + \vec{v}_i}{2}\right)t$$
$$2.8 \text{ m} = \left(\frac{v_f + 2.0 \text{ m/s}}{2}\right)1.5 \text{ s}$$
$$\vec{v}_f = \frac{2(2.8 \text{ m})}{1.5 \text{ s}} - 2.0 \text{ m/s}$$
$$= 1.7 \text{ m/s or } 1.7 \text{ m/s up the slope}$$

9.

$\vec{v}_i$	$\vec{v}_f$	$\vec{a}$	$\vec{d}$	t
2.2 m/s	−1.2 m/s	?	×	2.0 s

Consider up the slope as the positive direction.

$$\vec{a} = \frac{\vec{v}_f - \vec{v}_i}{t}$$
$$= \frac{(-1.2 \text{ m/s}) - 2.2 \text{ m/s}}{2.0 \text{ s}}$$
$$= -1.7 \text{ m/s}^2 \text{ or } 1.7 \text{ m/s}^2 \text{ down the incline}$$

11.

$\vec{v}_i$	$\vec{v}_f$	$\vec{a}$	$\vec{d}$	t
2.0 m/s	0	×	2.7 m	?

Consider up the slope to be the positive direction.

$$\vec{d} = \left(\frac{\vec{v}_f + \vec{v}_i}{2}\right)t$$
$$2.7 \text{ m} = \left(\frac{0 + 2.0 \text{ m/s}}{2}\right)t$$
$$t = \frac{2(2.7 \text{ m})}{2.0 \text{ m/s}}$$
$$= 2.70 \text{ s}$$

This is the time it takes for the ball to roll up the incline. Since it will take the same amount of time to come down, the total time is $2(2.70 \text{ s}) = 5.4 \text{ s}$.

13.

$\vec{v}_i$	$\vec{v}_f$	$\vec{a}$	$\vec{d}$	t
20.0 m/s	?	-9.81 m/s^2	-30.0 m	?

$$\vec{v}_f^{\,2} = \vec{v}_i^{\,2} + 2\vec{a}\vec{d}$$
$$= (20.0 \text{ m/s})^2 + 2(-9.81 \text{ m/s}^2)(-30.0 \text{ m})$$
$$= 988.6 \text{ m}^2/\text{s}^2$$
$$\vec{v}_f = \sqrt{988.6 \text{ m}^2/\text{s}^2}$$
$$= \pm 31.4 \text{ m/s} \Rightarrow -31.4 \text{ m/s or } 31.4 \text{ m/s down}$$

15.

$\vec{v}_i$	$\vec{v}_f$	$\vec{a}$	$\vec{d}$	t
11.0 m/s	?	-9.81 m/s^2	-5.00 m	?

Find $\vec{v}_f$.

$$\vec{v}_f^{\,2} = \vec{v}_i^{\,2} + 2\vec{a}\vec{d}$$
$$= (11.0 \text{ m/s})^2 + 2(-9.81 \text{ m/s}^2)(-5.00 \text{ m})$$
$$= 219.10 \text{ m}^2/\text{s}^2$$
$$\vec{v}_f = \sqrt{219.10 \text{ m}^2/\text{s}^2}$$
$$= \pm 14.8 \text{ m/s} \Rightarrow -14.80 \text{ m/s}$$
$$\text{or } 14.80 \text{ m/s down}$$

Now, find t.

$$\vec{a} = \frac{\vec{v}_f - \vec{v}_i}{t}$$
$$-9.81 \text{ m/s}^2 = \frac{(-14.80 \text{ m/s}) - 11.0 \text{ m/s}}{t}$$
$$t = \frac{(-14.80 \text{ m/s}) - 11.0 \text{ m/s}}{-9.81 \text{ m/s}^2}$$
$$= 2.63 \text{ s}$$

17.

$\vec{v}_i$	$\vec{v}_f$	$\vec{a}$	$\vec{d}$	t
0	?	-9.81 m/s^2	-25.0 m	$\times$

First, find $\vec{v}_f$.

$$\vec{v}_f^{\,2} = \vec{v}_i^{\,2} + 2\vec{a}\vec{d}$$
$$= 0 + 2(-9.81 \text{ m/s}^2)(-25.0 \text{ m})$$
$$= 490.5 \text{ m}^2/\text{s}^2$$
$$\vec{v}_f = \sqrt{490.5 \text{ m}^2/\text{s}^2}$$
$$= \pm 22.15 \text{ m/s} \Rightarrow -22.15 \text{ m/s}$$
$$\text{or } 22.15 \text{ m/s down}$$

Now, calculate the average velocity.

$$\vec{v}_{ave} = \frac{\vec{v}_f + \vec{v}_i}{2}$$
$$= \frac{(-22.15 \text{ m/s}) + 0}{2}$$
$$= -11.1 \text{ m/s or } 11.1 \text{ m/s down}$$

19. The horizontal velocity and distance pertaining to the object can be used to determine the time interval that the stone is in the air. Consider east as the positive direction.

$$\vec{v} = \frac{\vec{d}}{t}$$
$$t = \frac{\vec{d}}{\vec{v}}$$
$$= \frac{4.00 \text{ m}}{1.00 \text{ m/s}}$$
$$= 4.00 \text{ s}$$

Use this time to calculate the height above the water (displacement) from which the stone was dropped.

$\vec{v}_i$	$\vec{v}$	$\vec{a}$	$\vec{d}$	t
0	$\times$	-9.81 m/s^2	?	4.00 s

$$\vec{d} = \vec{v}_i t + \frac{1}{2}\vec{a}t^2$$
$$= 0 + \frac{1}{2}(-9.81 \text{ m/s}^2)(4.00 \text{ s})^2$$
$$= -78.5 \text{ m}$$

The object dropped from a height of 78.5 m above the water.

Practice Test

ANSWERS AND SOLUTIONS

1. The motion of a falling object is uniformly accelerated motion. This means that the acceleration of a falling object remains constant. Recall that the slope of a velocity-time graph is the acceleration. For acceleration to be constant, the slope of a velocity-time graph must be linear. Seeing as the stone is influenced by gravity $(a = g = 9.81 \text{ m/s}^2)$, the slope must be non-zero.

Furthermore, the stone is initially at rest, so the initial velocity must be zero. The only graph that displays all of these properties is graph B.

408

The fact that the slope is negative is irrelevant; this is merely a convention chosen when the graph was created. The remaining graphs represent uniform motion, non-uniformly accelerated motion, and uniformly accelerated motion with a non-zero initial velocity, respectively.

B is the correct answer.

3. The acceleration of a falling object is constant and non-zero. The only graph that displays these properties is graph A.

A is the correct answer.

5. Velocity is the slope of a position-time graph.

$$slope = \frac{rise}{run}$$
$$= \frac{y_2 - y_1}{x_2 - x_1}$$
$$= \frac{50.0 \text{ m} - 20.0 \text{ m}}{6.0 \text{ s} - 0 \text{ s}}$$
$$= 5.0 \text{ m/s}$$
$$\therefore \vec{v} = 5.0 \text{ m/s north}$$

C is the correct answer.

7. Velocity is a vector quantity; therefore it has direction. Once the object is released, gravity will act on it. The acceleration due to gravity is constant at –9.81 m/s^2. The baseball must have a positive initial velocity (as it travels up). When it reaches the highest point in its motion, the direction of the ball's motion will reverse. Therefore, the correct graph must show a change in the sign of the velocity. The only graph that displays this property accurately is graph A. While graph D does indeed show a change in sign of the velocity of the baseball, it shows infinitely high acceleration between the change, and not the constant –9.81 m/s^2.

A is the correct answer.

9. The slope of a position-time graph is the velocity. In this graph, the slope is decreasing.

C is the correct answer.

11.

$\vec{v}_i$	$\vec{v}_f$	$\vec{a}$	$\vec{d}$	t
2.0 m/s	0	?	2.7 m	×

Consider up the slope to be the positive direction.
$$\vec{v}_f^{\,2} = \vec{v}_i^{\,2} + 2\vec{a}\vec{d}$$
$$\vec{a} = \frac{\vec{v}_f^{\,2} - \vec{v}_i^{\,2}}{2\vec{d}}$$
$$\vec{a} = \frac{0 - (2.0 \text{ m/s})^2}{2(2.7 \text{ m})}$$
$$= -0.74 \text{ m/s}^2 \text{ or } 0.74 \text{ m/s}^2 \text{ down the slope}$$

B is the correct answer.

13.

$\vec{v}_i$	$\vec{v}_f$	$\vec{a}$	$\vec{d}$	t
15.0 m/s	×	–9.81 m/s^2	?	8.00 s

$$\vec{d} = \vec{v}_i t + \frac{1}{2}\vec{a}t^2$$
$$= (15.0 \text{ m/s})(8.00 \text{ s}) + \frac{1}{2}(-9.81 \text{ m/s}^2)(8.00 \text{ s})^2$$
$$= -1.94 \times 10^2 \text{ m}$$

Since the vertical displacement of the object was 194 m, the building must be 194 m tall.

B is the correct answer.

15. Convert 105 km/h to m/s.
$$(105 \text{ km/h})(1\,000 \text{ m/km})(1 \text{ h}/3\,600 \text{ s}) = 29.17 \text{ m/s}$$

$\vec{v}_i$	$\vec{v}_f$	$\vec{a}$	$\vec{d}$	t
0	29.17 m/s	×	×	9.0 s

Consider east as the positive direction.
$$\vec{v}_{ave} = \frac{\vec{v}_f + \vec{v}_i}{2}$$
$$= \frac{29.17 \text{ m/s} + 0 \text{ m/s}}{2}$$
$$= 15 \text{ m/s east}$$

B is the answer.

VECTOR KINEMATICS— PART B

Lesson 1—Addition of Vectors on a Plane

PRACTICE EXERCISES
ANSWERS AND SOLUTIONS

1. 4.0 m south + 3.0 m south = 7.0 m south

3.

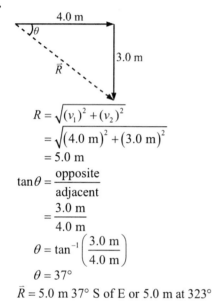

$$R = \sqrt{(v_1)^2 + (v_2)^2}$$
$$= \sqrt{(4.0 \text{ m})^2 + (3.0 \text{ m})^2}$$
$$= 5.0 \text{ m}$$

$$\tan\theta = \frac{\text{opposite}}{\text{adjacent}}$$
$$= \frac{3.0 \text{ m}}{4.0 \text{ m}}$$
$$\theta = \tan^{-1}\left(\frac{3.0 \text{ m}}{4.0 \text{ m}}\right)$$
$$\theta = 37°$$
$$\vec{R} = 5.0 \text{ m } 37° \text{ S of E or 5.0 m at } 323°$$

5.

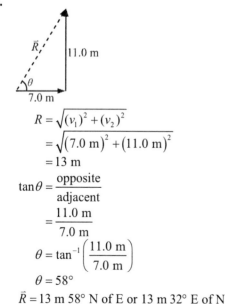

$$R = \sqrt{(v_1)^2 + (v_2)^2}$$
$$= \sqrt{(7.0 \text{ m})^2 + (11.0 \text{ m})^2}$$
$$= 13 \text{ m}$$

$$\tan\theta = \frac{\text{opposite}}{\text{adjacent}}$$
$$= \frac{11.0 \text{ m}}{7.0 \text{ m}}$$
$$\theta = \tan^{-1}\left(\frac{11.0 \text{ m}}{7.0 \text{ m}}\right)$$
$$\theta = 58°$$
$$\vec{R} = 13 \text{ m } 58° \text{ N of E or 13 m } 32° \text{ E of N}$$

7. First add the two displacements along the north-south direction. Consider north as the positive direction.

$$\vec{R}_y = 7.0 \text{ m south} + 8.0 \text{ m north}$$
$$= (-7.0 \text{ m}) + 8.0 \text{ m}$$
$$= 1.0 \text{ m or 1.0 m north}$$

Now add the perpendicular vectors to find the resultant.

$$R = \sqrt{(v_1)^2 + (v_2)^2}$$
$$= \sqrt{(6.0 \text{ m})^2 + (1.0 \text{ m})^2}$$
$$= 6.1 \text{ m}$$

$$\tan\theta = \frac{\text{opposite}}{\text{adjacent}}$$
$$= \frac{1.0 \text{ m}}{6.0 \text{ m}}$$
$$\theta = \tan^{-1}\left(\frac{1.0 \text{ m}}{6.0 \text{ m}}\right)$$
$$\theta = 9.5°$$
$$\vec{R} = 6.1 \text{ m } 9.5° \text{ N of E or 6.1 m } 81° \text{ E of N}$$

Lesson 2—Vector Components

PRACTICE EXERCISES
ANSWER AND SOLUTIONS

1. x-component = 0
y-component = 16.0 m or 16.0 m north

3. Consider north and east as the positive directions.

$$\sin\theta = \frac{\text{opposite}}{\text{hypotenuse}}$$
$$\sin\theta = \frac{R_x}{R}$$
$$R_x = R\sin\theta$$
$$= (20.0 \text{ m})\sin 38.0°$$
$$= 12.3 \text{ m}$$
$$\therefore \vec{R}_x = -12.3 \text{ m or 12.3 m west}$$

$$\cos\theta = \frac{\text{adjacent}}{\text{hypotenuse}}$$
$$\cos\theta = \frac{R_y}{R}$$
$$R_y = R\cos\theta$$
$$= (20.0 \text{ m})\cos 38.0°$$
$$= 15.8 \text{ m}$$
$$\therefore \vec{R}_y = 15.8 \text{ m or } 15.8 \text{ m north}$$

5. Consider north and east as the positive directions.
$$\vec{R}_1 = 8.00 \text{ m east}$$
$$\vec{R}_{1x} = 8.00 \text{ m or } 8.00 \text{ m east}$$
$$\vec{R}_{1y} = 0$$

Find the x- and y-components of 6.00 m 35.0° N of E.

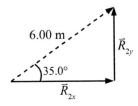

$$\cos\theta = \frac{\text{adjacent}}{\text{hypotenuse}}$$
$$\cos\theta = \frac{R_{2x}}{R_2}$$
$$R_{2x} = R_2\cos\theta$$
$$= (6.00 \text{ m})(\cos 35.0°)$$
$$= 4.915 \text{ m}$$
$$\vec{R}_{2x} = 4.915 \text{ m or } 4.915 \text{ m east}$$

$$\sin\theta = \frac{\text{opposite}}{\text{hypotenuse}}$$
$$\sin\theta = \frac{R_{2y}}{R_2}$$
$$R_{2y} = R_2\sin\theta$$
$$= (6.00 \text{ m})\sin 35.0°$$
$$= 3.441 \text{ m}$$
$$\vec{R}_{2y} = 3.441 \text{ m or } 3.441 \text{ m north}$$

Add x-components.
$$\vec{R}_x = \vec{R}_{1x} + \vec{R}_{2x}$$
$$= 8.00 \text{ m} + 4.915 \text{ m}$$
$$= 12.915 \text{ m}$$

Add y-components.
$$\vec{R}_y = \vec{R}_{1y} + \vec{R}_{2y}$$
$$= 0 \text{ m} + 3.441 \text{ m}$$
$$= 3.441 \text{ m}$$

Add $\vec{R}_x$ and $\vec{R}_y$.

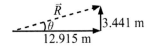

$$R = \sqrt{(R_x)^2 + (R_y)^2}$$
$$= \sqrt{(12.915 \text{ m})^2 + (3.441 \text{ m})^2}$$
$$= 13.4 \text{ m}$$
$$\tan\theta = \frac{\text{opposite}}{\text{adjacent}}$$
$$= \frac{R_y}{R_x}$$
$$= \frac{3.441 \text{ m}}{12.915 \text{ m}}$$
$$\theta = \tan^{-1}\left(\frac{3.441 \text{ m}}{12.915 \text{ m}}\right)$$
$$\theta = 14.9°$$
$$\vec{R} = 13.4 \text{ m } 14.9° \text{ N of E}$$

7. Find x- and y-components of 5.0 m 26° S of E.

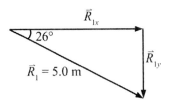

$$\cos\theta = \frac{\text{adjacent}}{\text{hypotenuse}}$$
$$\cos\theta = \frac{R_{1x}}{R_1}$$
$$R_{1x} = R_1\cos\theta$$
$$= (5.0 \text{ m})(\cos 26°)$$
$$= 4.49 \text{ m}$$
$$\vec{R}_{1x} = 4.49 \text{ m or } 4.49 \text{ m east}$$

$\sin \theta = \dfrac{\text{opposite}}{\text{hypotenuse}}$

$\sin \theta = \dfrac{R_{1y}}{R_1}$

$R_{1y} = R_1 \sin \theta$

$\quad = (5.0 \text{ m})(\sin 26°)$

$\quad = 2.19 \text{ m}$

$\vec{R}_{1y} = -2.19 \text{ m or } 2.19 \text{ m south}$

Find x- and y-components of 7.0 m 58° W of N (32° N of W).

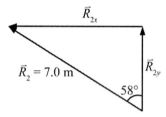

$\sin \theta = \dfrac{\text{opposite}}{\text{hypotenuse}}$

$\sin \theta = \dfrac{R_{2x}}{R_2}$

$R_{2x} = R_2 \sin \theta$

$\quad = (7.0 \text{ m})(\sin 58°)$

$\quad = 5.94 \text{ m}$

$\vec{R}_{2x} = -5.94 \text{ m or } 5.94 \text{ m west}$

$\cos \theta = \dfrac{\text{adjacent}}{\text{hypotenuse}}$

$\cos \theta = \dfrac{R_{2y}}{R_2}$

$R_{2y} = R_2 \cos \theta$

$\quad = (7.0 \text{ m})(\cos 58°)$

$\quad = 3.70 \text{ m}$

$\vec{R}_{2y} = 3.70 \text{ m or } 3.70 \text{ m north}$

Add x-components.

$\vec{R}_x = \vec{R}_{1x} + \vec{R}_{2x}$

$\quad = 4.49 \text{ m} + (-5.94 \text{ m})$

$\quad = -1.450 \text{ m or } 1.450 \text{ m west}$

Add y-components.

$\vec{R}_y = \vec{R}_{1y} + \vec{R}_{2y}$

$\quad = (-2.19 \text{ m}) + 3.71 \text{ m}$

$\quad = 1.520 \text{ m or } 1.520 \text{ m north}$

Add $\vec{R}_x$ and $\vec{R}_y$.

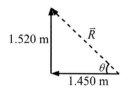

$R = \sqrt{(R_x)^2 + (R_y)^2}$

$\quad = \sqrt{(-1.450 \text{ m})^2 + (1.520 \text{ m})^2}$

$\quad = 2.1 \text{ m}$

$\tan \theta = \dfrac{R_x}{R_y}$

$\quad = \dfrac{1.520 \text{ m}}{1.450 \text{ m}}$

$\theta = \tan^{-1}\left(\dfrac{1.520 \text{ m}}{1.450 \text{ m}}\right)$

$\theta = 46°$

$\vec{R} = 2.1 \text{ m } 46° \text{ N of W}$

Lesson 3—Velocity Vectors and Navigation

PRACTICE EXERCISES
ANSWERS AND SOLUTIONS

1.

$R = \sqrt{(v_x)^2 + (v_y)^2}$

$\quad = \sqrt{(15.0 \text{ m/s})^2 + (11.0 \text{ m/s})^2}$

$\quad = 18.6 \text{ m/s}$

$\tan \theta = \dfrac{\text{opposite}}{\text{adjacent}}$

$\quad = \dfrac{11.0 \text{ m/s}}{15.0 \text{ m/s}}$

$\theta = \tan^{-1}\left(\dfrac{11.0 \text{ m/s}}{15.0 \text{ m/s}}\right)$

$\quad = 36.3°$

$\vec{R} = 18.6 \text{ m/s } 36.3° \text{ S of E}$

3. Find the *y*-component of 2.00 m/s at 35.0° above the horizontal.

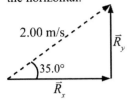

$$\vec{R}_y = R\sin\theta$$
$$= (2.00 \text{ m/s})(\sin 35.0°)$$
$$= 1.15 \text{ m/s}$$

5.

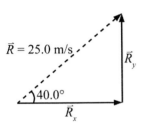

Find the *y*-component.
$$\sin\theta = \frac{R_y}{R}$$
$$R_y = R\sin\theta$$
$$= (25.0 \text{ m/s})(\sin 40.0°)$$
$$= 16.1 \text{ m/s}$$
$$\vec{R}_y = 16.1 \text{ m/s or } 16.1 \text{ m/s up}$$

7. 2.5 m/s south + 1.0 m/s south = 3.5 m/s south

9.

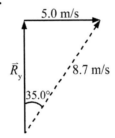

$$R = \sqrt{(v_1)^2 + (v_2)^2}$$
$$= \sqrt{(2.5 \text{ m/s})^2 + (1.0 \text{ m/s})^2}$$
$$= 2.7 \text{ m/s}$$
$$\tan\theta = \frac{\text{opposite}}{\text{adjacent}}$$
$$= \frac{1.0 \text{ m/s}}{2.5 \text{ m/s}}$$
$$\theta = \tan^{-1}\left(\frac{1.0 \text{ m/s}}{2.5 \text{ m/s}}\right)$$
$$= 22°$$
$$\vec{R} = 2.7 \text{ m/s } 22° \text{ S of W}$$

11.

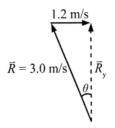

$$\sin\theta = \frac{\text{opposite}}{\text{hypotenuse}}$$
$$= \frac{R_x}{R}$$
$$= \frac{1.2 \text{ m/s}}{3.0 \text{ m/s}}$$
$$\theta = \sin^{-1}\left(\frac{1.2 \text{ m/s}}{3.0 \text{ m/s}}\right)$$
$$= 24° \text{ W of N}$$

13.

$$\tan\theta = \frac{\text{opposite}}{\text{adjacent}}$$
$$\text{adjacent} = \frac{\text{opposite}}{\tan\theta}$$
$$R_y = \frac{R_x}{\tan\theta}$$
$$R_y = \frac{5.0 \text{ m/s}}{\tan 35.0°}$$
$$= 7.1 \text{ m/s}$$

15. Only the velocity that is directed across the current of the river will act to move the boat across the river.

$$v = \frac{d}{t}$$
$$t = \frac{d}{v}$$
$$= \frac{2\,395 \text{ m}}{5.0 \text{ m/s}}$$
$$= 4.8 \times 10^2 \text{ s}$$

17. 2.5 m/s east + 2.0 m/s east = 4.5 m/s east

19.

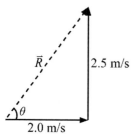

$$R = \sqrt{(v_1)^2 + (v_2)^2}$$
$$= \sqrt{(2.0 \text{ m/s})^2 + (2.5 \text{ m/s})^2}$$
$$= 3.2 \text{ m/s}$$

$$\tan\theta = \frac{\text{opposite}}{\text{adjacent}} = \frac{R_y}{R_x}$$
$$= \frac{2.5 \text{ m/s}}{2.0 \text{ m/s}}$$

$$\theta = \tan^{-1}\left(\frac{2.5 \text{ m/s}}{2.0 \text{ m/s}}\right)$$
$$= 51°$$
$$\vec{R} = 3.2 \text{ m/s } 51° \text{ N of E}$$

Lesson 4—Projectile Motion (Thrown Horizontally)

PRACTICE EXERCISES
ANSWER AND SOLUTIONS

NOTE: For all projectile motion problems in this section, consider down as the positive direction.

1. We are asked to find the horizontal component.

$$\therefore \text{ use } v = \frac{d}{t}$$

Find t from the vertical component.

v_0	v	a	d	t
0	×	9.81 m/s²	90.0 m	?

$$d = v_0 t + \frac{1}{2}at^2$$
$$90.0 \text{ m} = \frac{1}{2}\left(9.81 \text{ m/s}^2\right)t^2$$
$$t = \sqrt{\frac{2(90.0 \text{ m})}{9.81 \text{ m/s}^2}}$$
$$= 4.28 \text{ s}$$

$$v = \frac{d}{t}$$

Therefore the range of the object
$$d = vt$$
$$= (10.0 \text{ m/s})(4.29 \text{ s})$$
$$= 42.9 \text{ m}$$

3. We are asked to find the vertical component.

Find t from the horizontal component.

$$v = \frac{d}{t}$$

$$t = \frac{d}{v}$$
$$= \frac{100 \text{ m}}{18.0 \text{ m/s}}$$
$$= 5.56 \text{ s}$$

Vertical component

v_0	v	a	d	t
0	×	9.81 m/s²	?	5.56 s

$$d = v_0 t + \frac{1}{2}at^2$$
$$= \frac{1}{2}(9.81 \text{ m/s}^2)(5.56 \text{ s})^2$$
$$= 152 \text{ m}$$

5. We are asked to find the vertical component.

v_0	v	a	d	t
0	×	9.81 m/s²	?	5.50 s

$$d = v_0 t + \frac{1}{2}at^2$$
$$= \frac{1}{2}(9.81 \text{ m/s}^2)(5.50 \text{ s})^2$$
$$= 148 \text{ m}$$

7. a)

time (s)	displacement from t = 0 (x 10⁻² m)		displacement during time interval (x 10⁻³ m)		average velocity during time interval (x 10⁻² m/s)	
	horiz.	vert.	horiz.	vert.	horiz.	vert.
0	0	0				
0.10	0.5	0.15	5.0	1.5	5.0	1.5
0.20	1.0	0.30	5.0	1.5	5.0	1.5
0.30	1.5	0.70	5.0	4.0	5.0	4.0
0.40	2.0	1.1	5.0	4.0	5.0	4.0
0.50	2.5	1.6	5.0	5.0	5.0	5.0
0.60	3.0	2.2	5.0	6.0	5.0	6.0
0.70	3.5	2.9	5.0	7.0	5.0	7.0
0.80	4.0	3.7	5.0	8.0	5.0	8.0
0.90	4.5	4.6	5.0	9.0	5.0	9.0
1.00	5.0	5.6	5.0	10.0	5.0	10.0
1.10	5.5	6.7	5.0	11.0	5.0	11.0

b)

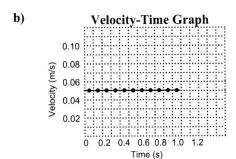

c)

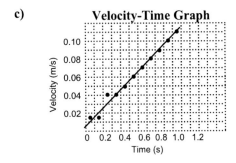

d) **i)** slope = 0

ii) slope = $\dfrac{\text{rise}}{\text{run}}$

$= \dfrac{0.10 \text{ m/s} - 0.01 \text{ m/s}}{0.95 \text{ s} - 0.05 \text{ s}}$

$= 0.10 \text{ m/s}^2$

Lesson 5—Projectiles—Thrown at an Angle

PRACTICE EXERCISES ANSWERS AND SOLUTIONS

1. We are asked to find the horizontal component. First, find the vertical and horizontal components of the velocity

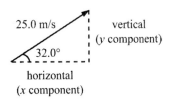

$\sin \theta = \dfrac{\text{opposite}}{\text{hypotenuse}}$

$\sin 40.0° = \dfrac{\text{vertical}}{18.0 \text{ m/s}}$

vertical component of velocity

$= (18.0 \text{ m/s})(\sin 40.0°)$

$= 11.6 \text{ m/s}$

$\cos \theta = \dfrac{\text{adjacent}}{\text{hypotenuse}}$

$\cos 40.0° = \dfrac{\text{horizontal}}{18.0 \text{ m/s}}$

horizontal component of velocity

$= (18.0 \text{ m/s})(\cos 40.0°)$

$= 13.8 \text{ m/s}$

Find t from vertical component

$\vec{v}_{y(i)}$	$\vec{v}_{y(f)}$	$\vec{a}$	d	t
11.6 m/s	−11.6 m/s	−9.81 m/s²	×	?

$\vec{a} = \dfrac{\vec{v}_{y(f)} - \vec{v}_{y(i)}}{t}$

$-9.81 \text{ m/s}^2 = \dfrac{-11.6 \text{ m/s} - 11.6 \text{ m/s}}{t}$

$t = \dfrac{-11.6 \text{ m/s} - 11.6 \text{ m/s}}{-9.81 \text{ m/s}^2}$

$= 2.36 \text{ s}$

Horizontal speed

$v_x = \dfrac{d}{t}$

Range

$d = v_x t$

$= (13.8 \text{ m/s})(2.36 \text{ s})$

$= 32.6 \text{ m}$

3. We are asked to find the horizontal component.

25.0 m/s — vertical (y component)

32.0°

horizontal (x component)

$\sin \theta = \dfrac{\text{opposite}}{\text{hypotenuse}}$

$\sin 32.0° = \dfrac{\text{vertical}}{25.0 \text{ m/s}}$

vertical component of velocity

$= (25.0 \text{ m/s})(\sin 32.0°)$

$= 13.2 \text{ m/s}$

$$\cos\theta = \frac{\text{adjacent}}{\text{hypotenuse}}$$

$$\cos 32.0° = \frac{\text{horizontal}}{25.0 \text{ m/s}}$$

horizontal component of velocity

$$= (25.0 \text{ m/s})(\cos 32.0°)$$
$$= 21.2 \text{ m/s}$$

Find t from the vertical component

$\vec{v}_{y(i)}$	$\vec{v}_{y(f)}$	$\vec{a}$	d	t
13.2 m/s	−13.2 m/s	−9.81 m/s²	×	?

$$\vec{a} = \frac{\vec{v}_{y(f)} - \vec{v}_{y(i)}}{t}$$

$$-9.81 \text{ m/s}^2 = \frac{-13.2 \text{ m/s} - 13.2 \text{ m/s}}{t}$$

$$t = 2.70 \text{ s}$$

Horizontal speed

$$v = \frac{d}{t}$$

Range

$$d = v_x t$$
$$= (21.2 \text{ m/s})(2.70 \text{ s})$$
$$= 57.3 \text{ m}$$

5.

v_0	v	$\vec{a}$	$\vec{d}$	t
?	0	−9.81 m/s²	5.75 m	×

$$v^2 = v_0^2 + 2ad$$
$$0 = v_0^2 + 2(-9.81 \text{ m/s}^2)(5.75 \text{ m})$$
$$0 = v_0^2 - 113 \text{ m}^2/\text{s}^2$$
$$v_0^2 = 113 \text{ m}^2/\text{s}^2$$
$$v_0 = 10.6 \text{ m/s}$$

NOTE: this is the initial vertical velocity

$$\sin\theta = \frac{\text{opposite}}{\text{hypotenuse}}$$

$$\sin 30.0° = \frac{10.6 \text{ m/s}}{v}$$

$$v = 21.1 \text{ m/s}$$

∴ the object was thrown at a velocity of 10.6 m/s at an angle of 30.0° to the horizontal.

7.

$\vec{v}_0$	$\vec{v}$	$\vec{a}$	$\vec{d}$	t
?	0	−9.81 m/s²	25.0 m	1.08 s

NOTE: Time to reach $v = 0$ will be
$2.15 \text{ s} \times 0.5 = 1.08 \text{ s}$

$$\vec{a} = \frac{\vec{v} - \vec{v}_0}{t}$$

$$-9.81 \text{ m/s}^2 = \frac{0 - \vec{v}_0}{1.08 \text{ s}}$$

$$\vec{v}_0 = 10.6 \text{ m/s up}$$

NOTE: This is the vertical component of the velocity.

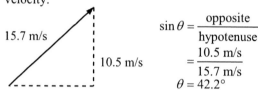

$$\sin\theta = \frac{\text{opposite}}{\text{hypotenuse}}$$
$$= \frac{10.5 \text{ m/s}}{15.7 \text{ m/s}}$$
$$\theta = 42.2°$$

9. a)

time (s)	displacement from t = 0 (x 10⁻² m)		displacement during time interval (x 10⁻² m)		average velocity during time interval (x 10⁻¹ m/s)	
	horiz.	vert.	horiz.	vert.	horiz.	vert.
0	0	0				
0.10	0.4	1.1	0.4	1.1	0.4	1.1
0.20	0.8	2.0	0.4	0.9	0.4	0.9
0.30	1.2	2.7	0.4	0.7	0.4	0.7
0.40	1.6	3.5	0.4	0.8	0.4	0.8
0.50	2.0	4.2	0.4	0.7	0.4	0.7
0.60	2.4	4.5	0.4	0.3	0.4	0.3
0.70	2.8	5.0	0.4	0.5	0.4	0.5
0.80	3.2	5.3	0.4	0.3	0.4	0.3
0.90	3.6	5.5	0.4	0.2	0.4	0.2
1.00	4.0	5.6	0.4	0.1	0.4	0.1
1.10	4.4	5.5	0.4	0.1	0.4	0.1
1.20	4.8	5.2	0.4	0.3	0.4	0.3
1.30	5.2	5.0	0.4	0.2	0.4	0.2
1.40	5.6	4.5	0.4	0.5	0.4	0.5
1.50	6.0	4.1	0.4	0.4	0.4	0.4
1.60	6.4	3.4	0.4	0.7	0.4	0.7
1.70	6.8	2.5	0.4	0.9	0.4	0.9
1.80	7.2	2.0	0.4	0.5	0.4	0.5
1.90	7.6	1.1	0.4	1.0	0.4	1.0
2.00	8.0	0	0.4	1.0	0.4	1.0

b)

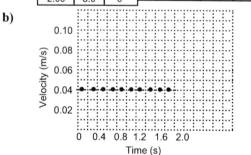

c)

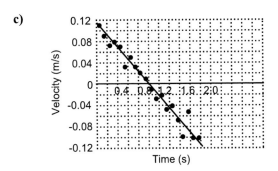

d) acceleration = slope of velocity-time graph

i) acceleration = 0

ii) slope = $\dfrac{\text{rise}}{\text{run}}$

$= \dfrac{(-0.10 - 0.10)\ \text{m/s}}{(0.15 - 0.05)\ \text{s}}$

$= 2.0\ \text{m/s}^2$

Acceleration = 2.0 m/s² downward

11. We are asked to find the vertical component.

First, we will find the vertical and horizontal components of the velocity.

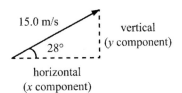

$\sin\theta = \dfrac{\text{opposite}}{\text{hypotenuse}}$

$\sin 28° = \dfrac{\text{vertical}}{15\ \text{m/s}}$

vertical component of the velocity

$= (15\ \text{m/s})(\sin 28°)$

$= 7.04\ \text{m/s}$

$\cos\theta = \dfrac{\text{adjacent}}{\text{hypotenuse}}$

$\cos 28° = \dfrac{\text{horizontal}}{15\ \text{m/s}}$

horizontal component of the velocity

$= (15\ \text{m/s})(\cos 28°)$

$= 13.2\ \text{m/s}$

Find t from the horizontal component.

speed $v = \dfrac{d}{t}$

$t = \dfrac{d}{v}$

$= \dfrac{32\ \text{m}}{13.2\ \text{m/s}}$

$= 2.42\ \text{s}$

Consider Vertical motion

$\vec{v}_0$	$\vec{v}$	$\vec{a}$	$\vec{d}$	t
7.04 m/s	×	−9.81 m/s²	?	2.42 s

$\vec{d} = \vec{v}_0 t + \dfrac{1}{2}\vec{a}t^2$

$= (7.04\ \text{m/s})(2.42\ \text{s}) + \dfrac{1}{2}(-9.81\ \text{m/s}^2)(2.42\ \text{s})^2$

$= 12\ \text{m high}$

Practice Test

ANSWERS AND SOLUTIONS

1. $\vec{d}_x = d\cos\theta$

Convert 33° W of S to 57° S of W

$\vec{d}_x = (12\ \text{m})(\cos 57°)$

$= -6.5\ \text{m}$

B is the answer.

3.

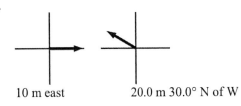

10 m east   20.0 m 30.0° N of W

Consider east and north directions as positive

$\vec{d}_{1x} = 10\ \text{m}$ $\vec{d}_{2x} = d_2\cos\theta$

$= (20\ \text{m})(\cos 30°)$

$= -17.3\ \text{m}$

$\vec{d}_{1y} = 0$ $\vec{d}_{2y} = d_2\sin\theta$

$= (20\ \text{m})(\sin 30°)$

$= 10\ \text{m}$

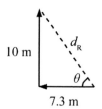

$$\sum d_x = 10 \text{ m} - 17.3 \text{ m}$$
$$= -7.3 \text{ m}$$
$$\sum d_y = 10 \text{ m}$$

Magnitude of the displacement is

$$d_R = \sqrt{d_x^2 + d_y^2}$$
$$= \sqrt{(7.3 \text{ m})^2 + (10 \text{ m})^2}$$
$$= 12.4 \text{ m}$$

A is the answer.

5.

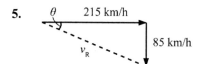

The speed is,

$$v_R = \sqrt{v_x^2 + v_y^2}$$
$$= \sqrt{(215 \text{ km/h})^2 + (85 \text{ km/h})^2}$$
$$= 231 \text{ km/h}$$

C is the answer.

7. A projectile has a vertical and a horizontal component which are independent of each other. The time that this projectile is in the air, it is accelerating uniformly toward the ground. Because the initial vertical velocity is zero, no matter how fast it is thrown horizontally, the time remains the same.

C is the answer.

9. The horizontal component of the motion is uniform motion (constant velocity) and the vertical component of the motion is uniform accelerated motion. Therefore, the horizontal component of the velocity remains constant, but the vertical component of the velocity depends on the angle.

A is the answer.

11. $v = 25.0$ m/s ⟋ $20.0°$

$$\vec{v}_x = v \cos\theta$$
$$= (25.0 \text{ m/s})(\cos 20.0°)$$
$$= 23.5 \text{ m/s}$$
$$\vec{v}_y = v \sin\theta$$
$$= (25.0 \text{ m/s})(\sin 20.0°)$$
$$= 8.55 \text{ m/s}$$

Find t from the magnitude of the horizontal component of velocity:

$$v_x = \frac{d_x}{t}$$
$$t = \frac{d_x}{v_x}$$
$$= \frac{25.0 \text{ m}}{23.5 \text{ m/s}}$$
$$= 1.06 \text{ s}$$

$\vec{v}_{yi}$	$\vec{v}_{yf}$	$\vec{a}$	$\vec{d}$	t
8.55 m/s		-9.81 m/s^2	?	1.06 s

$$\vec{d} = \vec{v}_{yi}t + \frac{1}{2}\vec{a}t^2$$
$$= (8.55 \text{ m/s})(1.06 \text{ s}) + \frac{1}{2}(-9.81 \text{ m/s}^2)(1.06 \text{ s})^2$$
$$= 3.55 \text{ m up}$$

At 3.55 m height above the ground, the object will hit the building.

A is the answer.

13. The horizontal component of a projectile represents uniform motion (constant velocity).

A is the answer.

15. We are only concerned about the vertical component in the projectile (baseball), and because the initial vertical velocity of this projectile is zero, it will hit the ground at the same time as it would if it were dropped.

C is the answer.

DYNAMICS

Lesson 1—Dynamics

PRACTICE EXERCISES
ANSWERS AND SOLUTIONS

Consider east and north directions as positive for the following solutions.

1. 2.0 N east + 3.0 N east = 5.0 N east

3.

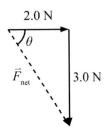

$$F_{net} = \sqrt{(F_x)^2 + (F_y)^2}$$
$$= \sqrt{(2.0 \text{ N})^2 + (3.0 \text{ N})^2}$$
$$= 3.6 \text{ N}$$
$$\tan\theta = \frac{\text{opposite}}{\text{adjacent}}$$
$$\theta = 56°$$
$$\vec{F}_{net} = 3.6 \text{ N } 56°\text{S of E}$$
$$\text{or}$$
$$3.6 \text{ N } 34° \text{ E of S (3.6 N } 304°)$$

5.

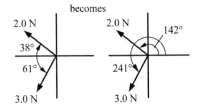

Find the x and y components of 2.0 N 39° N of W
$$\vec{F}_{1x} = \vec{F}_1 \cos\theta$$
$$= (2.0 \text{ N})(\cos 142°)$$
$$= -1.58 \text{ N}$$

$$\vec{F}_{1y} = \vec{F}_1 \sin\theta$$
$$= (2.0 \text{ N})(\sin 142°)$$
$$= 1.23 \text{ N}$$

Find the x and y components of 3.0 N 61° S of W
$$\vec{F}_{2x} = F_2\cos\theta$$
$$= (3.0 \text{ N})(\cos 241°)$$
$$= -1.45 \text{ N}$$

$$\vec{F}_{2y} = F_2\sin\theta$$
$$= (3.0 \text{ N})(\sin 241°)$$
$$= -2.62 \text{ N}$$

Add x components
$$\vec{F}_x = (-1.58 \text{ N}) + (-1.45 \text{ N})$$
$$= -3.03 \text{ N}$$

Add y components
$$\vec{F}_y = 1.23 \text{ N} + (-2.62 \text{ N})$$
$$= -1.39 \text{ N}$$

Add F_x and F_y, using Pythagoras theorem

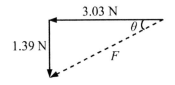

$$F_{net} = \sqrt{(F_x)^2 + (F_y)^2}$$
$$= \sqrt{(3.03 \text{ N})^2 + (1.39 \text{ N})^2}$$
$$= 3.3 \text{ N}$$
$$\tan\theta = \frac{F_y}{F_x}$$
$$= \frac{1.39 \text{ N}}{3.03 \text{ N}}$$
$$\theta = 25°$$

$$\vec{F}_{net} = 3.3 \text{ N } 25° \text{ S of W}$$
or 3.3 N 65° W of S (3.3 N 205°)

Lesson 2—Newton's First Law of Motion

PRACTICE EXERCISES
ANSWERS AND SOLUTIONS

1. $$\vec{F}_{net} = m\vec{a}$$
$$\vec{a} = \frac{\vec{F}_{net}}{m}$$
$$= \frac{9.0 \text{ N}}{20.0 \text{ kg}}$$
$$= 0.45 \text{ m/s}^2 \text{ east}$$

3. Magnitude of force is

$$\vec{F}_{net} = m\vec{a}$$
$$= (16.0 \text{ kg})(2.0 \text{ m/s}^2)$$
$$= 32 \text{ N}$$

5. $$\vec{F}_{net} = m\vec{a}$$
$$= (5.2 \text{ kg})(6.0 \text{ m/s}^2)$$
$$= 31 \text{ N}$$

7. Here south is considered as positive direction

$$a = \frac{\vec{v} - \vec{v}_0}{t}$$
$$= \frac{25.0 \text{ m/s} - 0}{10.0 \text{ s}}$$
$$= 2.50 \text{ m/s}^2$$
$$\vec{F}_{net} = m\vec{a}$$
$$= (925 \text{ kg})(2.5 \text{ m/s}^2 \text{ south})$$
$$= 2.31 \times 10^3 \text{ N south}$$

9. $$v^2 = v_0^2 + 2ad$$
$$(12 \text{ m/s})^2 = (5.0 \text{ m/s})^2 + 2(a)(94 \text{ m})$$
$$a = 0.633 \text{ m/s}^2$$
$$\vec{a} = 0.633 \text{ m/s}^2 \text{ east}$$

$$\vec{F}_{net} = m\vec{a}$$
$$= (1.20 \times 10^3 \text{ kg})(0.633 \text{ m/s}^2)$$
$$= 7.6 \times 10^2 \text{ N east}$$

11. a) $$\vec{F}_{net} = m\vec{a}$$
$$\vec{a} = \frac{\vec{F}_{net}}{m}$$
$$= \frac{6.6 \text{ N east}}{9.0 \text{ kg}}$$
$$= 0.73 \text{ m/s}^2 \text{ east}$$
$$v^2 = v_0^2 + 2ad$$
$$(12 \text{ m/s})^2 = 2(0.73 \text{ m/s}^2)d$$
$$d = 6.1 \text{ m}$$
$$\therefore d = 6.1 \text{ m east}$$

b) The magnitude of acceleration is

$$a = \frac{v - v_0}{t}$$
$$0.73 \text{ m/s}^2 = \frac{3.0 \text{ m/s} - 0}{t}$$
$$t = 4.1 \text{ s}$$

Lesson 3—Forces in Nature

PRACTICE EXERCISES
ANSWERS AND SOLUTIONS

1. $$\vec{F}_g = m\vec{g}$$
$$= (25.0 \text{ kg})(9.81 \text{ m/s}^2)$$
$$= 245 \text{ N down}$$

3. $$F_g = mg$$
$$g = \frac{F_g}{m}$$
$$= \frac{36.0 \text{ N}}{22.0 \text{ kg}}$$
$$= 1.64 \text{ m/s}^2$$

5. $$F_g = mg$$
$$m = \frac{F_g}{g}$$
$$= \frac{127 \text{ N}}{9.81 \text{ m/s}^2}$$
$$= 12.9 \text{ kg}$$

Lesson 4—Force Due to Gravity

PRACTICE EXERCISES
ANSWERS AND SOLUTIONS

1. $$F_N = F_g$$
$$= mg$$
$$= (14.0 \text{ kg})(9.81 \text{ m/s}^2)$$
$$= 137 \text{ N}$$

3. $$F_{fr} = \mu F_N$$
$$\mu = \frac{F_f}{F_N}$$
$$= \frac{3.0 \text{ N}}{20.0 \text{ N}}$$
$$= 0.15$$

5.

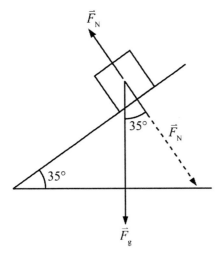

$$F_N = F_g \cos 35.0°$$
$$= (15.0 \text{ N})(\cos 35.0°)$$
$$= 12.3 \text{ N}$$
$$F_{fr} = \mu F_N$$
$$= (0.300)(12.3 \text{ N})$$
$$= 3.69 \text{ N}$$

Lesson 5—Applied Force or Tension

PRACTICE EXERCISES
ANSWERS AND SOLUTIONS

For the following sets of solution, magnitudes of the forces are considered.

1. $\vec{F}_{app}$

$$F_{net} = F_{app} - F_g$$
$$= 145 \text{ N} - mg$$
$$= 145 \text{ N} - (11.0 \text{ kg})(9.81 \text{ m/s}^2)$$
$$= 37.1 \text{ N}$$
$$F_{net} = ma$$
$$a = \frac{F_{net}}{m}$$
$$= \frac{37.1 \text{ N}}{11.0 \text{ kg}}$$
$$= 3.37 \text{ m/s}^2$$

$\vec{F}_g$

3. $\vec{F}_{app}$

$$F_g = mg$$
$$= (15.0 \text{ kg})(9.81 \text{ m/s}^2)$$
$$= 147 \text{ N}$$
$$F_{net} = ma$$
$$= (15.0 \text{ kg})(8.80 \text{ m/s}^2)$$
$$= 132 \text{ N}$$
$$F_{net} = F_{app} - F_g$$
$$F_{app} = F_{net} + F_g$$
$$= 132 \text{ N} + 147 \text{ N}$$
$$= 279 \text{ N}$$

$\vec{F}_g$

5.
$$v^2 = v_0^2 + 2ad$$
$$(4.0 \text{ ms})^2 = 2(a)(5.0\text{m})$$
$$a = 1.6 \text{ m/s}^2$$
$$\vec{F}_{net} = m\vec{a}$$
$$m = \frac{F_{net}}{a}$$
$$= \frac{12.0 \text{ N}}{1.6 \text{ m/s}^2}$$
$$= 7.5 \text{ kg}$$

7. a) $\vec{F}_T$

$$F_{net} = ma$$
$$= (1.20 \times 10^3 \text{ kg})(1.05 \text{ m/s}^2)$$
$$= 1.26 \times 10^3 \text{ N}$$
$$F_g = mg$$
$$= (1.20 \times 10^3 \text{ kg})(9.81 \text{ m/s}^2)$$
$$= 1.18 \times 10^4 \text{ N}$$
$$F_{net} = F_g - F_T$$
$$F_T = F_g - F_{net}$$
$$= 1.18 \times 10^4 \text{ N} - 1.26 \times 10^3 \text{ N}$$
$$= 1.05 \times 10^4 \text{ N}$$

$\vec{F}_g$

b)
$$F_{net} = F_T - F_g$$
$$F_T = F_{net} + F_g$$
$$= 1.26 \times 10^3 \text{ N} + 1.18 \times 10^4 \text{ N}$$
$$= 1.30 \times 10^4 \text{ N}$$

c)
$$F_{net} = F_T - F_g$$
Acceleration = 0; therefore $F_{net} = 0$
Therefore,
$$T = F_g$$
$$= mg$$
$$= (1.20 \times 10^3 \text{kg})(9.81 \text{ m/s}^2)$$
$$= 1.18 \times 10^4 \text{ N}$$

9. acceleration = 0; therefore $F_{net} = 0$

$$F_{net} = F_{app} - F_{fr}$$
$$0 = 90.0 \text{ N} - F_{fr}$$
$$F_{fr} = 90.0 \text{ N}$$

11.

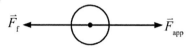

$$F_{net} = F_{app} - F_{fr}$$
$$= 2.5 \times 10^2 \text{ N} - 1.4 \times 10^2 \text{ N}$$
$$= 1.1 \times 10^2 \text{ N}$$
$$F_g = mg$$

Therefore

$$m = \frac{F_g}{g}$$
$$= \frac{1.0 \times 10^2 \text{ N}}{9.81 \text{ m/s}^2}$$
$$= 1.0 \times 10^1 \text{ kg}$$

The net force is acting along north.

$$\vec{F}_{net} = m\vec{a}$$
$$\vec{a} = \frac{\vec{F}_{net}}{m}$$
$$= \frac{1.1 \times 10^2 \text{ N north}}{1.0 \times 10^1 \text{ kg}}$$
$$= 1.1 \times 10^1 \text{ m/s}^2 \text{ north}$$

13. $F_{net} = ma$

$$a = \frac{F_{net}}{m}$$
$$= \frac{1.80 \times 10^4 \text{ N}}{1.5 \times 10^3 \text{ kg}}$$
$$= 1.2 \times 10^1 \text{ m/s}^2$$
$$v^2 = v_0^2 + 2ad$$
$$0 = (24.0 \text{ m/s})^2 + 2(1.2 \times 10^1 \text{ m/s}^2)d$$
$$d = 24.0 \text{ m}$$

15.

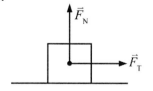

$$F_{net} = F_T = F_g = mg$$
$$= (1.5 \text{ kg})(9.81 \text{ m/s}^2)$$
$$= 14.7 \text{ N}$$

Again $F_{net} = ma$
Therefore,

$$a = \frac{F_{net}}{m}$$
$$= \frac{14.7 \text{ N}}{2.5 \text{ kg}}$$
$$= 5.9 \text{ m/s}^2$$

17.

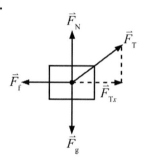

$$F_{Tx} = F_T (\cos 42.0°)$$
$$= (60.0 \text{ N})(\cos 42.0°)$$
$$= 44.6 \text{ N}$$
$$F_g = mg$$
$$m = \frac{F_g}{g}$$
$$= \frac{125 \text{ N}}{9.81 \text{ m/s}^2}$$
$$= 12.7 \text{ kg}$$

$$F_{net} = F_{Tx} - F_{fr}$$
$$= 44.6 \text{ N} - 15.0 \text{ N}$$
$$= 29.6 \text{ N}$$

Again
$$F_{net} = ma$$
Therefore

$$a = \frac{F_{net}}{m}$$
$$= \frac{29.6 \text{ N}}{12.7 \text{ kg}}$$
$$= 2.32 \text{ m/s}^2$$

19. $v^2 = v_0^2 + 2ad$

$0 = (3.0 \text{ m/s})^2 + 2(a)(8.0 \text{ m})$

$a = -0.56 \text{ m/s}^2$

Negative sign indicates that the puck is decelerating.

$\vec{F}_{net} = m\vec{a}$

$= (0.48 \text{ kg})(-0.56 \text{ m/s}^2)$

$= -0.27 \text{N}$ or 0.27 N south

21. a) $F_{net} = ma$

$a = \dfrac{F_{net}}{m}$

$= \dfrac{20.0 \text{ N}}{5.0 \text{ kg}}$

$= 4.0 \text{ m/s}^2$

b) $F_{net} = ma$

$= (3.0 \text{kg})(4.0 \text{ m/s}^2)$

$= 12$ N

23. a) $F_{fr} = \mu F_N$

$= \mu mg$

$= (0.35)(4.0 \text{ kg})(9.81 \text{ m/s}^2)$

$= 13.7$ N

$\vec{F}_f = 13.7 \text{ N} \longleftarrow \boxed{} \longrightarrow \vec{F}_{app} = 14.0 \text{ N}$

$F_{net} = F_{app} - F_{fr}$

$= 14.0 \text{ N} - 13.7 \text{ N}$

$= 0.28$ N

Again

$F_{net} = ma$

$a = \dfrac{F_{net}}{m}$

$= \dfrac{0.28 \text{ N}}{4.0 \text{ kg}}$

$= 0.070 \text{ m/s}^2$

b) Net force on 1.0 kg mass

$F_{net} = ma$

$= (1.0 \text{ kg})(0.070 \text{ m/s}^2)$

$= 0.070$ N

$F_{fr} = \mu F_N$

$= \mu mg$

$= (0.35)(1.0 \text{ kg})(9.81 \text{ m/s}^2)$

$= 3.43$ N

$\vec{F}_f = ? \longleftarrow \boxed{} \longrightarrow \vec{F}_{app} = ?$

$F_{net} = F_{app} - F_{fr}$

$F_{app} = F_{net} + F_{fr}$

$= 0.070 \text{ N} + 3.43 \text{ N}$

$= 3.5$ N

Lesson 6—Physics of an Inclined Plane

PRACTICE EXERCISES
ANSWERS AND SOLUTIONS

1.

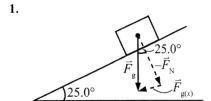

$\sin \theta = \dfrac{\text{opposite}}{\text{hypotenuse}}$

$\sin 25.0° = \dfrac{F_{g(x)}}{445 \text{ N}}$

$F_{g(x)} = (445 \text{ N})(\sin 25.0°)$

$= 188$ N

3.

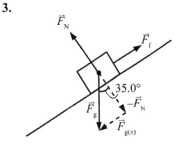

$\sin \theta = \dfrac{\text{opposite}}{\text{hypotenuse}}$

$\sin 35.0° = \dfrac{F_{g(x)}}{275 \text{ N}}$

$F_{g(x)} = (275 \text{ N})(\sin 35.0°)$

$= 158$ N

$F_{net} = F_{g(x)} - F_{fr}$

$= 158 \text{ N} - 96.0 \text{ N}$

$= 62.0$ N

$$F_g = mg$$
$$m = \frac{F_g}{g}$$
$$= \frac{275 \text{ N}}{9.81 \text{ m/s}^2}$$
$$= 28.0 \text{ kg}$$

$$F_{net} = ma$$
$$a = F_{g(x)}$$
$$= \frac{62.0 \text{ N}}{28.0 \text{ kg}}$$
$$= 2.21 \text{ m/s}^2$$

5.

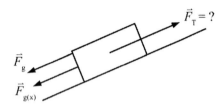

$$F_{fr} = \mu F_N = \mu F_g \cos\theta$$
$$= (0.180)(125 \text{ N})(\cos 23.0°)$$
$$= 20.7 \text{ N}$$

$$F_{g(x)} = F_g \sin\theta$$
$$= (125 \text{ N})(\sin 23.0°)$$
$$= 48.8 \text{ N}$$

$$F_T = F_f + F_{g(x)}$$
$$F_T = 20.7 \text{ N} + 48.8 \text{ N}$$
$$= 69.5 \text{ N}$$

7. a)
$$F_{fr} = \mu F_N = \mu F_g \cos\theta$$
$$= \mu mg\cos\theta$$
$$= (0.25)(1.0 \text{ kg})(9.81 \text{ m/s}^2)(\cos 30.0°)$$
$$= 2.12 \text{ N}$$

$$F_{net} = F_{g1} - F_{g2(x)} - F_{fr}$$
$$= 19.6 \text{ N} - 4.9 \text{ N} - 2.1 \text{ N}$$
$$= 12.6 \text{ N}$$

$$F_{net} = ma$$
$$a = \frac{F_{net}}{m}$$
$$= \frac{12.6 \text{ N}}{3.0 \text{ kg}}$$
$$= 4.2 \text{ m/s}^2$$

b)

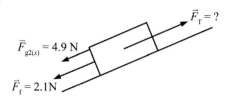

F_{net} on 1.0 kg mass
$$F_{net} = m_2 a$$
$$= (1.0 \text{ kg})(4.2 \text{ m/s}^2)$$
$$= 4.2 \text{ N}$$

$$F_{net} = F_T - F_{g2(x)} - F_{fr}$$
$$F_T = F_{net} + F_{g2(x)} + F_{fr}$$
$$= 4.2 \text{ N} + 4.9 \text{ N} + 2.1 \text{ N}$$
$$= 11.2 \text{ N} = 11 \text{ N}$$

Lesson 7—Newton's Third Law of Motion

PRACTICE EXERCISES
ANSWERS AND SOLUTIONS

1. Considering east direction as positive for this case
$$\vec{F}_1 = -\vec{F}_2$$
$$m_1 \vec{a}_1 = -m_2 \vec{a}_2$$
$$(38 \text{ kg})(0.60 \text{ m/s}^2) = -m_2 (-0.75 \text{ m/s}^2)$$
$$m_2 = 30.4 \text{ kg}$$
$$\approx 30 \text{ kg}$$

3.
$$a = \frac{v - v_0}{t}$$
$$= \frac{22 \text{ m/s} - 11 \text{ m/s}}{0.75 \text{ s}}$$
$$= 14.6 \text{ m/s}^2$$

$$F_{net} = ma$$
$$= (9.8 \times 10^3 \text{ kg})(14.6 \text{ m/s}^2)$$
$$= 1.4 \times 10^5 \text{ N}$$

According to Newton's third law
$$\vec{F}_{net} = 1.4 \times 10^5 \text{ N west}$$

Practice Test

ANSWERS AND SOLUTIONS

1. Newton's First Law states that an object will remain at constant velocity (including zero) unless acted on by an unbalanced force.

   B is the answer.

3. Newton's Second Law in part tells us that the acceleration of an object varies inversely with the mass. This graph shows an inverse relationship.

   C is the answer.

5. Mass is defined as the quantitative measure of an object's inertia. Mass does not depend on gravity.

   C is the answer.

7. If we ignore air friction, the acceleration of a falling object does not depend on the mass.

   D is the answer.

9. Mass is defined as the quantitative measure of an object's inertia.

   A is the answer.

11.

   $\vec{F}_f = 48\ \text{N} \longleftarrow \boxed{} \longrightarrow \vec{F}_T = 105\ \text{N}$

   $\begin{aligned} F_{net} &= F_T - F_{fr} \\ &= 105\ \text{N} - 48\ \text{N} \\ &= 57\ \text{N} \end{aligned}$

   $\begin{aligned} F_{net} &= ma \\ a &= \frac{F_{net}}{m} \\ &= \frac{57\ \text{N}}{95.0\ \text{kg}} \\ &= 0.600\ \text{m/s}^2 \end{aligned}$

   B is the answer.

13. $\begin{aligned} F_g &= mg \\ m &= \frac{F_g}{g} \\ &= \frac{12.0\ \text{N}}{9.81\ \text{m/s}^2} \\ &= 1.22\ \text{kg} \end{aligned}$

   B is the answer.

15.

   $\vec{F}_T \uparrow$

   $\vec{F}_g \downarrow$

   $\begin{aligned} F_g &= mg \\ &= (3.0\text{kg})(9.81\ \text{m/s}^2) \\ &= 29.4\ \text{N} \\ F_{net} &= F_T - F_g \\ &= 55\ \text{N} - 29.4\ \text{N} \\ &= 25.6\ \text{N} \end{aligned}$

   $\begin{aligned} F_{net} &= ma \\ a &= \frac{F_{net}}{m} \\ &= \frac{25.6\ \text{N}}{3.0\ \text{kg}} \\ &= 8.5\ \text{m/s}^2 \end{aligned}$

   A is the answer.

WORK, POWER, AND ENERGY

Lesson 1—Work

PRACTICE EXERCISES
ANSWERS AND SOLUTIONS

1. $W = Fd$
$= (20.0 \text{ N})(1.50 \text{ m})$
$= 30.0 \text{ J}$

3. $W = Fd$
$= (2.20 \text{ N})(0)$
$= 0$

5. Find horizontal component of the force.

$F = 75.0 \text{ N}$

$20.0°$

horizontal

$\cos \theta = \dfrac{\text{adjacent}}{\text{hypotenuse}}$

$\cos 20.0° = \dfrac{\text{horizontal}}{75.0 \text{ N}}$

$\text{horizontal} = (75.0 \text{ N})(\cos 20.0°)$

$= 70.5 \text{ N}$

$W = Fd$
$= (70.5 \text{ N})(10.0 \text{ m})$
$= 705 \text{ J}$

7. Here the force is the gravitational force and no displacement occurs parallel to the force. Therefore, work done on the box $= 0$

9. Find out work done against friction:
$W = F_{fr}d$
$= (3.8 \text{ N})(6.0 \text{ m})$
$= 22.8 \text{ J}$

Find out work done to accelerate from rest through a distance of 6.0 m:

$d = v_0 t + \dfrac{1}{2}at^2$

$6.0 \text{ m} = \dfrac{1}{2}(a)(4.0 \text{ s})^2$

$a = 0.75 \text{ m/s}^2$

$F = ma$
$= (25.0 \text{ kg})(0.75 \text{ m/s}^2)$
$= 18.8 \text{ N}$

$W = Fd$
$= (18.8 \text{ N})(6.0 \text{ m})$
$= 1.13 \times 10^2 \text{ J}$

Total work done $= 1.1 \times 10^2 \text{ J} + 22.8 \text{ J}$
$= 1.4 \times 10^2 \text{ J}$

11. $d = vt$
$= (2.00 \text{ m/s})(15.0 \text{ s})$
$= 30.0 \text{ m}$

$W = Fd$
$= (225 \text{ N})(30.0 \text{ m})$
$= 6.75 \times 10^3 \text{ J}$

13. $W = Fd$
$= (3.5 \text{ N})(16.0 \text{ m})$
$= 56 \text{ J}$

Lesson 2—Power

PRACTICE EXERCISES
ANSWERS AND SOLUTIONS

1. $W = mgh$
$= (45.0 \text{ kg})(9.81 \text{ m/s}^2)(6.0 \text{ m})$
$= 2.65 \times 10^3 \text{ J}$

$P = \dfrac{W}{t}$

$t = \dfrac{W}{P}$

$= \dfrac{2.65 \times 10^3 \text{ J}}{1.50 \times 10^3 \text{ W}}$

$= 1.8 \text{ s}$

3. $v_{average} = \dfrac{v + v_0}{2}$

$= \dfrac{3.00 \text{ m/s} + 0}{2}$

$= 1.50 \text{ m/s}$

$v^2 = v_0^2 + 2ad$

$(3.00 \text{ m/s})^2 = 2(a)(1.5 \text{ m})$

$a = 3.0 \text{ m/s}^2$

$F = ma$
$$= (2.00 \text{ kg})(3.0 \text{ m/s}^2)$$
$$= 6.0 \text{ N}$$

$P = Fv$
$$= (6.0 \text{ N})(1.50 \text{ m/s})$$
$$= 90 \text{ W}$$

5.
$$v^2 = v_0^{\ 2} + 2ad$$
$$(6.0 \text{ m/s})^2 = 2(a)(2.0 \text{ m})$$
$$a = 9.0 \text{ m/s}^2$$

$F_{\text{net}} = ma$
$$= (5.0 \text{ kg})(9.0 \text{ m/s}^2)$$
$$= 45 \text{ N}$$
$F_{\text{net}} = F_{\text{T}} - F_{\text{fr}}$
$F_{\text{T}} = F_{\text{net}} + F_{\text{fr}}$
$$= 45 \text{ N} + 4.0 \text{ N}$$
$$= 49 \text{ N}$$

$v_{\text{av}} = \dfrac{v + v_0}{2}$
$$= \dfrac{6.0 \text{ m/s} + 0}{2}$$
$$= 3.0 \text{ m/s}$$

$P = F_{\text{T}} v_{\text{av}}$
$$= (49 \text{ N})(3.0 \text{ m/s})$$
$$= 1.5 \times 10^2 \text{ W}$$

7. efficiency $= \dfrac{\text{power out}}{\text{power in}} \times 100\%$

power out $= \dfrac{\text{efficiency} \times \text{power in}}{100\%}$
$$= (0.82)(1.00 \times 10^5 \text{ W})$$
$$= 8.2 \times 10^4 \text{ W}$$

power $= \dfrac{mgh}{t}$

$t = \dfrac{mgh}{\text{power}}$
$$= \dfrac{(50.0 \text{ kg})(9.81 \text{ m/s}^2)(8.00 \text{ m})}{(8.2 \times 10^4 \text{ W})}$$
$$= 0.048 \text{ s}$$

Lesson 3—Potential Energy

PRACTICE EXERCISES
ANSWERS AND SOLUTIONS

1. $E_p = F_g d$
$$= (25.0 \text{ N})(2.10 \text{ m})$$
$$= 52.5 \text{ J}$$

3. $E_p = mgh$
$$= (2.75 \text{ kg})(9.81 \text{ m/s}^2)(7.00 \text{ m})$$
$$= 189 \text{ J}$$

5. $E_p = mgh$
$$= (2.0 \times 10^2 \text{ kg})(9.81 \text{ m/s}^2)(6.0 \text{ m})$$
$$= 1.2 \times 10^4 \text{ J}$$

Lesson 4—Kinetic Energy

PRACTICE EXERCISES
ANSWERS AND SOLUTIONS

1. $E_k = \dfrac{1}{2}mv^2$
$$= \dfrac{1}{2}(3.0 \text{ kg})(7.5 \text{ m/s})^2$$
$$= 84 \text{ J}$$

3. $v^2 = v_0^{\ 2} + 2ad$
$$= 2(2.5 \text{ m/s}^2)(15.0 \text{ m})$$
$$= 75 \text{ m}^2/\text{s}^2$$
$v = 8.66 \text{ m/s}$

$F_g = mg$
$m = \dfrac{F_g}{g}$
$$= \dfrac{10.0 \text{ N}}{9.80 \text{ m/s}^2}$$
$$= 1.02 \text{ kg}$$

$E_k = \dfrac{1}{2}mv^2$
$$= \dfrac{1}{2}(1.02 \text{ kg})(8.66 \text{ m/s})^2$$
$$= 38 \text{ J}$$

427

5. $F_g = mg$

$$m = \frac{F_g}{g}$$

$$= \frac{10.0 \text{ N}}{9.80 \text{ m/s}^2}$$

$$= 1.02 \text{ kg}$$

$$E_k = \frac{1}{2}mv^2$$

$$v = \sqrt{\frac{2E_k}{m}}$$

$$= \sqrt{\frac{2(3.00 \times 10^2 \text{ J})}{1.02 \text{ kg}}}$$

$$= 24.2 \text{ m/s}$$

Lesson 5—Work-Energy Theorem

PRACTICE EXERCISES
ANSWERS AND SOLUTIONS

The force in these equations is the net force.

1.

$$Fd = \frac{1}{2}m\left(v^2 - v_0^2\right)$$

$$(23.0 \text{ N})\left(5.0 \times 10^{-2} \text{ m}\right) = \frac{1}{2}(0.12 \text{ kg})(v^2 - 0)$$

$$v = \sqrt{\frac{2(23.0 \text{ N})(5.0 \times 10^{-2} \text{m})}{0.12 \text{ kg}}}$$

$$= 4.4 \text{ m/s}$$

3. Convert 5.00 km/h to m/s

$$= \frac{(5.00 \text{ km/h})(1\ 000 \text{ m/km})}{3\ 600 \text{ s/h}}$$

$$= 1.39 \text{ m/s}$$

$$W = Fd = \frac{1}{2}m\left(v_f^2 - v_0^2\right)$$

$$= \frac{1}{2}(1.10 \times 10^3 \text{ kg})\left((1.39 \text{ m/s})^2 - 0\right)$$

$$= 1.06 \times 10^3 \text{ J}$$

5.

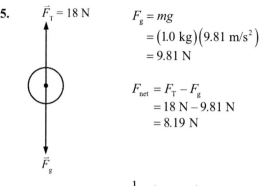

$\vec{F}_T = 18$ N

$\vec{F}_g$

$$F_g = mg$$

$$= (1.0 \text{ kg})\left(9.81 \text{ m/s}^2\right)$$

$$= 9.81 \text{ N}$$

$$F_{net} = F_T - F_g$$

$$= 18 \text{ N} - 9.81 \text{ N}$$

$$= 8.19 \text{ N}$$

$$F_{net}d = \frac{1}{2}m\left(v^2 - v_0^2\right)$$

$$(8.19 \text{ N})(0.30 \text{ m}) = \frac{1}{2}(1.0 \text{ kg})(v^2 - 0)$$

$$v = \sqrt{\frac{2(8.19 \text{ N})(0.30 \text{ m})}{1.0 \text{ kg}}}$$

$$= 2.2 \text{ m/s}$$

7.

$$Fd = \frac{1}{2}m\left(v^2 - v_0^2\right)$$

$$F(5.5 \text{ m}) = \frac{1}{2}(0.65 \text{ kg})\left(0 - (2.0 \text{ m/s})^2\right)$$

$$F = \frac{\frac{1}{2}(0.65 \text{ kg})\left(0 - (2.0 \text{ m/s})^2\right)}{5.5 \text{ m}}$$

$$= -0.24 \text{ N}$$

9.

$$Fd = \frac{1}{2}m\left(v^2 - v_0^2\right)$$

$$(35 \text{ N})(3.5 \text{ m}) = \frac{1}{2}(15 \text{ kg})(v^2 - 0)$$

$$v = \sqrt{\frac{2(35 \text{ N})(3.5 \text{ m})}{15 \text{ kg}}}$$

$$= 4.0 \text{ m/s}$$

11. Find net force

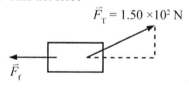

$\vec{F}_T = 1.50 \times 10^2$ N

$\vec{F}_f$

$$F_{Tx} = F_T \cos\theta$$

$$= \left(1.50 \times 10^2 \text{ N}\right)(\cos 25°)$$

$$= 135.9 \text{ N}$$

$$F_{Ty} = F_T \sin\theta$$

$$= \left(1.50 \times 10^2 \text{ N}\right)(\sin 25°)$$

$$= 63.39 \text{ N}$$

$$F_N + F_{Ty} = F_g$$
$$F_N = F_g - F_{Ty}$$
$$= (50.0 \text{ kg})(9.81 \text{ m/s}^2) - 63.39 \text{ N}$$
$$= 427.1 \text{ N}$$

$$F_{fr} = \mu F_N$$
$$= (50.0 \text{ kg})(9.81 \text{ m/s}^2) - 63.39$$
$$= 427.1 \text{ N}$$

$$F_{net} = F_{Tx} - F_{fr}$$
$$= 135.9 \text{ N} - 106.8 \text{ N}$$
$$= 29.1 \text{ N}$$

$$F_{net}d = \frac{1}{2}m(v^2 - v_0^2)$$
$$(29.1 \text{ N})(12.0 \text{ m}) = \frac{1}{2}(50.0 \text{ kg})(v^2 - 0)$$
$$v = \sqrt{\frac{2(29.1 \text{ N})(12.0 \text{ m})}{50.0 \text{ kg}}}$$
$$= 3.74 \text{ m/s}$$

13. Find net force:

$$F_{fr} = \mu F_N$$
$$= (0.35)(45.0 \text{ N})(9.81 \text{ m/s}^2)$$
$$= 154.5 \text{ N}$$

$$F_{net} = F_T - F_{fr}$$
$$= 192 \text{ N} - 154.5 \text{ N}$$
$$= 37.4 \text{ N}$$

$$F_{net}d = \frac{1}{2}m(v^2 - v_0^2)$$
$$(37.5 \text{ N})(8.0 \text{ m}) = \frac{1}{2}(45.0 \text{ kg})(v^2 - 0)$$
$$v = \sqrt{\frac{2(37.5 \text{ N})(8.0 \text{ m})}{45.0 \text{ kg}}}$$
$$= 3.7 \text{ m/s}$$

Lesson 6—Law of Conservation of Mechanical Energy

PRACTICE EXERCISES
ANSWERS AND SOLUTIONS

1.
$$\Delta E_k + \Delta E_p = 0$$
$$\Delta E_k = -\Delta E_p$$
$$\frac{1}{2}m(v^2 - v_0^2) = -mg\Delta h$$
$$\frac{1}{2}(v^2 - v_0^2) = -(9.81 \text{ m/s}^2)(\Delta h)$$
$$\Delta h = \frac{\frac{1}{2}(3.2 \text{ m/s})^2}{-9.81 \text{ m/s}^2}$$
$$= -0.52 \text{ m}$$

∴ the object is dropped from a height of 0.52 m.

3.
$$\Delta E_k + \Delta E_p = 0$$
$$\Delta E_k = -\Delta E_p$$
$$\frac{1}{2}m(v^2 - v_0^2) = -mg\Delta h$$
$$\frac{1}{2}(v^2 - v_0^2) = -g\Delta h$$
$$\frac{1}{2}((37.0 \text{ m/s})^2 - 0) = (9.81 \text{ m/s}^2)(\Delta h)$$
$$\Delta h = \frac{\frac{1}{2}(37.0 \text{ m/s})^2}{-9.81 \text{ m/s}^2}$$
$$= -69.8 \text{ m}$$

∴ The building was 69.8 m tall.

5.
$$\Delta E_k + \Delta E_p = 0$$
$$\Delta E_k = -\Delta E_p$$
$$\frac{1}{2}m(v^2 - v_0^2) = -mg\Delta h$$
$$\frac{1}{2}(v^2 - v_0^2) = -g\Delta h$$
$$\frac{1}{2}(v^2 - 0) = -(9.81 \text{ m/s}^2)(-4.0 \text{ m})$$
$$v = \sqrt{2(9.81 \text{ m/s}^2)(4.0 \text{ m})}$$
$$= 8.9 \text{ m/s}$$

7. Find Δh first:

$$\sin 30.0° = \frac{\Delta h}{12.0 \text{ m}}$$
$$\Delta h = 6.0 \text{ m}$$
$$\Delta E_k + \Delta E_p = 0$$
$$\Delta E_k = -\Delta E_p$$
$$\frac{1}{2}m(v^2 - v_0^2) = -mg\Delta h$$
$$\frac{1}{2}(v^2 - v_0^2) = -g\Delta h$$
$$\frac{1}{2}(v^2 - 0) = -(9.81 \text{ m/s}^2)(-6.0 \text{ m})$$
$$v = \sqrt{2(9.81 \text{ m/s}^2)(6.0 \text{ m})}$$
$$= 10.8 \text{ m/s}$$

9.
$$\Delta E_k + \Delta E_p = 0$$
$$\Delta E_k = -\Delta E_p$$
$$\frac{1}{2}m(v^2 - v_0^2) = -mg\Delta h$$
$$\frac{1}{2}(v^2 - v_0^2) = -g\Delta h$$
$$\frac{1}{2}(v^2 - 0) = -(9.81 \text{ m/s}^2)(-10.0 \text{ m})$$
$$v = \sqrt{2(9.81 \text{ m/s}^2)(10.0 \text{ m})}$$
$$= 14 \text{ m/s}$$

11.

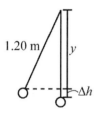

1.20 m, y, Δh

Find Δh first

$$\cos 25.0° = \frac{y}{1.20 \text{ m}}$$
$$y = 1.09$$

$$\therefore \Delta h = 1.20 \text{ m} - y$$
$$= 1.20 \text{ m} - 1.09 \text{ m}$$
$$= 0.112 \text{ m}$$

$$\Delta E_k + \Delta E_p = 0$$
$$\Delta E_k = -\Delta E_p$$
$$\frac{1}{2}m(v^2 - v_0^2) = -mg\Delta h$$
$$\frac{1}{2}(v^2 - v_0^2) = -g\Delta h$$
$$\frac{1}{2}(v^2 - 0) = -(9.81 \text{ m/s}^2)(-0.112 \text{ m})$$
$$v = \sqrt{2(9.81 \text{ m/s}^2)(-0.112 \text{ m})}$$
$$= 1.5 \text{ m/s}$$

13.
$$\Delta E_k + \Delta E_p = 0$$
$$\Delta E_k = -\Delta E_p$$
$$\frac{1}{2}m(v^2 - v_0^2) = -mg\Delta h$$
$$\frac{1}{2}(v^2 - v_0^2) = -g\Delta h$$
$$\frac{1}{2}(v^2 - 0) = -(9.81 \text{ m/s}^2)(-2.0 \text{ m})$$
$$v = \sqrt{2(9.81 \text{ m/s}^2)(-2.0 \text{ m})}$$
$$= 6.3 \text{ m/s}$$

Lesson 7—Law of Conservation of Energy

PRACTICE EXERCISES
ANSWERS AND SOLUTIONS

1.
$$\Delta E_k + \Delta E_p + \Delta TE = 0$$
$$\Delta E_k + \Delta E_p = -\Delta TE$$
$$\frac{1}{2}m(v^2 - v_0^2) + mg\Delta h = F_{ft}d$$

$$\frac{1}{2}(12 \text{ kg})(v^2 - 0) + (12 \text{ kg})(9.81 \text{ m/s}^2)(-6.0 \text{ m})$$
$$= -(5.0 \text{ N})(11.0 \text{ m})$$
$$(6.0 \text{ kg})(v^2) - 706.3 \text{ J} = -55.0 \text{ J}$$
$$(6.0 \text{ kg})(v^2) = 651.3 \text{ J}$$
$$v = \sqrt{\frac{651.3 \text{ J}}{6.0 \text{ kg}}}$$
$$= 10 \text{ m/s}$$

3. $\Delta E_k + \Delta E_p + \Delta TE =$ work done by external force

$\frac{1}{2}m(v^2 - v_0{}^2) + mg\Delta h =$ work done by external force

$\left(\begin{array}{c} \frac{1}{2}(12\ \text{kg})\left((8\ \text{m/s})^2 - (2\ \text{m/s})^2\right) \\ +0 + F_{fr}d \end{array}\right) = (85\ \text{N})(15\ \text{m})$

$360\ \text{J} + 0 + F_{fr}(15\ \text{m}) = 1\ 275\ \text{J}$

$F_{fr} = \dfrac{1\ 275\ \text{J} - 360\ \text{J}}{15\ \text{m}}$

$= 61\ \text{N}$

$F_{fr} = \mu F_N$

$\mu = \dfrac{F_{fr}}{F_N}$

$= \dfrac{61\ \text{N}}{(12\ \text{kg})(9.81\ \text{m/s}^2)}$

$= 0.52$

4. Find Δh

5. Find Δh

$\sin 30° = \dfrac{\Delta h}{0.850\ \text{m}}$

$\Delta h = 0.425\ \text{m}$

$\Delta E_k + \Delta E_p + \Delta TE = 0$

$\Delta E_k + \Delta E_p = -\Delta TE$

$\frac{1}{2}m(v^2 - v_0{}^2) + mg\Delta h = F_{fr}d$

$\left(\begin{array}{c} \frac{1}{2}(2.5\ \text{kg})(v^2 - 0) \\ +(2.5\ \text{kg})(9.81\ \text{m/s}^2)(-0.425\ \text{m}) \end{array}\right) = -(3.2\ \text{N})\ (0.850\ \text{m})$

$(1.25\ \text{kg})(v^2) - 10.42\ \text{J} = -2.72\ \text{J}$

$v = \sqrt{\dfrac{-2.72\ \text{J} + 10.42\ \text{J}}{1.25\ \text{kg}}}$

$= 2.5\ \text{m/s}$

7. Find Δh

$\sin 40° = \dfrac{\Delta h}{50.0\ \text{m}}$

$\Delta h = 32.1\ \text{m}$

$\Delta E_p = mgh$

$= (115\ \text{N})(32.1\ \text{m})$

$= 3.70 \times 10^3\ \text{J}$

9. a) $\Delta TE = F_{fr}d$

$= (17.9\ \text{N})(8.0\ \text{m})$

$= 1.4 \times 10^2\ \text{J}$

b) $\Delta E_k + \Delta E_p + \Delta TE = 0$

$\Delta E_k + \Delta E_p = -\Delta TE$

$\frac{1}{2}m(v^2 - v_0{}^2) + mg\Delta h = F_{fr}d$

$\left(\begin{array}{c} \frac{1}{2}(75.0\ \text{kg})(v^2 - 0) \\ +(75.0\ \text{kg})(9.81\ \text{m/s}^2)(-5.0\ \text{m}) \end{array}\right) = -(17.9\ \text{N})(8.0\ \text{m})$

$(37.5\ \text{kg})(v^2) - 3\ 679\ \text{J} = -143.2\ \text{J}$

$v = \sqrt{\dfrac{-143.2\ \text{J} + 3679\ \text{J}}{37.5\ \text{kg}}}$

$= 9.7\ \text{m/s}$

Practice Test

1. $E_k = \dfrac{1}{2}mv^2$

$\therefore E_k \propto v^2$

This mathematical expression tells us that if we double the speed, the kinetic energy will quadruple.

D is the answer.

3. When an object falls, it loses position and gains velocity. When it loses position, it loses potential energy. When it gains velocity, it gains kinetic energy.

A is the answer.

5. $E_k = \dfrac{1}{2}mv^2$

$E_k \propto m$, $E_k \propto v^2$

From this mathematical expression,
- if we double the mass, we double E_k.
- if we halve the speed, we "quarter" E_k.

  $\therefore$ if we double the mass and halve the speed, we halve the kinetic energy.

  C is the answer.

7. Work $= F_g d$, but F_g and d are perpendicular, $(F_g)x = 0$

$\therefore$ work $= 0$

C is the answer.

9. $E_k = \dfrac{1}{2}mv^2$

$E_k \propto v^2$ (velocity triples)
$\therefore E_k$ increases 9 times
$E_k = 9E$

D is the answer.

11. Work $= \Delta E_k$

$= \dfrac{1}{2}mv^2 - \dfrac{1}{2}mv_0^2$

$= \dfrac{1}{2}(2.50 \text{ kg})(10.0 \text{ m/s})^2$

$= 125$ J

C is the answer.

13. $E_p = mgh$

Note that from this equation, the potential energy of the student does not depend on the speed.

A is the answer.

15.

$$\Delta E_k + \Delta E_p = 0$$

$$\dfrac{1}{2}mv^2 - \dfrac{1}{2}mv_0^2 + mg\Delta h = 0$$

$$\dfrac{1}{2}v^2 (9.81 \text{ m/s}^2)(-0.40 \text{ m}) = 0$$

$$v_f = 2.8 \text{ m/s}$$

A is the answer.

MOMENTUM

Lesson 1—Momentum and Impulse

PRACTICE EXERCISES
ANSWERS AND SOLUTIONS

1. $\vec{p} = m\vec{v}$
$= (4.0 \text{ kg})(12.0 \text{ m/s east})$
$= 48 \text{ kg} \cdot \text{m/s east}$

3. $\vec{p} = m\vec{v}$
$m = \dfrac{\vec{p}}{\vec{v}}$
$= \dfrac{36.0 \text{ kg} \cdot \text{m/s south}}{8.0 \text{ m/s south}}$
$= 4.5 \text{ kg}$

5. $F_g = mg$
$m = \dfrac{F_g}{g}$
$= \dfrac{6.6 \text{ N}}{9.81 \text{ m/s}^2}$
$= 0.673 \text{ kg}$

$\vec{p} = m\vec{v}$
$= (0.673 \text{ kg})(3.0 \text{ m/s north})$
$= 2.0 \text{ kg} \cdot \text{m/s north}$

7. $\vec{a} = \dfrac{\vec{v} - \vec{v}_0}{t}$
$-9.81 \text{ m/s}^2 = \dfrac{\vec{v} - 0}{0.25 \text{ s}}$
$\vec{v} = -2.45 \text{ m/s}$

$\vec{p} = m\vec{v}$
$= (5.0 \text{ kg})(-2.45 \text{ m/s})$
$= -12 \text{ kg} \cdot \text{m/s}$
$= 12 \text{ kg} \cdot \text{m/s down}$

9. Impulse $= \vec{F}_{net} t$
$t = \dfrac{\text{Impulse}}{\vec{F}_{net}}$
$= \dfrac{7.00 \text{ N} \cdot \text{s west}}{11.2 \text{ N west}}$
$= 0.625 \text{ s}$

11. Magnitude of impulse
$\vec{F}_{net} t = m\Delta\vec{v}$
$(31.6 \text{ N})t = (15.0 \text{ kg})(10.0 \text{ m/s})$
$t = 4.75 \text{ s}$

13. Impulse $= m\Delta\vec{v}$
$= (5.00 \text{ kg})(15.0 \text{ m/s east})$
$= 75.0 \text{ kg} \cdot \text{m/s east}$

15. The magnitude of momentum
$p = mv$
$v = \dfrac{p}{m}$
$= \dfrac{6.0 \text{ kg} \cdot \text{m/s}}{3.0 \text{ kg}}$
$= 2.0 \text{ m/s}$
$v^2 = v_0^2 + 2ad$
$(2.0 \text{ m/s})^2 = 2(9.81 \text{ m/s}^2)d$
$d = 0.20 \text{ m}$

17. Consider up as positive,
$\vec{F}_{net} = m\vec{a}$
$\vec{a} = \dfrac{\vec{F}_{net}}{m}$
$= \dfrac{1.5 \times 10^5 \text{ N}}{9.5 \times 10^3 \text{ kg}}$
$= 15.8 \text{ m/s}^2$
$\vec{a} = \dfrac{\vec{v} - \vec{v}_0}{t}$
$15.8 \text{ m/s}^2 = \dfrac{\vec{v} - 0}{15 \text{ s}}$
$\vec{v} = 2.4 \times 10^2 \text{ m/s}$

or

$\vec{F}_{net} t = m\Delta\vec{v}$
$(1.5 \times 10^5 \text{ N})(15 \text{ s}) = (9.5 \times 10^3 \text{ kg})\vec{v}$
$\vec{v} = 2.4 \times 10^2 \text{ m/s}$

19. The magnitude of impulse
$F_{net} t = m\Delta v$
$(225 \text{ N})t = (1.0 \times 10^3 \text{ kg})(5.0 \text{ m/s} - 2.0 \text{ m/s})$
$t = 13 \text{ s}$

Lesson 2—Conservation of Momentum (Linear Interactions)

PRACTICE EXERCISES
ANSWERS AND SOLUTIONS

1. before collision

Consider right as positive and left as negative
$m_1 = 30.0$ kg $m_2 = 20.0$ kg
$\vec{v}_1 = 1.00$ m/s $\vec{v}_2 = -5.00$ m/s
$\vec{p}_1 = 30.0$ kg·m/s $\vec{p}_2 = -100$ kg·m/s

$\therefore \vec{P}_{sys(before)} = \vec{p}_1 + \vec{p}_2 = -70.0$ kg·m/s

after collision

$m_1 = 30.0$ kg $m_2 = 20.0$ kg
$\vec{v}'_1 = ?$ $\vec{v}'_2 = -1.25$ m/s
$\vec{p}'_1 = ?$ $\vec{p}'_2 = -25.0$ kg·m/s

$\vec{P}_{sys(after)} = \vec{P}_{sys(before)} = -70.0$ kg·m/s

$\vec{P}_{sys(after)} = \vec{p}'_1 + \vec{p}'_2 = -70.0$ kg·m/s
$\Rightarrow \vec{p}'_1 = -70.0$ kg·m/s $- (-25.0$ kg·m/s$)$
$\therefore \vec{p}'_1 = -45.0$ kg·m/s

$\vec{p}'_1 = m_1 \vec{v}'_1$
$\vec{v}'_1 = \dfrac{\vec{p}'_1}{m_1}$
$= \dfrac{-45.0 \text{ kg·m/s}}{30.0 \text{ kg}}$
$= -1.50$ m/s

The velocity of the 30.0 kg ball after the collision is 1.50 m/s left

3. before collision

$m_1 = 925$ kg $m_2 = ?$
$\vec{v}_1 = 18.0$ m/s $\vec{v}_2 = 0$ m/s
$\vec{p}_1 = 1.67 \times 10^4$ kg·m/s $\vec{p}_2 = 0$ kg·m/s

$\therefore \vec{P}_{before} = \vec{p}_1 + \vec{p}_2 = 1.67 \times 10^4$ kg·m/s

after collision

$m = ?$
$\vec{v} = 6.50$ m/s
$\vec{p} = \vec{P}_{after}$
$= 1.67 \times 10^4$ kg·m/s

$m = \dfrac{\vec{p}}{\vec{v}}$
$= \dfrac{1.67 \times 10^4 \text{ kg·m/s}}{6.50 \text{ kg}}$
$= 2.57 \times 10^3$ kg
$m_2 = 2.57 \times 10^3$ kg $= 925$ kg
$= 1.65 \times 10^3$ kg

5. before collision

Consider right as positive and left as negative
$m_1 = 40.0$ g
$\vec{v}_1 = 9.00$ m/s
$\vec{p}_1 = 3.60 \times 10^2$ g·m/s

$m_2 = 55.0$ g
$\vec{v}_2 = -6.00$ m/s
$\vec{p}_2 = -3.30 \times 10^2$ g·m/s

$\therefore \vec{P}_{before} = \vec{p}_1 + \vec{p}_2 = 3.00 \times 10^1$ g·m/s

after collision

$m = m_1 + m_2 = 95.0$ kg
$\vec{v} = ?$
$\vec{p} = \vec{P}_{after} = \vec{P}_{before} = 3.00 \times 10^1$ g·m/s

$\vec{v} = \dfrac{\vec{p}}{m}$
$= \dfrac{3.00 \times 10^1 \text{ g·m/s}}{95.0 \text{ g}}$
$= 0.316$ m/s right

7. before collision

$m = 1.13 \times 10^3$ kg
$v = 0$
$p = 0$
$\vec{p}_{before} = 0$

after collision

Consider east as positive
$m_L = 1.1 \times 10^3$ kg $m_P = 25$ kg
$\vec{v}_L = ?$ $\vec{v}_P = 325$ m/s
$\vec{p}_L = ?$ $\vec{p}_P = 8.13 \times 10^3$ kg·m/s

$\vec{P}_{after} = \vec{P}_{before} = 0$
$\vec{P}_{after} = \vec{p}_L + \vec{p}_P = 0$
$\vec{p}_L = -8.13 \times 10^3$ kg·m/s

$\vec{v}_L = \dfrac{p_L}{m_L}$

$= \dfrac{-8.13 \times 10^3 \text{ kg·m/s}}{1.1 \times 10^3 \text{ kg}}$

$= -7.4$ m/s
$= 7.4$ m/s west

9. before collision

$m = 7.0$ kg
$v = 0$
$p = 0$
$\vec{P}_{before} = 0$

after collision

Consider right as positive
$m_B = 5.0$ kg $m_A = 2.0$ kg
$\vec{v}_B = ?$ $\vec{v}_A = 10.0$ m/s
$\vec{p}_B = ?$ $\vec{p}_A = 20.0$ kg·m/s

$\vec{P}_{after} = \vec{P}_{before} = 0$

$\vec{P}_{after} = \vec{p}_A + \vec{p}_B = 0$
$\vec{p}_B = -20.0$ kg·m/s

$\vec{v}_B = \dfrac{\vec{p}_B}{m_B}$

$= \dfrac{-20.0 \text{ kg·m/s}}{5.0 \text{ kg}}$

$= 4.0$ m/s left

11. a)   before collision

Consider right as positive
$m_1 = 225$ g
$\vec{v}_1 = 30.0$ cm/s
$\vec{p}_1 = 6.75 \times 10^3$ g·cm/s

$m_2 = 125$ g
$\vec{v}_2 = 10.0$ cm/s
$\vec{p}_2 = 1.25 \times 10^3$ g·cm/s

$\therefore \vec{p}_{before} = \vec{p}_1 + \vec{p}_2 = 8.00 \times 10^3$ g·cm/s

after collision

$m_1 = 225$ g $m_2 = 125$ g
$\vec{v}_1' = ?$ $\vec{v}_2' = 24$ cm/s
$\vec{p}_1' = ?$ $\vec{p}_2' = 3.00 \times 10^3$ g·cm/s

$\vec{P}_{sys(after)} = \vec{P}_{sys(before)} = 8.00 \times 10^3$ g·cm/s
$\vec{p}_1' = 5.00 \times 10^3$ g·cm/s

$\vec{v}_1' = \dfrac{\vec{p}_1'}{m}$

$= \dfrac{5.00 \times 10^3 \text{ g·cm/s}}{225 \text{ g}}$

$= 22.2$ cm/s right

b)   Kinetic energy calculations, unlike momentum, require converting units to standard units. Also, consider speed.

before collision

$m_1 = 0.225$ kg $m_2 = 0.125$ kg
$v_1 = 0.300$ m/s $v_2 = 0.100$ m/s

after collision

 1   2

$m_1 = 0.225$ kg $m_2 = 0.125$ kg
$v_1' = 0.222$ m/s $v_2' = 0.240$ m/s

Kinetic energy of object 1 before

$$E_{k1} = \frac{1}{2}m_1 v_1^2$$
$$= \frac{1}{2}(0.225 \text{ kg})(0.300 \text{ m/s})^2$$
$$= 1.0125 \times 10^{-2} \text{ J}$$

Kinetic energy of object 2, before

$$E_{k2} = \frac{1}{2}m_2 v_2^2$$
$$= \frac{1}{2}(0.125 \text{ kg})(0.100 \text{ m/s})^2$$
$$= 6.25 \times 10^{-4} \text{ J}$$

Kinetic energy of object 1, after

$$E_{k1}' = \frac{1}{2}m_1 \left(v_1'\right)^2$$
$$= \frac{1}{2}(0.225 \text{ kg})(0.222 \text{ m/s})^2$$
$$= 5.5445 \times 10^{-3} \text{ J}$$

Kinetic energy of object 2, after

$$E_{k2}' = \frac{1}{2}m_2 \left(v_2'\right)^2$$
$$= \frac{1}{2}(0.125 \text{ kg})(0.240 \text{ m/s})^2$$
$$= 3.60 \times 10^{-3} \text{ J}$$

Total kinetic energy before collision
$$= 1.0125 \times 10^{-2} \text{ J} + 6.25 \times 10^{-4} \text{J}$$
$$= 1.075 \times 10^{-2} \text{ J}$$

Total kinetic energy after collision
$$= 5.5445 \times 10^{-3} \text{ J} + 3.60 \times 10^{-3} \text{ J}$$
$$= 9.1445 \times 10^{-3} \text{ J}$$

Mechanical (kinetic) energy lost in collision
$$= 1.075 \times 10^{-2} \text{ J} - 9.1445 \times 10^{-3} \text{ J}$$
$$= 1.61 \times 10^{-3} \text{ J}$$
$\therefore$ collision is inelastic.

Lesson 3—Two-Dimensional Interactions

PRACTICE EXERCISES ANSWERS AND SOLUTIONS

1.   before collision

 1   2

$m_1 = 2.0 \times 10^3$ kg
$\vec{v}_1 = 35$ km/h north
$\vec{p}_1 = 7.00 \times 10^4$ kg $\cdot$ km/h north

$m_2 = 1.4 \times 10^3$ kg
$\vec{v}_2 = 37.0$ m/s   west
$\vec{p}_2 = 28.0$ kg $\cdot$ m/s west

after collision

 1 + 2

$m = m_1 + m_2 = 3.4 \times 10^3$ kg
$\vec{v} = ?$
$\vec{p} = ?$

First find out the momentum of the system before collision ($\vec{p}_{\text{sys(before)}}$)

$p_2 = 5.18 \times 10^4$ kg·km/h

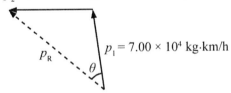

The magnitude of the resultant momentum is
$$p_R = \sqrt{p_1^2 + p_2^2}$$
$$= \sqrt{(7.00 \times 10^4 \text{ kg} \cdot \text{km/h})^2 + (5.18 \times 10^4 \text{ kg} \cdot \text{km/h})^2}$$
$$= 8.71 \times 10^4 \text{ kg} \cdot \text{km/h}$$

Now, find the direction
$$\tan \theta = \frac{p_2}{p_1}$$
$$= \frac{5.18 \times 10^4 \text{ kg} \cdot \text{km/h}}{7.00 \times 10^4 \text{ kg} \cdot \text{km/h}}$$
$$= 0.750$$
$$\theta = 36.5°$$

Therefore

$\vec{p}_{\text{sys(before)}} = \vec{p}_R$

$= 8.71 \times 10^4 \text{ kg} \cdot \text{km/h } 36.5° \text{ W of N}$

Again $\vec{p} = \vec{p}_{\text{sys(after)}} = \vec{p}_{\text{sys(before)}} = \vec{p}_R$

$\vec{v} = \dfrac{\vec{p}}{m}$

$= \dfrac{8.71 \times 0^4 \text{kg} \cdot \text{km/h } 36.5° \text{ W of N}}{3.4 \times 10^3 \text{ kg}}$

$= 26 \text{ km/h } 37° \text{ W of N}$

3. before collision

$m_1 = 4.0 \times 10^4 \text{ kg}$

$\vec{v}_1 = 8.0 \text{ m/s west}$

$\vec{p}_1 = 3.2 \times 10^5 \text{ kg} \cdot \text{m/s west}$

$m_2 = 3.0 \times 10^4 \text{ kg}$

$\vec{v}_2 = 5.0 \text{ m/s south}$

$\vec{p}_2 = 1.5 \times 10^5 \text{ kg} \cdot \text{m/s south}$

after collision

$m = m_1 + m_2 = 7.0 \times 10^4 \text{ kg}$

$\vec{v} = ?$

$\vec{p} = ?$

$p_1 = 3.2 \times 10^5 \text{ kg·m/s}$

$p_2 = 1.5 \times 10^5 \text{ kg·m/s}$

p_R

$p_R = \sqrt{p_1^2 + p_2^2}$

$= \sqrt{(3.2 \times 10^5 \text{ kg} \cdot \text{m/s})^2 + (1.5 \times 10^5 \text{ kg} \cdot \text{m/s})^2}$

$= 3.53 \times 10^5 \text{ kg} \cdot \text{m/s}$

$\tan\theta = \dfrac{p_2}{p_1}$

$= \dfrac{1.5 \times 10^5 \text{ kg} \cdot \text{m/s}}{3.2 \times 10^5 \text{ kg} \cdot \text{m/s}}$

$= 0.469$

$\theta = 25°$

$\vec{p} = \vec{p}_R = 3.53 \times 10^5 \text{ kg} \cdot \text{m/s } 26° \text{ S of W}$

$\vec{v} = \dfrac{\vec{p}}{m}$

$= \dfrac{3.53 \times 10^5 \text{ kg} \cdot \text{m/s } 26° \text{ S of W}}{7.0 \times 10^4 \text{ kg}}$

$= 5.0 \times 10^1 \text{ m/s } 25° \text{ S of W}$

5. a) before collision

$m_1 = 15.0 \text{ kg}$ $m_2 = 10.0 \text{ kg}$

$\vec{v}_1 = 7.0 \text{ m/s east}$ $\vec{v}_2 = 0$

$\vec{p}_1 = 105 \text{ kg} \cdot \text{m/s east}$ $\vec{p}_2 = 0$

before collision

$m_1 = 15.0 \text{ kg}$

$\vec{v}_1' = 4.2 \text{ m/s } 20.0° \text{ S of E}$

$\vec{p}_1' = 63 \text{ kg} \cdot \text{m/s } 20.0° \text{ S of E}$

$m_2 = 10.0 \text{ kg}$

$\vec{v}_2' = ?$

$\vec{p}_2' = ?$

$p_{\text{after}} = p_{\text{before}}$

$p_{\text{before}} = 105 \text{ kg} \cdot \text{m/s east}$

$\therefore p_{\text{after}} = 105 \text{ kg} \cdot \text{m/s east}$

Find horizontal and vertical components of 63 kg·m/s 20.0° S of E

20.0° S of E = 340° heading counter clockwise from positive x-axis

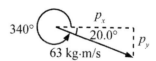

$\vec{p}_{1x}' = p_{1x}' \cos\theta$

$= (63 \text{ kg} \cdot \text{m/s})(\cos 340°)$

$= 59.2 \text{ kg} \cdot \text{m/s}$

$\vec{p}_{1y}' = p_1' \sin\theta$

$= (63 \text{ kg} \cdot \text{m/s})(\sin 340°)$

$= -21.5 \text{ kg} \cdot \text{m/s}$

After collision, the 10.0 kg object must have a horizontal component of

105 kg·m/s – 59.2 kg·m/s = 45.8 kg·m/s east

After collision, the 10.0 kg object must have a vertical component of

0 – (–21.5 kg·m/s) = 21.5 kg·m/s north

Now, add 45.8 kg·m/s east and
21.5 kg·m/s north using Pythagoras theorem.

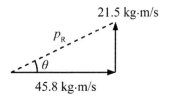

$$p_R = \sqrt{(p_x)^2 + (p_y)^2}$$
$$= \sqrt{(45.8 \text{ kg} \cdot \text{m/s})^2 + (21.5 \text{ kg} \cdot \text{m/s})^2}$$
$$= 50.6 \text{ kg} \cdot \text{m/s}$$

Magnitude of velocity

$$v_2 = \frac{p_2}{m}$$
$$= \frac{50.6 \text{ kg} \cdot \text{m/s}}{10.0 \text{ kg}}$$
$$= 5.1 \text{ m/s}$$

Now find out the direction using

$$\tan \theta = \frac{p_y}{p_x}$$
$$= \frac{21.5 \text{ kg} \cdot \text{m/s}}{45.8 \text{ kg} \cdot \text{m/s}}$$
$$\theta = 25° \text{ N of E}$$
$$\bar{v}_2 = 5.1 \text{ m/s } 25° \text{ N of E}$$

b)

before collision

$m_1 = 15.0 \text{ kg}$ $m_2 = 10.0 \text{ kg}$
$v_1 = 7.0 \text{ m/s}$ $v_2 = 0$

after collision

        2

$m_1' = 15.0 \text{ kg}$ $m_2' = 10.0 \text{ kg}$
$v_1' = 4.2 \text{ m/s}$ $v_2' = 5.1 \text{ m/s}$

Kinetic energy of object 1, before
$$E_{k1} = \frac{1}{2} m_1 v_1^2$$
$$= \frac{1}{2}(15.0 \text{ kg})(7.0 \text{ m/s})^2$$
$$= 3.7 \times 10^2 \text{ J}$$

Kinetic energy of object 1, after
$$E_{k1}' = \frac{1}{2} m_1 \left(v_1'\right)^2$$
$$= \frac{1}{2}(15.0 \text{ kg})(4.2 \text{ m/s})^2$$
$$= 1.3 \times 10^2 \text{ J}$$

Kinetic energy of object 2, before
$$E_{k2} = \frac{1}{2} m_2 v_2^2$$
$$= \frac{1}{2}(10.0 \text{ kg})(0)^2$$
$$= 0$$

Kinetic energy of object 2, after
$$E_{k2}' = \frac{1}{2} m_2' \left(v_2'\right)^2$$
$$= \frac{1}{2}(10.0 \text{ kg})(5.1 \text{ m/s})^2$$
$$= 1.30 \times 10^2 \text{ J}$$

Total kinetic energy before collision
$$= 3.7 \times 10^2 \text{ J} + 0$$
$$= 3.7 \times 10^2 \text{ J}$$

Total kinetic energy after collision
$$= 1.3 \times 10^2 \text{ J} + 1.3 \times 10^2 \text{ J}$$
$$= 2.6 \times 10^2 \text{ J}$$

Mechanical (kinetic) energy lost in collision is
$3.7 \times 10^2 \text{ J} - 2.6 \times 10^2 \text{ J} = 1.1 \times 10^2 \text{ J}$,
∴ collision is inelastic. Kinetic energy was not conserved.

c) Most of the loss in mechanical energy was converted to thermal energy—some to sound, etc.

Practice Test

ANSWERS AND SOLUTIONS

1. $E_k = \frac{1}{2}mv^2$

Since both the mass and the velocity remain constant, the kinetic energy remains constant.

$E_p = mgh$
Since the height (h) increases, the gravitational potential energy increases.

$p = mv$
Like kinetic energy, since both the mass and the velocity remain constant, the momentum remains constant.

D is the answer.

3. $\left.\begin{array}{l} E_k = \frac{1}{2}mv^2 \\ p = mv \end{array}\right\}$ since $v = 0$, $E_k = 0$ and $p = 0$

As we see above, if the velocity is zero, an object cannot have kinetic energy or momentum, but it can have position; therefore, it can have potential energy.

D is the answer.

5. If the object has momentum, it has mass and velocity; and if it has mass and velocity, it has kinetic energy also.

Mechanical energy is the sum of the gravitational potential energy and the kinetic energy. Therefore, if it has kinetic energy, it must also have mechanical energy.

Note: The object does not need to have potential energy.

A is the answer.

7. $E_k = \frac{1}{2}mv^2$

$\therefore v = \sqrt{\frac{2E_k}{m}}$

Again magnitude of the momentum
$p = mv$

$\therefore p = m\left(\sqrt{\frac{2E_k}{m}}\right)$

$p^2 = \frac{m^2 2E_k}{m}$

$p = \sqrt{m2E_k}$ or $\sqrt{2mE_k}$

B is the answer.

9. If the object slides along a horizontal frictionless surface, there will be no acceleration (i.e., constant velocity). If the velocity remains constant, all of these quantities remain constant.

D is the answer.

11. Find the velocity of the spacecraft.

before collision

$m = 1.30 \times 10^2 \text{ kg} + 2.80 \times 10^3 \text{ kg}$
$\quad = 2.93 \times 10^3 \text{ kg}$
$\bar{v} = 0$
$\bar{p} = m\bar{v}$
$\quad = 0$

after collision

$m_1 = 1.30 \times 10^2 \text{ kg}$
$\bar{v}_1 = 9.00 \text{ m/s}$
$\bar{p}_1 = 1.17 \times 10^3 \text{ kg·m/s}$

$m_2 = 2.80 \times 10^3 \text{ kg}$
$\bar{v}_2 = ?$
$\bar{p}_2 = -1.17 \times 10^3 \text{ kg·m/s}$

$$\vec{v}_2 = \frac{\vec{p}_2}{m_2}$$

$$= \frac{-1.17 \times 10^3 \text{ kg} \cdot \text{m/s}}{2.80 \times 10^3 \text{ kg}}$$

$$= -0.418 \text{ m/s}$$

∴ relative velocity of the astronaut with respect to the spacecraft is

9.00 m/s − (− 0.418 m/s) = 9.42 m/s

$$v = \frac{d}{t}$$

$$t = \frac{d}{v}$$

$$= \frac{22.0 \text{ m}}{9.42 \text{ m/s}}$$

$$= 2.34 \text{ s}$$

C is the answer.

13. A perfect elastic collision is defined as a collision in which both kinetic energy and momentum are conserved.

C is the answer.

15.

before collision

car 1   car 2

Consider east as positive

$m_1 = 1.1 \times 10^3$ kg

$\vec{v}_1 = 25$ km/h

$\vec{p}_1 = 2.75 \times 10^4$ kg·km/h

$m_2 = 2.3 \times 10^3$ kg

$\vec{v}_2 = -15$ km/h

$\vec{p}_2 = -3.45 \times 10^4$ kg · km/h

$\vec{p}_{\text{before}} = \vec{p}_1 + \vec{p}_2 = -7.0 \times 10^3$ kg·km/h

after collision

$m = 3.4 \times 10^3$ kg

$\vec{v} = ?$

$\vec{p} = -7.0 \times 10^3$ kg·km/h

$$\vec{v} = \frac{\vec{p}}{m}$$

$$= \frac{-7.0 \times 10^3 \text{ kg} \cdot \text{km/h}}{3.4 \times 10^3 \text{ kg}}$$

$$= -2.1 \text{ km/h or } 2.1 \text{ km/h west}$$

B is the answer.

EQUILIBRIUM

Lesson 1—The First Condition of Equilibrium

PRACTICE EXERCISES
ANSWERS AND SOLUTIONS

1.

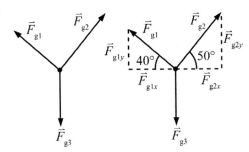

$$F_{g1x} = F_{g1}\cos\theta_1 \qquad F_{g1y} = F_{g1}\sin\theta_1$$
$$= F_{g1}\cos40° \qquad = F_{g1}\sin40°$$
$$= 0.766F_{g1} \qquad = 0.643F_{g1}$$

$$F_{g2x} = F_{g2}\cos\theta_2 \qquad F_{g2y} = F_{g2}\sin\theta_2$$
$$= F_{g2}\cos50° \qquad = F_{g2}\sin50°$$
$$= 0.643F_{g2} \qquad = 0.766F_{g2}$$

$$\sum \vec{F}_x = 0$$
$$F_{g2x} - F_{g1x} = 0$$
$$0.643F_{g2} - 0.766F_{g1} = 0$$
$$F_g = \frac{0.766\,F_{g1}}{0.643}$$
$$F_{g2} = 1.19F_{g1}$$
$$\sum \vec{F}_y = 0$$

$$F_{g1y} + F_{g2y} - F_{g3} = 0$$
$$0.643F_{g1} + 0.766F_{g2} - 12\text{ N} = 0$$
$$1.55F_{g1} = 12\text{ N}$$
$$F_{g1} = 7.74\text{ N}$$

Again $F_{g2} = 1.19F_{g1}$
$$= (1.19)(7.74\text{ N})$$
$$= 9.21\text{ N} = 9.2\text{ N}$$

3.

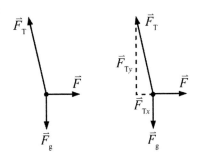

$$F_{Tx} = F_T\cos\theta \qquad F_{Ty} = F_T\sin\theta$$
$$= F_T\cos63.0° \qquad = F_T\sin63.0°$$
$$= 0.454F_T \qquad = 0.891F_T$$

$$\sum \vec{F}_y = 0$$
$$F_{Ty} - F_g = 0$$
$$F_{Ty} = F_g = 20.0\text{ N}$$
$$F_T = \frac{F_{Ty}}{0.891} = \frac{20.0\text{ N}}{0.891}$$
$$= 22.4\text{ N}$$
$$\sum \vec{F}_x = 0$$
$$F_{app} - F_{Tx} = 0$$
$$F_{app} - 0.454F_T = 0$$
$$F_{app} = (0.454)(22.4\text{ N})$$
$$= 10.2\text{ N}$$

5.

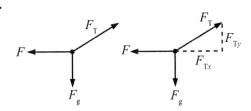

$$F_{Tx} = F_T\cos\theta \qquad F_{Ty} = F_T\sin\theta$$
$$= F_T\cos30° \qquad = F_T\sin30°$$
$$= 0.866F_T \qquad = 0.500F_T$$

$$F = F_{fr} = \mu mg\cos\theta$$
$$= (0.27)(15\text{ kg})(9.81\text{ m/s})(\cos 0)$$
$$= 39.7\text{ N}$$

$$\sum \vec{F}_x = 0$$
$$F_{Tx} - F = 0$$
$$F_{Tx} = 39.7\text{ N}$$
$$F_{Tx} = 0.866F_T$$
$$F_T = \frac{F_{Tx}}{0.866} = \frac{39.7\text{ N}}{0.866}$$
$$= 45.9\text{ N}$$

$$\sum \bar{F}_y = 0$$
$$F_{Ty} - F_g = 0$$
$$0.500 F_T = F_g$$
$$\Rightarrow F_g = (0.500)(45.9\ \text{N})$$
$$= 22.9\ \text{N}$$

$$F_g = mg$$
$$m = \frac{F_g}{g} = \frac{22.9\ \text{N}}{9.81\ \text{m/s}^2}$$
$$= 2.3\ \text{kg}$$

7.

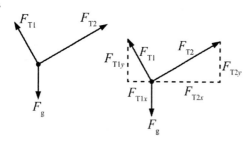

$$F_{T1x} = F_{T1}\cos\theta_1 \qquad F_{T1y} = F_{T1}\sin\theta_1$$
$$= (96\ \text{N})\cos 60° \qquad = (96\ \text{N})\sin 60°$$
$$= 48\ \text{N} \qquad = 83\ \text{N}$$

$$F_{T2x} = F_{T2}\cos\theta_2 \qquad F_{T2y} = F_{T2}\sin\theta_2$$
$$= F_{T2}\cos 30° \qquad = F_{T2}\sin 30°$$
$$= 0.866 F_{T2} \qquad = 0.500 F_{T2}$$

$$\sum \bar{F}_x = 0$$
$$F_{T2x} - F_{T1x} = 0$$
$$48\ \text{N} = 0.866\ T_2$$
$$F_{T2} = \frac{48\ \text{N}}{0.866}$$
$$= 55.43\ \text{N} \approx 55\ \text{N}$$

$$\sum \bar{F}_y = 0$$
$$F_{T1y} + F_{T2y} - F_g = 0$$
$$83\ \text{N} + 0.500 F_{T2} = F_g$$
$$83\ \text{N} + (0.500)(55\ \text{N}) = F_g$$

9.

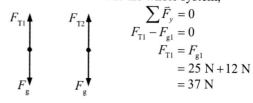

For the whole system,
$$\sum \bar{F}_y = 0$$
$$F_{T1} - F_{g1} = 0$$
$$F_{T1} = F_{g1}$$
$$= 25\ \text{N} + 12\ \text{N}$$
$$= 37\ \text{N}$$

For the lower block,
$$\sum \bar{F}_y = 0$$
$$F_{T2} - F_g = 0$$
$$F_{T2} = F_g$$
$$= 12\ \text{N}$$

10.

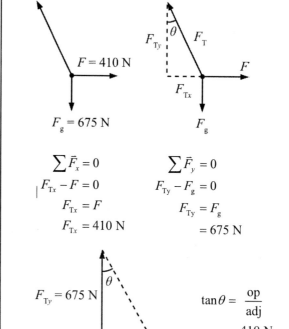

$$\sum \bar{F}_x = 0 \qquad \sum \bar{F}_y = 0$$
$$F_{Tx} - F = 0 \qquad F_{Ty} - F_g = 0$$
$$F_{Tx} = F \qquad F_{Ty} = F_g$$
$$F_{Tx} = 410\ \text{N} \qquad = 675\ \text{N}$$

$$\tan\theta = \frac{\text{op}}{\text{adj}}$$
$$= \frac{410\ \text{N}}{675\ \text{N}}$$
$$\therefore \theta = 31.3°$$

Lesson 2—The Second Condition of Equilibrium

PRACTICE EXERCISES
ANSWERS AND SOLUTIONS

1. $$\tau = rF\sin\theta$$
$$F = \frac{\tau}{r\sin\theta}$$
$$= \frac{45\ \text{N}\cdot\text{m}}{(0.35\ \text{m})(\sin 90°)}$$
$$= 129\ \text{N or } 1.3\times 10^2\ \text{N}$$

3.

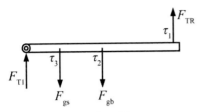

Point of rotation is arbitrary

a)
$$\sum \tau = 0$$
$$\tau_1 - \tau_2 - \tau_3 = 0$$
$$r_1 F_1 \sin\theta_1 - r_2 F_2 \sin\theta_2 - r_3 F_3 \sin\theta_3 = 0$$

$$(5.00 \text{ m})(F_{TR})\sin 90°$$
$$-(2.50 \text{ m})(250 \text{ N})\sin 90°$$
$$-(1.50 \text{ m})(650 \text{ N})\sin 90° = 0$$
$$(5.00 \text{ m})(F_{TR}) - 625 \text{ N} - 975 \text{ N} = 0$$
$$\Rightarrow F_{TR} = \frac{(625 \text{ N}\cdot\text{m} + 975 \text{ N}\cdot\text{m})}{5.00 \text{ m}}$$
$$\therefore F_{TR} = 320 \text{ N}$$

b)
$$\sum F_x = 0$$
$$F_{TR} + F_{TL} - F_{gs} - F_{gb} = 0$$
$$320 \text{ N} + F_{TL} - 650 \text{ N} - 250 \text{ N} = 0$$
$$F_{TL} = 900\text{N} - 320 \text{ N}$$
$$\therefore F_{TL} = 580 \text{ N}$$

5.

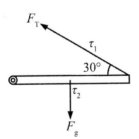

$$\sum \tau = 0$$
$$\tau_1 - \tau_2 = 0$$
$$r_1 F_1 \sin\theta_1 - r_2 F_2 \sin\theta_2 = 0$$
$$(L)(F_T)\sin 30° - \left(\tfrac{1}{2}L\right)(F_{gb})\sin 90° = 0$$
$$0.500 F_T - 100 \text{ N} = 0$$
$$0.500 F_T = 100 \text{ N}$$

$$F_T = \frac{100 \text{ N}}{0.500}$$
$$= 200 \text{ N}$$
$$= 2.0 \times 10^2 \text{ N}$$

Practice Test

ANSWERS AND SOLUTIONS

1. Force of friction depends on the surfaces (coefficient of friction, μ) and the normal force ($F_N = mg\cos\theta$).

   $$\therefore \; F_{fr} = \mu mg \cos\theta$$

   A is the answer.

3. Rotational motion is related to torque.

   B is the answer.

5. We say that an object is at equilibrium when there is no acceleration (rotational or translational).

   B is the answer.

7. If there is no net force, there is no translational acceleration. If there is no torque, there is no rotational acceleration.

   A is the answer.

9.

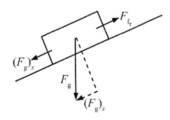

$$F_{net} = 0$$
$$F_{net} = F_{g(x)} - F_{fr}$$
$$F_{fr} = F_{g(x)}$$
$$F_{g(x)} = F_g \sin\theta$$
$$= (3.0 \text{ N})(9.81 \text{ m/s}^2)(\sin 37°)$$
$$= 17.7 \text{ N}$$
$$F_{fr} = \mu mg \sin\theta$$
$$\mu = \frac{F_{fr}}{mg\cos\theta}$$
$$= \frac{(17.7 \text{ N})}{(3.0 \text{ kg})(9.81 \text{ m/s}^2)(\cos 37°)}$$
$$= 0.75$$

B is the answer.

CIRCULAR MOTION AND GRAVITATION

Lesson 1—Uniform Circular Motion

PRACTICE EXERCISES
ANSWERS AND SOLUTIONS

---

1. $F_c = \dfrac{mv^2}{r}$

$= \dfrac{(925 \text{ kg})(22 \text{ m/s})^2}{75 \text{ m}}$

$= 6.0 \times 10^3 \text{ N}$

3. $F_c = \dfrac{mv^2}{r}$

$= \dfrac{(822 \text{ kg})(28.0 \text{ m/s})^2}{105 \text{ m}}$

$= 6.14 \times 10^3 \text{ N}$

5. $F_c = \dfrac{mv^2}{r}$

$v^2 = \dfrac{\left(2.00 \times 10^{-2} \text{ m}\right)\left(4.60 \times 10^{-14} \text{ N}\right)}{(9.11 \times 10^{-31} \text{ kg})}$

$v = \sqrt{\dfrac{(4.60 \times 10^{-14} \text{ N})(2.00 \times 10^{-2} \text{ m})}{9.11 \times 10^{-31} \text{ kg}}}$

$= 3.18 \times 10^7 \text{ m/s}$

7. $F_c = \dfrac{mv^2}{r}$

$= \dfrac{(2.7 \times 0^3 \text{ kg})(4.7 \times 10^3 \text{ m/s})^2}{1.8 \times 10^7 \text{ m}}$

$= 3.3 \times 10^3 \text{ N}$

9. Speed

$2r = \text{Diameter}$

$r = \dfrac{30.0 \times 10^{-2} \text{ m}}{2}$

$= 15.0 \times 10^{-2} \text{ m}$

$T = \dfrac{1}{f}$

$f = 33\frac{1}{3} \text{ rev/minute} \times \dfrac{1 \text{ m}}{60 \text{ s}}$

$= \dfrac{33\frac{1}{3}}{60} \text{ Hz}$

$T = \dfrac{60}{33\frac{1}{3} \text{ Hz}}$

$= 1.80 \text{ s}$

$v = \dfrac{2\pi r}{T}$

$= \dfrac{2\pi(15.0 \times 10^{-2} \text{ m})}{1.80 \text{ s}}$

$= 0.524 \text{ m/s}$

Acceleration

$a_c = \dfrac{v^2}{r}$

$= \dfrac{(0.524 \text{ m/s})^2}{15.0 \times 10^{-2} \text{ m}}$

$= 1.83 \text{ m/s}^2$

11. a) $F_N = mg$

$= \left(932 \text{ kg}\right)\left(9.81 \text{ m/s}^2\right)$

$= 9143 \text{ N}$

$F_{fr} = \mu F_N$

$= \left(0.95\right)\left(9143 \text{ N}\right)$

$= 8.69 \times 10^3 \text{ N}$

$F_c = \dfrac{mv^2}{r}$

$8.69 \times 10^3 \text{ N} = \dfrac{(932 \text{ kg})(v^2)}{82 \text{ m}}$

$v = \sqrt{\dfrac{(8.69 \times 10^3 \text{ N})(82 \text{ m})}{932 \text{ kg}}}$

$= 28 \text{ m/s}$

---

b) $F_{\text{fr}} = \mu F_{\text{N}}$
$\quad = (0.40)(9143 \text{ N})$
$\quad = 3.66 \times 10^3 \text{ N}$

$$F_{\text{c}} = \frac{mv^2}{r}$$

$$3.66 \times 10^3 \text{ N} = \frac{(932 \text{ kg})(v^2)}{82 \text{ m}}$$

$$v = \sqrt{\frac{(3.66 \times 10^3 \text{ N})(82 \text{ m})}{932 \text{ kg}}}$$

$$= 18 \text{ m/s}$$

Vertical Circular Motion

PRACTICE EXERCISES
ANSWERS AND SOLUTIONS

1.

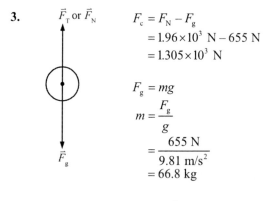

$F_{\text{T}} = 0$
$\therefore F_{\text{c}} = F_{\text{g}}$
$$\frac{mv^2}{r} = mg$$
$$v = \sqrt{rg}$$
$$= \sqrt{(5.00 \text{ m})(9.81 \text{ m/s}^2)}$$
$$= 7.00 \text{ m/s}$$

3.

$F_{\text{c}} = F_{\text{N}} - F_{\text{g}}$
$\quad = 1.96 \times 10^3 \text{ N} - 655 \text{ N}$
$\quad = 1.305 \times 10^3 \text{ N}$

$F_{\text{g}} = mg$
$$m = \frac{F_{\text{g}}}{g}$$
$$= \frac{655 \text{ N}}{9.81 \text{ m/s}^2}$$
$$= 66.8 \text{ kg}$$

$$F_{\text{c}} = \frac{mv^2}{r}$$
$$v = \sqrt{\frac{F_{\text{c}} r}{m}}$$
$$= \sqrt{\frac{(1.305 \times 10^3 \text{ N})(18.0 \text{ m})}{66.8 \text{ kg}}}$$
$$= 18.7 \text{ m/s}$$

5.

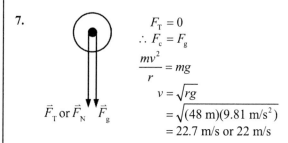

$F_{\text{g}} = mg$
$\quad = (1.50 \text{ kg})(9.81 \text{ m/s}^2)$
$\quad = 14.7 \text{ N}$

$F_{\text{c}} = F_{\text{T}} - F_{\text{g}}$
$\quad = 186 \text{ N} - 14.7 \text{ N}$
$\quad = 171 \text{ N}$
$$F_{\text{c}} = \frac{mv^2}{r}$$
$$v = \sqrt{\frac{F_{\text{c}} r}{m}}$$
$$= \sqrt{\frac{(171 \text{ N})(1.90 \text{ m})}{1.50 \text{ kg}}}$$
$$= 14.7 \text{ m/s}$$

7.

$F_{\text{T}} = 0$
$\therefore F_{\text{c}} = F_{\text{g}}$
$$\frac{mv^2}{r} = mg$$
$$v = \sqrt{rg}$$
$$= \sqrt{(48 \text{ m})(9.81 \text{ m/s}^2)}$$
$$= 22.7 \text{ m/s or } 22 \text{ m/s}$$

9. a)

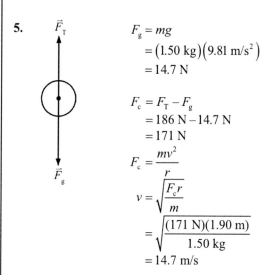

High	Low
$F_{\text{c}} = F_{\text{T}} + F_{\text{g}}$	$F_{\text{c}} = F_{\text{T}} - F_{\text{g}}$
$F_{\text{T}} = F_{\text{c}} - F_{\text{g}}$	$F_{\text{T}} = F_{\text{c}} + F_{\text{g}}$

It is clear from the above formulas that the tension in the string greater at its low point than at its high point

b) $F_g = mg$
$$= (2.5 \text{ kg})(9.81 \text{ m/s}^2)$$
$$= 24.5 \text{ N}$$

$$F_c = \frac{mv^2}{r}$$
$$= \frac{(2.5 \text{ kg})(12 \text{ m/s})^2}{0.75 \text{ m}}$$
$$= 4.8 \times 10^2 \text{ N}$$

i) The tension of the string at its low point is
$$F_T = F_c + F_g$$
$$= 480 \text{ N} + 24.5 \text{ N}$$
$$= 5.0 \times 10^2 \text{ N}$$

ii) The tension of the string at its high point is
$$F_T = F_c - F_g$$
$$= 480 \text{ N} - 24.5 \text{ N}$$
$$= 4.6 \times 10^2 \text{ N}$$

Lesson 3—Newton's Law of Universal Gravitation

PRACTICE EXERCISES ANSWERS AND SOLUTIONS

1. $F_g = \dfrac{Gm_1 m_2}{r^2}$
$$= \frac{\left(6.67 \times 10^{-11} \dfrac{\text{N} \cdot \text{m}^2}{\text{kg}^2}\right)(70.0 \text{ kg})(52.0 \text{ kg})}{(1.50 \text{ m})^2}$$
$$= 1.08 \times 10^{-7} \text{ N}$$

3. $F_g = \dfrac{Gm_1 m_2}{r^2}$

As both the objects have equal mass,
$$m^2 = \frac{F_g r^2}{G}$$
$$= \frac{(2.30 \times 10^{-8} \text{ N})(10.0 \text{ m})^2}{6.67 \times 10^{-11} \dfrac{\text{N} \cdot \text{m}^2}{\text{kg}^2}}$$
$$= 3.45 \times 10^4 \text{ kg}^2$$
$$m = 1.86 \times 10^2 \text{ kg}$$

5. $F_g = \dfrac{Gm_1 m_2}{r^2}$
$$m_2 = \frac{F_g r^2}{Gm_1}$$
$$= \frac{(3.2 \times 10^{-6} \text{ N})(2.1 \times 10^{-1} \text{ m})^2}{\left(6.67 \times 10^{-11} \dfrac{\text{N} \cdot \text{m}^2}{\text{kg}^2}\right)(5.5 \times 10^1 \text{ kg})}$$
$$= 3.8 \times 10^1 \text{ N}$$

7. $F_g = \dfrac{Gm_1 m_2}{r^2}$
$$= \frac{\left(6.67 \times 10^{-11} \dfrac{\text{N} \cdot \text{m}^2}{\text{kg}^2}\right)(5.98 \times 10^{24} \text{ kg})(70.0 \text{ kg})}{(6.38 \times 10^6 \text{ m})^2}$$
$$= 6.86 \times 10^2 \text{ N}$$

9. $F_g = \dfrac{Gm_1 m_2}{r^2}$
$$F_g \propto \frac{1}{r^2}$$

Distance changes by a factor of:
$$\frac{\text{to}}{\text{from}} = \frac{1.276 \times 10^7 \text{ m}}{6.38 \times 10^6 \text{ m}}$$
$$= 2.00$$

Distance changes by a factor of 2.00

$\therefore F_g$ changes by a factor of $0.250 = \dfrac{1}{(2.00)^2}$

$$F_g = (6.86 \times 10^2 \text{ N})(0.250)$$
$$= 1.72 \times 10^2 \text{ N}$$

11.

$F_{g1} = F_{g2}$, and since these forces are in opposite directions, the net force will be zero.

13. $F_g = \dfrac{Gm_1m_2}{r^2}$

$F_g \propto \dfrac{m_1m_2}{r^2}$

$\propto \dfrac{(2)(2)}{(3)^2}$

$\propto 0.444$

$F_{g(new)} = \left(3.24 \times 10^{-7} \text{ N}\right)(0.444)$

$\qquad\quad = 1.44 \times 10^{-7} \text{ N}$

Lesson 4—Gravitational Fields

ANSWERS AND SOLUTIONS
PRACTICE EXERCISES

1. $g = \dfrac{GM}{r^2}$

$= \dfrac{Gm_M}{r^2}$

$= \dfrac{\left(6.67 \times 10^{-11} \; \dfrac{\text{N} \cdot \text{m}^2}{\text{kg}^2}\right)(6.37 \times 10^{23} \text{ kg})}{(3.43 \times 10^6 \text{ m})^2}$

$= 3.61 \text{ N/kg}$

3. $g = \dfrac{F_g}{m}$

$= \dfrac{63.5 \text{ N}}{22.5 \text{ kg}}$

$= 2.82 \text{ N/kg}$

5. $g = \dfrac{GM}{r^2}$

$g \propto \dfrac{1}{r^2}$

$\propto \dfrac{1}{(2)^2}$

$\propto 0.25$

$g_{new} = \left(9.81 \text{ N/kg}\right)(0.25)$

$\qquad = 2.45 \text{ N/kg}$

7.

$g_A = \dfrac{GM}{r_A^{\,2}}$

$g_B = \dfrac{GM}{r_B^{\,2}}$

$\dfrac{g_A}{g_B} = \dfrac{r_B^{\,2}}{r_A^{\,2}}$

$r_A^{\,2} = r_B^{\,2}\dfrac{g_B}{g_A}$

$r_A = r_B\sqrt{\dfrac{1}{1.20}} \qquad (\because g_A = 1.20 g_B)$

$r_A = (0.913)r_B$

Lesson 5—Gravitational Potential Energy

PRACTICE EXERCISES
ANSWERS AND SOLUTIONS

1. $E_p = -\dfrac{Gm_E m_s}{r}$

$= -\dfrac{\left(6.67 \times 10^{-11} \; \dfrac{\text{N} \cdot \text{m}^2}{\text{kg}^2}\right)(5.98 \times 10^{24} \text{ kg})}{9.90 \times 10^6 \text{ m}} \times (5.00 \times 10^3 \text{ kg})$

$== -2.01 \times 10^{11} \text{ J}$

3. $W = \Delta E_p$

Therefore, answer is the same as in 2

$\Delta E_p = 1.11 \times 10^{11} \text{ J}$

5. $E_p = -\dfrac{Gm_E m_o}{r}$

$= -\dfrac{\left(6.67 \times 10^{-11} \; \dfrac{\text{N} \cdot \text{m}^2}{\text{kg}^2}\right)(5.98 \times 10^{24} \text{ kg})(10.0 \text{ kg})}{6.38 \times 10^6 \text{ m}}$

$= -6.25 \times 10^8 \text{ J}$

7. mechanical energy $= E_k + E_p$

$$E_k = \frac{1}{2}mv^2$$
$$= \frac{1}{2}(2.50 \times 10^3 \text{ kg})(7.60 \times 10^3 \text{ m/s})^2$$
$$= 7.22 \times 10^{10} \text{ J}$$

$$\Delta E_p = Gm_em_s\left(\frac{1}{r_i} - \frac{1}{r_f}\right)$$
$$= \left(6.67 \times 10^{-11} \frac{\text{N} \cdot \text{m}^2}{\text{kg}^2}\right)(5.98 \times 10^{24} \text{ kg})(2.50 \times 10^3 \text{ kg})$$
$$\times \left(\frac{1}{6.38 \times 10^6 \text{ m}} - \frac{1}{6.90 \times 10^6 \text{ m}}\right)$$
$$= 1.18 \times 10^{10} \text{ J}$$

mechanical energy
$$E_k + E_p = 7.22 \times 10^{10} \text{ J} + 1.18 \times 10^{10} \text{ J}$$
$$= 8.40 \times 10^{10} \text{ J}$$

Lesson 6—Launching

PRACTICE EXERCISES
ANSWERS AND SOLUTIONS

1. $$v = \sqrt{\frac{2GM}{r}}$$
$$= \sqrt{\frac{2(6.67 \times 10^{-11} \text{ N} \cdot \text{m}^2/\text{kg}^2)(7.35 \times 10^{22} \text{ kg})}{(1.74 \times 10^6 \text{ m})}}$$
$$= 2.37 \times 10^3 \text{ m/s}$$

3. $$v = \sqrt{\frac{2GM}{r}}$$
$$M = \frac{v^2 r}{2G}$$
$$= \frac{(9.0 \times 10^3 \text{ m/s})^2 (7.2 \times 10^6 \text{ m})}{2(6.67 \times 10^{-11} \text{ N} \cdot \text{m}^2/\text{kg}^2)}$$
$$= 4.37 \times 10^{24} \text{ kg}$$

Lesson 7—Satellites in Orbit

PRACTICE EXERCISES
ANSWERS AND SOLUTIONS

1. $$F_c = F_g$$
$$\frac{m_m v^2}{r} = \frac{Gm_E m_m}{r^2}$$

or

$$v = \sqrt{\frac{Gm_E}{r}}$$
$$= \sqrt{\frac{\left(6.67 \times 10^{-11} \frac{\text{N} \cdot \text{m}^2}{\text{kg}^2}\right)(5.98 \times 10^{24} \text{ kg})}{3.84 \times 10^8 \text{ m}}}$$
$$= 1.02 \times 10^3 \text{ m/s}$$

3. $$F_c = F_g$$
$$\frac{m_s v^2}{r} = \frac{Gm_J m_s}{r^2}$$

or

$$v = \sqrt{\frac{Gm_J}{r}}$$
$$= \sqrt{\frac{\left(6.67 \times 10^{-11} \frac{\text{N} \cdot \text{m}^2}{\text{kg}^2}\right)(1.90 \times 10^{27} \text{ kg})}{(5.60 \times 10^6 \text{ m} + 7.18 \times 10^7 \text{ m})}}$$
$$= 4.06 \times 10^4 \text{ m/s}$$

5. $$T = \frac{2\pi r^{\frac{3}{2}}}{\sqrt{Gm}}$$
$$= \frac{(2\pi)(2.3 \times 10^{11} \text{ m})^{\frac{3}{2}}}{\sqrt{\left(6.67 \times 10^{-11} \frac{\text{N} \cdot \text{m}^2}{\text{kg}^2}\right)(1.98 \times 10^{30} \text{ kg})}}$$
$$= 6.0 \times 10^7 \text{ s or } 1.9 \text{ Earth years}$$

Practice Test

ANSWERS AND SOLUTIONS

1.

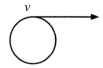

In circular motion, the velocity is tangent to the path.

C is the answer.

3.

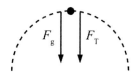

A is the answer.

5. $F_g = \dfrac{Gm_1m_2}{r^2}$ or $F_g \propto \dfrac{1}{r^2}$ (r is doubled, because the final distance from Earth's centre is $2r$)

$\therefore F_g \propto \dfrac{1}{4}$

$F_g' = \dfrac{2.0\ \text{N}}{4}$

$\quad = 0.50\ \text{N}$

A is the answer.

7. We cannot use $E_p = mgh$ in this case because g is not constant—g decreases as the distance from the earth increases.

B is the answer.

9. Centripetal force is the net force causing an object to travel in a circle.

C is the answer.

11. $F_g = mg$

- From equation above, the weight depends on the mass. Because B has twice the mass, it has twice the weight.
- The acceleration due to gravity on both objects is the same but B has twice the mass; therefore B has twice the weight of A on the moon.
- All objects experience the same acceleration due to gravity.

B is the answer.

13. Refer to question 12.

C is the answer.

15. $E_p = -\dfrac{Gm_1m_2}{r}$

$= \dfrac{\left(6.67 \times 10^{-11}\ \dfrac{\text{N} \cdot \text{m}^2}{\text{kg}^2}\right)(5.98 \times 10^{24}\ \text{kg})(1.25 \times 10^3\ \text{kg})}{4.00 \times 10^6\ \text{m} + 6.38 \times 10^6\ \text{m}}$

$= -4.80 \times 10^{10}\ \text{J}$

A is the answer.

ELECTROSTATICS

Lesson 1—Electric Forces

PRACTICE EXERCISES
ANSWERS AND SOLUTIONS

1.
$$F_g = \frac{Gm_1m_2}{r^2}$$
$$= \frac{\left(6.67 \times 10^{-11} \dfrac{N \cdot m^2}{kg^2}\right)(70.0\ kg)(52.0\ kg)}{(1.50\ m)^2}$$
$$= 1.08 \times 10^{-7}\ N$$

3.
$$F_e = \frac{kq_1q_2}{r^2}$$
$$= \frac{\left(9.00 \times 10^9 \dfrac{N \cdot m^2}{C^2}\right)(4.00 \times 10^{-6}\ C)}{} \\ \frac{\times (3.00 \times 10^{-6}\ C)}{(2.00 \times 10^{-2}\ m)^2}$$
$$= 2.70 \times 10^2\ N$$

5.
$$F_e = \frac{kq_1q_2}{r^2}$$
$$r^2 = \frac{kq_1q_2}{F_e}$$
$$= \frac{\left(9.00 \times 10^9 \dfrac{N \cdot m^2}{C^2}\right)(2.0 \times 10^{-6}\ C)}{} \\ \frac{\times (4.0 \times 10^{-6}\ C)}{(5.6 \times 10^{-1}\ N)^2}$$
$$= 1.28 \times 10^{-1}\ m^2$$
$$r = 3.6 \times 10^{-1}\ m$$

7.
$$F_e = \frac{kq_1q_2}{r^2}$$
$$F_e \propto \frac{q_1q_2}{r^2}$$
$$\propto \frac{(3)(3)}{(2)^2}$$
$$\propto 2.25$$

$$F_e = \left(4.5 \times 10^{-3}\ N\right)(2 \cdot 25)$$
$$= 1.0 \times 10^{-2}\ N$$

9.
$$F_e = \frac{kq_1q_2}{r^2}$$
$$F_e \alpha \frac{1}{r^2}$$

Distance changes by a factor of:
$$\frac{to}{from} = \frac{4.04 \times 10^{-1}\ m}{3.11 \times 10^{-1}\ m}$$
$$= 1.30$$

Distance increases by a factor of 1.30.
$$F_e \propto \frac{1}{(1.30)^2}$$
$$\propto 0.592$$

$$F_e' = \left(5.2 \times 10^{-4}\ N\right)(0.592)$$
$$= 3.1 \times 10^{-4}\ N$$

11.

$$F_2 = \frac{kq_1q_2}{r^2}$$
$$= \frac{\left(9.00 \times 10^9 \dfrac{N \cdot m^2}{C^2}\right)(1.50 \times 10^{-6}\ C)^2}{(2.00 \times 10^{-1}\ m)^2}$$
$$= 5.06\ 10^{-1}\ N$$

13.
$$F_{A\ on\ B} = \frac{q2}{r_1^2}$$
$$F_{C\ on\ B} = \frac{q2}{r_2^2}$$
$$\frac{F_{C\ on\ B}}{F_{A\ on\ B}} = \frac{r_1^2}{r_2^2}$$
$$= \frac{(1.5\ cm)^2}{(4.5\ cm)^2}$$
$$= 0.11$$

Lesson 2—Electric Fields

PRACTICE EXERCISES
ANSWERS AND SOLUTIONS

1. $|\vec{E}| = \dfrac{kq_1}{r^2}$

$= \dfrac{\left(9.00 \times 10^9 \ \dfrac{N \cdot m^2}{C^2}\right)(8.00 \times 10^{-6} \ C)}{(7.50 \times 10^{-1} \ m)^2}$

$= 1.28 \times 10^5 \ N/C$

3. $|\vec{E}| = \dfrac{kq_1}{r^2}$

$r = \sqrt{\dfrac{kq}{|\vec{E}|}}$

$= \sqrt{\dfrac{\left(9.00 \times 10^9 \ \dfrac{N \cdot m^2}{C^2}\right)(4.60 \times 10^{-6} \ C)}{2.75 \times 10^5 \ N/C}}$

$= 3.88 \times 10^{-1} \ m$

5. $F_e \propto q$

$\dfrac{to}{from} = \dfrac{1.60 \times 10^{-19} \ C}{3.20 \times 10^{-19} \ C}$

$= 0.500$

$F_e = (0.500)(0.250 \ N)$

$= 0.125 \ N$

7. $|\vec{E}| = \dfrac{F_e}{q}$

$= (3.20 \times 10^{-19} \ C)(7.60 \times 10^4 \ N/C)$

$= 2.43 \times 10^{-14} \ N$

$F_e = ma$

$a = \dfrac{F_e}{m}$

$= \dfrac{2.43 \times 10^{-14} \ N}{6.65 \times 10^{-27} \ kg}$

$= 3.65 \times 10^{12} \ m/s^2$

9.

$|\vec{E_1}| = \dfrac{kq_1}{r_1^{\ 2}}$

$= \dfrac{\left(9.00 \times 10^9 \ \dfrac{N \cdot m^2}{C^2}\right)(3.0 \times 10^{-6} \ C)}{(4.0 \times 10^{-1} \ m)^2}$

$= 1.688 \times 10^5 \ N/C$

$|\vec{E_2}| = \dfrac{kq_2}{r_2^{\ 2}}$

$= \dfrac{\left(9.00 \times 10^9 \ \dfrac{N \cdot m^2}{C^2}\right)(6.0 \times 10^{-6} \ C)}{(4.0 \times 10^{-1} \ m)^2}$

$= 3.375 \ 10^5 \ N/C$

$\vec{E}_{net} = \vec{E_1} + \vec{E_2}$

$= 1.688 \times 10^5 \ N/C - 3.375 \times 10^5 \ N/C$

$= -1.7 \times 10^5 \ N/C \ \text{towards left}$

$|\vec{E}_{net}| = 1.7 \times 10^5 \ N/C$

11. $F_e = ma$

$= (9.11 \times 10^{-31} \ kg)(7.50 \times 10^{12} \ m/s^2)$

$= 6.83 \times 10^{-18} \ N$

$|\vec{E}| = \dfrac{F_e}{q}$

$= \dfrac{6.83 \times 10^{-18} \ N}{1.60 \times 10^{-19} \ C}$

$= 4.27 \times 10^1 \ N/C$

13. $|\vec{E}| = \dfrac{kq}{r^2}$

$|\vec{E}| \propto \dfrac{1}{r^2}$

$r^2 \propto \dfrac{1}{|\vec{E}|} \Rightarrow r = \sqrt{\dfrac{1}{|\vec{E}|}}$

Field is changed by a factor of:

$\dfrac{To}{From} = \dfrac{4.20 \times 10^4 \ N/C}{2.10 \times 10^6 \ N/C}$

$= 2.00$

$|\vec{E}|$ changes by a factor of 2.00

$\therefore \ r$ changes by a factor of $\sqrt{\dfrac{1}{2.00}} = 0.707$

$r' = (7.50 \times 10^{-1} \ m)(0.707)$

$= 5.30 \times 0^{-1} \ m$

Lesson 3—Electric Potential due to a Point

PRACTICE EXERCISES
ANSWERS AND SOLUTIONS

1. $V = \dfrac{kq_1}{r}$

$$= \dfrac{\left(9.00 \times 10^9 \; \dfrac{\text{N} \cdot \text{m}^2}{\text{C}^2}\right)(2.5 \times 10^{-6} \; \text{C})}{6.0 \times 10^{-2} \; \text{m}}$$

$$= 3.8 \times 10^5 \; \text{V}$$

3. $V_1 = \dfrac{kq_1}{r_1}$

$$= \dfrac{\left(9.00 \times 10^9 \; \dfrac{\text{N} \cdot \text{m}^2}{\text{C}^2}\right)(5.0 \times 10^{-6} \; \text{C})}{45 \times 10^{-2} \; \text{m}}$$

$$= 9.99 \times 10^4 \; \text{V}$$

$V_2 = \dfrac{kq_1}{r_2}$

$$= \dfrac{\left(9.00 \times 10^9 \; \dfrac{\text{N} \cdot \text{m}^2}{\text{C}^2}\right)(5.0 \times 10^{-6} \; \text{C})}{15 \times 10^{-2} \; \text{m}}$$

$$= 3.00 \times 10^5 \; \text{V}$$

$\Delta V = V_2 - V_1$
$$= 3.00 \times 10^5 \; \text{V} - 9.99 \times 10^4 \; \text{V}$$
$$= 2.00 \times 10^5 \; \text{V}$$

$W = \Delta E = qV$
$$= \left(0.030 \times 10^{-6} \; \text{C}\right)\left(2.00 \times 10^5 \; \text{V}\right)$$
$$= 6.0 \times 10^{-3} \; \text{J}$$

5. $V_1 = \dfrac{kq_1}{r_1}$

$$= \dfrac{\left(9.00 \times 10^9 \; \dfrac{\text{N} \cdot \text{m}^2}{\text{C}^2}\right)(1.0 \times 10^{-6} \; \text{C})}{7.5 \times 10^{-2} \; \text{m}}$$

$$= 1.20 \times 10^5 \; \text{V}$$

$V_2 = \dfrac{kq_2}{r_2}$

$$= \dfrac{\left(9.00 \times 10^9 \; \dfrac{\text{N} \cdot \text{m}^2}{\text{C}^2}\right)(-3.0 \times 10^{-6} \; \text{C})}{17.5 \times 10^{-2} \; \text{m}}$$

$$= -1.54 \times 10^5 \; \text{V}$$

$V_3 = \dfrac{kq_3}{r_3}$

$$= \dfrac{\left(9.00 \times 10^9 \; \dfrac{\text{N} \cdot \text{m}^2}{\text{C}^2}\right)(-5.0 \times 10^{-6} \; \text{C})}{27.5 \times 10^{-2} \; \text{m}}$$

$$= -1.63 \times 10^5 \; \text{V}$$

$V_T = V_1 + V_2 + V_3$
$$= 1.20 \times 10^5 \; \text{V} + \left(-1.54 \times 10^5 \; \text{V}\right) + \left(-1.63 \times 10^5 \; \text{V}\right)$$
$$= -2.0 \times 10^5 \; \text{V}$$

7. $E_k + E_p = E_k' + E_p'$
$$0 + E_p = E_k' + E_p'$$

$$\frac{kq_1q_2}{r} = \frac{1}{2}m_1(v_1')^2 + \frac{1}{2}m_2(v_2')^2 + \frac{kq_1q_2}{r'}$$

$$\frac{kq_1q_2}{r} = m(v')^2 + \frac{kq_1q_2}{r'} \quad (\because m_1 = m_2)$$

$$v' = \sqrt{\dfrac{\dfrac{kq_1q_2}{r} - \dfrac{kq_1q_2}{r'}}{m}} \quad \ldots \ldots (1)$$

$$\frac{kq_1q_2}{r} = \dfrac{\left(9.00 \times 10^9 \; \dfrac{\text{N} \cdot \text{m}^2}{\text{C}^2}\right)(3.20 \times 10^{-19} \; \text{C})^2}{2.5 \times 10^{-12} \; \text{m}}$$
$$= 3.69 \times 10^{-17} \; \text{N} \cdot \text{m}$$

$$\frac{kq_1q_2}{r'} = \dfrac{\left(9.00 \times 10^9 \; \dfrac{\text{N} \cdot \text{m}^2}{\text{C}^2}\right)(3.20 \times 10^{-19} \; \text{C})^2}{0.75 \; \text{m}}$$
$$= 1.23 \times 10^{-27} \; \text{N} \cdot \text{m}$$

Inserting the values in equation (1)

$$v' = \sqrt{\dfrac{3.69 \times 10^{-16} \; \text{N} \cdot \text{m} - 1.23 \times 10^{-27} \; \text{N} \cdot \text{m}}{6.65 \times 10^{-27} \; \text{kg}}}$$
$$= 2.4 \times 10^5 \; \text{m/s}$$

Lesson 4—Potential Difference

PRACTICE EXERCISES
ANSWERS AND SOLUTIONS

1. $\left|\vec{E}\right| = \dfrac{V}{d}$

    $= \dfrac{12.0 \text{ V}}{9.00 \times 10^{-2} \text{ m}}$

    $= 1.33 \times 10^{2} \text{ V/m}$

3. $\left|\vec{E}\right| = \dfrac{V}{d}$

    $V = \left|\vec{E}\right| d$

    $\therefore V = \left(2.0 \times 10^{3} \text{ V/m}\right)\left(7.3 \times 10^{-2} \text{ m}\right)$

    $= 1.5 \times 10^{2} \text{ V}$

5. $V = \dfrac{\Delta E_{k}}{q}$

    $\Delta E_{k} = qV$

    $= \left(1.60 \times 10^{-19} \text{ C}\right)\left(7.20 \times 10^{2} \text{ V}\right)$

    $= 1.15 \times 10^{-16} \text{ J}$

7. Because there is no change in the potential energy of the proton, there is no work done.

9. $V = \dfrac{\Delta E_{k}}{q}$

    $V \propto \Delta E$

    Energy is changed by a factor of:

    $\dfrac{\text{to}}{\text{from}} = \dfrac{9.00 \times 10^{-17} \text{ J}}{3.00 \times 10^{-17} \text{ J}}$

    $= 3.00$

    The energy changes by a factor of 3.00.
    $\therefore$ potential difference is changed by a factor of 3.00

    $V' = \left(4.20 \times 10^{2} \text{ V}\right)\left(3.00\right)$

    $= 1.26 \times 10^{3} \text{ V}$

11. Find initial energy:

    $E_{k1} = \dfrac{1}{2}mv_{1}^{2}$

    $= \dfrac{1}{2}(9.11 \times 10^{-31} \text{ kg})(5.0 \times 10^{5} \text{ m/s})^{2}$

    $= 1.14 \times 10^{-19} \text{ J}$

    Find energy of electron at plate:

    $E_{k2} = \dfrac{1}{2}mv_{2}^{2}$

    $= \dfrac{1}{2}(9.11 \times 10^{-31} \text{ kg})(1.0 \times 10^{5} \text{ m/s})^{2}$

    $= 4.56 \times 10^{-21} \text{ J}$

    $\Delta E = 1.14 \times 10^{-19} \text{ J} - 4.56 \times 10^{-21} \text{ J}$

    $= 1.09 \times 10^{-19} \text{ J}$

    $V = \dfrac{\Delta E}{q}$

    $= \dfrac{1.09 \times 10^{-19} \text{ J}}{1.60 \times 10^{-19} \text{ C}}$

    $= 6.8 \times 10^{-1} \text{ V}$

13. $\left|\vec{E}\right| = \dfrac{V}{d}$

    $= \dfrac{3.00 \times 10^{2} \text{ V}}{5.00 \times 10^{-2} \text{ m}}$

    $= 6.00 \times 10^{3} \text{ V/m}$

15. Uniform accelerated motion:

    $v_{i} = 0$

    $t = 2.50 \times 10^{-5} \text{ s}$

    $d = 4.00 \times 10^{-2} \text{ m}$

    $d = v_{i}t + \dfrac{1}{2}at^{2}$

    $a = \dfrac{2d}{t^{2}}$

    $= \dfrac{2(4.00 \times 10^{-2} \text{ m})}{(2.50 \times 10^{-5} \text{ s})^{2}}$

    $= 1.28 \times 10^{8} \text{ m/s}^{2}$

    $F_{net} = F_{e} = ma$

    $= \left(6.65 \times 10^{-27} \text{ kg}\right)\left(1.28 \times 10^{8} \text{ m/s}^{2}\right)$

    $= 8.51 \times 10^{-19} \text{ N}$

    $\left|\vec{E}\right| = \dfrac{F_{e}}{q}$

    $= \dfrac{8.51 \times 10^{-19} \text{ N}}{3.20 \times 10^{-19} \text{ C}}$

    $= 2.66 \text{ N/C}$

17. When a charged object is moved perpendicular to an electric field, no work is done.

19. $E_k = \dfrac{1}{2}mv^2$

$\Delta E = qV$

$qV = \dfrac{1}{2}mv^2$

$v^2 \propto V$ or $V \propto v^2$

speed changes by a factor of:

$\dfrac{\text{To}}{\text{From}} = \dfrac{7.25 \times 10^4 \text{ m/s}}{2.90 \times 10^4 \text{ m/s}}$

$= 2.50$

$\therefore V$ changes by a factor of $(2.50)^2 = 6.25$

$V' = (6.25)(2.50 \times 10^5 \text{ V})$

$= 1.56 \times 10^6 \text{ V}$

21. **a)** $|\bar{E}| = \dfrac{V}{d}$

$= \dfrac{12.0 \text{ V}}{2.00 \times 10^{-2} \text{ m}}$

$= 6.00 \times 10^2 \text{ V/m}$

$F_e = q|E|$

$= (3.20 \times 0^{-19} \text{ C})(6.00 \times 10^2 \text{ V/m})$

$= 1.92 \times 10^{-16} \text{ N}$

b) $F_g = mg$

$= (6.65 \times 10^{-27} \text{ kg})(9.81 \text{ N/kg})$

$= 6.52 \times 10^{-26} \text{ N}$

c) $F_{net} = F_e - F_g$

$= 1.92 \times 10^{-16} \text{ N} - 6.52 \times 10^{-26} \text{ N}$

$= 1.92 \times 10^{-16} \text{ N}$

d) $F_{net} = ma$

$a = \dfrac{F_{net}}{m}$

$= \dfrac{1.92 \times 10^{-16} \text{ N}}{6.65 \times 10^{-27} \text{ kg}}$

$= 2.89 \times 10^{10} \text{ m/s}^2$

e) $F_e = F_g$

$F_e = 6.52 \times 10^{-26} \text{ N}$

$|\bar{E}| = \dfrac{F_e}{q}$

$= \dfrac{6.52 \times 10^{-26} \text{ N}}{3.20 \times 10^{-19} \text{ C}}$

$= 2.04 \times 10^{-7} \text{ N/C}$

$V = |\bar{E}|d$

$= (2.04 \times 10^{-7} \text{ N/C})(2.00 \times 10^{-2} \text{ m})$

$= 4.07 \times 10^{-9} \text{ V}$

23. Find how long the electron will be in the electric field:

$v = \dfrac{d}{t}$

$t = \dfrac{d}{v}$

$= \dfrac{14.0 \times 10^{-2} \text{ m}}{8.70 \times 10^6 \text{ m/s}}$

$= 1.61 \times 10^{-8} \text{ s}$

Find the electric force on the electron:

$F_e = q|\bar{E}|$

$= (1.60 \times 10^{-19} \text{ C})(1.32 \times 10^3 \text{ N/C})$

$= 2.11 \times 10^{-16} \text{ N}$

$F_{net} = ma$

$a = \dfrac{F_{net}}{m}$

$= \dfrac{2.11 \times 10^{-16} \text{ N}}{9.11 \times 10^{-31} \text{ kg}}$

$= 2.32 \times 10^{-14} \text{ m/s}^2$

Now find out vertical component of displacement of the electron:

$v_i = 0$

$t = 1.61 \times 10^{-8} \text{ s}$

$a = 2.32 \times 10^{-14} \text{ m/s}^2$

Magnitude of displacement

$d = v_i t + \dfrac{1}{2}at^2$

$= \dfrac{1}{2}(2.32 \times 10^{14} \text{ m/s}^2)(1.61 \times 10^{-8} \text{ s})^2$

$= 3.00 \times 10^{-2} \text{ m}$

Practice Test

ANSWERS AND SOLUTIONS

1.

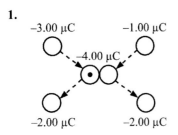

−3.00 μC   −1.00 μC
−4.00 μC
−2.00 μC   −2.00 μC

$$F_e = \frac{kq_1q_2}{r^2}$$

$$= \frac{\left(9.00 \times 10^9 \ \dfrac{\text{N} \cdot \text{m}^2}{\text{C}^2}\right)(2.00 \times 10^{-6} \ \text{C})(2.00 \times 10^{-6} \ \text{C})}{(2.00 \times 10^{-2} \ \text{m})^2}$$

$$= 90.0 \ \text{N}$$

D is the answer.

3. $F_e = \dfrac{kq_1q_2}{r^2}$ or $F_e \propto \dfrac{1}{r^2}$

r decreases by $\dfrac{1}{3}$

$\therefore \ r^2$ changes by 0.111
F_e changes by 9 times
New force $= 9.0F$

D is the answer.

5. $F_{net} = ma$
  $a \propto F_{net}$

In this case the net force is the electric force.

$$F_{net} = F_e = \frac{kq_1q_2}{r^2}$$

$$= \frac{\left(9.00 \times 10^9 \ \dfrac{\text{N} \cdot \text{m}^2}{\text{C}^2}\right)(3.00 \times 10^{-6} \ \text{C})^2}{(2.00 \times 10^{-2} \ \text{m})^2}$$

$$= 2.03 \times 10^2 \ \text{N}$$

$$a = \frac{F_{net}}{m}$$

$$= \frac{2.02 \times 10^2 \ \text{N}}{5.00 \times 10^{-4} \ \text{kg}}$$

$$= 4.05 \times 10^5 \ \text{m/s}^2$$

C is the answer.

7.
$$\Delta E_k + \Delta E_p = 0$$
$$\frac{1}{2}mv^2 - \frac{1}{2}mv_0{}^2 + qV = 0$$
$$\frac{1}{2}(6.65 \times 10^{-27} \ \text{kg})v^2$$
$$+ (3.20 \times 10^{-19} \ \text{C})(-2.00 \times 10^3 \ \text{V}) = 0$$
$$v = 4.39 \times 10^5 \ \text{m/s}$$

B is the answer.

9. Electric potential is defined as electric potential energy per charge.

C is the answer.

11. The direction of an electric field is defined in terms of the direction of the electric force on a positive test charge.

A is the answer.

13. $V = \dfrac{kq_1}{r}$

$V \propto \dfrac{1}{r}$

This is an inverse relationship.

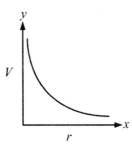

A is the answer.

455

ELECTRIC CIRCUITS

Lesson 1—Electric Current

**PRACTICE EXERCISES
ANSWERS AND SOLUTIONS**

1. $I = \dfrac{q}{t}$

    $q = It$

    $= (3.60\text{A})(15.3 \text{ s})$

    $= 55.1 \text{ C}$

    $e^- = \dfrac{q}{1.60 \times 10^{-19} \text{ C}}$

    $= \dfrac{55.1 \text{ C}}{1.60 \times 10^{-19} \text{ C}}$

    $= 3.44 \times 10^{20}$

3. $I = \dfrac{q}{t}$

    $= \dfrac{5.60 \text{ C}}{15.4 \text{ s}}$

    $= 3.64 \times 10^{-1} \text{A}$

5. $P = I^2 R$

    $= (11.0 \text{ A})^2 (7.20 \text{ W})$

    $= 8.71 \times 10^2 \text{ W}$

    $P = \dfrac{\Delta E}{t}$

    $\Delta E = Pt$

    $= (8.71 \times 10^2 \text{ W})(25.0 \text{ s})$

    $= 2.18 \times 10^4 \text{ J}$

7. $P = IV$

    $I = \dfrac{P}{V}$

    $= \dfrac{4.00 \times 10^2 \text{ W}}{1.20 \times 10^2 \text{ V}}$

    $= 3.33 \text{ A}$

9. **a)** $V = IR$

    $= (20.0\text{A})(6.00 \ \Omega)$

    $= 1.20 \times 10^2 \text{ V}$

    b) $q = It$

    $= (20.0 \text{ A})(60.0 \text{ s})$

    $= 1200 \text{ C}$

    $e^- = \dfrac{\text{total charge}}{\text{charge on 1 e}^-}$

    $= \dfrac{1 \ 200 \text{ C}}{1.60 \times 10^{-19} \text{ C}}$

    $= 7.50 \times 10^{21}$

11. $P = \dfrac{\Delta E}{t}$

    $\Delta E = Pt$

    $= (1.0 \text{ kW})(5.0 \text{ h})$

    $= 5.0 \text{ kW} \cdot \text{h}$

    $\text{cost} = (\$0.060)(5.0 \text{ kW} \cdot \text{h})$

    $= \$0.30$

13. $W = mgh$

    $= (45 \text{ kg})(9.81 \text{ m/s}^2)(9.0 \text{ m})$

    $= 3973 \text{ J}$

    $25\% \text{ of } 7.5 \times 10^2 \text{ W} = 187.5 \text{ W}$

    $P = \dfrac{W}{t}$

    $t = \dfrac{W}{P}$

    $= \dfrac{3 \ 973 \text{ J}}{187.5 \text{ W}}$

    $= 21 \text{ s}$

Lesson 2—Electric Circuits

**PRACTICE EXERCISES
ANSWERS AND SOLUTIONS**

1. In a series circuit:

    $I = I_1 = I_2 = I_3$

    $I_1 = 1.7 \text{ A}$

    $I_2 = 1.7 \text{ A}$

    $I_3 = 1.7 \text{ A}$

3. In a series circuit:
    $$V = V_1 + V_2$$
    $$12.0 \text{ V} = 8.0 \text{ V} + V_2$$
    $$V_2 = 4.0 \text{ V}$$

5. At first consider the series circuit:
    $$V = V_1 + V_2$$
    $$45.0 \text{ V} = 11.0 \text{ V} + V_2$$
    $$V_2 = 45.0 \text{ V} - 11.0 \text{ V}$$
    $$= 34.0 \text{ V}$$

    Then consider the parallel circuit:
    $$V_2 = V_3$$
    $$34.0 \text{ V} = V_2 = V_3$$
    $$\therefore V_3 = 34.0 \text{ V}$$

7. In a parallel circuit:
    $$\frac{1}{R_{eq}} = \frac{1}{R_1} + \frac{1}{R_2}$$
    $$= \frac{1}{6.0 \ \Omega} + \frac{1}{8.0 \ \Omega}$$
    $$R_{eq} = 3.4 \ \Omega$$

9. In a series circuit:
    $$R_{eq} = R_1 + R_2 + R_3$$
    $$= 9.0 \ \Omega + 3.0 \ \Omega + 12.0 \ \Omega$$
    $$= 24.0 \ \Omega$$

11. In a parallel circuit:
    $$\frac{1}{R_{eq}} = \frac{1}{R_1} + \frac{1}{R_2} + \frac{1}{R_3}$$
    $$\frac{1}{2.0 \ \Omega} = \frac{1}{4.5 \ \Omega} + \frac{1}{9.0 \ \Omega} + \frac{1}{R_3}$$
    $$\frac{1}{R_3} = \frac{1}{2.0 \ \Omega} - \left(\frac{1}{4.5 \ \Omega} + \frac{1}{9.0 \ \Omega} \right)$$
    $$R_3 = 6.0 \ \Omega$$

13. a) In a series circuit:
    $$R_{eq} = R_1 + R_2$$
    $$= 10.0 \ \Omega + 15.0 \ \Omega$$
    $$= 25.0 \ \Omega$$

    $$I = \frac{V}{R_{eq}}$$
    $$= \frac{30.0 \text{ V}}{25.0 \ \Omega}$$
    $$= 1.20 \text{ A}$$

$$I = I_1 = I_2$$
$$\therefore I_1 = 1.20 \text{ A}$$
$$I_2 = 1.20 \text{ A}$$

b) $$P = I^2 R_1$$
    $$= (1.20 \text{ A})^2 (10.0 \ \Omega)$$
    $$= 14.4 \text{ W}$$

15. a) In a parallel circuit:
    $$\frac{1}{R_{eq}} = \frac{1}{R_1} + \frac{1}{R_2}$$
    $$= \frac{1}{6.0 \ \Omega} + \frac{1}{8.0 \ \Omega}$$
    $$R_{eq} = 3.43 \ \Omega$$

    In the 2nd circuit:
    $$I_2 = \frac{V_2}{R_2}$$
    $$= \frac{12.0 \text{ V}}{8.0 \ \Omega}$$
    $$= 1.5 \text{ A}$$
    $$I_1 = \frac{V}{R_{eq}}$$
    $$= \frac{12.0 \text{ V}}{3.43 \ \Omega}$$
    $$= 3.5 \text{ A}$$

    b) $$P = I^2 R$$
        $$= (3.5 \text{ A})^2 (3.43 \ \Omega)$$
        $$= 42 \text{ W}$$

17. a) In a series circuit:
    $$R_{eq} = R_1 + R_2 + R_3$$
    $$= 2.0 \ \Omega + 2.5 \ \Omega + 3.0 \ \Omega$$
    $$= 7.5 \ \Omega$$

    $$V = IR$$
    $$= IR_{eq}$$
    $$= (8.0 \text{ A})(7.5 \ \Omega)$$
    $$= 6.0 \times 10^1 \text{ V}$$

    b) $$P = I^2 R$$
        $$= (8.0 \text{ A})^2 (7.5 \text{ W})$$
        $$= 4.8 \times 10^2 \text{ W}$$

19.

$$I_1 = \frac{V}{R_{eq(total)}}$$

$$R_{eq(total)} = \frac{V}{I_{eq}}$$
$$= \frac{90.0 \text{ V}}{4.5 \text{ A}}$$
$$= 20.0 \text{ } \Omega$$

Add R_1 and R_2 for parallel circuit I:

$$\frac{1}{R^I_{eq}} = \frac{1}{20.0 \text{ } \Omega} + \frac{1}{10.0 \text{ } \Omega}$$
$$R^I_{eq} = 6.67 \text{ } \Omega$$

Add R_4 and R_5 for parallel circuit II:

$$\frac{1}{R^{II}_{eq}} = \frac{1}{20.0 \text{ } \Omega} + \frac{1}{10.0 \text{ } \Omega}$$
$$R^{II}_{eq} = 6.67 \text{ } \Omega$$

Find R_3 :

In a series circuit:
$$R_{eq(total)} = R^I_{eq} + R^{II}_{eq} + R_3$$
$$R_3 = R_{eq(total)} - \left(R^I_{eq} + R^{II}_{eq} \right)$$
$$= 20.0 \text{ } \Omega - (6.67 \text{ } \Omega + 6.67 \text{ } \Omega)$$
$$= 6.7 \text{ } \Omega$$

Now, find the current:
$$I_3 = 4.5 \text{ A}$$

The sum of the current through R_1 and R_2 is also 4.5 A.

Since $I \alpha \frac{1}{R}$, the current through R_1 will be 0.50 the current through R_2.

Let $I_{R_2} = I_2$

$$I_{T(through R_1 \text{ and } R_2)} = I_{R_1} + I_{R_2}$$
$$4.5 \text{ A} = 0.50 \, I_2 + I_2$$
$$4.5 \text{ A} = 1.50 \, I_2$$
$$I_2 = 1.5 \text{ A}$$

In this problem:
$$I_4 = I_2 = 1.5 \text{ A}$$

21. Find total resistance of the circuit:

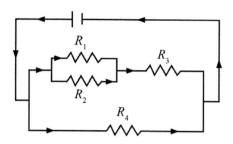

Add R_1 and R_2
$$\frac{1}{R_{eq(1)}} = \frac{1}{R_1} + \frac{1}{R_2}$$
$$= \frac{1}{12 \text{ } \Omega} + \frac{1}{12 \text{ } \Omega}$$
$$R_{eq(1)} = 6.0 \text{ } \Omega$$

Add 6.0 Ω to R_3
$$R_{eq(2)} = 6.0 \text{ W} + 12 \text{ W}$$
$$= 18 \text{ W}$$

Add 18 Ω to R_4
$$\frac{1}{R_{eq(3)}} = \frac{1}{12 \text{ } \Omega} + \frac{1}{18 \text{ } \Omega}$$
$$R_{eq(3)} = 7.2 \text{ } \Omega$$

Find power dissipated by the circuit:
$$P = \frac{V^2}{R}$$
$$= \frac{(120 \text{ V})^2}{7.2 \text{ } \Omega}$$
$$= 2.0 \times 10^3 \text{ W}$$

Find energy used in 4.0 h
$$P = \frac{\Delta E}{t}$$
$$\Delta E = Pt$$
$$= \left(2.0 \times 10^4 \text{ W} \right) (4.0 \text{ h} \times 3600 \text{ s/h})$$
$$= 2.9 \times 10^7 \text{ J}$$

Use: $\Delta E = mc\Delta T$
$$\Delta T = \frac{\Delta E}{mC}$$
$$= \frac{2.9 \times 10^7 \text{ J}}{(200 \text{ kg})(4.19 \times 10^3 \text{ J/kg} \cdot \text{C})}$$
$$= 34° \text{ C}$$

Final temperature:
$$T_f = T_i + \Delta T$$
$$= 15°\text{C} + 34°\text{C}$$
$$= 49°\text{C}$$

Lesson 3—Electromotive Force (EMF)

PRACTICE EXERCISES
ANSWERS AND SOLUTIONS

1. $V = \mathcal{E} - Ir$
   $= 1.5 \text{ V} - (1.0 \text{ A})(0.50 \text{ }\Omega)$
   $= 1.5 \text{ V} - 0.50 \text{ V}$
   $= 1.0 \text{ V}$

3. Current flowing to battery
   $V = \mathcal{E} + Ir$
   $= 24 \text{ V} + (24 \text{ A})(0.25 \text{ }\Omega)$
   $= 30 \text{ V}$

5. $V = \mathcal{E} - Ir$
   $r = \dfrac{\mathcal{E} - V}{I}$
   $= \dfrac{120 \text{ V} - 115 \text{ V}}{12 \text{ A}}$
   $= 0.42 \text{ }\Omega$

Practice Test

ANSWERS AND SOLUTIONS

1. $V = IR$
   $= (9.0 \text{ A})(5.0 \text{ }\Omega)$
   $= 45 \text{ V}$

   C is the answer.

3. $P = \dfrac{\Delta E}{t}$
   $\Delta E = Pt$
   $= (775 \text{ W})(60 \text{ s/min})(15 \text{ min})$
   $= 7.0 \times 10^5 \text{ J}$

   D is the answer.

5. $R_{eq} = R_1 + R_2$
   $= 5.00 \text{ W} + 7.50 \text{ W}$
   $= 12.5 \text{ W}$

   D is the answer.

7. For every electron that passes through R_2, two electrons will pass through R_3 (R_3 has $\frac{1}{2}$ the resistance). This means that for every three electrons that pass through this circuit, one electron passes through R_2, i.e., $\frac{1}{3}$ of the total current passes through R_2.

   Current through R_2 is
   $I_{R_2} = \dfrac{1}{3} \times 9.0 \text{ A}$
   $= 3.0 \text{ A}$

   A is the answer.

9. The voltage across each resistor must be the same (Kirchhoff's laws).

   D is the answer.

11. By adding R_2 in series, we increase the resistance of the circuit, $R_{eq} = R_1 + R_2$, and if we increase the resistance of the circuit, we decrease the current through the circuit
    $I = \dfrac{V}{R}$

    D is the answer.

13. Add parallel resistors first:
    $\dfrac{1}{R_{eq(p)}} = \dfrac{1}{R_2} + \dfrac{1}{R_3}$
    $= \dfrac{1}{4.0 \text{ }\Omega} + \dfrac{1}{2.0 \text{ }\Omega}$
    $R_{eq(p)} = 1.33 \text{ }\Omega$

    Now add in the series resistor:
    $R_{eq(s)} = 1.33 \text{ }\Omega + R_1$
    $= 1.33 \text{ }\Omega + 5.0 \text{ }\Omega$
    $= 6.33 \text{ }\Omega$
    $\doteq 6.3 \text{ }\Omega$

    C is the answer.

MAGNETIC FORCES AND FIELDS

Lesson 1—Magnetic Fields

PRACTICE EXERCISES
ANSWERS AND SOLUTIONS

1. $B = \mu_0 In$

$= \dfrac{\left(4\pi \times 10^{-7} \dfrac{\text{T} \cdot \text{m}}{\text{A}}\right)(1.25 \text{ A})(1800)}{25.0 \times 10^{-2} \text{ m}}$

$= 1.13 \times 10^{-2} \text{ T}$

3. $\dfrac{775 \text{ turns}}{30.0 \text{ cm}} = \dfrac{n}{100 \text{ cm}}$

$n = 2\ 583$

$B = \mu_0 In$

$I = \dfrac{B}{\mu_0 n}$

$= \dfrac{0.100 \text{ T}}{\left(4\pi \times 10^{-7} \dfrac{\text{T} \cdot \text{m}}{\text{A}}\right)(2\ 583)}$

$= 31 \text{ A}$

Lesson 2—Magnetism

PRACTICE EXERCISES
ANSWERS AND SOLUTIONS

1. $F_m = qvB_\perp$

$B_\perp = \dfrac{F_m}{qv}$

$= \dfrac{9.50 \times 10^{-14} \text{ N}}{(1.60 \times 10^{-19} \text{ C})(2.10 \times 10^5 \text{ m/s})}$

$= 2.83 \text{ T}$

3. $F_m = qvB_\perp$

$= \left(1.60 \times 10^{-19} \text{ C}\right)\left(3.52 \times 10^5 \text{ m/s}\right)$

$\times \left(2.80 \times 10^{-1} \text{ T}\right)$

$= 1.58 \times 10^{-14} \text{ N}$

$\vec{F}_m = 1.58 \times 10^{-14} \text{ N west}$

5. $F_m = qvB_\perp$

$B_\perp = \dfrac{F_m}{qv}$

$= \dfrac{1.70 \times 10^{-14} \text{ N}}{(1.60 \times 10^{-19} \text{ C})(1.40 \times 10^4 \text{ m/s})}$

$= 5.59 \text{ T}$

$\vec{B}_\perp = 5.59 \text{ T up}$

7. The alpha particle is moving parallel to the magnetic field.

$\therefore$ there is no force.

$F_m = qvB\sin\theta$

$= 0$

9. $\Delta E = qV$

$= \left(1.60 \times 10^{-19} \text{ C}\right)\left(1.70 \times 10^3 \text{ V}\right)$

$= 2.72 \times 10^{-16} \text{ J}$

$E_k = \dfrac{1}{2}mv^2$

$v = \sqrt{\dfrac{2E_k}{m}}$

$= \sqrt{\dfrac{2(2.72 \times 10^{-16})}{9.11 \times 10^{-31} \text{ kg}}}$

$= 2.44 \times 10^7 \text{ m/s}$

$F_m = qvB_\perp$

$= \left(1.60 \times 10^{-19} \text{ C}\right)\left(2.44 \times 10^7 \text{ m/s}\right)$

$\times \left(2.50 \times 10^{-1} \text{ T}\right)$

$= 9.77 \times 10^{-13} \text{ N}$

11. $F_m = qvB_\perp$

$= \left(1.60 \times 10^{-19} \text{ C}\right)\left(6.20 \times 10^5 \text{ m/s}\right)$

$\times \left(2.30 \times 10^{-1} \text{ T}\right)$

$= 2.28 \times 10^{-14} \text{ N}$

$F = ma$

$a = \dfrac{F}{m}$

$a = \dfrac{F_m}{m}$

$= \dfrac{2.28 \times 10^{-14} \text{ N}}{9.11 \times 10^{-31} \text{ kg}}$

$= 2.50 \times 10^{16} \text{ m/s}^2$

Lesson 3—Thomson's Experiment, Cathode Rays

PRACTICE EXERCISES
ANSWERS AND SOLUTIONS

1. $F_m = F_c$

$qvB_\perp = \dfrac{mv^2}{r}$

$v = \dfrac{qB_\perp r}{m}$

$= \dfrac{(3.20\times10^{-19}\text{ C})(4.22\times10^{-1}\text{ T})(1.50\times10^{-3}\text{ m})}{6.65\times10^{-27}\text{ kg}}$

$= 3.05\times10^4$ m/s

3. $F_m = F_c$

$qvB_\perp = \dfrac{mv^2}{r}$

$\dfrac{q}{m} = \dfrac{v}{B_\perp r}$

$= \dfrac{(3.60\times10^5\text{ m/s})}{(6.10\times10^{-1}\text{ T})(7.40\times10^{-2}\text{ m})}$

$= 7.98\times10^6$ C/kg

5. $F_e = F_m$

$q|\vec{E}| = qvB_\perp$

$v = \dfrac{|\vec{E}|}{B_\perp}$

$= \dfrac{2.10\times10^5\text{ N/C}}{6.50\times10^{-1}\text{ T}}$

$= 3.23\times10^5$ m/s

7. $V = \dfrac{\Delta E}{q}$

$\Delta E = qV$

$= \left(1.60\times10^{-19}\text{ C}\right)\left(2.50\times10^3\text{ V}\right)$

$= 4.00\times10^{-16}$ J

$E_k = \dfrac{1}{2}mv^2$

$v = \sqrt{\dfrac{2E_k}{m}}$

$= \sqrt{\dfrac{2(4.00\times10^{-16}\text{ J})}{9.11\times10^{-31}\text{ kg}}}$

$= 2.96\times10^7$ m/s

9. $V = \dfrac{\Delta E}{q}$

$\Delta E = qV$

$= (1.00\times10^{-14}\text{ C})(1.40\times10^3\text{ V})$

$= 2.24\times10^{-16}$ J

$E_k = \dfrac{1}{2}mv^2$

$v = \sqrt{\dfrac{2E_k}{m}}$

$= \sqrt{\dfrac{2(2.24\times10^{-16}\text{ J})}{9.11\times10^{-31}\text{ kg}}}$

$= 2.23\times10^7$ m/s

$F_m = F_c$

$qvB_\perp = \dfrac{mv^2}{r}$

$r = \dfrac{mv}{qB_\perp}$

$= \dfrac{(9.11\times10^{-31}\text{ kg})(2.23\times10^7\text{ m/s})}{(1.60\times10^{-19}\text{ C})(2.20\times10^{-2}\text{ T})}$

$= 5.74\times10^{-3}$ m

11. $F_m = F_c$

$qvB_\perp = \dfrac{mv^2}{r}$

$q = \dfrac{mv}{rB_\perp}$

$= \dfrac{(8.4\times10^{-27}\text{ kg})(5.6\times10^5\text{ m/s})}{(3.5\times10^{-2}\text{ m})(2.8\times10^{-1}\text{ T})}$

$= 4.8\times10^{-19}$ C

$\#\,e^- = \dfrac{4.8\times10^{-19}\text{ C}}{1.6\times10^{-19}\text{ C}}$

$= 3$

13. $F_m = F_c$

$qvB_\perp = \dfrac{mv^2}{r}$

$v = \dfrac{qB_\perp r}{m}$

$v = \dfrac{(1.60\times10^{-19}\text{ C})(0.75\text{ T})(0.30\text{ m})}{1.67\times10^{-27}\text{ kg}}$

$= 2.16\times10^7$ m/s

15. $F_m = F_c$

$$qvB_\perp = \frac{mv^2}{r}$$

$$v = \frac{qB_\perp r}{m}$$

$$= (1.0 \times 10^4 \text{ C/kg})(9.10 \times 10^{-1} \text{ T})(0.240 \text{ m})$$

$$= 2.4 \times 10^3 \text{ m/s}$$

$$d = C = 2\pi r$$

$$= 2\pi(0.240 \text{ m})$$

$$= 1.51 \text{ m}$$

$$v = \frac{d}{t}$$

$$t = \frac{d}{v}$$

$$= \frac{1.51 \text{ m}}{2.40 \times 10^3 \text{ m/s}}$$

$$= 6.28 \times 10^{-4} \text{ s}$$

Lesson 4—Magnetic Flux

PRACTICE EXERCISES
ANSWERS AND SOLUTIONS

1. area $= \pi r^2$

$$= \pi(5.0 \times 10^{-2} \text{ m})^2$$

$$= 7.85 \times 10^{-3} \text{ m}^2$$

$$\Phi = BA\cos\theta$$

$$= (7.85 \times 10^{-3} \text{ m}^2)(3.2 \times 10^{-3} \text{ T})$$

$$= 2.5 \times 10^{-5} \text{ Wb}$$

3. $\Phi_f = BA\cos\theta$

$$= (2.2 \times 10^{-2} \text{ T})(0)(\cos 90°)$$

$$= 0$$

$$\Phi_0 = BA\cos\theta$$

$$= (2.2 \times 10^{-2} \text{ T})(2.5 \times 10^{-3} \text{ m}^2)(\cos 0°)$$

$$= 5.5 \times 10^{-5} \text{ Wb}$$

$$\Delta\Phi = \Phi_f - \Phi_0$$

$$= 0 - 5.5 \times 10^{-5} \text{ Wb}$$

$$= -5.5 \times 10^{-5} \text{ Wb}$$

$$\varepsilon = -N\frac{\Delta\Phi}{\Delta t}$$

$$= -\left(\frac{-5.5 \times 10^{-5} \text{ Wb}}{0.10 \text{ s}}\right)$$

$$= 5.5 \times 10^{-4} \text{ V}$$

Direction: clockwise

5. $\varepsilon = -N\frac{\Delta\Phi}{\Delta t}$

$$\Delta\Phi = -\frac{\varepsilon(\Delta t)}{N}$$

$$= -\frac{(0.92 \text{ V})(0.12 \text{ s})}{100}$$

$$= -1.10 \times 10^{-3} \text{ Wb}$$

$$\Phi = BA\cos\theta$$

$$B = \frac{\Phi}{A\cos\theta}$$

$$= \frac{-1.10 \times 10^{-3} \text{ Wb}}{4.0 \times 10^{-3} \text{ m}^2}$$

$$= 2.8 \times 10^{-1} \text{ T}$$

7. $\Phi_0 = BA\cos\theta$

$$= (0.40 \text{ T})(5.0 \times 10^{-3} \text{ m}^2)(\cos 0°)$$

$$= 2.0 \times 10^{-3} \text{ Wb}$$

$$\Phi_f = BA\cos\theta$$

$$= (0)(5.0 \times 10^{-3} \text{ m}^2)(\cos 0°)$$

$$= 0$$

$$\Delta\Phi = \Phi_f - \Phi_0$$

$$= 0 - 2.0 \times 10^{-3} \text{ Wb}$$

$$= -2.0 \times 10^{-3} \text{ Wb}$$

$$\varepsilon = -N\frac{\Delta\Phi}{\Delta t}$$

$$= -(25)\left(\frac{-2.0 \times 10^{-3} \text{ Wb}}{1.0 \text{ s}}\right)$$

$$= 5.0 \times 10^{-2} \text{ V}$$

Lesson 5—Back EMF

PRACTICE QUESTIONS—
ANSWERS AND SOLUTIONS

1. $V_{back} = \varepsilon - Ir$

$$= 120 \text{ V} - (12.0 \text{ A})(6.0 \text{ Ω})$$

$$= 48 \text{ V}$$

3. a) $V_{back} = \varepsilon - Ir$

$$= 120 \text{ V} - (9.0 \text{ A})(5.0 \text{ Ω})$$

$$= 75 \text{ V}$$

b) no back emf

c) initial

$$V_{back} = 0$$

$$V_{back} = \varepsilon - Ir$$

$$0 = 120 \text{ V} - I(5.0 \text{ Ω})$$

$$I = \frac{120 \text{ V}}{5.0 \text{ Ω}}$$

$$= 24 \text{ A}$$

5. 45.0 V

We can use $\varepsilon = -N\dfrac{\Delta\Phi}{\Delta t}$, which tells us that the induced emf varies directly with the rate of change in the magnetic flux. The back emf is the emf induced by the motor. Therefore, if the rate of rotation is halved, the back emf is halved.

Lesson 6—Electromagnetic Induction

CLASS EXERCISES
ANSWERS AND SOLUTIONS

1. $\varepsilon = B_\perp lv$
$= (0.75 \text{ T})(0.35 \text{ m})(1.5 \text{ m/s})$
$= 0.39 \text{ V}$

3. $\varepsilon = B_\perp lv$
$= (0.150 \text{ T})(0.220 \text{ m})(1.25 \text{ m/s})$
$= 0.0413 \text{ V}$
$\varepsilon = IR$
$I = \dfrac{\varepsilon}{R}$
$= \dfrac{0.0413 \text{ V}}{2.25 \text{ }\Omega}$
$= 1.83 \times 10^{-2} \text{ A}$
counter-clockwise

5. $\varepsilon = B_\perp lv$
$= (0.950 \text{ T})(0.300 \text{ m})(1.50 \text{ m/s})$
$= 0.428 \text{ V}$
$\varepsilon = IR$
$I = \dfrac{\varepsilon}{R}$
$= \dfrac{0.428 \text{ V}}{3.25 \text{ }\Omega}$
$= 0.132 \text{ A}$
$F_m = BIl$
$= (0.950\text{T})(0.132 \text{ A})(0.300 \text{ m})$
$= 3.75 \times 10^{-2} \text{ N}$

7. $\varepsilon = B_\perp lv$
$= (0.600 \text{ T})(0.300 \text{ m})(3.00 \text{ m/s})$
$= 0.540 \text{ V}$
$P = \dfrac{\varepsilon^2}{R}$
$= \dfrac{(0.540 \text{ V})^2}{2.25 \text{ }\Omega}$
$= 0.130 \text{ W}$
$P = \dfrac{W}{t}$
$W = Pt$
$= (0.130\text{W})(15.0 \text{ s})$
$= 1.94 \text{ J}$

9. $\varepsilon = B_\perp lv$
$= (0.95 \text{ T})(1.0 \text{ m})(3.0 \text{ m/s})$
$= 2.85 \text{ V}$
$P = \dfrac{\varepsilon^2}{R}$
$\dfrac{(2.85 \text{ V})^2}{45.0 \text{ }\Omega}$
$= 0.181 \text{ W}$

$P = \dfrac{W}{t}$
$W = Pt$
$= (0.181 \text{ W})(1.0 \times 10^{-2} \text{ s})$
$= 1.8 \times 10^{-3} \text{ J}$

11. a) $\varepsilon = B_\perp lv$
$= (1.30 \text{ T})(0.625 \text{ m})(1.80 \text{ m/s})$
$= 1.463 \text{ V}$
$\varepsilon = IR$
$I = \dfrac{\varepsilon}{R}$
$= \dfrac{1.463 \text{ V}}{1.50 \text{ }\Omega}$
$= 0.975 \text{ A}$

b) clockwise

Lesson 7—Transformers

PRACTICE EXERCISES
ANSWERS AND SOLUTIONS

1.
$$\frac{I_s}{I_p} = \frac{N_p}{N_s}$$
$$\frac{0.95\ A}{0.25\ A} = \frac{1.0 \times 10^3}{N_s}$$
$$N_s = 2.6 \times 10^2$$

3. a) $P_p = I_p V_p$
$$I_p = \frac{P_p}{V_p}$$
$$= \frac{2.4 \times 10^3\ W}{3.6 \times 10^3\ V}$$
$$= 0.67\ A$$

b) $P_s = I_s V_s$
$$I_s = \frac{P_s}{V_s}$$
$$= \frac{2.4 \times 10^3\ W}{1.20 \times 10^2\ V}$$
$$= 2.0 \times 10^1\ A$$

5. $P_p = I_p V_p$
$$= (3.0\,A)(1.20 \times 10^2\ V)$$
$$= 3.6 \times 10^2\ W$$

Power delivered to the secondary coil is also 3.6×10^2 W
(same in both cells)

7. $P_p = I_p V_p$
$$= (1.0\ A)(1.20 \times 10^2\ V)$$
$$= 1.2 \times 10^2\ W$$

The power in the secondary coil is also 1.2×10^2 W
(same in both cells)

Practice Test

ANSWERS AND SOLUTIONS

1. i) False.
Lenz's law tells us that the induced field will oppose the original change of flux of the magnet.

ii) True.
The induced magnetic field inside the solenoid must oppose the motion of the magnet. That means that the left side of the solenoid is the induced magnetic north. Use the right hand rule. Point your thumb of your right hand to the left. Your fingers now curl in the direction of the electric current. For this to happen, the current flows from A to B through G.

D is the answer.

3. i) False. Law of Conservation of Energy tells us that this is false. A transformer cannot create energy.

ii) False.
$$\frac{N_p}{N_s} = \frac{I_s}{I_p}$$
$$\frac{1}{10} = \frac{I_s}{I_p}$$

This tells us that the current in the primary coil is 10 times that of the secondary coil.

B is the answer.

5. A transformer makes use of the principle of electromagnetic induction. This means that there must be a change in the magnetic field inside the secondary coil. In order to change this magnetic field, a switch is placed in the primary circuit.

C is the answer.

7. Use the right hand rule. The opposing magnetic force must be in the opposite direction to its motion (i.e., to the left). Place palm of hand to the left along the conductor, and the fingers into the page (in the direction of the magnetic field). Your thumb will now point up along the conductor. This is the direction of the induced electric current.

$$\varepsilon = B_\perp lv \quad \text{and} \quad I = \frac{\varepsilon}{R}$$

From these mathematical relationships, if the velocity decreases, the current also decreases.

D is the answer.

9. Use the right hand rule. Point thumb east. Point fingers north. Then the palm is directed up.

A is the answer.

11. Use the left hand rule (electrons). Point thumb north. When your fingers curl over your thumb, they are pointing west.

B is the answer.

13. A generator converts mechanical energy to electric energy.

A is the answer.

15. Transformers operate on the principle of electromagnetic induction as do generators.

D is the answer.

17. Apply Lenz's Law here. Use the right hand rule for conventional current.

D is the answer.

19. Cathode rays are a beam of electrons.

B is the answer.

21. This equation tells us that the radius of deflection (the smaller the radius, the greater the deflection) depends on the mass, velocity, charge, and magnetic field.

$$F_m = F_c$$
$$qvB_\perp = \frac{mv^2}{R}$$
$$R = \frac{mv}{qB_\perp}$$

i) True. Decrease the mass, the radius decreases.

ii) True. Increase the charge, the radius decreases.

iii) False. Increase the mass, the radius increases.

C is the answer.

NOTES

Student Notes and Problems

APPENDICES

NOTES

468

PHYSICS DATA TABLES

EQUATIONS AND CONSTANTS USED IN THIS BOOK

KINEMATICS

$$\vec{v} = \frac{\vec{d}}{t} \qquad \vec{a} = \frac{\vec{v}_f - \vec{v}_i}{t} \qquad \vec{d} = \left(\frac{\vec{v}_f + \vec{v}_i}{2}\right)t$$

$$\vec{d} = \vec{v}_i t + \frac{1}{2}\vec{a}t^2 \qquad v_f^2 = v_i^2 + 2\vec{a}\vec{d} \qquad \vec{v}_{ave} = \frac{\vec{v}_f + \vec{v}_i}{2}$$

WORK AND ENERGY

$$W = Fd \qquad E_k = \frac{1}{2}mv^2 \qquad E_p = mgh$$

$$F_f = \mu F_N \qquad P = \frac{W}{t} \ \text{ or } \ \frac{\Delta E}{t}$$

MOMENTUM AND IMPULSE

$$\vec{p} = m\vec{v} \qquad \vec{F}\Delta t = m\Delta\vec{v}$$

FORCES AND FIELDS

$$\vec{F}_g = m\vec{g} \qquad \vec{g} = \frac{Gm}{r^2} \qquad \vec{a}_c = \frac{v^2}{r}$$

$$\vec{F}_c = \frac{mv^2}{r} \qquad v = \frac{2\pi r}{T} \qquad \vec{F}_g = \frac{Gm_1 m_2}{r^2}$$

$$E_p = -\frac{Gm_1 m_2}{r} \qquad \vec{F}_e = \frac{kq_1 q_2}{r^2} \qquad V = \frac{kq}{r}$$

$$V = \frac{\Delta E_p}{q} \qquad \left|\vec{E}\right| = \frac{F_e}{q} = \frac{V}{d} \qquad \left|\vec{E}\right| = \frac{kq}{r^2}$$

ELECTRIC CIRCUITS

$$V = IR \qquad R_{eq\,series} = R_1 + R_2 + \dots \qquad \frac{1}{R_{eq\,parallel}} = \frac{1}{R_1} + \frac{1}{R_2} + \dots$$

$$P = IV \qquad P = I^2 R \qquad P = \frac{V^2}{R}$$

$$V_{terminal} = \mathcal{E} - Ir \qquad P = \frac{W}{t} \qquad \text{Efficiency} = \frac{\text{power out}}{\text{power in}} \times 100\%$$

ELECTROMAGNETISM

$$F_{\text{m}} = qvB_{\perp}$$

$$F_{\text{m}} = B_{\perp}Il$$

$$B = \mu_0 In$$

$$\mathcal{E} = B_{\perp}lv$$

$$\Phi = BA\cos\theta$$

$$\mathcal{E} = -N\frac{\Delta\Phi}{\Delta t}$$

$$V_{\text{back}} = \mathcal{E} - Ir$$

$$\frac{V_{\text{s}}}{V_{\text{p}}} = \frac{N_{\text{s}}}{N_{\text{p}}} = \frac{I_{\text{p}}}{I_{\text{s}}}$$

CONSTANTS

Acceleration due to gravity near Earth	$g = 9.81 \text{ m/s}^2$
Gravitational field near Earth	$g = 9.81 \text{ N/kg}$
Gravitational constant	$G = 6.67 \times 10^{-11} \text{ N} \cdot \text{m}^2/\text{kg}^2$
Index of refraction (air)	$n = 1.00$
Coulomb's constant	$k = 8.99 \times 10^9 \text{ N} \cdot \text{m}^2/\text{C}^2$
Permeability of free space	$\mu_0 = 4\pi \times 10^{-7} \text{ T} \cdot \text{m/A}$
Elementary charge	$e = 1.60 \times 10^{-19} \text{ C}$
Electron volt	$1 \text{ eV} = 1.60 \times 10^{-19} \text{ J}$

Earth's mass	$m_{\text{E}} = 5.98 \times 10^{24} \text{ kg}$
Earth's radius	$r_{\text{E}} = 6.38 \times 10^6 \text{ m}$
Sun's mass	$m_{\text{s}} = 1.99 \times 10^{30} \text{ kg}$
Sun's radius	$r_{\text{s}} = 6.96 \times 10^8 \text{ m}$

Particles	Rest Mass	Charge
Alpha particle	$6.65 \times 10^{-27} \text{ kg}$	$3.20 \times 10^{-19} \text{ C}$
Electron	$9.11 \times 10^{-31} \text{ kg}$	$-1.60 \times 10^{-19} \text{ C}$
Neutron	$1.67 \times 10^{-27} \text{ kg}$	0
Proton	$1.67 \times 10^{-27} \text{ kg}$	$1.60 \times 10^{-19} \text{ C}$

PREFIXES

Name	Symbol	Multiplier	Name	Symbol	Multiplier
yotta-	Y	10^{24}	deci-	d	10^{-1}
tera-	T	10^{12}	centi-	c	10^{-2}
giga-	G	10^{9}	milli-	m	10^{-3}
mega-	M	10^{6}	micro-	μ	10^{-6}
kilo-	k	10^{3}	nano-	n	10^{-9}
hecto-	h	10^{2}	pico-	p	10^{-12}
deca-	da	10^{1}	femto-	f	10^{-15}

Legend for Elements

☐ Metallic solids ☐ Gases
▨ Non-metallic solids ■ Liquids

Note: the legend denotes the physical state of the elements at exactly 101.325 kPa and 298.15 K.

Atomic number → 29
Electronegativity → 1.9   63.55 Atomic molar mass (g/mol)*
Symbol → Cu   2+,1+ Most stable ion charges
Name → copper

*Based on $^{12}_{6}C$
( ) indicates mass of most stable isotope

*The variability of the isotopic mix of lead prevents precision in measurement beyond tenths of a gram per mole.

Table of Common Polyatomic Ions

acetate (ethanoate)	CH_3COO^-	chromate	CrO_4^{2-}	phosphate	PO_4^{3-}
ammonium	NH_4^+	dichromate	$Cr_2O_7^{2-}$	hydrogen phosphate	HPO_4^{2-}
benzoate	$C_6H_5COO^-$	cyanide	CN^-	dihydrogen phosphate	$H_2PO_4^-$
borate	BO_3^{3-}	hydroxide	OH^-	silicate	SiO_3^{2-}
carbide	C_2^{2-}	iodate	IO_3^-	sulfate	SO_4^{2-}
carbonate	CO_3^{2-}	nitrate	NO_3^-	hydrogen sulfate	HSO_4^-
hydrogen carbonate (bicarbonate)	HCO_3^-	nitrite	NO_2^-	sulfite	SO_3^{2-}
perchlorate	ClO_4^-	oxalate	$OOCCOO^{2-}$	hydrogen sulfite	HSO_3^-
chlorate	ClO_3^-	hydrogen oxalate	$HOOCCOO^-$	hydrogen sulfide	HS^-
chlorite	ClO_2^-	permanganate	MnO_4^-	thiocyanate	SCN^-
hypochlorite	OCl^- or ClO^-	peroxide	O_2^{2-}	thiosulfate	$S_2O_3^{2-}$
		persulfide	S_2^{2-}		

Group 1: H 1.01 1+,1-; Li 6.94 1+; Na 22.99 1+; K 39.10 1+; Rb 85.47 1+; Cs 132.91 1+; Fr (223) 1+

Group 2: Be 9.01 2+; Mg 24.31 2+; Ca 40.08 2+; Sr 87.62 2+; Ba 137.33 2+; Ra (226) 2+

Lanthanide and actinide series begin

| 58 140.12 Ce cerium 1.1 3+ | 59 140.90 Pr praseodymium 1.1 3+ | 60 144.24 Nd neodymium 1.1 3+ | 61 (145) Pm promethium 3+ | 62 150.36 Sm samarium 3+,2+ | 63 151.96 Eu europium 3+,2+ | 64 157.25 Gd gadolinium 1.2 3+ | 65 158.93 Tb terbium 3+ | 66 162.50 Dy dysprosium 3+ | 67 164.93 Ho holmium 3+ | 68 167.26 Er erbium 1.2 3+ | 69 168.93 Tm thulium 3+ | 70 173.04 Yb ytterbium 3+,2+ | 71 174.97 Lu lutetium 3+,2+ |

| 90 232.04 Th thorium 1.3 4+ | 91 231.04 Pa protactinium 1.5 5+,4+ | 92 238.03 U uranium 1.7 6+,4+ | 93 (237) Np neptunium 1.3 5+ | 94 (244) Pu plutonium 1.3 4+,6+ | 95 (243) Am americium 3+,4+ | 96 (247) Cm curium 3+ | 97 (247) Bk berkelium 3+ | 98 (251) Cf californium 3+ | 99 (252) Es einsteinium 3+ | 100 (257) Fm fermium 3+ | 101 (258) Md mendelevium 2+,3+ | 102 (259) No nobelium 2+ | 103 (262) Lr lawrencium 3+ |

Credits

Every effort has been made to provide proper acknowledgement of the original source and to comply with copyright law. However, some attempts to establish original copyright ownership may have been unsuccessful. If copyright ownership can be identified, please notify Castle Rock Research Corp so that appropriate corrective action can be taken.

Some images in this document are from www.clipart.com, copyright (c) 2009 Jupiterimages Corporation.

NOTES

474

NOTES

NOTES